NOVELL'S

Guide to Troubleshooting NDS™

NOVELL'S

Guide to Troubleshooting
NDS™

PETER KUO AND JIM HENDERSON

Novell Press, San Jose

Novell's Guide to Troubleshooting NDS™

Published by
Novell Press
2211 North First Street
San Jose, CA 95131

Copyright © 1999 Novell, Inc. All rights reserved. No part of this book, including interior design, cover design, and icons, may be reproduced or transmitted in any form, by any means (electronic, photocopying, recording, or otherwise) without the prior written permission of the publisher.

ISBN: 0-7645-4579-5

Printed in the United States of America

10 9 8 7 6 5 4 3

1B/RT/QZ/ZZ/FC

Distributed in the United States by IDG Books Worldwide, Inc.

Distributed by CDG Books Canada Inc. for Canada; by Transworld Publishers Limited in the United Kingdom; by IDG Norge Books for Norway; by IDG Sweden Books for Sweden; by IDG Books Australia Publishing Corporation Pty. Ltd. for Australia and New Zealand; by TransQuest Publishers Pte Ltd. for Singapore, Malaysia, Thailand, Indonesia, and Hong Kong; by Gotop Information Inc. for Taiwan; by ICG Muse, Inc. for Japan; by Norma Comunicaciones S.A. for Colombia; by Intersoft for South Africa; by Eyrolles for France; by International Thomson Publishing for Germany, Austria, and Switzerland; by Distribuidora Cuspide for Argentina; by LR International for Brazil; by Galileo Libros for Chile; by Ediciones ZETA S.C.R. Ltda. for Peru; by WS Computer Publishing Corporation, Inc., for the Philippines; by Contemporanea de Ediciones for Venezuela; by Express Computer Distributors for the Caribbean and West Indies; by Micronesia Media Distributor, Inc. for Micronesia; by Grupo Editorial Norma S.A. for Guatemala; by Chips Computadoras S.A. de C.V. for Mexico; by Editorial Norma de Panama S.A. for Panama; by American Bookshops for Finland.

For general information on IDG Books Worldwide's books in the U.S., please call our Consumer Customer Service department at 800-762-2974. For reseller information, including discounts and premium sales, please call our Reseller Customer Service department at 800-434-3422.

For information on where to purchase IDG Books Worldwide's books outside the U.S., please contact our International Sales department at 317-596-5530 or fax 317-596-5692.

For consumer information on foreign language translations, please contact our Customer Service department at 800-434-3422, fax 317-596-5692, or e-mail rights@idgbooks.com.

For information on licensing foreign or domestic rights, please phone +1-650-655-3109.

For sales inquiries and special prices for bulk quantities, please contact our Sales department at 650-655-3200 or write to IDG Books Worldwide, 919 E. Hillsdale Blvd., Suite 400, Foster City, CA 94404.

For information on using IDG Books Worldwide's books in the classroom or for ordering examination copies, please contact our Educational Sales department at 800-434-2086 or fax 317-596-5499.

For press review copies, author interviews, or other publicity information, please contact our Public Relations department at 650-655-3000 or fax 650-655-3299.

For authorization to photocopy items for corporate, personal, or educational use, please contact Novell, Inc., Copyright Permission, 1555 North Technology Way, Mail Stop ORM-C-311, Orem, UT 84097-2395; or fax 801-228-7077.

For general information on Novell Press books in the U.S., including information on discounts and premiums, contact IDG Books Worldwide at 800-434-3422 or 650-655-3200. For information on where to purchase Novell Press books outside the U.S., contact IDG Books International at 650-655-3021 or fax 650-655-3295.

Library of Congress Cataloging-in-Publication Data

Kuo, Peter, 1959–
  Novell's guide to troubleshooting NDS / Peter Kuo and Jim Henderson
      p.   cm.
      ISBN 0-7645-4579-5 (alk. paper)
      1. NetWare (Computer file) 2. Directory services (Computer network technology) 3. Local area networks—Management.
      I. Henderson, Jim, 1970–   . II. Title.   III. Title: Guide to troubleshooting NDS.
TK5105.8.N65K87   1999
005.7'1369—dc21   99-34587
                                                        CIP

John Kilcullen, *CEO, IDG Books Worldwide, Inc.*
Steven Berkowitz, *President, IDG Books Worldwide, Inc.*
Richard Swadley, *Senior Vice President & Publisher, Technology*

The IDG Books Worldwide logo is a registered trademark or trademark under exclusive license to IDG Books Worldwide, Inc. from International Data Group, Inc. in the United States and/or other countries.

Marcy Shanti, *Publisher, Novell Press, Novell, Inc.*

Novell Press and the Novell Press logo are trademarks of Novell, Inc.

Welcome to Novell Press

Novell Press, the world's leading provider of networking books, is the premier source for the most timely and useful information in the networking industry. Novell Press books cover fundamental networking issues as they emerge — from today's Novell and third-party products to the concepts and strategies that will guide the industry's future. The result is a broad spectrum of titles for the benefit of those involved in networking at any level: end user, department administrator, developer, systems manager, or network architect.

Novell Press books are written by experts with the full participation of Novell's technical, managerial, and marketing staff. The books are exhaustively reviewed by Novell's own technicians and are published only on the basis of final released software, never on prereleased versions.

Novell Press at IDG Books Worldwide is an exciting partnership between two companies at the forefront of the knowledge and communications revolution. The Press is implementing an ambitious publishing program to develop new networking titles centered on the current versions of NetWare, GroupWise, BorderManager, ManageWise, and networking integration products.

Novell Press books are translated into several languages and sold throughout the world.

Marcy Shanti
Publisher
Novell Press, Novell, Inc.

Novell Press

Publisher
Marcy Shanti

IDG Books Worldwide

Acquisitions Editor
Jim Sumser

Development Editors
Brian MacDonald
Diane Puri
Bob MacSweeney

Technical Editor
Ken Neff

Copy Editors
Karyn DiCastri
Larisa North

Illustrator
Trevor Wilson

Production
Publication Services, Inc.

Proofreading and Indexing
Publication Services, Inc.

About the Author

Peter Kuo, president of DreamLAN Network Consulting Ltd. (http://www.dreamlan.com), is a Master CNI and Master CNE. He has been working with NetWare since the early 1980s, and has been working with NDS since NetWare 4.0 was still in beta. Peter has assisted many companies in implementing large-scale NDS trees and has been developing NDS-aware applications since 1995. Peter is also a volunteer SysOp for the Novell Support Connection and Novell DeveloperNet forums.

Jim Henderson started working with computer networks in 1989 at a small university in Daytona Beach, Florida. Jim, a programmer of several years, wrote several utilities to customize the NetWare environment for the academic computer lab. After leaving school, he went to work for a company that was one of the first to deploy NetWare 4.0 in production. During that time, Jim became a volunteer SysOp for Novell on CompuServe, and has supported NDS for Novell since 1993. He is currently employed by a Fortune 500 company based in Salt Lake City, and is responsible for the overall health and maintenance of the corporate NDS tree.

To my old physics professors, Dr. Kenneth G. McNeill and Dr. James W. Jury, who introduced me to the art and techniques of troubleshooting. — PK

For Mom, Dad, Amy, and Kenny, for all of their support — *past, present, and future.* — JH

Preface

In 1993, Novell became the first company to integrate directory services — Novell Directory Services (NDS) — with its server operating system. Since then, NDS has been ported to the major enterprise server platforms, and today NDS remains the dominant leader as a general-purpose enterprise directory in the LAN market, deployed in 80 percent of Fortune 500 companies.

Novell Directory Services is a multiple-platform, distributed database that stores information about the hardware and software resources available on your network. It provides network users, administrators, and application developers with seamless, global access to all network resources. NDS also provides a flexible directory database schema, unmatched network security, and a consistent cross-platform development environment.

NDS uses objects to represent all network resources and maintains them in a hierarchical directory tree. By pointing, clicking, and dragging, you can make changes to those directory trees without downing network servers. You can easily manage multiple trees, maintain and repair the network-wide directory from a client workstation, and automatically update distributed NDS replicas on all NetWare 4 and NetWare 5 servers.

Because NDS is the core of your NetWare 4 and NetWare 5 networks, it is important to have a firm handle on how it works and know what actions to take if there is a problem. What's more, good network administrators work proactively to prevent trouble from developing in the first place. This book is your comprehensive troubleshooting guide for Novell Directory Services.

You'll find this book to be a rich and definitive source of information for NDS troubleshooting methodologies. No matter the size of your NDS tree, you'll find this book to be indispensable. Topics covered in this book range from the fundamentals of Novell Directory Services and its new features to troubleshooting and proactive management of the internal operations of NDS. The information presented in this book will help you maintain and troubleshoot all aspects of Novell Directory Services.

What You'll Learn from Reading This Book

This book is written for all LAN administrators, system administrators, consultants, resellers, and any others who design, implement, and support NDS networks.

Using this book, you will learn basic to complex concepts and techniques on diagnosing and repairing NDS issues. Whether your interest lies solely in understanding how NDS processes function or in knowing how to deal with specific NDS problems, you will find this book to be the definitive source.

How This Book Is Organized

This book is organized into four logical parts: "NDS Foundations," "Understand the Error Codes and NDS Processes," "Troubleshoot and Resolve the Problem," and "Manage NDS to Prevent Problems."

Part I, "NDS Foundations," includes an overview of Novell Directory Services basics, such as objects, partitions, and time synchronization. Part I also provides readers with a comprehensive look at NDS classes and how these classes are used to build objects in the Directory tree. An understanding of NDS objects is a prerequisite to using the full potential of NDS and the information in the rest of this book.

Part II, "Understanding the Error Codes and NDS Processes," describes in great detail the internal operations of Novell Directory Services and associated error codes.

Part III, "Troubleshoot and Resolve the Problem," provides a thorough discussion on troubleshooting Novell Directory Services using various tools and utilities included with NetWare and available from third-party vendors. This section covers how to use the DSREPAIR, DSVIEW, DSTRACE, and other utilities during troubleshooting operations.

Additionally, this section covers NDS data recovery procedures and techniques, including the combination of various tools to diagnose, troubleshoot, and resolve problems. We conclude this section by applying the tools and techniques discussed to real-world examples.

Part IV, "Manage NDS to Prevent Problems," rounds out the many day-to-day aspects of NDS that you will need to know in order to proactively prevent problems. Topics include upgrading to NetWare 5 from the NDS point of view, and providing a comprehensive NDS security plan for your network. By proactively managing your NDS tree, you can prevent many problems; this section will show you how.

The four appendixes include valuable information that you can use as a handy reference, as follows:

▶ Appendix A, "NDS Error Codes," provides an exhaustive listing of all of the NDS error codes and their explanations. This listing of error codes helps you identify problems and determine resolution steps.

▶ Appendix B, "DS Verbs," provides information on the NDS verbs used by DSTRACE.

▶ Appendix C, "NDS Classes, Objects, and Attributes," contains NDS schema information for the various object classes and attribute definitions found in NetWare 4 and NetWare 5.

▶ Appendix D, "NDS Resources," lists resources used during the development of this book — third-party software products, good NDS Resources found on the Internet, and other publications covering related subject matter.

All the information and techniques presented in this book have been gathered from hands-on, real-world experiences learned from working with customers from around the world. Being SysOps for the Novell Support Connection Forums exposed us to a wide range of NDS implementations and issues. In this book, we share with you a selected number of the most frequently encountered NDS problems, and steps toward troubleshooting and fixing them.

Acknowledgments

Writing a book about troubleshooting Novell Directory Services requires not only knowing the current information that needs to be put into print, but knowing the people who can either provide, or nudge us in the direction of, the correct information. Without the people behind the NDS codes and folks from the DS Support team at Novell, much of the information in this book would not have come to light.

We appreciate the backing we received from the various groups at Novell. In particular, we thank Paul Reiner (who told us NDS was a "slam-dunk" so many years ago), DeAnne Higley, Gary Hein, and especially David Smith, for their insights into the inner workings of Novell Directory Services. We're grateful that Kim Groneman (Chief Grasshopper Herder) tolerated our disappearance from the Novell Support Connection Forums for days at a time when we were busy meeting the book schedule. We also would like to thank Marcel Cox, one of our fellow SysOps, for keeping us on our toes with new and interesting NDS problems.

We'd like to thank the folks at IDG Books Worldwide and Novell Press, who provided much-needed guidance throughout the project. Brian MacDonald, our development editor, did an outstanding job in providing the necessary prodding, shaping, and formatting of the book. Ken Neff, our technical editor, worked very hard to ensure this book was as technically accurate as possible. This book would never have been written if not for our acquisitions editor, Jim Sumser, who recognized the need for such a book.

Peter would like to extend a special thanks to a few people. First, thanks to Amy and Kenny for time-sharing Jim with me on this writing endeavor. I owe you another big hug, Amy. Second, thanks to SAS, LT, and JWO for *not* calling me a "glutton for punishment" when I told them I took on this book project. Finally, thanks to Dad and Mom for stocking the fridge with food and Classic Coke for my midnight writing marathons.

Jim would also like to extend his gratitude to several people who helped make this book possible. First and foremost, my wife Amy and stepson Kenny, who endured long nights, lots of pacing during writing sessions when I suffered from major writer's block, and a frequent lack of hot water due to all the showers I took when I *really* couldn't think of what to write. Many thanks also to my teammates Glen Wright, Michael Niesen, and Ryan Cox, all of whom patiently listened while

I ranted about NDS-related topics, sometimes at very inopportune times. I also would like to recognize Jeff Tibbitts for his assistance in discovering new ways to convert NLIST output into UIMPORT data files, and Stephen Robinson for sharing administration tips and tricks he discovered while working as one of our network administrators. Last but certainly not least, I would also like to thank Les Schalla for providing me the opportunity to be part of this exceptional team. The experience I have gained these past few years has been invaluable. And Les, you still owe me a lunch.

Contents at a Glance

Contents

## PART I

NDS Foundations

## CHAPTER 1

The Four Basics of NDS Troubleshooting

The purpose of troubleshooting is the timely restoration of essential services. Troubleshooting is part science, part art, and part pure luck. There have been many attempts made to reduce troubleshooting to a set of procedures and flowcharts; however, given the diversity of problems, no one has come up with a procedure or flowchart that covers every possible situation.

The key to successful troubleshooting is to develop the ability to break down a problem ("it doesn't work") into its elemental parts ("it works when I do this but doesn't when I do that.") This ability is the cumulation of personal experience and knowledge gained by exchanging war stories with others who have "been there, done that, and got the T-shirt." It is the combination of knowledge and experience (and some dumb luck doesn't hurt either) that will help you to develop an efficient on-the-spot strategy to tackle each problem. This same divide-and-conquer technique can be applied to troubleshooting Novell Directory Services (NDS) problems.

The Troubleshooting Process

A typical troubleshooting model consists of these five steps:

1. Gather information.
2. Develop a plan of attack.
3. Execute the plan.
4. Evaluate the results; go back to Step 1 if necessary.
5. Document the solution.

The material presented in this book focuses on the first three steps of the process.

In order to be able to break down an NDS error into its elemental parts, it is necessary to have an understanding of how NDS functions. Regardless of the nature and cause of your NDS issue, there are four rules you can follow that will make your NDS troubleshooting efforts much easier. This chapter briefly outlines and explains each of the four rules. The rest of this book covers in detail the various information and tools that you need to troubleshoot and resolve all NDS errors. Chapter 11, in particular, illustrates how you can use the knowledge presented in this book to solve a number of real-world NDS issues.

You can easily modify the four basics we outlined here for troubleshooting other problems, such as NetWare OS abends. You can also see Novell's Guide to Resolving Critical Server Issues, by Brad Dayley and Rich Jensen, from IDG Books Worldwide.

TIP

A solid understanding and reasonable application of the following NDS troubleshooting doctrines will assist you to quickly and efficiently identify the cause and restore any disruptions in your NDS tree:

- ▸ Don't panic

- ▸ Understand the error codes and NDS processes

- ▸ Troubleshoot and resolve the problem

- ▸ Manage NDS to prevent problems

Don't Panic!

Whenever an essential network service is down, you are generally under pressure to restore it, quickly. When the service is NDS, the pressure is much higher, because it can potentially affect all your users; however, the first rule of dealing with NDS issues is — don't panic!

Often, the NDS errors you encounter are transitional, and NDS will self-heal; furthermore, sometimes the NDS error condition is a secondary result of other network-related problems. For example, a -625 (unable to communicate) error is not a true NDS error but a by-product of a network communication problem. So, without first trying to understand the cause of the NDS error, if you start performing NDS-related "corrections," such as running DSREPAIR needlessly, you could *cause* NDS errors where there weren't any to start with.

The roots of many NetWare 4 and NetWare 5 administrators are from NetWare 3 with the bindery. While certain actions can be easily performed with the bindery, you can't and shouldn't treat NDS the same way. You need to keep in mind that Novell Directory Services is implemented as a *globally distributed, replicated, loosely consistent* database. The primary challenge in maintaining a globally distributed database is keeping all the information up-to-date when changes are made. For example, when you create a new user in a container, the change must be propagated to all servers holding a replica of that container; however, the loose-consistency nature of NDS means that the NDS database is not necessarily in strict synchronization all of the time.

When major changes are made in NDS, such as moving a server object or splitting a partition, it can take some time for the changes to propagate to all replicas; thus, there can be periods of time during which the information in one replica is different from that in another replica. But the information held by the replicas do eventually converge to an identical state, making NDS consistent once again. Because NDS is replicated, you shouldn't perform any partition-related operations when any of the servers holding a replica of the affected partition(s) are not available. If you do, you'll get NDS into a *stuck state,* where it is unable to complete the operation because it can't communicate the change to some servers.

As the old saying goes, "haste makes waste." You should *always* allow NDS sufficient time to perform what it is designed to do: replicate data without flooding the network with NDS traffic.

Understand the Error Codes and NDS Processes

In order to keep an application's file size (and thus, memory requirement) down, the trade-off is often to substitute comprehensive error and debugging messages with cryptic error codes. For example, instead of telling you "The NDS object you're searching for doesn't exist in the current context", a -601 error is displayed instead. If you don't have ready access to these error codes, your effort in determining the cause of your NDS error can be greatly hampered. In addition to needing the book, you'll also need to understand the processes involved when an error code is generated. Some could be a *legal* error condition, designating that there is not an actual error, while others designate a real error. For example, if you have enabled DSTRACE at the server console with the +ERR option, you may see a -601 error when an application is searching for an object in multiple containers. In such a case, they are legal errors but are expected. On the other hand, if you receive a -618 (NDS database inconsistent) error, it could mean real trouble; therefore, it is essential to know what the various error codes mean and to understand the processes that generate them.

You'll find a list of all published NDS error codes and their explanations in Chapter 5. A discussion about NDS processes can be found in Chapter 6.

TIP

An important side benefit of developing this understanding is your ability to determine if the problem is indeed NDS related or if it's caused by other sources, such as network communication faults. This ability saves you from going on a wild goose chase.

Troubleshoot and Resolve the Problem

Once you've determine the cause of your NDS trouble and formulated an attack plan, it's time to select your weapons. NetWare ships a wide range of utilities, such as DSREPAIR, NDS Manager, and DSTRACE, that you can use to troubleshoot and fix your NDS tree. Also, there are a number of third party tools that fill the gap in areas that Novell-supplied utilities don't cover; however, you need to know the capabilities of these tools and use the one best suitable for the task. Refer to Chapters 7 and 8 for more details.

Manage NDS to Prevent Problems

As most of you know, troubleshooting is a *reactive network management* process: you're on the defensive and are trying to stop the bleeding. Seasoned network managers tell you that the best network management tactic is a proactive one: you take actions to actively and properly manage your NDS so that problems don't occur. Treat the health of your NDS tree as you would your family's health — prevention is better than cure.

Refer to Chapters 12, 13, and 14 for details on proactive NDS management tips and information. Of particular interest to security-conscious network administrators is Chapter 15; in this chapter, we discuss various techniques in detecting intruders and minimizing NDS security risks.

Summary

This chapter introduced four NDS troubleshooting doctrines that can assist you to quickly and efficiently identify the cause and restore any disruptions in your NDS tree:

- ▸ Don't panic

- ▸ Understand the error codes and NDS processes

- ▸ Troubleshoot and resolve the problem

- ▸ Manage NDS to prevent problems

You'll find in-depth discussion of these topics in the remainder of this book. Before going into them, however, Chapter 2 provides a quick review of NDS terminology and basics that you should know before proceeding with the rest of this book.

NDS Basics

Troubleshooting and managing NDS can be a difficult task if you do not understand how it works. In preparation for the advanced information presented in this book, you need to achieve a baseline understanding of certain terms and concepts.

In this chapter, we provide this baseline, including

- ▸ NDS Database Structure

- ▸ Partition and Replica Types

- ▸ Bindery Services

- ▸ Time Synchronization

NDS Database Structure

In this section, we discuss the components that make up the NDS database structure. Specifically, we discuss classes, attributes, and syntaxes.

NDS is an inherently object-oriented structure, made up of objects that receive attributes from other objects. This idea is referred to as *inheritance* in object-oriented paradigms. The collection of all of the class and attribute definitions for a tree are referred to as the *schema*.

Classes

A *class* in NDS defines an object type, not a specific object, in terms of *attributes* or *flags*, which we discuss later in this chapter. Classes you might be familiar with are the user class, the print queue class, or the NCP server class. These definitions contain lists of attributes used to make up the class. The class definition is a blueprint or set of rules for how to make an object of a specified class.

There are two types of classes: The *effective* class and the *noneffective* class. An effective class is a class used to make an object that shows up in the NDS tree. The examples of a user, print queue, and NCP server are examples of effective classes. If you search the tree with the NetWare Administrator utility, you can find objects that are these types.

A noneffective class is a class used to define classes that do not appear in the tree but are used to build other classes. Examples of noneffective classes would be the person, queue, and NCP server classes, as shown in Figure 2.1.

All classes in NDS have common elements, which are part of the *top* class. This class is unique in that it has no parent classes, or *super classes*. All of the classes that make up the NDS tree, however, contain attributes defined in the top class.

▶ · ◀

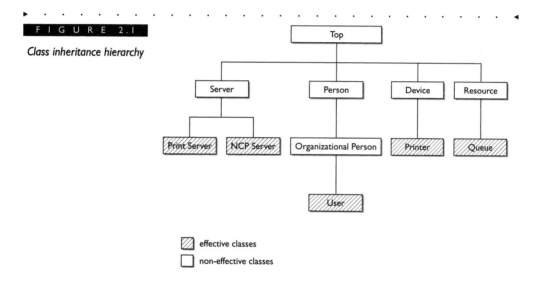

FIGURE 2.1

Class inheritance hierarchy

You may have deduced that classes alone are not enough to define objects in the tree. Think of a class as a type of box, and in order to have meaning, the box needs to have something in it. This thing in the box, in the NDS world, is called an *attribute*.

Attributes

Attributes are used to define aspects of an object. Examples of attributes associated with a user class object are *surname, full name,* and *network address.* Each of these holds a piece of information relevant to the user-class object in question.

It is also important to understand aspects of certain attributes. An aspect of a *mandatory* attribute is that it is required in order for the object to be created — if a *mandatory* attribute is missing, the object cannot be created. An aspect of a surname attribute is that it is required when creating a user — if you do not define a user's surname, you will be unable to create the user.

Loss of a mandatory attribute after creation of the object causes the object's class attribute to be changed to Unknown. Figure 2.2 shows a view of NetWare Administrator with several unknown objects in the tree. The Unknown class is designated by yellow circles with a question mark, making the unknown class easy to spot in NetWare Administrator.

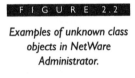

F I G U R E   2 . 2

Examples of unknown class objects in NetWare Administrator.

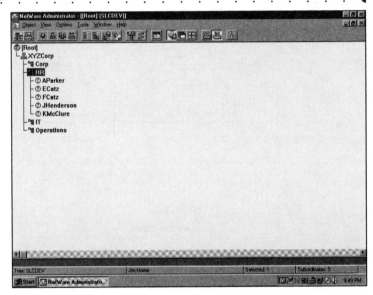

NOTE

It is important to recognize that there is a second type of object in NetWare Administrator that many people mistake for an unknown class object. This type of object appears in a white box with a question mark in it. This particular type of object is not of unknown class but just means that the necessary snap-in component for NetWare Administrator is not available and, consequently, that the object cannot be administered with NetWare Administrator.

The opposite of a mandatory attribute is an *optional* attribute. As the name implies, this is an attribute that is not necessary to create the object in question. The full name attribute of the user class is an example of an optional attribute. It can be present in the object that has been created, or it can be omitted.

Attributes can also be single-valued or multivalued. A single-valued attribute, such as the surname attribute, can only contain one value. If you change this value, the old value is replaced with the new one. A multivalued attribute is an attribute that can contain a number of entries. The network address attribute is such an attribute. It contains one entry for every workstation a user has logged into, and when you look at the list in NetWare Administrator, you see multiple values listed, one for each station the user is logged into.

Attribute data can be represented in many different forms in the NDS database. When defining an attribute, you also need to define the format used to store the data. This format is called a *syntax*.

Syntaxes

The last important piece of the database structure is syntax. Syntax defines the format the data in an attribute is in. Table 2.1 lists several examples of typical syntaxes included in every tree.

TABLE 2.1

Syntax Examples

SYNTAX (FROM C HEADER FILE)	DEFINITION	EXAMPLE ATTRIBUTE	EXAMPLE VALUE
SYN_CI_STRING	A list of characters that ignores whether the letters are upper or lower case when used in a comparison. CI stands for *case insensitive.*	Full Name	John Smith
SYN_NETWORK _ADDRESS	An IPX network address, represented in base 16 and made up of three components: the network number, node number, and socket. These components are typically delimited with : characters.	Network Address	84123001: 10005A627 D95:4088

Continued

T A B L E 2.1

Syntax Examples
(continued)

SYNTAX (FROM C HEADER FILE)	DEFINITION	EXAMPLE ATTRIBUTE	EXAMPLE VALUE
SYN_OCTET_STREAM	A list of binary data, represented in base 16 and used to represent information in a proprietary format.	CA Public Key	00 20 80 FF C3 11 98
SYN_INTEGER	A value represented by a number.	Login Maximum Simultaneous	10
SYN_BOOLEAN	A true/false or yes/no value.	Password Required	TRUE

Partition and Replica Types

Now that you have an understanding of what makes up the NDS database, we should look at how the database is distributed.

The NDS database is a loosely consistent partitioned database. This means that the data can be divided into many different logical pieces, called *partitions*, and you can put a copy, or *replica*, of any partition on a number of servers. The DS.NLM module keeps the information in different replicas synchronized, but at any given point in time, the information in one replica may not match the information in another replica; however, the DS.NLM module handles the discrepancy between copies by maintaining information about which copy has the most current changes and propagating, or replicating, this information to the servers with older information. It is important to note that the NDS database is continually converging to a consistent state. Once it completes synchronization on a partition, the partition is consistent until the next time data is changed.

When you first installed your server, the system created a number of special partitions on the SYS: volume. These partitions are:

- The System Partition

- The Schema Partition

- ▸ The External Reference Partition

- ▸ The Bindery Partition

In addition, it may have added a user-defined partition automatically if the server is one of the first three servers installed in the partition.

The System Partition

The system partition keeps track of the information specific to the local server. This information is not synchronized with other servers in the tree. This is the partition that the limber process operates on. See Chapter 6 for more information about the system partition.

Information contained in this partition includes:

- ▸ Information on where the server is located in the NDS tree, including the fully qualified distinguished name and object type identifiers. For example, on my server, the name recorded here would be CN=BETELGEUSE.O=Home.

- ▸ The state of background processes if the server is running DS.NLM 5.95 or later (for NetWare 4.11 and NetWare 4.2) or any version of DS on NetWare 5.0.

The Schema Partition

The schema partition keeps track of all of the object class and attribute definition information for the server. This information is synchronized between servers using a process called *schema skulk* or *schema sync*. The schema sync process starts with the server that contains the master replica of the [Root] partition and propagates to the other servers with a copy of the [Root]. Then it continues with the servers in the child partitions until all servers have received a copy of the schema.

· · · · ·
15

The External Reference Partition

The external reference partition contains information about objects that don't really exist on the local server. In Figure 2.3, server BETELGEUSE holds the master replica of the [Root] partition, server ANDROMEDA holds the master replica of the subordinate O=Home partition, and server RIGEL holds the master replica of the O=XYZCorp partition. The user CN=JimH in the O=Home partition has a group membership to the group CN=Users in the O=XYZCorp container.

▶ . . . . ◀

FIGURE 2.3

Tree partitioning/replication example for external reference discussion

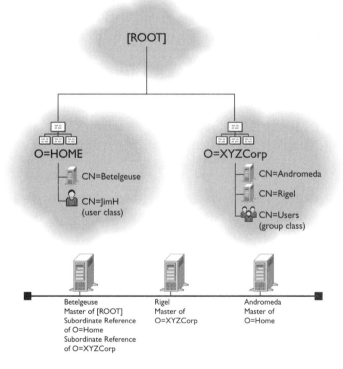

In this example, there would be an external reference created on RIGEL, for the object CN=Users.O=XYZCorp, on server ANDROMEDA, and on the object CN=JimH.O=Home. These objects would be contained in the external reference partitions of the respective servers.

The Bindery Partition

All servers keep track of NetWare server Service Advertising Protocol (SAP) traffic, and every server has a SUPERVISOR user maintained for backwards compatibility to NetWare 2.*x* and NetWare 3.*x*. This information is maintained in the server's *bindery partition*.

The bindery partition is not replicated to all servers but is kept specific to the server in question.

User-Defined Partitions

The last type of partition is the user-defined partition. This is the most common type of partition and likely the type you are already familiar with.

In Figure 2.3, we discussed the external reference partition, but this figure also demonstrates the user-defined partition type as well. In Figure 2.3, the master partition of [Root] is on server BETELGEUSE, the master replica of O=Home is on server ANDROMEDA, and the master of O=XYZCorp is on server RIGEL. Each of these partitions is a user-defined partition, even though the server BETELGEUSE got the master replica of the [Root] partition automatically during the installation of the server.

IMPORTANT

Many administrators do not realize it, but even without a user-defined partition on the system, the SUPERVISOR account exists on the server. If you later set up a bindery context for the server using the SET BINDERY CONTEXT console SET parameter, make sure you change the SUPERVISOR password to something you know; otherwise, it is possible for an old administrator to break into your system.

The user-defined partition type consists of four replica types:

▶ Master

▶ Read/Write

▶ Read-Only

▶ Subordinate Reference

The replica types are used to represent an actual copy of a partition in the NDS tree.

Master Replica

The master replica is the first copy of a new partition. When you install a new server into a new tree, this server automatically receives a master replica of the [Root] partition. If you then create a new partition in the NDS Manager utility, the already installed server receives the master copy of this partition as well, because it has the master of the parent partition.

As we will discuss in Chapter 6, the master replica must be available for certain partition operations, such as a partition join, partition split, or object/partition move.

Read/Write Replica

The read/write replica is created if a master replica already exists and you need to have a copy of the partition on a server. Referring back to Figure 2.3, if we were to add a copy of [Root] to server RIGEL, this replica would most likely be a read/write replica. It could be a read-only replica, but then it could not be used as a copy that could be modified from a workstation utility.

Read-Only Replica

The read-only replica time is seldom — if ever — used. It was added because Novell built NDS on the X.500 directory standard, and the standard specified read-only replicas

Use of read-only replicas is strongly discouraged. They do not provide any advantages with regard to traffic management, because they actually can generate more traffic than a read/write replica.

Any change directed at a server that holds a read-only replica of a partition ends up being redirected by the server to a server with a read/write or master replica. The change would then be synchronized back to the server through the normal synchronization process.

Subordinate Reference

The subordinate reference, or *subref*, replica type is the only user-defined replica type that is not actually placed manually. It is created automatically by the synchronization process when a server holds a parent partition but not a master.

Referring back to Figure 2.3, the replication scheme laid out is as follows:

Server	Partition/Replica
BETELGEUSE	Master of [Root]
ANDROMEDA	Master of O=Home
RIGEL	Master of O=XYZCorp

In this case, there would be two subordinate reference partitions on BETELGEUSE: one for O=Home and one for O=XYZCorp.

The actual replication scheme would look like this:

Server	Partition/Replica
BETELGEUSE	Master of [Root]
	Subref of O=Home
	Subref of O=XYZCorp
ANDROMEDA	Master of O=Home
RIGEL	Master of O=XYZCorp

As a rule of thumb for determining where a subordinate reference partition is going to be placed, remember that it will be placed everywhere the master is but where the child partition is not.

The placement of subordinate reference partitions is critical to the operation of *tree walking*, or the process of navigating the tree. When attempting to walk from O=Home to O=XYZCorp, in order to read the group object CN=Users, the client finds its way back to [Root] by looking at where there are subordinate reference replicas of O=Home and discovers that BETELGEUSE contains one. It then will ask BETELGEUSE how to find O=XYZCorp, at which time it will discover that BETELGEUSE also holds a subordinate reference of O=XYZCorp. From this partition's replica list, it will discover that RIGEL holds the master of O=XYZCorp and will ask RIGEL for the information needed.

NOTE

The subordinate reference partition type only contains the root object in the partition, commonly referred to as the *partition root* object. This object keeps track of the replica list for the partition and is used by the clients to perform the tree walking operation.

▶ . . . . ◀

Bindery Services

Bindery services, also referred to occasionally as *bindery emulation mode*, are used to provide backward compatibility to NetWare 2.*x* and NetWare 3.*x* services. The most common uses for bindery services are:

- ▶ To support software that requires a login as the SUPERVISOR object in order to install it.

- ▶ To support older printing devices, such as HP JetDirect cards, manufactured before NDS was released. These devices typically work on a bindery print queue.

Bindery services are enabled with the SET BINDERY CONTEXT console command. In order to use this command, you must have a master or read/write replica of the partition that holds the bindery objects created by the service. Failure to hold the objects will result in bindery services not being enabled for this container, and the following error message will be displayed:

```
Bindery context OU=WEST.O=XYZCORP set, illegal replica type.

Error: The Bindery context container must be set to a

location that is present in a replica on this server.
Bindery context NOT set.

Bindery Context is set to: O=XYZCORP
```

▶ . . . . ◀

Time Synchronization

Time synchronization, while not a service provided by NDS, is a very important part of maintaining the integrity of the NDS tree. Every time a change is made to an object, the change is time stamped in order to allow the change to be made on all servers holding a copy of that object in the proper sequence. Without time synchronization, it would be possible to set up two servers with different times but holding copies of the same objects. In this case, you could change a user's password on one server and this change might not be propagated to the second server properly, and the user would be forced to log in with his or her old password.

There are four time-server types:

▸ Single Reference

▸ Reference

▸ Primary

▸ Secondary

Single Reference Time Server

The single reference time-server type is typically used in a small network, where one server holds the definitive time for the entire network. If you need to change the time for some reason, you would change the time at the single reference server.

NOTE

It is generally recommended that if you change the time on the network, you should use the SET TIMESYNC TIME ADJUSTMENT console command and not the SET TIME console command.

You can think about the relationship of a single reference time server and a secondary time server as a master-slave relationship. The single reference server decides unilaterally what time it is and tells the rest of the servers on the network that it is correct.

Figure 2.4 shows a sample time-server configuration using a single reference time server and multiple secondary time servers.

Reference Time Server

A reference time server is typically used in larger network environments. A reference server participates in a polling process to determine what the correct time is. While a reference server has more weight than other servers in the polling process, it is part of this process and, if the polling servers determine the time on the reference server is too far off, they disregard the time change and maintain correct time.

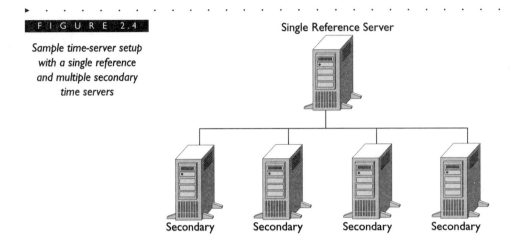

FIGURE 2.4

Sample time-server setup with a single reference and multiple secondary time servers

Single Reference Server

Secondary   Secondary   Secondary   Secondary

Reference time servers typically are used to talk to external time sources, such as an atomic clock, in order to maintain accurate time. One reference time server is allowed per NDS tree.

Primary Time Server

Primary time servers are used in the polling process with a reference time server. Typically, more than one primary time server is used in conjunction with a reference time server. Primary time servers are best used when positioned geographically to allow time synchronization to continue with other servers even if a link is down to the reference time server.

In Figure 2.5, you can see a sample reference/primary/secondary time server configuration. Note that the secondary time servers can get their time from the reference or any of the primary time servers.

Secondary Time Server

The last type of time server is a secondary time server. This type of time server receives its time from another server on the network — it does not matter whether it is a single reference, reference, or primary time server. Secondary time servers do not participate in polling and are essentially slaves to the time synchronization process.

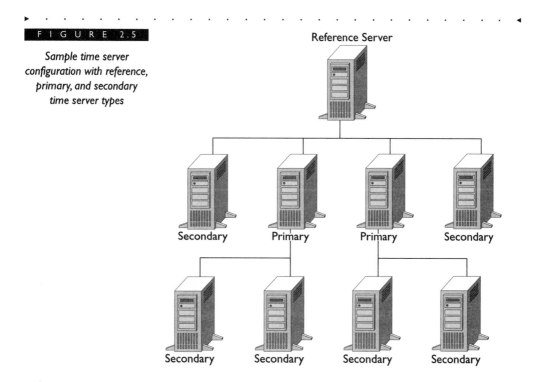

Sample time server configuration with reference, primary, and secondary time server types

Reference Server

Secondary   Primary   Primary   Secondary

Secondary   Secondary   Secondary   Secondary

Summary

In this chapter, we established a base of information necessary to begin looking at NDS tree design and troubleshooting. Starting with classes, attributes, and syntaxes, we examined how the database is structured and discussed the partitioning and replication features of NDS. Last, we looked at why time synchronization is important to the NDS database.

In Chapter 3, we examine the actual data store used by NDS: the Directory Information Base (DIB).

Directory Information Base

Just as you don't really need to know how a combustion engine works in order to drive a car, it is not necessary for you to have an intricate knowledge of the NDS database file structures in order to use, manage, and troubleshoot NDS; however, knowing that the NDS database is made up of a number of files and knowing what components make up the NDS database can make troubleshooting easier. Though this chapter is by no means an in-depth technical view of the NDS database files, it will give you an idea of what these file names are, where they are located, and what their purpose is.

The set of NDS database files is officially known as the *Directory Information Base* (DIB). Often times, these files are simply referred to as *NDS files;* however, in a number of Novell utilities, such as DSREPAIR, the term *DIB* is used.

NetWare 4 DIB

The main NetWare 4 DIB set is comprised of four files:

▸ PARTITIO.NDS

▸ ENTRY.NDS

▸ VALUE.NDS

▸ BLOCK.NDS

PARTITIO.NDS

The PARTITIO.NDS file contains information specific to partitions that are stored on that server. This data is server centric, because it has no correlation with the data in the PARTITIO.NDS file on another server. The file contains the following information that helps NDS replicate and synchronize data between servers:

▸ **Partition ID**. The hexadecimal number assigned to a replica (by NetWare) when it is created. This number is used to associate an object with its partition.

▸ **Partition Root Object**. The hexadecimal object ID number of the object that is the root of the partition.

▸ **Replica Type**. The type of replica (such as Master or Read/Write).

▸ **Replica State**. The state of the replica (such as On or Split).

▸ **Replica Flags**. Used by NDS synchronization processes.

▸ **Next Timestamp**. The minimum value of the next timestamp the server issues to an object in the partition.

You can look up this information using DSREPAIR. From the Main menu, select Advanced Options and then Replica and Partition Operations. Select any one of the partitions from the displayed list. Choose Display Replica Information. The resulting log file shows the data from the PARTITIO.NDS file in a readable format, as shown in Figure 3.1.

FIGURE 3.1

DSREPAIR log file showing information about the [Root] partition

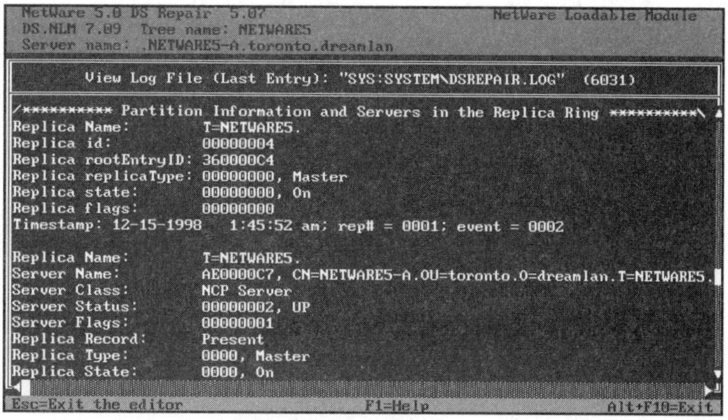

```
NetWare 5.0 DS Repair  5.07                          NetWare Loadable Module
DS.NLM 7.09  Tree name: NETWARE5
Server name: .NETWARE5-A.toronto.dreamlan

┌───────── View Log File (Last Entry): "SYS:SYSTEM\DSREPAIR.LOG"  (6031) ─────────┐
│ /********** Partition Information and Servers in the Replica Ring **********\  ▲
│ Replica Name:        T=NETWARE5.
│ Replica id:          00000004
│ Replica rootEntryID: 360000C4
│ Replica replicaType: 00000000, Master
│ Replica state:       00000000, On
│ Replica flags:       00000000
│ Timestamp: 12-15-1998  1:45:52 am; rep# = 0001; event = 0002
│
│ Replica Name:        T=NETWARE5.
│ Server Name:         AE0000C7, CN=NETWARE5-A.OU=toronto.O=dreamlan.T=NETWARE5.
│ Server Class:        NCP Server
│ Server Status:       00000002, UP
│ Server Flags:        00000001
│ Replica Record:      Present
│ Replica Type:        0000, Master
│ Replica State:       0000, On                                                 ▼
│ ◄                                                                          ►
│ Esc=Exit the editor              F1=Help                    Alt+F10=Exit
```

ENTRY.NDS

All objects stored on the server are located within the ENTRY.NDS file. Each object has a record entry in the file. Each record contains the following information:

- **Object Name**. The typed relative distinguished name of the object — for example, CN=Peter.

- **Partition ID**. The hexadecimal id of the partition in which the object belongs. This corresponds to the records in the PARTITIO.NDS file.

- **Base Object Class**. Pointer to the record within the ENTRY.NDS file containing the schema definition (such as user), which is used as the object's base object class.

- **Creation Time**. The timestamp of when this object was created.

- **Parent Object**. A pointer to the record within the ENTRY.NDS file containing the object that is the parent of the current object. For example, if the current object's full name is CN=Peter.OU=DREAMLAN.O=North_America, this field points to OU=DREAMLAN.O=North_America, which is the parent of the CN=Peter object.

- **Sibling Object**. Pointer to the record within ENTRY.NDS file for the object that is a sibling object.

NOTE

A sibling object is an object that has the same parent object (or name context) as another object. For example, CN=Peter.OU=DREAMLAN.O=North_America is a sibling object to CN=Jim.OU=DREAMLAN.O=North_America, because both objects have the same parent object, OU=DREAMLAN.O=North_America.

- **First Child Object**. Pointer to the record within ENTRY.NDS file for the object that is the first child object. If the current object is a leaf object, such as a user, then there is no child object.

- **Last Child Object**. Pointer to the record within ENTRY.NDS file for the object that is the last child object. If the current object is a leaf object, such as a user, then there is no child object.

▶ **First NDS Attribute**. Pointer to the record within VALUES.NDS file containing the object's first attribute.

▶ **Subordinate Count**. Number of records that are subordinate to, that is, reference, the current object. In essence, this is the number of child objects this object has. For example, if the current object is a container and has four user objects and two OUs, the subordinate count is six.

▶ **Object Flags**. A set of flags identifying the characteristics of the object. The following are the possible flags:

  • **Alias** indicates the object is an alias to another object.

  • **Backlinked** indicates the object is an external reference that has established a backlink.

An external reference is a placeholder used to store information about an object that is not contained in a partition held by the server. See Chapter 6 for more information about external references and backlinks.

NOTE

  • **Partition** indicates the object is a partition root object.

  • **Present** indicates the object is present in the NDS tree.

  • **Not Present**, indicates the object is no longer considered by NDS to exist within the tree, but its record still exists in the DIB because the janitor process hasn't purged it yet. See the "Delete" and "Obits" sections in Chapter 6 for more information.

VALUES.NDS

The VALUES.NDS file contains (attribute) values associated with records in the ENTRY.NDS file. The structure of the VALUES.NDS file is similar to that of ENTRY.NDS. The following information is stored in the VALUES.NDS file:

▶ **Object Name**. Pointer to the object record in the ENTRY.NDS file to which this attribute is associated.

▶ **Attribute**. Pointer to the record within the ENTRY.NDS file containing the schema attribute definition (such as surname) for this attribute.

▶ **Next Value**. Pointer to the record within VALUES.NDS file containing the attribute's next value if the attribute is multivalued.

▶ **Next Attribute**. Pointer to the record within VALUES.NDS file containing the next attribute assigned to the object.

▶ **First Block**. Each VALUES.NDS record can hold up to 16 bytes of data (such as the number of days before a password expires). If the data for an attribute's value doesn't fit in a single VALUES.NDS record, the extra data is stored in a record in the BLOCK.NDS file. The First Block is a pointer to a record in this file that holds the first block of overflow data.

▶ **Modification Timestamp**. Contains the timestamp on when the attribute value was created or last modified.

▶ **Attribute Value**. The data associated with the attribute. If the attribute's data type or syntax is stream (SYN_STREAM), the filename containing the stream data is recorded instead.

NOTE

All stream data, such as login scripts, are stored in individual files, where the file name is a hexadecimal number and the file extension is .000. The hexadecimal number in the filename has no direct relation to the hexadecimal object id of the NDS object to which the hex number in the filename is associated. For example, the container login script for OU=DREAMLAN (whose object id is 0x01000124) is stored in a stream file named 0004B3C0.000, and the Print Job Configuration information associated with the same container is stored in a stream file called 0031B000.000.

▶ **Attribute Flags**. A set of flags identifying the characteristics of the attribute. The following are the possible flags:

   • **Base Object Class** indicates that the value in the record is the value used as the base object class for the object that this attribute is associated with.

- **Naming** indicates that the value in the record is used as the relative distinguished name of the object that this attribute is associated with.

- **Present** indicates the object is present in the NDS tree.

- **Not Present** indicates the object is no longer considered by NDS to exist within the tree, but its record still exists in the DIB because the janitor process hasn't purged it yet. See the "Delete" and "Obits" sections in Chapter 6 for more information.

BLOCK.NDS

The BLOCK.NDS file is used to store the value of an object's attribute that exceeds 16 bytes in size. Each record in BLOCK.NDS consists of the following fields:

▶ **Attribute Name**. Pointer to the attribute record in VALUE.NDS file to which this data block is associated.

▶ **Value**. The value or data for the attribute. Each record in BLOCK.NDS can hold up to 108 bytes of data.

▶ **Next Block**. If the data is larger than 124 bytes (16 bytes in the VALUE.NDS file and 108 bytes in the first block of BLOCK.NDS), additional records in the BLOCK.NDS file is used for the excess data. The next block points to the next record within the BLOCK.NDS file containing data for the attribute.

If you are familiar with database structures, you'll readily recognize that the NDS DIB set is implemented as a set of linked lists. The link generally starts in the ENTRY.NDS file and is then linked to VALUE.NDS and then to BLOCK.NDS. Using linked lists, NDS can easily insert data into the DIB by simply adjusting the pointers accordingly. Any nodes (elements in the list) that are deleted can be easily reused; therefore, there is generally no need to repack the DIB, unless you have deleted a large number of objects. Even then, you may not see much of a size reduction of the DIB because only empty nodes at the end of the lists are deleted.

To reduce the chance of pointer corruption and data integrity, NDS transactions are protected by NetWare Transaction Tracking System (TTS); therefore, if for some reason the server's TTS mechanism is disabled, DS.NLM automatically shuts down the DIB. Because TTS uses disk space on the SYS: volume to create transaction log files, it is essential that you ensure the SYS: volume always has sufficient free disk space, or else you risk shutting down NDS.

You can easily look up the object and attribute information using Novell's DSVIEW NLM. This NLM is not included with NetWare, but can generally be found included with the DS.NLM updates. At the time of this writing, DSVIEW for NetWare 5 is not available, because DSVIEW is NDS-version specific. The DSVIEW screen in Figure 3.2 shows the information related to the login intruder limit attribute, such as timestamp and syntax.

FIGURE 3.2

Examining NDS DIB
using DSVIEW

```
Key<Action> 1<Next Attribute> 2<Next Value> 3<View Entry>
            4<Previous Attribute/Value> 5<Toggle Display Mode>
            6<Go To Entry> ESC<Return to Main Menu>

********------ Value Information ------********

Entry ID: 01000124   "O=DreamLAN"
Attribute Name: "Login Intruder Limit"

Value Flags:  Present
TimeStamp: 98/10/27 00:38:26; rep# = 0001; event = 04D2

syntax: Integer
2,  0x00000002

More Attributes: Yes     More Attribute Values: No
```

NOTE   By default, **DSREPAIR** saves the old **DIB** files after a repair operation. The four files mentioned previously are renamed with a **.OLD** extension. Because of the backup **DIB** files, you have essentially doubled your **DIB** size after you run **DSREPAIR**. Do keep this in mind if you're low on disk space on the **SYS:** volume.

NetWare 5 DIB

The names of the four core NDS files are changed in NetWare 5, but their functions remain the same as their cousins in NetWare 4. Also, two new DS-related files are also added to NetWare 5. The NetWare 5 DIB is comprised of the following files:

- **0.DSD**. This file contains the same type of data as and performs the same function as the ENTRY.NDS in NetWare 4.

- **1.DSD**. This file contains the same type of data as and performs the same function as the VALUE.NDS.

- **2.DSD**. This file contains the same type of data as and performs the same function as BLOCK.NDS.

- **3.DSD**. This file contains the same type of data as and performs the same function as PARTITIO.NDS.

- **0.DSB**. This is a look-up table that holds the names of the .DSD files to facilitate faster server start.

IMPORTANT

The 0.DSB file is 28 bytes in size, and if it's missing or corrupted, the NetWare 5 server displays a -723 or -736 error on boot-up. You can copy this file from another server or download 0DSB.EXE from Novell's Support Connection Web site.

- **NLSLIST.DAT**. This file contains NetWare 5 licensing (both server and connection) data used by Novell Licensing Services (NLS).

In NetWare 4, DSREPAIR renames old DIB files with an .OLD extension. Under NetWare 5, however, DSREPAIR renames the old DIB .DSD files to files with a .DOD extension, and the 0.DSB file is renamed to 0.DOB.

NOTE

A complete definition of object classes, object types, and attributes found in NetWare 4.11 and NetWare 5 is in Appendix B.

▶ . . . . ◀

Locating the DIB

Many administrators often wonder where NetWare stores the DIB files. These files are located in the SYS:_NETWARE directory. This is a system-protected directory that can't be accessed using standard utilities such as FILER; however, you can easily view the content of this directory using RCONSOLE:

1. Use RCONSOLE to connect to your server.

2. Press Alt-F1 to bring up the Available Options menu.

3. Select Directory Scan and enter SYS:_NETWARE as the name for the directory to scan.

4. A list of DIB and stream files is displayed.

Figure 3.3 shows the contents of the SYS:_NETWARE directory on a NetWare 5 server. On a NetWare 4.11 server, the output is similar, but the file names are different, as we noted earlier.

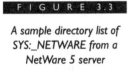

FIGURE 3.3

A sample directory list of SYS:_NETWARE from a NetWare 5 server

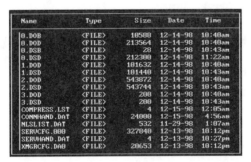

Name	Type	Size	Date	Time
0.DOB	<FILE>	10588	12-14-98	10:40am
0.DOD	<FILE>	213564	12-14-98	10:40am
0.DSB	<FILE>	28	12-14-98	10:43am
0.DSD	<FILE>	212300	12-14-98	11:22am
1.DOD	<FILE>	101632	12-14-98	10:40am
1.DSD	<FILE>	101440	12-14-98	10:43am
2.DOD	<FILE>	543872	12-14-98	10:40am
2.DSD	<FILE>	543744	12-14-98	10:43am
3.DOD	<FILE>	200	12-14-98	10:40am
3.DSD	<FILE>	200	12-14-98	10:43am
COMPRESS.LST	<FILE>	4	12-15-98	12:05am
CONNHAND.DAT	<FILE>	24000	12-15-98	4:56am
NLSLIST.DAT	<FILE>	532	11-29-98	1:07am
SERVCFG.000	<FILE>	327840	12-13-98	10:12pm
SERVHAND.DAT	<FILE>	4	12-13-98	10:27pm
XMGRCFG.DA0	<FILE>	20653	12-13-98	10:12pm

▶ . . . . ◀

Backing Up the DIB

In a single-server environment, it is possible to back up your NDS by making a copy of the DIB files. This is analogous to backing up the bindery in the old NetWare 2 and NetWare 3 environment, because all the data is located on a single server. Backing up the NDS by making a copy of the DIB files is *not* a good idea at all, however, if you have a multiserver environment. Because the NDS database is often in a loosely synchronized, loosely consistent state, you can't guarantee the DIB on a given server has full data integrity at the time you make a copy of the files.

In a multiserver configuration, it is best to use a Storage Management Service (SMS)-compliant backup application to back up the NDS via proper API calls. You can learn more about SMS and other tools that back up and restore NDS in Chapter 8.

Summary

This chapter presented the organization and a high-level look at the file structure of the NDS database in NetWare 4 and NetWare 5. We have identified the file name differences between the two operation systems and shown you how you can view, using DSREPAIR and DSVIEW, some of the information recorded and used by NDS that are not displayed by conventional utilities such as NetWare Administrator.

## CHAPTER 4

Don't Panic

In fact, the very best advice it has to offer in these situations is to be found on the cover, where it says in those now notoriously large and famously friendly letters "DON'T PANIC."

—Douglas Adams,
The Original Hitchhiker Radio Scripts

While Adams's book is a work of fiction, the advice given has great practical value. In the world of networking and dealing with critical problems, the absolute worst thing you can do is panic. This is especially true when working with NDS. In traditional network troubleshooting, changes that are made are typically easy to undo. For example, if you are working with a routing problem, you can change a setting in the router that disables packet forwarding on a particular interface and observe the change in the environment, and if the change does not affect the problem the way you thought it would, you can change the setting back.

When working with NDS, however, many changes are easy to make but extremely difficult to undo. As you will see in later chapters, it takes a thorough understanding of what makes NDS work combined with a full understanding of what the problem actually is to determine a proper course of corrective action.

It is not uncommon for inexperienced administrators to run into a situation that demands immediate attention. Critical NDS problems tend to be highly visible — either because the problem affects users' ability to log in and do the work that makes your company run or a major piece of functionality is affected. Printing, for example, might be offline, so users can work on documents, but they cannot print out the sales reports that upper management likes to see every day by 10:00A.M.

In this sort of highly visible (not to mention high stress) environment, it is very easy to fall into the trap of doing something for the sake of doing something. Upper management doesn't understand the intricacies of what makes the network tick, but they certainly can identify when the person who is responsible for fixing the problem isn't doing anything about it.

Or so they believe.

Doing something for the sake of doing something is nearly always counterproductive. It is easy to make a change at the server, and when upper management wants to know what you are doing about the problem, you can say "I changed this, this, and this." It is an easy out, but it can make the problem resolution take much longer because new factors introduced to the problem have made the problem worse.

This book is about the technical aspects of working with NDS and fixing problems, but we want to diverge for a second and talk about how to deal with the difficult situation of working with people.

Dealing with People

The vast majority of technical people in our industry prefer working with machines to working with people. This statement is based largely on many discussions we have had with administrators, engineers, and consultants while working in this industry.

Computers are easy to work with. They do what they are told — even if that does not equate to what you want — they will wait for you while you go have lunch, and they never have a bad attitude or demand that you do something *right now*.

Conversely, people can be difficult to work with. They do not necessarily do what they are told, will interrupt your lunch to have you work on a project they forgot needed to be done *right now*, and when things are not going their way, they can have a very bad attitude.

People skills are a very important part of a system administrator's job. You have to be a salesperson, a diplomat, and a teacher. It is very difficult to do any of these things well if you have a hard time dealing with people and communicating effectively with them.

Take some time to learn how to interact with the people you work with. Learning how to communicate with them outside of a crisis situation will help you know how to effectively communicate with them in a crisis situation. Learn the best way to tell people that they are in your way, and learn to tell them that continually interrupting your thought process, by asking when the system is going to be operational again, is not going to help you get things running again. Different people react differently to being told this, so it is important that you know how best to communicate this with the people who will invariably come down to find out what is going on.

In addition to learning to deal with people effectively, it is also important to handle your own stress in a crisis situation.

▶ . . . . ◀

Dealing with Stress

Your own stress can be the biggest detriment to getting a problem resolved. Stress creates an environment that is not conducive to clear thinking, and being able to think clearly about what you are seeing in order to reason through the problem is absolutely critical.

Some techniques you can use to clear your head and perform a type of mental soft reset include

▶ Take a walk while DSREPAIR (or some other automated process) is doing a repair.

▶ Close your eyes and count to ten when you're in front of the server exhibiting the problem.

▶ Laugh. This one sometimes brings on strange looks from coworkers, but it really works. Laughter is one of the best stress relievers there is.

▶ Stretch. Stretch out the tension in your neck and shoulders; it will help you relax.

Other people use other techniques—the important thing is to learn what works for you. When in a crisis situation, it is important that the stress relief you use for yourself is something that can be applied quickly. Going cycling might be a great stress reliever for you, but in a crisis situation, this is not likely to be a viable option.

Once you're calm and in control of the situation, you can begin to address the problem by starting to understand NDS processes and error codes.

Understanding the Error Codes and NDS Processes

## CHAPTER 5

NDS Error Codes Explained

NDS errors occur during the processing of an NDS request or the execution of an NDS background process. These errors can happen as a result of hardware or software failure, data inconsistency, or unexpected responses received; therefore, when troubleshooting a problem, it is essential that you know from where the error originated, the condition that caused the error, and what the error code or message means. Unfortunately computer-generated error messages are notoriously cryptic at best and frequently don't provide the source of the error. For example, an NDS error can be generated from one of three possible sources:

▶ The DS service running on the NetWare server

▶ The client application (workstation-based or server-based)

▶ The DS Agent running on the NetWare server.

It gets even more frustrating if there can be multiple causes resulting in the same error code.

NOTE

Each NDS-capable NetWare server runs both the DS service (which processes NDS requests locally) and the DS Agent (DSA) service. The DSA _tree-walks_ and queries other DS servers on behalf of the requesting client — which can be either a workstation or another server — if the local server doesn't have the requested information.

By examining the code number returned or associated with the error message, you can determine the most likely source (the server, the client, or the DSA) and the possible cause of the NDS error. Do keep in mind that the information provided here does not necessarily give remedies but just a developer's explanation of the error. There are several factors that can help you to identify the root cause of the error and then eliminate or correct the error, including

▶ An understanding of NDS processes (see Chapter 6)

▶ An understanding of NDS error code definitions and possible conditions under which they can occur

▶ Familiarity with the NDS tree that is experiencing the error

▸ Familiarity with the placement of the replicas

▸ Familiarity with NDS diagnostic and repair tools, such as DSTRACE, DSVIEW, and DSREPAIR (see Chapter 7)

This chapter provides information to help you understand the more commonly encountered NDS error codes. You can use this as a starting point to further determine the actual cause of the problem and then formulate a corrective action plan. An exhaustive listing and explanation of all of the published NDS error codes is presented in Appendix A.

Types and Causes of NDS Errors

The first step in dealing with NDS problems is to understand the nature of the error. NDS errors can be categorized into *transitory NDS errors* or *recurring NDS errors*. These terms refer to the conditions that cause an NDS error to occur and not to the NDS error code reported in response to the conditions. In addition to understanding the nature of an NDS error, an understanding of the types of conditions that can cause NDS errors to occur is essential to help you to narrow down the area in which to concentrate your troubleshooting efforts.

NOTE

Not all NDS errors are bad errors. Some errors are considered *normal* **errors. A normal error — perhaps a better term is** *informational error* **— is one that logically happens in the DS. Examples are the collisions and DSA common request errors you see in DSTRACE. These informational errors are displayed to help you see how NDS handles processes such as user logins and changes in the DS. For example, DSTRACE shows a -601 error (no such object) when a user tries to log in using a wrong context — this is an error from a programming point of view, but it's not an error from the NDS operation's point of view.**

Transitory NDS Errors

Transitory NDS errors are those errors that occur on an intermittent basis or that occur only for a short time and do not reoccur. These errors are generally caused by conditions external to the server that reports the error; however, transitory errors may occur due to data inconsistency between different replicas of the same partition.

A commonly encountered transitory NDS error is error code -625 (transport failure). It is caused by communication failure between two servers that hold replicas of the same partition. The communication fault may be due to a down WAN connection or a disruption of the LAN (such as beaconing in a Token Ring environment). Both of these error conditions are external to the servers, out of the control of NDS, and can't be resolved by NDS; however, once the communication link is reestablished, the NDS -625 error automatically stops and does not reoccur unless the link is down again.

In a well-maintained, healthy NDS tree, most of the NDS errors are of the transitory type; therefore, when you're presented with an NDS error it is best to remember not to panic and to give NDS some time (say, up to 30 minutes) to see if the error can be auto-corrected.

Recurring NDS Errors

A recurring NDS error is an error that results from a permanent error condition that can't be correctly resolved without human intervention. Errors of this type persist until the cause of the error is identified and corrected. It is important to note that not all recurring errors are attributed to NDS or the NDS databases.

Although most of the time error -625 is a transitory error, it can also be a recurring error. For example, if a server holding a replica of a partition is removed from the network without going through the proper procedure, the replica ring becomes inconsistent, because the servers in the replica ring are not aware that the server is no longer available and will continue to attempt to synchronize update with this server. The resulting -625 error continues to be reported until the replica ring is repaired.

X-REF

For the procedure on repairing replica ring inconsistency, see Chapter 11.

Another common recurring NDS error is -601 (no such object). This is caused by an NDS user attempting to access a nonexistent NDS object; for example, if the user is trying to log in but the context of the object is wrong. The user will continue to receive this -601 error code after each attempt. Do keep in mind that this -601 error code may also be transitory, depending on the cause of the error.

NDS Error-Causing Conditions

NDS errors can be divided into three categories: informational messages, communication-related errors, and errors due to data inconsistency. Informational "errors" are nonfatal errors that are returned by DS to the requesting client to inform it of the following conditions:

▸ The request cannot be processed at this time due to outstanding operation. For example, you're trying to perform a partitioning operation while a previous one is still in progress.

▸ The request cannot be processed due to insufficient NDS rights. For example, if the requesting client doesn't have the Browse object right to an object, a -601 (no such object) error will be returned, even though the object does exist.

▸ The information provided in the request is invalid or is missing some mandatory fields.

▸ The request references a nonexistent object or object class.

▸ An unexpected response was received while processing the request. For example, it cannot connect to another server for tree-walking purposes (error -635).

Communication-related errors are those errors resulting from LAN or WAN failures. Given that NDS is a distributed and replicated database, NDS must be able to communicate with other servers within the same NDS tree. Any failure in the underlying hardware and software to provide the capability to communicate between servers results in disruption of NDS processes and operations. Fortunately, communication-related NDS errors are generally transitory and are resolved once the communication capability between servers is restored. Some possible causes of communication-related NDS errors are as follows:

- ▸ Faulty LAN drivers

- ▸ Faulty LAN/WAN hardware, such as cabling and network cards

- ▸ Unreliable network infrastructure, such as slow or often congested WAN links

- ▸ Incorrect server (internal) network address contained in the NDS database of a server (perhaps the server didn't get updated by other servers in the replica ring due to other errors)

- ▸ Duplicate server internal network addresses

- ▸ Route and/or SAP filtering

Communication errors can result in NDS data inconsistency, such as a user object exists in one replica but not in another. This is due to replicas of the same partition being out of sync; however, such inconsistencies are transitory in nature and will self-correct once communication is reestablished. On the other hand, NDS data inconsistency can be of the recurring type. For example, if the schema or one of the NDS database files on a server is corrupted, the resulting data inconsistency can't be rectified automatically by DS, and manual intervention is required.

To correctly identify the condition under which a specific NDS error occurs, you need to know the meaning of the reported error code and the source of the error code. The rest of this chapter is dedicated to describing NDS error codes and the possible conditions under which they occur. The discussions are divided into the following categories, based on the error code grouping:

- ▸ Directory Services OS error codes (-1 through -255)

- ▸ Directory Services client error codes (-301 through -399)

- ▸ Directory Services NLM client library error codes (-400 through -599)

- ▸ Directory Services Agent error codes (-601 through -799)

Error codes between -255 and -300 are currently reserved for future use.

NOTE

A detailed discussion about the NDS processes that generate the errors is found in Chapter 6.

◄ . . . . ◄

Directory Services OS Error Codes

Error codes -1 through -255 are operating system-related errors (such as from the file system, IPX, bindery NCP, and other OS services) returned through Directory Services. The OS error codes are one byte in size and are mapped to -1 to -255 when returned as a Directory Services error. For example, when an application makes an NDS API call but didn't allocate a large enough buffer for the data to be returned by the server, it results in a -119 (buffer too small) error.

You normally do *not* come across these OS-related DS error codes, because the applications should trap them and take appropriate action; however, should the program fail to trap the error, you may encounter these error codes.

In general, the error codes listed in this section are of more interest to programmers writing NDS-aware applications than they are to network administrators.

NOTE

Table 5.1 lists the OS-related errors that you are most likely to see and what they mean. You can find a complete list of all the OS-related errors in Appendix A.

TABLE 5.1

Common OS-related NDS
Error Codes

DECIMAL	HEXADECIMAL	CONSTANT
-131	0xFFFFFF7D	DSERR_HARD_IO_ERROR
-149	0xFFFFFF6B	DSERR_FILE_DETACHED
-150	0xFFFFFF6A	DSERR_NO_ALLOC_SPACE

Continued

TABLE 5.1

Common OS-related NDS
Error Eodes (continued)

DECIMAL	HEXADECIMAL	CONSTANT
-188	0xFFFFFF44	DSERR_LOGIN_SIGNING_REQUIRED
-189	0xFFFFFF43	DSERR_LOGIN_ENCRYPT_REQUIRED
-190	0xFFFFFF42	DSERR_INVALID_DATA_STREAM
-191	0xFFFFFF41	DSERR_INVALID_NAME_SPACE
-192	0xFFFFFF40	DSERR_NO_ACCOUNTING_PRIVILEGES
-193	0xFFFFFF3F	DSERR_NO_ACCOUNT_BALANCE
-194	0xFFFFFF3E	DSERR_CREDIT_LIMIT_EXCEEDED
-195	0xFFFFFF3D	DSERR_TOO_MANY_HOLDS
-196	0xFFFFFF3C	DSERR_ACCOUNTING_DISABLED
-197	0xFFFFFF3B	DSERR_LOGIN_LOCKOUT
-198	0xFFFFFF3A	DSERR_NO_CONSOLE_RIGHTS
-239	0xFFFFFF11	DSERR_ILLEGAL_NAME

Pay special attention to error -149, an internal auditing error that should generally not happen in the first place unless there's internal system corruption. If you do encounter it, you need to contact Novell for a resolution to this error. Error -150 is important because it suggests the server doesn't have sufficient dynamic memory to process the current auditing request; this error could be due to RAM shortage or memory fragmentation on the server. If you encounter a -239 error, it means the server received a request made with an object or property name containing illegal characters, such as a control character, comma, colon, semicolon, slash, backslash, question mark, asterisk, or tilde. This error may also be due to the fact that DS.NLM can't map the supplied object or attribute name to its unicode representation and could be a result of missing or corrupted unicode files in the SYS:LOGIN\NLS directory. You'll find some of these OS-related error codes (such as -254 and -255) have multiple meanings. And because -001 to -255 are NetWare OS error codes reported as DS errors, you need to be aware of the context under which the error code is returned in order to correctly interpret the cause of the error.

Directory Services Client Library Error Codes

Error code -301 through -399 are errors returned by Directory Services client API library functions. For example, when an application makes a call to an API function using an invalid object name (such as CN=Test.O=ABC.O=TopLevel) a -314 (invalid object name) error will be returned.

Similar to the Directory Services OS errors, you normally do *not* come across these client API DS error codes, because the applications should have trapped them and taken appropriate action; however, should the program fail to trap the error, you may encounter these error codes. Sometimes, the error code is shown as part of the error message displayed by the application. For example, Novell-supplied applications, such as NWAdmin and NETADMIN, display error messages as follows:

```
NWDS-4.0-code_number error message
```

or

```
Return Code: 1910:code_number error message
```

NOTE **In general, the error codes listed in this section are of more interest to programmers writing NDS-aware applications than they are to network administrators.**

Table 5.2 lists some common Directory Services client API library error codes.

TABLE 5.2

*Common Directory Services
Client API Library
Error Codes*

DECIMAL	HEXADECIMAL	CONSTANT
-301	0xFFFFFED3	ERR_NOT_ENOUGH_MEMORY
-302	0xFFFFFED2	ERR_BAD_KEY
-318	0xFFFFFEC2	ERR_COUNTRY_NAME_TOO_LONG
-319	0xFFFFFEC1	ERR_SYSTEM_ERROR
-320	0xFFFFFEC0	ERR_CANT_ADD_ROOT

Continued

T A B L E 5.2

Common Directory Services
Client API Library
Error Codes (continued)

DECIMAL	HEXIDECIMAL	CONSTANT
-321	0xFFFFFEBF	ERR_UNABLE_TO_ATTACH
-338	0xFFFFFEAE	ERR_INVALID_PASSWORD_CHARS
-339	0xFFFFFEAD	ERR_FAILED_SERVER_AUTHENT
-345	0xFFFFFEA7	ERR_INVALID_DS_VERSION
-346	0xFFFFFEA6	ERR_UNICODE_TRANSLATION
-347	0xFFFFFEA5	ERR_SCHEMA_NAME_TOO_LONG
-348	0xFFFFFEA4	ERR_UNICODE_FILE_NOT_FOUND

Error -301 means the application is unable to allocate memory. This suggests the client (workstation) may be low on memory or the application has repeatedly allocated buffers and failed to release them (memory leak); therefore, if you still receive this error code after closing all other applications running on the client, there's a good chance the application has a memory leak and you need to contact the vendor for an update.

Error -348 means the application can't locate the required unicode file or files. This error can be due to one of two reasons. The first reason is that NDS stores all characters using unicode representation, NDS-aware applications need access to country-code and code-page specific unicode files. Often, a programmer may hardcode the country-code information into the software (typically country code 1 and code page 437, for the United States). When you try to run such an application on a workstation that's configured for, say, German, it may fail with error -348, because the necessary unicode files may not have been installed. In North America, a workstation's default country setting is

▸ Country code = 001 (United States)

▸ Code page = 437 (United States)

The unicode files needed are

```
UNI_437.001  UNI_COL.001  UNI_MON.001  437_UNI.001
```

If you set the code page to 850 instead of 437 (the default), then the required unicode files needed are

```
UNI_850.001  UNI_COL.001  UNI_MON.001  850_UNI.001
```

Sometimes even when the programmer retrieves the country information during run-time, you may still encounter the -348 error. Different operating system platforms use different code pages, even if the country code is the same. For example, the default DOS country setting in North America is country code 1 and code page 850; however, the default Windows NT North America country setting is country code 1 and code page 1252. As a result, if you try to run a DOS-based NDS-aware application in the Command Prompt box on Windows NT, you may receive the -348 error because the unicode files for code page 850 are not found.

Secondly, NDS-aware applications search for unicode files in the following locations, in the order listed:

1. The directory in which the NDS-aware application resides

2. The NLS directory directly under the directory in which the NDS-aware application resides (this is why you have NLS directories in LOGIN and PUBLIC)

3. Your search drives

For example, if the application is installed in SYS:NDSAPP, the application looks, in the following order, at SYS:NDSAPPS, SYS:NDSAPPS\NLS, and your search drives. Therefore, you have to ensure the unicode files can be found in one of the above locations.

▶ · ◀

Directory Services NLM Client Library Error Codes

Error code -400 through -599 are errors returned by Directory Services NLM-specific API library functions. They are typically generated by DS.NLM and DSREPAIR.NLM; however, certain NDS processes require the functionality from

NLMs such as TIMESYNC.NLM and UNICODE.NLM. If one of these supporting NLMs encounters an error, the error may be passed back to NDS, and DS.NLM will report the error instead.

You generally do not encounter these error codes, because they are mostly trapped and handled by the NLMs. But in case you do encounter these error codes, they are included here for your reference.

 In general, the error codes listed in this section are of more interest to programmers writing NDS-aware applications than they are to network administrators.

NOTE

Table 5.3 shows common Directory Services client API library error codes specific to NLMs.

TABLE 5.3

*Common Directory Services
Client API Library Error
Codes Specific to NLMs*

DECIMAL	HEXADECIMAL	CONSTANT
-400	0xFFFFFE70	ERR_BAD_SERVICE_CONNECTION
-401	0xFFFFFE6F	ERR_BAD_NETWORK
-402	0xFFFFFE6E	ERR_BAD_ADDRESS
-405	0xFFFFFE6B	ERR_BAD_SERVER_NAME
-406	0xFFFFFE6A	ERR_BAD_USER_NAME
-408	0xFFFFFE68	ERR_NO_MEMORY
-412	0xFFFFFE64	ERR_CONNECTION_ABORTED
-413	0xFFFFFE63	ERR_TIMEOUT
-414	0xFFFFFE62	ERR_CHECKSUM

Directory Services Agent Error Codes

Error codes -601 through -799 are errors returned by the Directory Services Agent (DSA) that are running on the NetWare (NDS) server. The DSA errors are what you generally see in the DSTRACE screen and reported by various NDS utilities, such as NetWare Administrator; therefore, you should be versed in these error codes.

Table 5.4 shows some of the common error codes returned by DSA.

TABLE 5.4

Common DSA Error Codes

DECIMAL	HEXADECIMAL	CONSTANT
-601	0xFFFFFDA7	ERR_NO_SUCH_ENTRY
-602	0xFFFFFDA6	ERR_NO_SUCH_VALUE
-603	0xFFFFFDA5	ERR_NO_SUCH_ATTRIBUTE
-624	0xFFFFFD90	ERR_REPLICA_ALREADY_EXISTS
-625	0xFFFFFD8F	ERR_TRANSPORT_FAILURE
-626	0xFFFFFD8E	ERR_ALL_REFERRALS_FAILED
-654	0xFFFFFD72	ERR_PARTITION_BUSY
-659	0xFFFFFD6D	ERR_TIME_NOT_SYNCHRONIZED
-666	0xFFFFFD66	ERR_INCOMPATIBLE_DS_VERSION
-672	0xFFFFFD60	ERR_NO_ACCESS
-698	0xFFFFFD46	ERR_REPLICA_IN_SKULK
-715	0xFFFFFD35	ERR_CHECKSUM_FAILURE

The -601 error is perhaps the most common NDS error code. This error refers to the fact that the specified object is not found on the server replying to the request. The specified object context could be wrong, or the client doesn't have sufficient rights (such as Browse) to the object. If you see this in a DSTRACE screen, it simply means the server handling the request doesn't have the information and will have to perform a tree-walk; therefore, in most cases, a -601 error is an informational error.

Errors -602 and -603 mean the requested attribute value or attribute, respectively, is not found on the server replying to the request. The client may not have sufficient rights to the data. Unlike the -601 error, however, no tree-walking will be performed to look for the information elsewhere.

Next to the -601 error, -625 is probably the second most commonly reported error by DSA. Error -625 means the reporting server is unable to communicate with the target server. This is generally a result of target server being down, a LAN/WAN outage, or some sort of routing problem.

The -698 error code is another one of the informational errors. It means an attempt to start the NDS Replica Synchronization process with a target server was made, but the target server was busy synchronizing with another server. This is a transitory error, and the NDS Replica Synchronization process will reschedule. You'll see this error on partitions that have a large replica ring (say, ten or more servers) or have slow or busy server in the replica ring.

A routing problem could result in a misleading -715 error code, which means The NDS checksum in the request packet is invalid. We have encountered one instance where a duplicate IPX network address on the network caused NDS to erroneously report a -715 error . After removing the duplicate route, NDS resolved the -715 error without further intervention, such as the need to run DSREPAIR.

▶ · ◀

Summary

This chapter presented a discussion of the various error types and some possible sources. The errors were broken into following categories: errors returned by the DS service running on the NetWare server, errors returned by the client application (workstation-based or server-based), and errors returned by the DS agent running on the NetWare server.

Chapter 6 provides you with an in-depth look at the common NDS processes and helps explain the causes of the errors.

Understanding Common NDS Processes

In Chapter 1, we defined Novell Directory Services (NDS) as a loosely consistent distributed database. Several background processes ensure the integrity of the data in the NDS database and must run smoothly to provide consistent operation. There are also several processes you initiate with administration tools such as NetWare Administrator and NDS Manager to manage objects, partitions, and replicas.

In this chapter, we will look at the most common of these processes in order to develop a better understanding of how they work. Through understanding how they work, it becomes much easier to determine a proper course of action to resolve problems in NDS.

This chapter goes into some detail about the processes themselves. For step-by-step level detail of the operation of a specific process, please refer to Novell's "LogicSource for NDS" CD-ROM. See Appendix D for information on how to get "LogicSource for NDS."

Before we talk about the processes themselves, though, we need to discuss obituaries, which NDS uses to keep track of the state of some of the operations.

Obituaries

Some of the most common problems in NDS are caused by obituaries not being processed properly. Any number of reasons can cause obituaries to not be processed, ranging from a down server or communication link to an invalid backlink list in an object. By understanding the background processes and how obituaries are used by certain processes, it is easier to determine the best course of action to correct a problem.

Many of the most common NDS problems are caused by problems with obituaries purging, but they initially appear to be caused by something else.

Obituaries are used by NDS to keep track of the state of certain operations — such as object and partition move operations, object deletions, and object restores. Table 6.1 shows the different obituary types and when NDS generates them.

TABLE 6.1

Obituary Types and Classes

OBITUARY TYPE	OBITUARY CLASS	DESCRIPTION
Restored	Primary	Created when an object is restored from a backup.
Dead	Primary	Created when an object is deleted.
Moved	Primary	Created when an object is moved from one container to another. This obituary is created for the object's original location.
Inhibit Move	Informational	Created when an object is moved from one container to another. This obituary is created for the object's destination location.
Old RDN	Informational	Created when an object is renamed. This obituary is created for the old object name.
New RDN	Primary	Created when an object is renamed. This obituary is created for the new object name.
Backlink	Secondary	Created when an object stored as an external reference has a primary obituary created for it.
Tree Old RDN	Informational	Created when a partition root object is renamed. This is a special case of the Old RDN obituary type.
Tree New RDN	Special Case	Created when a partition root object is renamed. This is a special case of the New RDN Obituary type.
Purge All	Special Case	Created internally by NDS to identify objects that have attribute values that need to be purged.
Move Subtree	Special Case	Created when a partition root object is moved from one container to another.

In addition to the obituary types and classes, obituaries move through four distinct states. These states are always executed in the same order to ensure obituaries are processed by the servers properly and then purged from the system. Obituary advancement through the four states occurs during the synchronization process. By observing the synchronization process, you can see the obituaries actually being purged. Listing 6.1 shows where obituaries appear in the synchronization process. Notice how the object Pkuo.West.XYZCorp has two obituary entries: one of type 2 and one of type 6. The stage is shown in the flags field.

L I S T I N G   6 . 1

Obituary state advancement

SYNC: Start sync of partition <[Root]> state:[0] type:[0]

SYNC: Start outbound sync with (#=2, state=0, type=1) [010000C3]
<RIGEL.West.XYZCorp>

SYNC: Using version 5 on server <CN=RIGEL>

SENDING TO ---> CN=RIGEL

SYNC: sending updates to server <CN=RIGEL>

SYNC:[010000B8][(22:20:00),2,1] ORION.East.XYZCorp (NCP Server)

SYNC:[010002A4][(19:49:49),2,1] JimH.West.XYZCorp(User)

SYNC:[010000C3][(08:31:47),1,1] RIGEL.West.XYZCorp (NCP Server)

SYNC: [150002E4] obituary for PKuo.West.XYZCorp

valueTime=36905EB9,1,20 type=2, flags=0, oldCTS=36905E6F,1,1

valueTime=36905EB9,1,21 type=6, flags=0, oldCTS=36905E6F,1,1

SYNC:[150002E4][(00:04:05),1,1] PKuo.West.XYZCorp (User)

SYNC: [0E0002BC] obituary for PKuo.East.XYZCorp

valueTime=36905EB9,1,17 type=3, flags=0, oldCTS=36905EB9,1,1

SYNC:[0E0002BC][(23:24:57),1,1] PKuo.East.XYZCorp (User)

SYNC: Objects: 7, total changes: 74, sent to server <CN=RIGEL>

SYNC: update to server <CN=RIGEL> successfully completed

Merged transitive vector for [010000C3] <RIGEL.West.XYZCorp> succeeded

SYNC: SkulkPartition for <[Root]> succeeded

SYNC: End sync of partition <[Root]> All processed = YES.

The stages that an obituary passes through before it is deleted are shown in Table 6.2. The four stages are always followed in the order presented.

TABLE 6.2	OBITUARY STAGE	FLAGS VALUE	DESCRIPTION
Obituary processing stage definitions	Issued	0	Initial stage
	Notified	1	Servers needing secondary obituaries have been notified of the primary obituary
	OK to Purge	2	All servers have been notified
	Purgeable	4	All servers are ready to purge the value or object

You may notice a couple of weird things about the information in Table 6.2. The first oddity is the flags values—the progression is 0, 1, 2, 4. This field is what is referred to as a *bit field*. The software checks specific bits rather than for specific integer values.

The second thing that may appear strange is the Issued and OK to Purge states; these states indicate the beginning or end of another stage, rather than their own processing procedure. Stage 0 is initially set when an obituary is set; this change is then replicated to all servers. Once the replication cycle is complete, DS knows that all servers are at stage 0, and it can go ahead and start the notification process. A change in the obituary is made, and this information is replicated to the other servers that need to be notified. After all servers have been notified, the obituary is set to stage 2, meaning that stage 1 has completed. When all servers have received a flag indicating it is okay to purge, the servers mark the obituaries purgeable, and this change is replicated to all of the servers. At this point, the individual servers process the actual purge process, but because all servers have to report the obituary as purgeable, no additional notification needs to be done once the obituaries have actually been purged.

These four stages actually describe a multiserver transaction processing system. You can think of the processing of obituaries as a synchronized transaction taking place nearly simultaneously on multiple servers.

Because obituaries are the source of most NDS problems, you need a good understanding of obituaries to understand background processes, which we discuss next.

▶ . . . . ◀

Background Processes

The DS.NLM module maintains the database through several background processes running on each server. These processes run automatically and generally do not need to be manually invoked. There are cases where there is benefit in forcing a process to run, but as a general rule, you should not force them to run unless it is really necessary. As we discussed in Chapter 4, doing something for the sake of doing something is frequently not a good idea.

Synchronization

The synchronization process, sometimes referred to as the *skulker*, is the process that keeps the information in multiple replicas of the NDS database current on all servers. Listing 6.2 shows a sample of the sync process as shown by the DSTRACE screen.

LISTING 6.2

Sample synchronization process

```
SYNC: Start sync of partition <[Root]> state:[0] type:[0]

SYNC: Start outbound sync with (#=2, state=0, type=1)
[010000C3]<RIGEL.West.XYZCorp>

(21:11:57) SYNC: failed to communicate with server <CN=RIGEL> ERROR: -625

SYNC: SkulkPartition for <[Root]> succeeded

SYNC: End sync of partition <[Root]> All processed = NO.
```

Listing 6.2 demonstrates a failed synchronization condition. The local server is attempting to contact the server named CN=Rigel.OU=West.O=XYZCorp, but is unable to complete the synchronization process. The error -625 indicates a transport failure — also known as a communications failure. To correct this problem, the easiest way to proceed is to verify that the target server is up and that the communications links between the two servers are working properly.

A successful synchronization between the two servers is shown in Listing 6.3.

LISTING 6.3
Successful synchronization

```
SYNC: Start sync of partition <[Root]> state:[0] type:[0]

SYNC: Start outbound sync with (#=2, state=0, type=1)
[010000C3]<RIGEL.West.XYZCorp>

SYNC: Using version 5 on server <CN=RIGEL>

SENDING TO ---> CN=RIGEL

SYNC: sending updates to server <CN=RIGEL>

SYNC:[010000B7][(20:02:16),1,3] XYZCorp (Organization)

SYNC:[010000B8][(22:20:00),2,1] ORION.East.XYZCorp (NCP Server)

SYNC:[0100029A][(20:02:50),2,1] Jim.East.XYZCorp (User)

SYNC:[0100029B][(19:50:43),2,1] Amy.East.XYZCorp (User)

SYNC:[010002A4][(19:49:49),2,1] Kenny.East.XYZCorp (User)

SYNC:[010002A8][(19:58:46),2,1] WINNT.Scripts.East.XYZCorp (Profile)

SYNC:[100002E1][(02:36:26),1,1] WIN98.Scripts.East.XYZCorp (Profile)

SYNC: Objects: 7, total changes: 25, sent to server <CN=RIGEL>

SYNC: update to server <CN=RIGEL> successfully completed

Merged transitive vector for [010000C3]<RIGEL.West.XYZCorp> succeeded

SYNC: SkulkPartition for <[Root]> succeeded

SYNC: End sync of partition <[Root]> All processed = YES.
```

This time the servers are talking to each other, and there are a few updates that need to be sent from one server to the other. Listing 6.3 demonstrates a successful synchronization cycle on the [Root] partition of the tree.

Nontransitive Synchronization in NetWare 4

In NetWare 4.*x*, all servers that hold a replica of an NDS partition have to communicate with all of the other servers that hold a replica of the partition. Figure 6.1 shows the type of communication that has to take place in order for synchronization to be completely successful on all NetWare 4.*x* servers.

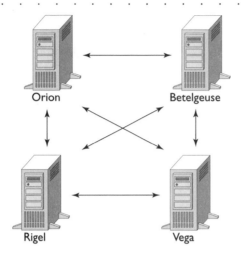

FIGURE 6.1

NetWare 4 replica synchronization between 4 servers (nontransitive)

Orion   Betelgeuse

Rigel   Vega

As becomes apparent, the number of synchronization processes that must complete grows exponentially as replicas are added. The amount of traffic generated can be tremendous.

In fact, the number of communications vectors is $n \times (n-1)$, where n represents the number of replicas in the replica ring. Thus, at 27 replicas, a total of 27×26, or 702, communications vectors exist.

Transitive Synchronization in NetWare 5

In NetWare 5, Novell introduced the idea of transitive synchronization. Transitive synchronization introduces a synchronization methodology where a server doesn't have to contact every other server in the replica list. It can enable other servers to ensure synchronization is complete, as demonstrated in Figure 6.2.

The reduction in traffic in a transitive synchronization environment is very significant, and the completion of the entire synchronization cycle is reduced. Ideally, this would create a scenario where the vector count would simply equal $n-1$, so with 27 replicas, only 26 communications vectors would be needed. Table 6.3 shows the difference in vectors between transitive and nontransitive synchronization.

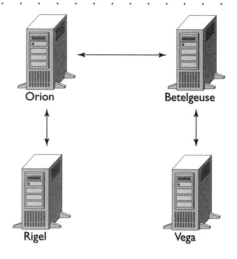

FIGURE 6.2

NetWare 5 replica synchronization between 4 servers (transitive)

Orion   Betelgeuse

Rigel   Vega

TABLE 6.3	SERVERS IN REPLICA RING	NONTRANSITIVE VECTORS	TRANSITIVE VECTORS
Communications Vectors with Transitive and Nontransitive Synchronization	2	2	1
	3	6	2
	4	12	3
	5	20	4
	6	30	5
	7	42	6
	8	56	7
	9	72	8
	10	90	9

This example represents the ideal number of synchronization vectors when using transitive synchronization. As you can see in Table 6.3, the number of communications vectors with transitive synchronization is significantly smaller than when using nontransitive synchronization. It is possible that the number of vectors could increase, depending on the network design and availability of services. The actual number of synchronization vectors with transitive synchronization could be larger but will still be smaller than without transitive synchronization.

Schema Synchronization

Schema synchronization works a little differently than the standard object synchronization. Schema sync is set up so changes propagate from servers starting near the [Root] of the tree and then work down to the extreme branches of the tree. Figure 6.3 depicts a small tree with 5 servers and 3 partitions.

FIGURE 6.3

Schema synchronization

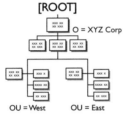

Partition	Master	Read/Write	Subref
[ROOT]	Betelgeuse	Rigel Andromeda	
OU = West	Orion	Vega	Betelgeuse Rigel Andromeda
OU = East	Vega	Rigel	Betelgeuse Andromeda

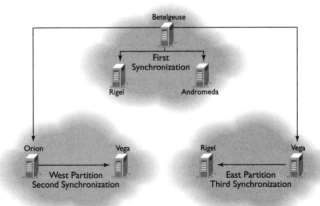

In Figure 6.3, a change made to the schema would start with ORION, because it holds the master of the [Root] partition. Once this server has been updated, it sends the schema changes out to the other servers that hold copies of [Root]: RIGEL and ANDROMEDA. After all servers in the [Root] partition have received the updates, DS sends the updates to the other servers in the tree. It does this by looking at the servers that hold copies of [Root] and reading the replica list information to find out what other replicas are out there.

By looking at the replica list on RIGEL, for example, DS.NLM can determine that there are two child partitions — OU=West.O=XYZCorp and OU=East.O=XYZCorp. By looking at the replica list on RIGEL to determine what other servers are in the tree, DS determines that the servers VEGA and ORION also need to be updated. During the determination of this, note that VEGA and RIGEL are listed twice because of the replication scheme in this tree; even though RIGEL receives an update in the first round of schema synchronization, after VEGA receives the updates to the schema, RIGEL is again checked to see if its schema is current. If the schema is not current, it is updated.

TIP

Schema updates are normally not something to be concerned about unless the change is being made because of an update in the DS.NLM module. In cases where Novell has introduced a schema change in a new version of DS.NLM, update the module on the server that holds the master of [Root] first and then update the rest of your servers after the schema update has completed.

Janitor

The NDS Janitor process is responsible for a number of different tasks, including

▸ Scheduling the Flat Cleaner

▸ Issuing console messages when synthetic time is issued

▸ Optimizing the local NDS database

▸ Updating and verifying the inherited ACL attributes of partition root objects

▸ Updating the status attribute in the NDS database for the local server

• • • • •

▶ Ensuring that the local server is registered with another server to receive schema updates if there is no local replica

▶ Validating the partition nearest to [Root] on the server and the replica depth of this partition.

The Janitor has responsibility for some fairly critical tasks. By default the Janitor process runs every two minutes, though it doesn't perform every task in its list each time it runs. Scheduling the Flat Cleaner, for example, only happens once every sixty minutes.

Synthetic time is used by NDS to manage situations where the current timestamp on an object is later than the current time. The Janitor process checks the timestamps on the objects in the server, and when a new timestamp is needed for an object. If an object in the server's replicas has a timestamp greater than the current server time, the Janitor process notifies the operating system, and a message is generated on the system console:

```
1-02-98   6:33:58 pm:     DS-5.99-12

Synthetic Time is being issued on partition "NW5TEST."
```

IMPORTANT

Synthetic time being issued is not always a critical problem. If a server's time is set back from within a few hours to a few days, it is not necessary to correct the problem. This situation is a case where waiting is a better solution than doing something. Using DSREPAIR to repair timestamps is a serious step to take that actually destroys replicas on all servers except the server with the master replica. Once all nonmaster replicas are destroyed, the replicas are recreated.

The optimization steps that the Janitor takes includes rehashing the database information to enable it to perform lookups more quickly and validating the server's authentication credentials and resetting them if they are no longer valid.

Updating the inherited ACL attribute values starts with the first partition in the partition database. Once the Janitor has located the partition, it validates that the parent object is not an external reference and looks at the ACL to determine if any of the attribute values have been modified. If they have, it validates whether or not the attribute is inheritable, and if it is, it recalculates the inherited ACL attribute values. The Janitor process continues this process with the rest of the partitions on the server.

Updating the status attribute involves validating that the NDS attribute Status is set to up. Because the server that performs the validation is up and running, it always checks for an up value. If it is set to down, the Janitor updates the attribute. Figure 6.4 shows where in NetWare Administrator you see the result of this operation.

▶ · ◀

F I G U R E   6.4

Server status value shown in NetWare Administrator

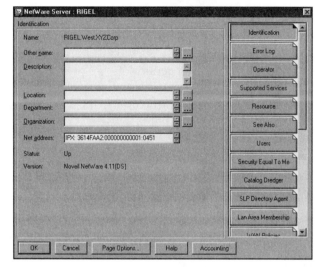

Ensuring the server can receive schema updates if it holds no replicas is particularly important. Even if a server has no local replicas, it still receives information for external references used to grant rights in the file system. In order to handle this properly, the server needs to know about all the different class definitions in case an extended class object receives rights to the file system. Equally important is the need for the schema partition to be maintained in case a new replica is added to the server later. If the server does not have current information on the schema, and a replica is added to the server, many objects will change to unknown objects in the local database, which can cause problems with object administration if this copy of the object is read by the administration tools.

Flat Cleaner

The Flat Cleaner is scheduled by the Janitor and by default runs every sixty minutes. Responsibilities of the Flat Cleaner include

- ▶ Purging unused objects and attributes stored in the bindery partition or external reference partition

- ▶ Purging obituaries that have reached the purgeable state

- ▶ Revalidating the Status and Version attributes of servers in all partitions the server has the master replica of

- ▶ Verifying that all objects in the user defined partitions on the server have valid Public Keys and CA Public Keys

The bindery partition, as described in Chapter 2, is the partition that is used to store information about the bindery SUPERVISOR user. This partition also stores the SAP information received from IPX networks connected to the server. If a service is removed from the network, the SAP table in the server needs to be updated — this is one of the tasks the Flat Cleaner is responsible for.

Obituaries that have reached the purgeable stage are removed from the database: all servers that needed to be notified of an obituary have been notified and the obituary has progressed through its life to a stage where all servers have agreed that NDS is done with the obituary.

The Flat Cleaner is responsible for validating the up state of all servers it holds the master copy of in NDS. As we discussed earlier, the Janitor is responsible for setting the server Status attribute to up. The Flat Cleaner is responsible for setting the Status attribute to down if necessary.

To understand the process better, we'll look at two servers, ORION and RIGEL. ORION holds the master copy of [Root], the only partition in the tree.

If RIGEL ABENDs and is down when ORION's Flat Cleaner process runs, ORION sets the status attribute for RIGEL to down. When RIGEL is restarted, it runs its Janitor process, checks the status attribute, and sees that it is set to down. Because the server is no longer down, RIGEL changes the status attribute to up.

The Flat Cleaner also performs a check to validate all Public Keys and CA Public Keys for objects the server holds. If it finds an invalid or missing key, it attempts to create new keys for the object. The Public Key and CA Public Key attribute values are used by NDS during the authentication process; if these keys are not valid on user objects, the user (or an administrator) has to change their password to fix the problem. If, however, these keys are corrupted on a container object, server-to-server authentication would be disrupted and synchronization would not occur.

Limber

The last of the automated processes is the Limber process. Primary responsibilities of the limber process include:

▸ Verifying the network address for the server in all partitions the server holds a replica of

▸ Validating that the relative distinguished name for the server is correct on the server holding the master partition of the replica the server exists in

▸ Updating and maintaining the Version attribute for the server in the NDS database

▸ Verifying the network address for the server is correct in the server's NDS object.

TIP

These operations perform verifications on the replica list information and server network addresses. If a replica list is inconsistent, forcing the limber process to run using the command SET DSTRACE=*L on the server that appears to have the problem may correct the problem.

As mentioned in Chapter 2, some of the information maintained by the Limber process is stored in part in the local System partition. These processes are considered to be secondary functions of the Limber process, but are nonetheless important:

- Verifying the directory tree name stored in the server's system partition is correct

- If the server does not hold a writable replica of the partition its own NDS object is in, verifying that the external reference for this object is valid and checking that the backlink attribute is valid on a server that holds a writable copy of the server object

- Checking to ensure the server's public key–private key credentials are correct.

The Limber process is one of the background processes that cannot have its schedule interval changed. If the Limber process' primary operations complete successfully, it reschedules itself to run again in three hours. If the primary operations have not completed successfully, it reschedules itself to run again in five minutes.

Manual Object-Related Processes

Now that we have reviewed the major background processes, we'll examine the processes that you invoke using the administrative utilities. The first set of such processes is object-related processes. In this section, we examine the creation, renaming, deletion, and movement of objects in the NDS tree.

Create Object

Object creation is a fairly straightforward process. In NetWare Administrator, you select the context where you want the new object to be placed and either press Insert or right-click the container you want to create the object in and select Create from the menu. NetWare Administrator asks you for the object class, and once this is selected, you are presented with an appropriate dialog box to enter the mandatory attributes of the object.

From the server's perspective, object creation is also a simple process. The client generates a Directory Services Agent (DSA) request 7 (Add Entry) as shown in Listing 6.5.

The request buffer is filled with the information entered in the create object dialog box. In the listings in this section, this information is seen on the server processing the client request by using the commands:

SET DSTRACE=+DSA

SET DSTRACE=+BUFFERS

The information shown in the request buffer is in unicode format, which is a two-byte character format. For English language objects, unicode fills the first byte with 00. In Listings 6.4 and 6.5, you can see the object name starting at offset 19, followed by the mandatory attribute Surname (offset 39) and its value (offset 63). Lastly, we see the object class attribute and the value USER. This is the minimum information needed to create a user object and is passed directly to the DS Agent from NetWare Administrator.

LISTING 6.4

*DS agent add entry request
shown on the server processing
the client request*

```
DSA: DSACommonRequest(7) conn:3 for client <JIM>

DSA REQUEST BUFFER:

02 00 00 00 00 00 00 00 FF FF FF FF E3 02 00 12  ................

0A 00 00 00 50 00 4B 00 75 00 6F 00 00 00 00 00  ....P.K.u.o.....

02 00 00 00 10 00 00 00 53 00 75 00 72 00 6E 00  ........S.u.r.n.

61 00 6D 00 65 00 00 00 01 00 00 00 08 00 00 00  a.m.e...........

4B 00 75 00 6F 00 00 00 1A 00 00 00 4F 00 62 00  K.u.o.......O.b.

6A 00 65 00 63 00 74 00 20 00 43 00 6C 00 61 00  j.e.c.t...C.l.a.

73 00 73 00 00 00 00 00 01 00 00 00 0A 00 00 00  s.s.............

55 00 53 00 45 00 52 00 00 00                    U.S.E.R...
```

If the object already exists, the server replies as shown in Listing 6.5.

DS agent add entry request
with failure

```
DSA: DSACommonRequest(7) conn:3 for client <JIM>

DSA REQUEST BUFFER:

02 00 00 00 00 00 00 00 FF FF FF FF E3 02 00 12  ...............

0A 00 00 00 50 00 4B 00 75 00 6F 00 00 00 00 00  ....P.K.u.o.....

02 00 00 00 10 00 00 00 53 00 75 00 72 00 6E 00  ........S.u.r.n.

61 00 6D 00 65 00 00 00 01 00 00 00 08 00 00 00  a.m.e...........

4B 00 75 00 6F 00 00 00 1A 00 00 00 4F 00 62 00  K.u.o.......O.b.

6A 00 65 00 63 00 74 00 20 00 43 00 6C 00 61 00  j.e.c.t...C.l.a.

73 00 73 00 00 00 00 00 01 00 00 00 0A 00 00 00  s.s.............

55 00 53 00 45 00 52 00 00 00                    U.S.E.R...

DSA REPLY BUFFER:

DSA: DSACommonRequest(7): returning ERROR -606
```

The error code -606 is defined as ERR_ENTRY_ALREADY_EXISTS. This makes sense, because the object does in fact already exist in the specified context.

Object creation can take place on any writable replica. Once the create request is completed on the server the workstation contacts, the object is queued up for the next synchronization cycle and sent out to the other servers in the replica ring. As discussed in the section on synchronization, this synchronization cycle is either transitive or nontransitive, depending on the version of NetWare running on the servers in the replica ring.

Rename Object

Renaming an object is also a fairly simple process. The request is actually broken down into two parts — a resolve name request, shown in Listing 6.6, and the actual rename operation, shown in Listing 6.7. In this example, we rename the object *PKuo* to *JimH*. This operation requires that the client be able to contact a server holding a writable copy of the object being renamed.

L I S T I N G 6.6

Object resolve name request issued during an object rename operation

```
DSA: DSACommonRequest(1) conn:3 for client <JIM>

DSA REQUEST BUFFER:

00 00 00 00 24 20 00 00 00 00 00 00 30 00 00 00    ...........0...

50 00 4B 00 75 00 6F 00 2E 00 4F 00 55 00 3D 00    P.K.u.o...O.U...

45 00 61 00 73 00 74 00 2E 00 4F 00 3D 00 58 00    E.a.s.t...O...X.

59 00 5A 00 43 00 6F 00 72 00 70 00 00 00 00 00    Y.Z.C.o.r.p.....

02 00 00 00 00 00 00 00 08 00 00 00 02 00 00 00    ...............

00 00 00 00 08 00 00 00                            ........

DSA REPLY BUFFER:

01 00 00 00 BC 02 00 0E 01 00 00 00 00 00 00 00    ...............

0C 00 00 00 84 12 30 01 00 00 00 00 00 01 04 51    ......0........Q
```

The reply sent to the resolve name request returns the object ID of the object being renamed, starting at offset 4 in reverse-byte order, as shown in bold in listing 6.7. In this example, the entry being renamed is entry ID 0E0002BC. The server responding also includes its network address in the reply buffer. In this example, the address is shown at offset 20. The offset is not byte-reversed and includes the network, node, and socket address. In this example, the address is 84123001:000000000001:0451.

L I S T I N G 6.7

Object rename request

```
DSA: DSACommonRequest(10) conn:3 for client <JIM>

DSA REQUEST BUFFER:

00 00 00 00 BC 02 00 0E 01 00 00 00 0A 00 00 00  ...............

4A 00 69 00 6D 00 48 00 00 00 6F 00               J.i.m.H...o.

DSA REPLY BUFFER:
```

Once the requested information is returned, the client sends the rename request to the server that replied to the read request. The request buffer for the rename request does not include the old object name, rather it uses the object's ID retrieved from the resolve name request that occurred at the start of the rename operation. This object ID is again put at offset 4 in reverse-byte order. In Listing 6.8, this is 0E0002BC, the same object ID returned by the read request. In a rename operation, the object ID in the rename request always matches the ID read in the initial resolve name request. This is how the client knows which object is being renamed.

In a multiple server environment, the rename operation sets in motion a series of events to ensure the rename operation is synchronized properly. The old object ID has an Old RDN obituary issued for it in order to start processing the purge of the old name from the DS database. At the same time, a New RDN obituary is issued for the new object name.

If a server is down, it is possible to see the obituaries that have been issued for the rename operation. By loading DSREPAIR with a -A parameter, you can view the current obituaries and their states on the server by performing an external reference check. Listing 6.8 shows the information written to the DSREPAIR log file about the two obituaries that have been created by renaming the object *PKuo* to *JimH*.

From our discussion about obituaries, we can also see a backlink obituary was created, because server RIGEL contains either a real copy or an external reference of the object.

LISTING 6.8

DSREPAIR log file showing
obituaries created by a rename
operation

```
/******************************************************************************/

Netware 4.1 Directory Services Repair 4.56 , DS 5.99

Log file for server "ORION.East.XYZCorp" in tree "NW5TEST"

External Reference Check

Start:  Sunday, January 3, 1999  10:01:50 pm Local Time

Found obituary at VID: 0002E540, EID: 0E0002BA, DN:
CN=PKuo.OU=East.O=XYZCorp.NW5TEST

    TV:  1-03-1999 21:45:55 0001, Type = 0005 NEW_RDN, Flags = 0000

    RDN: CN=JimH

Found obituary at VID: 00032540, EID: 0E0002BA, DN:
CN=PKuo.OU=East.O=XYZCorp.NW5TEST

    TV:  1-03-1999 21:45:55 0001, Type = 0006 BACKLINK, Flags = 0000

    Backlink: Type = 00000005 NEW_RDN, RemoteID = FFFFFFFF, ServerID = 010000C3,
CN=RIGEL.OU=West.O=XYZCorp.NW5TEST

Found obituary at VID: 00032D00, EID: 0E0002BC, DN:
CN=JimH.OU=East.O=XYZCorp.NW5TEST

    TV:  1-03-1999 21:45:55 0001, Type = 0004 OLD_RDN, Flags = 0000

    RDN: CN=Pkuo

Checked 0 external references


*** END ***
```

The obituaries that are issued do not prevent you from performing other operations on the object. In fact, once an object is renamed, it is possible to create a new object using the original object's name.

TIP

Because the Old RDN and New RDN obituary types do not hold up other operations, these obituaries can hang around for a very long time and not be detected. Periodically checking the state of obituaries using DSREPAIR helps ensure the obituaries are being advanced and purged properly by the Flat Cleaner.

Delete Object

Deleting an object from the tree is very similar to renaming an object in the tree. As with the rename operation, this operation requires that the client be able to communicate with any server that holds a writable copy of the object.

First, a resolve name request is sent similar to the one that appeared before the rename operation in Listing 6.6. As with the rename object operation, the reply buffer includes both the object ID of the object being deleted and the network address of the server that responded to the request. Once this information is returned, the client requests the actual deletion of the object using DS request 8 (Remove Entry). This request is shown in Listing 6.9

LISTING 6.9

DS remove entry request

```
DSA: DSACommonRequest(8) conn:3 for client <JIM>

DSA REQUEST BUFFER:

00 00 00 00 BA 02 00 10                          ........

DSA REPLY BUFFER:
```

We again see the object ID passed into the request starting at offset 4, in reverse-byte order. This request is for object ID 010002BA to be deleted. The object ID requested again corresponds to the object ID returned by the resolve name request at offset 4.

Object deletion creates an obituary of class dead. Again using DSREPAIR with the -A switch and checking external references, we can see the obituaries created by deleting the object. Listing 6.10 shows the log file entries resulting from this operation.

L I S T I N G   6 . 1 0

DSREPAIR log showing
obituaries created by a delete

```
/*********************************************************************/

Netware 4.1 Directory Services Repair 4.56 , DS 5.99

Log file for server "ORION.East.XYZCorp" in tree "NW5TEST"

External Reference Check

Start:   Sunday, January 3, 1999   10:49:10 pm Local Time

Found obituary at VID: 00019540, EID: 110002BA, DN:
CN=JimH.OU=East.O=XYZCorp.NW5TEST

   TV:  1-03-1999 22:41:51 0001, Type = 0001 DEAD, Flags = 0000

Found obituary at VID: 0001FCC0, EID: 110002BA, DN:
CN=JimH.OU=East.O=XYZCorp.NW5TEST

   TV:  1-03-1999 22:41:51 0001, Type = 0006 BACKLINK, Flags = 0000

   Backlink: Type = 00000001 DEAD, RemoteID = FFFFFFFF, ServerID = 010000C3,
CN=RIGEL.OU=West.O=XYZCorp.NW5TEST

Checked 0 external references


*** END ***
```

As with a rename request, a backlink obituary is generated in addition to the dead obituary. As with the rename operation, these obituaries do not cause any delay in creating an object with the same name.

Move Object

The final object-level operation we will examine is the move-object operation. This operation is more complex than the other operations and differs slightly because of the added complexity.

The first difference between moving an object and any other object-level operation is that a move request requires communication with the server that holds the master replica of the object. If an object is moved across a partition boundary, communication with the servers that hold the master replicas of both partitions is required. Additionally, those servers must be able to communicate with each other in order for the object's data to be moved from one partition to the other.

For simplicity, we will examine an object move within a partition, because the operation does not vary much from a single server operation to a multiserver operation.

In Listing 6.11, we start by reading object information for the source organizational unit and destination organizational unit. The request is made for the objects by ID, and the reply buffers contain information about the object: the container class and the full DN of the container in question.

L I S T I N G   6.11

*DS read entry information
requests for the source and
destination containers in
preparation for an object move*

```
DSA: DSACommonRequest(2) conn:3 for client <JIM>

DSA REQUEST BUFFER:

02 00 00 00 01 00 00 00 1D 28 00 00 E3 02 00 12  ...............

DSA REPLY BUFFER:

1D 28 00 00 04 00 00 00 01 00 00 00 4F E3 8F 36  ...........O..6

28 00 00 00 4F 00 72 00 67 00 61 00 6E 00 69 00  ....O.r.g.a.n.i.

7A 00 61 00 74 00 69 00 6F 00 6E 00 61 00 6C 00  z.a.t.i.o.n.a.l.

20 00 55 00 6E 00 69 00 74 00 00 00 1A 00 00 00  ..U.n.i.t.......

45 00 61 00 73 00 74 00 2E 00 58 00 59 00 5A 00  E.a.s.t...X.Y.Z.

43 00 6F 00 72 00 70 00 00 00                    C.o.r.p...

DSA: DSACommonRequest(2) conn:3 for client <JIM>

DSA REQUEST BUFFER:

02 00 00 00 00 00 00 00 1D 28 02 00 E2 02 00 12  ...............

DSA REPLY BUFFER:

1D 28 02 00 04 00 00 00 01 00 00 00 5B E3 8F 36  ..............6
```

```
28 00 00 00 4F 00 72 00 67 00 61 00 6E 00 69 00   ....O.r.g.a.n.i.

7A 00 61 00 74 00 69 00 6F 00 6E 00 61 00 6C 00   z.a.t.i.o.n.a.l.

20 00 55 00 6E 00 69 00 74 00 00 00 24 00 00 00   ..U.n.i.t.......

4F 00 55 00 3D 00 57 00 65 00 73 00 74 00 2E 00   O.U...W.e.s.t...

4F 00 3D 00 58 00 59 00 5A 00 43 00 6F 00 72 00   O...X.Y.Z.C.o.r.

70 00 00 00 28 00 00 00 4F 00 72 00 67 00 61 00   p.......O.r.g.a.

6E 00 69 00 7A 00 61 00 74 00 69 00 6F 00 6E 00   n.i.z.a.t.i.o.n.

61 00 6C 00 20 00 55 00 6E 00 69 00 74 00 00 00   a.l...U.n.i.t...
```

These requests validate that the source and target containers are known to the client as well as ensure that the client is communicating with the server that holds the master copy of the object and the server that will hold the master copy of the object. Next, we see a read request to obtain information on the actual object being moved. This is shown in Listing 6.12.

L I S T I N G   6.12

DS read entry information for the object being moved.

```
DSA: DSACommonRequest(2) conn:3 for client <JIM>

DSA REQUEST BUFFER:

02 00 00 00 00 00 00 00 1D 28 02 00 BC 02 00 0E   ...............

DSA REPLY BUFFER:

1D 28 02 00 00 00 00 00 00 00 00 00 6F 5E 90 36   ............o..6

0A 00 00 00 55 00 73 00 65 00 72 00 00 00 00 00   ....U.s.e.r.....

34 00 00 00 43 00 4E 00 3D 00 50 00 4B 00 75 00   4...C.N...P.K.u.

6F 00 2E 00 4F 00 55 00 3D 00 57 00 65 00 73 00   o...O.U...W.e.s.

74 00 2E 00 4F 00 3D 00 58 00 59 00 5A 00 43 00   t...O...X.Y.Z.C.

6F 00 72 00 70 00 00 00 0A 00 00 00 55 00 73 00   o.r.p.......U.s.

65 00 72 00 00 00                                 e.r...
```

The next step in the move process is to issue a start move operation. This request, shown in Listing 6.13, involves the name of the object and the server involved in the communications. Starting at offset 16, you can see the object name, and at offset 32, the fully qualified distinguished name of the server.

L I S T I N G 6 . 1 3

DS start move operation

```
DSA: DSACommonRequest(42) conn:3 for client <JIM>

DSA REQUEST BUFFER:

00 00 00 00 00 00 00 00 E3 02 00 12 0A 00 00 00 ...............
50 00 4B 00 75 00 6F 00 00 00 0C 01 2A 00 00 00 P.K.u.o.........
43 00 4E 00 3D 00 42 00 45 00 54 00 45 00 4C 00 C.N...B.E.T.E.L.
47 00 45 00 55 00 53 00 45 00 2E 00 4F 00 55 00 G.E.U.S.E...O.U.
3D 00 6F 00 6D 00 65 00 45 00 61 00 73 00 3D 00 ..E.a.s.t...O...
58 00 59 00 5A 00 43 00 6F 00 72 00 70 00 00 00 X.Y.Z.C.o.r.p...
C8 00                                           ..

DSA REPLY BUFFER:
```

At this point, the obituaries are issued for the moved object as well as for the object in its new location. Listing 6.14 shows the DSREPAIR log from performing a verification of external references.

Now we see more differences between the move operation and the previously described object operations. The Inhibit Move obituary issued for the new object blocks most further operations on the object, including rename, delete, and move. It is possible to change attributes in the object, but all other requests receive an error -637: previous move in progress. This is one of the more common error messages received while performing administrative tasks. From understanding how the move process operates, you can now understand what a -637 error means and know what needs to be done to resolve the situation.

LISTING 6.14

*Obituaries issued due to the
move operation*

```
/***************************************************************************/

Netware 4.1 Directory Services Repair 4.56 , DS 5.99

Log file for server "ORION.East.XYZCorp" in tree "NW5TEST"

External Reference Check

Start:   Sunday, January 3, 1999  11:48:14 pm Local Time

Found obituary at VID: 0002E7C0, EID: 0E0002BC, DN:
CN=PKuo.OU=East.O=XYZCorp.NW5TEST

   TV:   1-03-1999 23:24:57 0001, Type = 0003 INHIBIT_MOVE, Flags = 0000

Found obituary at VID: 00017F80, EID: 150002E4, DN:
CN=PKuo.OU=West.O=XYZCorp.NW5TEST

   TV:   1-03-1999 23:24:57 0001, Type = 0002 MOVED, Flags = 0000

   MoveObit: destID = 0E0002BC, CN=PKuo.OU=East.O=XYZCorp.NW5TEST

Found obituary at VID: 00032D00, EID: 150002E4, DN:
CN=PKuo.OU=West.O=XYZCorp.NW5TEST

   TV:   1-03-1999 23:24:57 0001, Type = 0006 BACKLINK, Flags = 0000

   Backlink: Type = 00000002 MOVED, RemoteID = FFFFFFFF, ServerID = 010000C3,
CN=RIGEL.OU=West.O=XYZCorp.NW5TEST

Checked 0 external references
```

*** END ***

NOTE **While the target object can only be manipulated in a minimal number of ways because of the Inhibit Move obituary, a new object with the same name can be created in the original location. The Moved obituary type does not prevent object creation.**

As with the previous object operations, we also have a Backlink obituary created.

Once the move is complete, DS requests that the move be finished. This initiates the purge process for the Move Inhibit and Moved obituaries. Listing 6.15 shows this request.

L I S T I N G   6 . 1 5

DS finish move operation

```
DSA: DSACommonRequest(43) conn:3 for client <JIM>

DSA REQUEST BUFFER:

00 00 00 00 01 00 00 00 BC 02 00 0E E3 02 00 12  ................

0A 00 00 00 50 00 4B 00 75 00 6F 00 00 00 6F 00  ....P.K.u.o...o.

2A 00 00 00 43 00 4E 00 3D 00 42 00 45 00 54 00  ....C.N...B.E.T.

45 00 4C 00 47 00 45 00 55 00 53 00 45 00 2E 00  E.L.G.E.U.S.E...

4F 00 55 00 3D 00 6F 00 6D 00 65 00 45 00 61 00  O.U...E.a.t...

73 00 3D 00 58 00 59 00 5A 00 43 00 6F 00 72 00  O...X.Y.Z.C.o.r.

70 00 00 00 65 00                                 p...e.
```

The finish move operation completes, and the obituary purge process begins. Once the obituaries are purged, you will be able to proceed with other move operations as well as renaming the object or deleting it. Listing 6.16 demonstrates the server response to a delete request on the object that was moved.

L I S T I N G   6 . 1 6

*Delete request on an object
with a previous move in
progress*

```
DSA: DSACommonRequest(8) conn:16 for client <JIM>

DSA REQUEST BUFFER:

00 00 00 00 BC 02 00 0E                           ........

DSA REPLY BUFFER:

DSA: DSACommonRequest(8): returning ERROR -637
```

The error message in the reply buffer is expected in this case: the -637 error is defined as ERR_PREVIOUS_MOVE_IN_PROGRESS. This error is reported because the obituaries created for the move request have not purged, even though the finish move operation has executed successfully.

Manual Partition and Replication Processes

Partitioning and replication operations all require communications with the server that holds the master replica or replicas. In this section, we examine the common operations used in manipulating partitions and replicas.

IMPORTANT

While many of these operations function even if some of the servers in the replica ring are unavailable, it is not recommended that they be performed until connectivity can be verified. Even though the impact to users is not noticeable if everything proceeds normally, these operations should be considered to be major changes to your tree.

Prior to initiating a partition or replica operation, it is a good idea to verify communication to all servers that will be involved in the operation. This is easiest to do from NDS Manager. NDS Manager has a couple of different options that are useful here — the check synchronization option, shown in Figure 6.5, and the partition continuity option, shown in Figure 6.6.

FIGURE 6.5

NDS Manager check synchronization option

As you can see in Figure 6.5, the check synchronization option shows a quick overview of synchronization status. This status is obtained by reading a single server and seeing what that server recorded the last synchronization status as. If the last synchronization status was All Processed=YES, the synchronization is determined to have been successful. If the status was All Processed=NO, the synchronization failed.

This basic check shows you high-level problems in synchronization, but in order to really determine the status, you should check each server in the replica ring. The partition continuity option provides this information in depth.

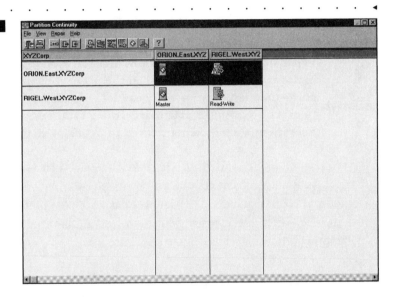

FIGURE 6.6

NDS Manager partition
continuity option

Figure 6.6 shows a normal status for partition continuity. In this figure, the two servers have been checked and each replica list has been verified. Serious problems in replica list consistency are easily spotted here, because each row in the table should be identical. If the rows are not identical, there is a serious problem you need to look into.

Synchronization errors between one server and another also are apparent here. If there is a synchronization problem reported between two servers, the error is shown in the square that would be the intersection of the source server and the destination server.

Figure 6.6 shows such an error. In this case, the source server is the server ORION.East.XYZCorp, and the destination server is RIGEL.West.XYZCorp. At the intersection in the grid for ORION (as the source) and RIGEL (as the destination), a special icon is displayed that indicates an error condition. By double clicking in the square that shows the error, a synchronization status window is presented that shows a number of different pieces of information, including:

- Partition name

- Server read

- Replica number

- Replica type

- Replica state

- Time and date of the last successful sync

- A referral address — this is equal to the network address of the server being read

- The current sync error

If a sync error exists, a box next to the sync error with a question mark is available, and clicking the button will bring up a help message describing the error and how it may be corrected.

Once you have verified that the involved replicas are properly synchronized, you can then proceed with a partitioning/replication operation. We'll start by examining the split partition operation.

Split Partition

The split partition operation is the process that is used to create a new partition. When you install the first NetWare server in a tree, the [Root] partition is created automatically — any other partitions created are split off of the [Root] partition.

The information reported by the DSTRACE screen is fairly minimal — watching the operation entails using the command **SET DSTRACE=+PART**. This enables the trace screens for all partitioning operations. Listing 6.17 shows the information presented during a split operation.

LISTING 6.17

Split partition operation

```
SPLITTING — BEGIN STATE 0

(20:28:39)

*** DSALowLevelSplit <[Root]> and <XYZCorp> ***


Successfully split all partitions in ring.

ADDED 010000B6 and 0C0000BC to partition busy list.

SPLITTING — END STATE 0

*CNTL: This server is the new master for [0C0000BC]<XYZCorp>

*CNTL: SetNewMaster for [0C0000BC]<XYZCorp> succeeded.

Turning replicas on after changing replica type.
```

While a split partition operation is being performed, further partitioning and replication operations are suspended. The split partition is reported in NDS Manager, and further operations result in an error -654, ERR_PARTITION_BUSY, until the replicas are turned on. This operation is indicated in the last line of Listing 6.17.

You may have noticed lines 7 and 8 in the previous listing, indicating the server that we did the trace on became the master replica for the new partition. This is to be expected, because this server holds the master of the parent partition. When performing a split operation, the servers that end up with replicas are the same as the ones that hold replicas of the parent partition. After the replicas are turned on, you can manipulate the replicas by adding, removing, or changing the replica types.

Figure 6.7 provides a good before-and-after view of what the split partition looks like. The shaded areas represent partitions. In the top half of Figure 6.7, you see the entire tree as a single partition. After the split operation is complete, the partitions appear as shown in the bottom half of the figure: a single partition for the [Root] partition and a separate partition starting at XYZCorp and containing the rest of the tree.

▶ • ◀

Tree NetWare 5 test before and after the partition is created

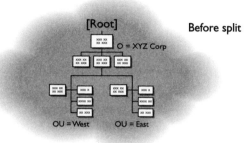

Before split

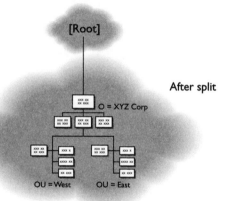

After split

Merge Partition

Merging a partition — also referred to as joining a partition — is the reverse of a partition split. This takes a parent-and-child partition and merges them into a single partition. In this case, the bottom half of Figure 6.7 shows the partitions before the merge, and the top half shows the single partition after the merge.

As Listing 6.18 shows, there are actually two operations that take place during a join — a *join up* operation and a *join down* operation. The join up operation is the joining of the child partition with the parent; the join down operation is the process of the parent joining with the child partition.

DSTRACE messages from a join
operation

```
(20:28:08)*** DSAStartJoin <XYZCorp> to <[Root]> ***

JOINING DOWN — BEGIN STATE 0

JOINING DOWN — END STATE 0

JOINING UP — BEGIN STATE 0

JOINING UP — END STATE 0

JOINING DOWN — BEGIN STATE 1

PARENT REPORTING CHILD IS STILL IN STATE 1

JOINING UP — BEGIN STATE 1

JOINING UP — END STATE 1

JOINING DOWN — BEGIN STATE 1

JOIN: Reassigning unowned replica changes for [010000B6]<[Root]> succeeded,
total values reassigned 1

 (20:28:12)

*** DSALowLevelJoin <[Root]> and <XYZCorp> ***


ADDED 010000B6 to partition busy list.

JOINING DOWN — END STATE 1
```

The merge operation results in a single partition where there were two; however, the replicas for each of the old partitions have to be dealt with in such a way that bindery services on all servers are not disrupted. When merging partitions together, it is very important to determine where the new partition's replicas are going to be: If you have, for example, 8 servers involved in the merge operation, you will end up with 8 replicas of the new partition. This may not be desirable, so you will want to examine where these new replicas will be and what services would be affected on each server if you were to remove the replica from this server.

Move Partition

Moving a partition is very similar to moving an object — in fact, the operation uses the same code within the DS.NLM module to perform the operation. The biggest difference is that the move partition operation also generates create replica operations, which in turn result in object synchronization operations. This is a fairly complex operation, and more so than the other operations, you must make sure you have no synchronization problems in the partitions involved.

IMPORTANT

There can be a total of three existing partitions affected by a move operation: two parent partitions and the partition being moved. It is important to verify the synchronization of all three partitions before initiating a move operation.

There are two rules to remember when moving partitions:

▶ Moving a partition cannot violate containment rules for the partition root object.

▶ The partition moved must not have any child partitions.

Figure 6.8 shows an example of a violation of the first rule. This move operation is invalid because the containment rules are violated. O=XYZCorp cannot be moved into O=DIV1, because an organization cannot contain another organization.

By extension of the second rule, it is not possible to move a partition to be subordinate to a child partition. In Figure 6.9, it is not possible to move the OU=West container under the OU=IT container, because OU=IT is a child partition to OU=West.

Next we need to talk about things you need to watch out for when moving a partition.

Important Considerations for Partition Moves

NetWare 5 introduces several objects into the tree at the time of installation, depending on which additional services are installed on the server. In addition, other Novell products or third-party products may also create dependencies on a server's location in the tree. When moving a partition, it is useful to determine which objects will be affected by a server's move if this server should be in the

F I G U R E   6.8

An organization cannot contain another organization.

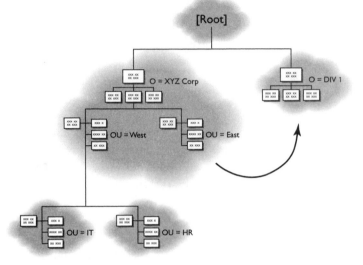

F I G U R E   6.9

You cannot move a partition that has child partitions.

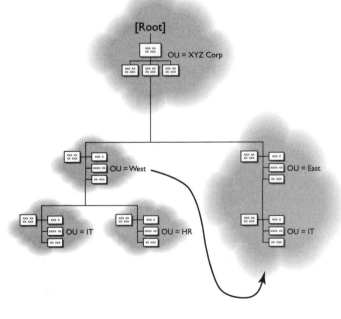

partition being moved. References to objects within the partition being moved may not be changed. We'll look at a few NetWare 5 specific examples.

NetWare 5 introduces the Secure Authentication Service (SAS). This add-on creates an object in the tree and references the server that hosts the service. When a partition containing this service is moved, you need to recreate the object by unloading the SAS.NLM module, loading SASI.NLM (the SAS installation utility), and logging in with sufficient rights to recreate the SAS object in the tree.

The NDPS Broker service also has dependencies on the server location—a broker object is created in the tree in the server's container. When the server object is moved, shut down, and brought back up in the new location, the broker service will not start properly.

WARNING

Of particular significance is NetWare 5's license service. If you should relocate a partition that contains license information for NetWare 5 servers, you will need to reassign the license files to the servers. This requires reinstalling the license service on the server or servers that have moved as a result of the partition move operation.

There are many other add-on services that can be affected by the move operation. The best thing to do is check all of your nonuser objects and see what references a server. Moving a server object—and a partition, by extension—is not a trivial operation and has widespread impact in most production environments.

The Move Partition Process

The partition move operation consists of two parts: the move partition request and the finish partition move request.

The move partition request is sent by the client to schedule the move. This process performs several verification operations, including

- ► Ensuring the user has create object rights to the destination container the partition is being moved to.

- ► Verifying there is not an object in the destination container with the same name as the partition root object being moved

- ► Verifying that the affected replicas are all available to perform a partition operation

▶ Ensuring that the Transaction Tracking Service (TTS) is available on all servers involved in the move operation. NDS operations are currently dependant on TTS, and if it is not available, NDS cannot function.

Once this is completed, the servers handle the finish partition move request. This process has two functions:

▶ Moving the partition root object and all subordinate objects from one context to another valid context

▶ Notifying the server that holds the master replica of the partition that the partition has moved.

This process also performs several verification operations, including verifying that the partition root object being moved and all subordinate objects do not have an Inhibit Move obituary on them. If there is such an obituary within the partition, the process aborts with an error -637, ERR_PREVIOUS_MOVE_IN_PROGRESS.

A second verification process involves testing to see if the partition root object is the [Root] object for the tree. It is not possible to move the [Root] object, and attempting to do so will result in a -641 error, ERR_INVALID_REQUEST.

NOTE

A further test can also cause a -641 error to be generated — attempting to move an object that is not a partition root. This is not something that the standard administration utilities will not allow, but the check is there to prevent third-party developers from creating utilities that could attempt this sort of illegal move.

A further test is done to verify that the servers involved in the move are running at least DS.NLM 4.63 — it is *highly* recommended that you be running a current version of DS.NLM before attempting a move operation. Novell made changes to the DS code that are involved in partition moves, and using versions older than 4.63 with versions newer than 4.63 causes the move to fail. Mixing versions in this manner causes an error -666, ERR_INCOMPATABLE_DS_VERSION, to be reported.

NOTE

The version of DS.NLM is checked on all servers holding real replicas of the partition root object and all servers holding an external reference of the partition root object.

Next, DS checks to verify the containment rules are not being violated by the move. The DS Agent finds a server with a copy of [Root] and asks for the class definition for the destination parent object's class; if the partition root object being moved is in the containment list of the destination, the move is allowed to proceed. Otherwise, an error -611, ERR_ILLEGAL_CONTAINMENT, is generated and the process aborts.

Another verification is done to ensure the partition root object's distinguished name and the distinguished names of all subordinate objects do not exceed the maximum length of 256 unicode characters (512 bytes). If any of the objects affected have a distinguished name that exceeds this length, an error -610, ERR_ILLEGAL_DS_NAME, is returned.

NOTE

In the check of the objects that are subordinate to the partition root object, the actual returned code may be a -353, ERR_DN_TOO_LONG. This error code means the same thing as a -610 but is reported by the client library instead.

A further step in the move process is the submission of a third process to the destination server: an NDS start tree move request. This request actually performs the move operation and is responsible for moving both the partition root object and all of the child objects to the new location.

Once the move is completed and the partition root object being moved has been locked to prevent other partition operations from occurring, the replica synchronization and backlinker processes are scheduled and, once successfully scheduled, the partition root object is unlocked.

Moving a partition also causes the creation and deletion of subordinate reference replicas — these are needed to provide connectivity between partitions, as discussed in Chapter 2. The old subordinate reference replicas will be deleted from the servers that hold them, and new subordinate reference replicas will be created to provide connectivity to the new location.

Rename Partition

The rename partition operation is very similar to the rename object operation, except the obituaries that are issued are different — rather than the Old RDN and New RDN obituaries being issued, the obituaries issued are Tree Old RDN and Tree New RDN. Renaming a partition is really a special case of the object rename operation, because the only object directly affected is the partition root object.

The rename partition operation is one operation that can hold up any other type of partition or replication operation. NDS checks for this condition before attempting the add replica, delete replica, split partition, join partition, and change partition type operations.

Create Replica

Creating a replica, also known as an add replica request, requires communication with each server in the replica ring for the partition being affected. An inability to communicate with a server in the replica ring results in a -625 error, ERR_TRANSPORT_FAILURE, or a -636 error, ERR_UNREACHABLE_SERVER.

NOTE

If a server has a subordinate reference replica and you wish to put a readable replica on the server, the operation you need to use is the create replica operation, not the change replica type operation. This is because a subordinate reference replica is not a real copy of the partition, but rather contains just enough information for NDS operations such as tree walking.

Creating a replica of a partition involves making changes to the local partition database and then performing a synchronization of all objects in the partition to the server receiving the new replica. Problems can occur for two reasons:

▶ Communication cannot be established or maintained with a server in the replica ring

▶ If the server being examined to determine the location of the master replica does not have a replica attribute, error -602, ERR_NO_SUCH_VALUE, is returned and the operation is aborted.

Delete Replica

Deleting a replica is similar in requirements to the create replica operation. This operation requires all servers in the replica ring be reachable. The request is processed by the server holding the master replica of the partition.

The verification routines ensure the replica being removed is a read/write or read-only replica. If the replica in question is the master, an error -656, ERR_CRUCIAL_REPLICA, is returned.

A lock is placed on the partition during the operation. Unlike other operations, this lock is left in place for a number of steps, including an immediate synchronization that is scheduled to ensure all objects in the replica being moved have been synchronized. This ensures that information in the objects stored in the replica being deleted does not get lost if it is newer than the information in other replicas.

Change Replica Type

The final operation we examine is the change replica type operation. Compared to the other operations we have looked at in this chapter, this operation is relatively simple.

The change replica type operation is easiest to perform from the NDS Manager utility. Figure 6.10 shows the NDS Manager dialog box used during this operation.

Change replica type dialog box

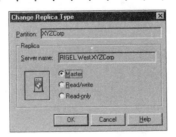

As discussed earlier, changing a replica type from a subordinate reference to a master, read/write or read-only replica is treated as a create replica operation. The option to change a replica type is not presented if a server containing a subordinate reference replica of the specified partition is selected.

In Figure 6.10, you can see the replica types available for changing the selected server's replica type. Because we have selected the server RIGEL.West.XYZCorp, and this server currently holds a read/write replica of the option, we have the option of making it a master, leaving it as a read/write or changing it to a read-only.

 Even though the option is presented to change the replica type to a read/write replica, if you select this option, the OK button is disabled, because the replica already is a read/write replica.
NOTE

Changing the master to a read/write or changing a read/write or read-only replica to a master actually causes two changes to be made: one to change the master to a read/write replica, and the other to change the read/write or read-only replica to the master. This is done because there cannot be two master replicas for a given partition.

This operation generally occurs very quickly, because no replicas need to be created or deleted in order to change the replica. The replica ring is updated on all servers holding a replica (including subordinate reference replicas), and the server or servers affected have a change made in their partition entry tables to reflect the change in replica type.

Summary

In this chapter, we examined NDS' use of obituaries and the major NDS background processes. We also examined several object-related and partitioning-replication-related operations to see how NDS actually performs these operations. Understanding how these processes operate lays a foundation for understanding how to effectively troubleshoot and resolve problems.

In the next part of the book, we will examine how to use this information to troubleshoot and resolve issues with NDS using the different tools available. We also will examine ways to combine tools using different techniques in order to streamline the troubleshooting-resolution process.

## PART III

Troubleshoot and Resolve the Problem

## CHAPTER 7

Diagnosis Tools

Regardless of the type of troubleshooting you need to perform, having the right tools is essential. You can't troubleshoot effectively if you can't see what and where the error is. This chapter introduces you to the various server- and workstation-based diagnosis tools and utilities included with the NetWare 4 and NetWare 5 operating systems and additional artilleries available from either Novell sources or third parties.

▶ · ◀

Server Tools

It is important to keep in mind that NDS is a global, distributed name service whose database exists as a set of files that are stored on one or more NetWare servers. These servers continually exchange updates and other time-sensitive information. If a server's local copy of the NDS information is corrupted, it may prevent the rest of the servers in the same NDS tree from communicating NDS changes; therefore, NetWare is shipped with a number of server-centric diagnosis tools that can help you to determine if the local NDS database has problems and repair the errors automatically if possible. The features of these utilities are discussed in the following sections, and specific applications of the tools can be found in later chapters.

DSREPAIR

One of the most commonly used NDS diagnostic utilities is DSREPAIR. It is an NLM provided with NetWare 4 and NetWare 5 operating systems to check for and to correct problems in the NDS database on a server-centric basis.

NOTE

The DSREPAIR NLM is frequently updated to include new functionalities and bug fixes; therefore, you should use the latest version whenever possible. Generally, new versions of DSREPAIR are included with new versions of DS.NLM releases. Check http://support.novell.com **for information about newer releases of DSREPAIR.**

The opening screen of DSREPAIR offers you five options:

- Unattended full repair

- Time synchronization

- Report synchronization status

- View repair log file

- Advanced options menu

The version of DSREPAIR, along with the name of the current NDS tree and server name, is shown at the top of the menu.

The unattended full repair option automatically performs all the possible repair operations that don't require user input. You can select the items to be checked or repaired using the Repair Local Database option in the Advanced Repair Options menu. A log file (called DSREPAIR.LOG) located in the SYS:SYSTEM directory records all actions during the repair operation so you can later determine what was done.

During the repair of the local database, the NDS database (on the server running DSREPAIR only) is locked, making it inaccessible to the client or any other use until the repair is completed. That means new users will not be able to authenticate to this server while users already logged in will be able to continue to access other (non-NDS) resources on this server.

NOTE

The unattended full repair goes through the following four major diagnostic and repair procedures:

- Local NDS data (database is locked during this phase)

- Validation of all network addresses (database is not locked)

- Validation of remote server IDs (database is not locked)

- Consistency check of replica rings (database is not locked)

A status menu is displayed (see Figure 7.1) during the repair operation. The same information is recorded in the log file. When the repair operations are completed, the log file is automatically displayed, so you can determine what repairs were done and what the state of the database is following the repair operation.

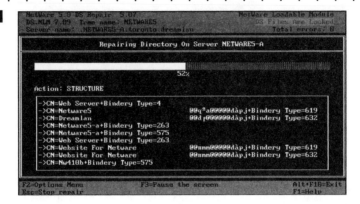

DSREPAIR status screen

TIP

You can initiate an unattended repair option from the command-line by loading DSREPAIR with the -U option switch. The NLM will unload itself when the operation is completed.

The time synchronization check procedure contacts every server known to this server's local database and looks up information about NDS (such as the version of DS.NLM), time sychnronization status, and server status. The retrieved data is displayed on the screen (see Figure 7.2) and recorded to the log file as a table.

The table shows the following information:

▸ **Server name**. This field shows the absolute distinguished name of the server responding to the query. NetWare 5's DSREPAIR reports the server names with a leading period (that is, NETWARE5-A.toronto.dreamlan) while NetWare 4's shows the server names without the leading period.

▸ **DS.NLM version**. This field lists the version of DS.NLM that's running on the reporting server. This is useful in determining, at a glance, the versions of DS you have running on your NDS tree.

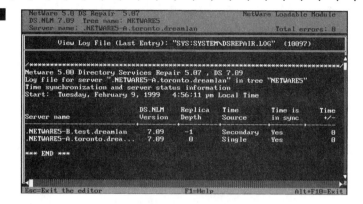

FIGURE 7.2

Sample time
synchronization check
report

▸ **Replica depth**. This entry shows a −1 if the reporting server holds no
replica (as is the case for server NETWARE5-B). A 0 indicates the server
contains a replica of the [Root] partition (as is the case for server
NETWARE5-A), and a positive integer that indicates how many levels
away from the [Root] the first replica is on the reporting server.

▸ **Time source**. The name of this field is misleading. What this field shows
is *not* the time source, but rather the time server *type* of the queried server
(such as single reference, primary, and so on). The information provided
in this field can be useful in determining if time synchronization has been
configured properly.

▸ **Time is in sync flag**. A Yes here indicates the reporting server's time is in
synchronization with the network time. A No status means either the
reporting server can't communicate with its time source or that its time is
not in agreement with the network time.

NOTE

**If a server reports time not in synchronization for a short period of
time (perhaps 24 hours), there's nothing to worry about, because the
server's internal clock generally will not drift significantly; however,
you should determine and resolve this problem at your earliest
convenience. All servers in the tree must be time-synchronized, or**

NDS can't resolve synchronization collisions properly, which may lead to NDS data inconsistency.

▶ **Time delta.** This field reports the time difference between the server running DSREPAIR and the queried server. With time synchronization working correctly and no network communication errors, all servers should be, by default, within two seconds of each other. (This threshold is determined by the timesync synchronization radius server SET command whose default value is 2000 milliseconds; this setting may be increased if you have slow WAN links, such as satellite hops.) This field reports up to 999 minutes and 59 seconds, or approximately 16.5 hours, in the form MINUTES:SECONDS. If the time difference is greater than that, the maximum value is displayed as "999:59".

The report synchronization status process checks the synchronization status, by examining the Sync Up To attribute of the partition root object, of all partitions that have a replica stored on the local server. Each server in the replica ring is queried and any errors found is displayed (see Figure 7.3) and logged to the DSREPAIR.LOG file.

▶ . . . . ◀

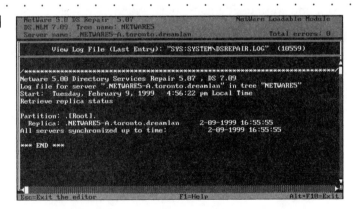

In the log file, each partition has its own section. The section starts off with the name of the partition and ends with the "All servers synchronized up to time" — this is the time stamp according to the master replica of that partition and is not an average of all reported sync up to times for that replica ring. In the sample shown in Figure 7.4, there is only one partition, [Root]. Below the partition name, each replica known to the local server is identified by a server name. The key to note here is that a synchronization status is only available for the servers that hold replicas according to this local database.

TIP **By comparing the status reports of all servers within the replica ring, you can easily determine the consistency of the ring. For example, each server in the replica ring should report the same number of replicas (regardless of the replica type, including SubRefs) for a particular partition.**

To the right of each replica entry, one of the following is displayed:

▶ The date and time of the last successful synchronization

▶ The date and time of the last successful synchronization with an error code (such as -625) and a designation of whether the error was local or remote to the server in question

The following is an example of a replica synchronization report that contains some errors:

```
Partition: .O=Europe.

   Replica: CN=NETWARE5-D.OU=Consulting.OU=Toro...   2-09-1999 22:18:46

   Replica: CN=NW411B.OU=Consulting.O=North_...    ******** ********  -625

   Replica: CN=NETWARE5-C.OU=Toronto.O=North_...   2-09-1999 22:17:41

   Server: CN=NW411B.OU=Consulting.OU=Toro...    2-09-1999 22:10:05  -621 Remote


All servers synchronized up to time:         2-09-1999 22:17:41
```

In this example, there are three servers in the replica ring: NW411B, NETWARE5-C, and NETWARE5-D. The first error suggests that the local server isn't able to obtain a replica synchronization status from the NW411B server and an error -625 is returned; -625 indicates some kind of communication error. The second error means that server NETWARE5-C last successfully synchronized at 22:17:41, and it failed to synchronize at 22:10:05 with the replica stored on server

NW411B due to error -621. Error -621 means TTS is disabled. This could be a result of SYS volume out of disk space or SYS volume that was dismounted. And combined with the -625 error when the synchronization check is performed, chances are good that there was a problem with NW411B's SYS volume and the server has been taken down since — thus the -625 error.

Use the view report log file option to examine the DSREPAIR.LOG file without having to first exit out of DSREPAIR. Through the log file and login configuration option in the Advanced options menu, you can disable the logging, enable the logging, delete the log file, change the name of the log file, or change the location in which the log file is to be stored. When viewing the log file using this option, you'll start with the beginning of the file; when operations, such as time synchronization check, are completed the most recent entry (which contain information from the operation that was just performed) of the log file is displayed instead.

NOTE

Every time any DSREPAIR operation is performed, new information is appended to the log file; therefore, you should keep track of the size of this DSREPAIR.LOG file, because it can quickly grow to be many megabytes in size. The size of the file is displayed in parentheses at the end of the log file title line.

TIP

You can use the -L command-line switch to specify an alternate directory path and filename for the log file (for example, -L SYS:LOGFILES\DS.LOG); the path can be any NetWare volume or DOS drive. You can also use -RL instead. Unlike the -L option, however, -RL causes the existing file to be overwritten instead of new data being appended.

The advanced options menu is what you'd select when you need to perform specific repair or diagnostic operations. This menu option allows you to manually control a number of individual repair operations and global repair functions in the NDS tree. Also available are diagnostic information about the local NDS database and the overall status of your NDS tree. The Advanced options menu in NetWare 5's version of DSREPAIR provides the following additional selections (see Figure 7.4):

> ▸ **Log file and login configuration**. Configure options for the DSREPAIR log file (such as enabling or disabling logging and setting the log file's size limit). Also you can use this option to login to the Directory Services tree

which is required by some operations (the login is valid only for the duration when the DSREPAIR NLM is loaded; the login name and password are not stored for later use).

▸ **Repair local database**. Repairs the Directory Services database files stored on this server.

▸ **Servers known to this database**. Performs verification operations on servers that are known to this database: time synchronization, network addresses, and server status check.

▸ **Replica and partition operations**. This selection provides functions to repair replicas, replica rings, and server objects. It also dynamically displays each server's last synchronization time.

▸ **Check volume objects and trustees**. Perform checks on all mounted volumes for valid volume objects and valid trustees on the volumes.

▸ **Check external references**. Check for illegal external references.

▸ **Security equivalence synchronization**. Allows you to synchronize security equivalence attributes throughout the global tree.

▸ **Global schema operations**. Provides functions to update the schema in the tree.

▸ **View repair log file**. View the log file which is optionally created when repair operations are performed.

▸ **Create a database dump file**. This option copies the Directory Services database files into a single file in compressed format that is to be used for off-line repairs and diagnostics by Novell Technical Support. This option is not meant to be a backup method for your NDS database.

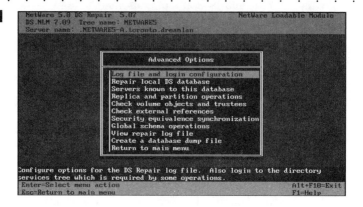

FIGURE 7.4

*DSREPAIR's advanced
options menu*

We'll briefly discuss each of these functions and highlight some of their more salient features; you'll find their applications in later chapters.

The repair local database function works with the NDS files stored on the local server. It is analogous to running Bindfix in the NetWare 3 environment. You can control the following repair options:

▶ **Pause on errors.** Set to Yes if you wish DSREPAIR to pause its operation after each error message. The default is No.

▶ **Validate mail directories.** Choose Yes to check the mail directories on volume SYS for users who no longer exist and deletes those directories. The default is Yes.

▶ **Validate stream syntax files.** Set to Yes if you wish to verify that the stream syntax files are associated with valid NDS objects and delete those that are not. A stream file is a file containing a series of data bytes. An example of a stream file is the login script associated with a user object. The default is Yes.

▶ **Check local references.** Choose Yes to check local reference properties to ensure they are valid and to check for duplicate time stamps. Using this option will slow down the repair process. The default is Yes.

▸ **Rebuild operational schema.** Choose Yes to check the schema for valid object class and attribute definitions. DSREPAIR will check for any invalid classes and/or attributes found in the predefined (base) schema on this server. You generally need not enable this option unless your server's schema is corrupted; it has no effect on extended schema definitions. The default is No.

▸ **Conserve disk space.** Choose Yes to remove the backup files before and after the repair. These files can help recover a damaged database but take up disk space. The default is No.

NOTE

All repairs are performed on a temporary copy of the NDS database files, which are renamed at the end when you commit to save the database on which repairs have been made. With the conserve disk space option enabled, when DSREPAIR saves the changed database, it renames the previous database files to a .OLD extension and the temporary files (which have a .TMP extension) are renamed to the appropriate names (see Chapter 3 for naming conventions). One important note is that the .OLD files are not preserved if a .OLD file set exists that is less than 72 hours old. This is to provide some reference point to go back if you run into trouble while running multiple DSREPAIRs within 72 hours.

▸ **Exit automatically upon completion**. Set to Yes to immediately exit DSREPAIR and open the local Directory Services database files after completing the repairs. The default is No.

During the repair operation, DSREPAIR performs an extensive analysis of the database. It checks for invalid partitions and partition roots and will fix any errors found. For each partition, it checks all objects in the partition for valid containment and for consistency with the schema. All illegal attributes are removed. DSREPAIR changes any object that is missing a mandatory attribute (such as a user object missing the Last Name attribute) to unknown. It checks all attribute syntaxes for consistency and also checks for invalid checksum and links in the database records.

NOTE

Like running VRepair, you should run **DSREPAIR** until it reports no more errors. You may need to run **DSREPAIR** multiple times until you get zero errors. There have been varying opinions about how often to run **DSREPAIR**. From our experience, you don't need to run **DSREPAIR** on a daily or even weekly basis as part of your regular network maintenance. Running it on a quarterly basis should do under normal circumstances, and even then, only after a large number of changes have been made to your tree.

NOTE

If case you wonder how long a typical **DSREPAIR** operation takes, our experience showed that for a Pentium P-133 server, with a moderately fast **SCSI** drive (not **RAID-5**), that has 3,000 objects in the local replicas, it takes about 15 minutes to perform a local database repair.

The Unattended full repair option in the main DSREPAIR menu executes all of the preceding checks and repairs, using the default parameter settings.

The servers known to this database option lists all the servers known to the local NDS database. The server names are obtained from the NCP Server objects found in the replicas that are stored in the server and are not learned through SAP (Service Advertising Protocol) or SLP (Service Locator Protocol). If this server holds a replica of [Root], then this list most likely contains all the servers in the tree. If, however, the server doesn't contain a replica of [Root], the list will be a subset of the servers in the NDS tree.

The servers known to this database list shows the local status and local ID for each server in the list (see Figure 7.5). The local status field reports the state of the listed server as known to this server. If the state is up, it is active; if it is down, some sort of communication problem has occurred recently. Upon selecting a server from the list, several options become available:

- ▸ **Time synchronization and server status.** This option performs the same task as the time synchronization option found in the main DSREPAIR menu.

- ▸ **Repair all network addresses.** For each of the listed servers, DSREPAIR compares the server's network address found in the SAP table with that found in the local NDS database. If they are different, the entries in the

NDS database are updated with the value from the SAP table. If DSREPAIR can't find the server in the SAP table, no repair is done.

▶ **Repair selected server's network address.** This operation is identical to the repair all network addresses function, except that only the selected server's network address is checked and repaired.

▶ **View entire server name.** DSREPAIR log file and status screen show only the first 35 characters in a server name. Use this option to verify the entire distinguished name, which can be as long as 256 bytes.

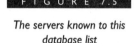

FIGURE 7.5

The servers known to this database list

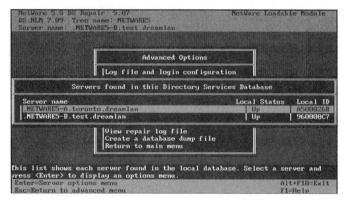

The replica and partition operation function is probably the most powerful of all DSREPAIR options, because you can destroy a replica just as easily as you can repair one. The initial opening screen of this option displays a list of all replicas stored on the local server. Shown in a table is each replica along with its replica type (master, read/write, read-only, or subordinate) and replica state (on or off), because it is stored on this server. After selecting a replica to work with, a list of replica-related functions is displayed (see Figure 7.6). The uses of these functions are discussed in Chapter 11.

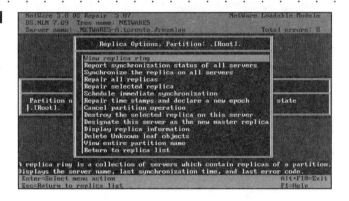

F I G U R E 7.6

Replica and partition options menu. The options indicated are activated only when you load DSREPAIR with the -A command-line switch.

TIP

To protect you from exercising some of the more destructive options in DSREPAIR inadvertently, such as editing a replica ring or repairing time stamps and declaring a new time epoch, these options are not automatically listed in the advanced options menu: You need to load DSREPAIR with the -A switch to toggle these special options on for selection.

The check volume objects and trustees option checks the association of all mounted volumes (including CD-ROM volumes and those mounted through NFS) on the current server with volume objects in the tree. If DSREPAIR doesn't find a matching volume object for a given mounted volume, one will be created. Once the association between the volumes and its objects are verified, file system trustee assignments for that volume are verified.

The check external references option validates all entries found in the external reference partition and attempts to locate a backlink for each entry. This operation will also display obituary information for all obituaries contained in the local database. You'll learn in Chapter 11 how to apply this information for troubleshooting obituary problems.

The Security equivalence synchronization operation forces the synchronization of security equivalence attributes throughout the whole tree. The process walks the tree and checks each object for an Equivalent To Me attribute and for the corresponding object referenced by this attribute for a Security Equals attribute. You'd not normally require to exercise this option unless you find security equivalences are not properly linked or you have NetWare 4.0x servers—The

Equivalent To Me attribute was introduced in NetWare 4.10 and is managed and synchronized by NetWare 4.10 and higher servers, but NetWare 4.0x servers do not manage this attribute, and thus they must be synchronized manually using this DSREPAIR option.

You must log in with a user ID that has sufficient rights to walk the tree and read/write rights to the Equivalent To Me and Security Equals attributes on all objects in the tree. If not, the operation will first report that the attributes are not synchronized and then will fail if an update is requested.

NOTE

The functionality of global schema operations changed somewhat between NetWare 4 and NetWare 5's DSREPAIR. In the NetWare 4 versions, this option can update the operational (base) schema on all servers within the tree or on only the root server—the root server is the server that contains the master of [Root]. You can also use this option to import schema definitions (including extensions) from a remote tree so that the schemas for both trees are identical prior to a tree merge. If the -A switch was used, you have the additional option to update the schemas on all NetWare 4.0x servers within the current tree as well as to declare a new epoch on the schema.

Declaring a new schema epoch will cause the server holding the master of [Root] to time stamp the schema and resend it to all servers in the tree. You should use extreme caution when using this option. If the schema is bad, and you force it to be sent, then you will corrupt the tree. This can also generate a lot of traffic on the wire; furthermore, if the receiving server contains schema that was not in the new epoch, objects and attributes that use the schema will be changed to the unknown object class or attribute.

WARNING

The global schema operations in NetWare 5's version of DSREPAIR performs the following tasks: update this server's schema by requesting any schema changes made in the next 24 hours from the server holding the master of [Root], import schema from a remote tree, and reset the local schema by requesting a complete copy of the schema from the server holding the master of [Root]. After the local server receives the schema updates, it will then remove any additional schema it has that did not get updated. As a result, any objects and attributes that used the old schema will be changed to the unknown object class or attribute. If the -A switch was used, you can also declare a new schema epoch.

The create a database dump file feature allows you to take a snapshot copy of the server's NDS database files. The snapshot stores the data in a compressed format which can be used by Novell Technical Support for off-line diagnostics and repair purposes. You should, however, not use this option as a means to back up your NDS, because DSREPAIR doesn't have an option to restore the component files of this dump file.

Shown in Table 7.1 is a summary of documented DSREPAIR command-line switches and some more commonly known and used undocumented switches. Because some of these switches are undocumented, their availability and their functions may be changed by Novell without any notice.

T A B L E   7 . 1

DSREPAIR Command-line
Switches

SWITCH	DOCUMENTED	DESCRIPTION
-A	No	Enables the advanced mode for DSREPAIR.
-L <filename>	Yes	Specifies an alternate directory path and filename for the log file, for example, -L SYS:LOGFILES\DS.LOG. The path can be any NetWare volume or DOS drive.
-M	No	Report move inhibit obituaries.
-N <integer>	No	Specifies number of days from which you want to purge the network address property on a user class object, for example, -N 4 for four days. The range is from 1–7, with one being today and seven being one week ago. When you set the day any network address property older than the number of days chosen will be purged.
-RC <filename>	No	Create DIB dump file followed by optional dump file name, for example, -RC SYS:BACKUP\SAVE.DIB; the default is SYS:SYSTEM\DSREPAIR.DIB
-RD	No	Allows for an automated repair of the local database.
-RI	No	Verify remote server IDs.

SWITCH	DOCUMENTED	DESCRIPTION
RL <*filename*>	No	Specifies an alternate directory path and filename for the log file, for example, -RL SYS:LOGFILES\DS.LOG. The path can be any NetWare volume or DOS drive. Unlike the -L option, the existing file is overwritten instead of being appended to.
-RN	No	Repair network addresses.
-RV	No	Repair volume objects.
-RVT	No	Repair volume objects and trustees.
-U	Yes	Perform unattended repair. Unload NLM when finished.

Some of you may have heard of or have even used some killer switches (-Kx or -XKx, such as -K2 or -XK2) in DSREPAIR to fix stubborn NDS issues. These switches are not listed in Table 7.1 because inappropriate use of these killer switches could result in damage to part or all of your NDS tree.

 Unless directly instructed by Novell Technical Support, avoid using the DSREPAIR killer switches.

WARNING

DSTRACE

DSTRACE is a troubleshooting aid built into DS.NLM by Novell's NDS Engineering Team to help in the development and debugging processes. It has since been made known to all that such a tool is available for diagnosing NDS synchronization problems. Because of its origin as an engineering tool, DSTRACE can sometimes display a lot of obscure information that is difficult to interpret.

In NetWare 4 context, DSTRACE really referred to a group of SET commands available at the server console although DSTRACE was often referred to as a utility. However, in NetWare 5, DSTRACE is now an NLM utility (called the NDS Trace Event Monitor) that provides expanded monitoring capabilities compared to its predecessor. Once it is loaded, you can use DSTRACE to monitor synchronization status and errors. DSTRACE is primarily used to determine and track the health of NDS, because it communicates with the other NetWare servers in the network.

To enable DSTRACE on a NetWare 5 server, simply type **DSTRACE** at the server console. After DSTRACE is enabled, you can type **HELP DSTRACE** which will display a list of options:

```
DSTRACE - Novell Directory Services Trace Event Monitor.


    USAGE: DSTRACE {Options}


    Options:

        {taglist}               List of qualified event tags.

        ON                      Enable tracing to target device.

        OFF                     Disable tracing to target device.

        FILE                    Change command target to log file.

        SCREEN                  Change command target to trace screen.

        INLINE                  Display events inline.

        JOURNAL                 Display events on a background thread.

        FMAX={size}             Specify maximum disk file size.

        FNAME={name}            Specify disk file name.


    Examples:

        DSTRACE INLINE

        DSTRACE SCREEN ON +AL +CB -FR

        DSTRACE FMAX=10240 FNAME=DBTRACE.LOG


    Notes:

        All event type tags and keywords (except DSTRACE) may be shortened. To

        display the current configuration and a list of event tag names, enter

        'DSTRACE' with no options. The default tag qualifier is '+'.
```

Once DSTRACE is loaded and you enabled its tracing using the DSTRACE SCREEN ON command, an alternate console screen is created where DS event information is displayed. You can specify what you would like DSTRACE data to display. Select a wide variety of information to view by specifying the DSTRACE command followed by a filter list. The list of possible filters and their current settings is displayed by typing just **DSTRACE** at the console. The following is a sample of that screen:

```
DSTRACE Configuration:


Trace mode is JOURNAL.   Trace Screen is ON.   Trace File is OFF.

File Size: 0 (unlimited). File Name: DSTRACE.LOG.


*Key: [OFF]   [SCREEN]   [FILE]   [BOTH]


TAGS: Show Event Tags      TIME: Show Event Times     ABUF: Agent Buffers

ALOC: Memory Allocation    AREQ: Agent Requests       AUMN: Audit

AUNC: Audit NCPs           AUSK: Audit Skulk          AUTH: Authentication

BASE: Base Set             BEMU: Bindery Emulator     BLNK: Backlinker

CBUF: Client Buffers       CHNG: Change Cache         COLL: Collisions

DRLK: Dist Ref Links       FRAG: Packet Fragmenter    INIT: Initialization

INSP: Inspector            JNTR: Janitor              LMBR: Limber

LDAP: LDAP                 LOCK: Locking              LOST: Lost Entries

MISC: Miscellaneous        MOVE: Move                 NCPE: NCP Engine

PART: Partition            PURG: Purger               RECM: Record Manager

RSLV: Resolve Name         SAPM: Srvc Advertising     SCMA: Schema

SPKT: Server Packets       SKLK: Skulker              STRM: Streams

SYNC: Inbound Sync         THRD: Threads              TVEC: Time Vector

VCLN: Virtual Client       WANM: WAN Traffic Mgr
```

The status of each filter (enabled or disabled) is denoted by a different color.

▸ Dimmed: the filter is disabled.

▸ Blue: the information associated with this filter is displayed to the console screen only.

▸ Green: the information associated with this filter is recorded to the log file only.

▸ Cyan: the information associated with this filter is displayed to the console screen and is also recorded in the log file.

To enable a filter, you simply type **DSTRACE** followed by the filter name or item you want to view. If you specified the filter without specifying a + (to enable) or – (to disable) in front of the filter name, a + is assumed; therefore, DSTRACE +SYNC is the same as DSTRACE SYNC. When a filter name is specified without qualifying it with either SCREEN or FILE, then the action is applied to both devices. That means DSTRACE +SYNC enables the displaying of inbound synchronization information on the trace screen as well as have that data recorded to the log file; DSTRACE FILE -SYNC turns off the recording of inbound synchronization data to the log file.

TIP

You can abbreviate the filter names to just the first two letters (sometimes three in order to keep it unique) of the name. For example, you can use either DSTRACE -TIME or DSTRACE -TI.

If you also work with NetWare 4 servers, the procedures for enabling the DSTRACE screen and setting the filters are slightly different from what was previously described. In NetWare 4, you must use SET commands exclusively when working with DSTRACE; there is no menu interface. The following commands start and stop DSTRACE and its file logging function on a NetWare 4 server:

▸ **SET DSTRACE=ON.** Activates the trace screen.

▸ **SET DSTRACE=OFF.** Deactivates the trace screen.

▶ **SET TTF=ON.** Enables the recording of DSTRACE information to the log file, SYS:SYSTEM\DSTRACE.DBG.

▶ **SET TTF=OFF.** Closes the DSTRACE log file so it can be viewed.

WARNING
You should not leave the TTF (Trace To File) function run attended. Due to the amount of information DSTRACE collects, the DSTRACE.DBG file can become very large quite quickly and could fill up your SYS volume in a matter of hours or days.

In general, the DSTRACE screen shows you five main things about each partition that exists on the server where you run the command:

▶ Name of the partition

▶ Name of the server with which the synchronization is being performed

▶ The state and type of the partition

▶ The NDS process currently taking place

▶ Whether or not the process completed successfully

The following is a sample DSTRACE screen output, with these five items highlighted in bold:

```
[1999/02/18 22:04:01] Sync - using version 6 on server
<.NETWARE5-A.toronto.dreamlan.NETWARE5.>.
[1999/02/18 22:04:01] Sending to   ---->
.NETWARE5-A.toronto.dreamlan.NETWARE5.
[1999/02/18 22:04:01] Sync - sending updates to server
<.NETWARE5-A.toronto.dreamlan.NETWARE5.>.
[1999/02/18 22:04:01] Start outbound sync from change cache
with (1) <.NETWARE5-A.toronto.dreamlan.NETWARE5.> state:0
type:1
```

```
[1999/02/18 22:04:01] Sync - [1c0000c6]
```

<.test.dreamlan.NETWARE5.> [1998/11/29 0:22:13, 1, 1].

```
[1999/02/18 22:04:01] 1999/02/18 22:04:01 * SchemaPurger
processing deleted classes.
```

```
[1999/02/18 22:04:01] End sync out to
```

.NETWARE5-A.toronto.dreamlan.NETWARE5. from change cache,
rep:1 state:0 type:1, success

```
[1999/02/18 22:04:01] Sync - Process: Send updates to
```

<.NETWARE5-A.toronto.dreamlan.NETWARE5.> succeeded.

```
[1999/02/18 22:04:01] 1999/02/18 22:04:01 * SchemaPurger
processing deleted attributes.
```

```
[1999/02/18 22:04:01] SkulkPartition for
```

.test.dreamlan.NETWARE5. succeeded.

```
[1999/02/18 22:04:01] Sync - Partition
```

.test.dreamlan.NETWARE5. All processed = YES

```
[1999/02/18 22:04:01] All processed = YES.
```

```
[1999/02/18 22:04:14] Start updating inherited ACLs...
```

```
[1999/02/18 22:04:14] Update inherited ACLs succeeded.
```

This example shows that an outbound synchronization for partition Test.DreamLAN occurred and is targeted at server NETWARE5-A.Toronto.DreamLAN. The replica on NETWARE5-A is On (state 0) and has a read/write (type 1) replica of the partition in question. The synchronization process was successful.

To assist you in noticing error messages among the vast amount of data being displayed on the DSTRACE screen, key information and error codes are shown in color to help stand out from the other information. For example, DSTRACE.NLM displays partition and server names in blue, while the success and All processed=YES messages (actually just the word *YES*) are in green; error are shown in red. Not all problems show up as color coded, but in most cases the colors do help you sort through the massive amount of information.

For backward compatibility, all DSTRACE SET commands you learned in NetWare 4 are accepted and work on NetWare 5 servers.

NOTE

DSTRACE has a number of SET commands that you can use to manipulate the display to show you more or less information about the various NDS processes. There are also commands to initiate certain synchronization processes, such as limber, and for tuning certain NDS parameters on the server. These DSTRACE SET commands can be divided into four groups: basic functions (such as starting and stopping DSTRACE), setting filters, initiating NDS background processes, and tuning parameters (server-centric).

None of the DSTRACE SET commands are case sensitive.

NOTE

The DSTRACE SET commands (SET DSTRACE=command) that control the basic functions of the DSTRACE include the following commands:

- ▸ **ON**. Starts the NDS trace screen with basic trace messages.

- ▸ **OFF**. Disables the trace screen.

- ▸ **ALL**. Starts the NDS trace screen with all the trace messages.

- ▸ **AGENT**. Starts the NDS trace screen with the trace messages that are equivalent to the ON, BACKLINK, DSAGENT, JANITOR, RESNAME, and VCLIENT flags.

- ▸ **CHECKSUM**. Enables Transport Dependent Checksumming (TDC). This is useful in networks where there are routers that fragment and rebuild data packets. This option ensures data integrity of the reassembled packets. (This option is not supported if you're using ETHERNET_802.3 frame type.)

- ▸ **NOCHECKSUM**. Disable TDC.

▶ **DEBUG**. Turns on a predefined set of trace messages typically used for debugging. The flags set are ON, BACKLINK, ERRORS, EMU, FRAGGER, INIT, INSPECTOR, JANITOR, LIMBER, MISC, PART, RECMAN, REPAIR, SCHEMA, SKULKER, STREAMS, and VCLIENT.

▶ **NODEBUG**. Leaves the trace screen enabled but turns off all debugging messages previously set. It leaves the messages set to the ON command option.

WARNING

The SET DSTRACE=ON command activates the trace screen from DS.NLM (called Directory Services screen) while the DSTRACE SCREEN ON command activates the trace screen from DSTRACE.NLM (called DSTRACE Console screen). On a NetWare 5 server, because you can issue both commands, you can end up with two trace screens showing the same information.

Shown in Table 7.2 is a list of DSTRACE filters. They can be used in place of the filter list available from DSTRACE.NLM, with a few exceptions. For example, there are no corresponding DSTRACE SET commands for WAN Traffic Manager. These filters are turned on by using a + (for example, SET DSTRACE=+BLINK) and turned off by using a − (for example, SET DSTRACE=-AUTHEN).

T A B L E   7.2

DSTRACE Filters

DSTRACE FILTER	DESCRIPTION
AUDIT	Enables messages and information related to auditing. **Caution:** In many cases, this will cause the server to drop into the debugger if auditing encounters an error.
AUTHEN	Enables messages that are displayed while authenticating connections to the server by workstations or servers.
BACKLINK (BLINK)	Enables messages related to verification of backlinks and external references. The backlink process resolves external references to make sure there is a real object in NDS. For real NDS objects the backlink process makes sure that an external reference exists for each backlink attribute.
BUFFERS	Displays messages associated with the request and reply buffers used by the DSA.

DSTRACE FILTER	DESCRIPTION
COLLISION (COLL)	Displays messages when duplicate changes are attempted on the same object. Collisions are normal errors in NDS.
DSAGENT (DSA, DSWIRE)	Enables messages relating to inbound client requests and what action is requested.
EMU	Enables messages relating to bindery services (emulation).
ERRORS (ERR, E)	Displays error messages to show what the error was and where it came from.
FRAGGER (FRAG)	Shows fragger debug messages. The fragger breaks up and rebuilds DS NCP packets (which can be up to 64K in size) into packets that can be transmitted on the network.
IN	Displays messages related to inbound synchronization traffic.
INIT	Enables the showing of messages that occur during the process of initializing or opening the local NDS database.
INSPECTOR (I)	Displays messages related to the inspector process, which verifies the DS name service and object integrity on the local server. The inspector is part of the janitor process. If errors are detected, it could mean that you need to run DSREPAIR. Be aware that messages reported by this process may not all be actual errors. For this reason, you need to understand what the messages mean.
JANITOR (J)	Enables messages related to the janitor process. The janitor controls the removal of deleted objects. It also finds the status and version of NCP servers and other miscellaneous record management data.
LIMBER	Displays messages related to the limber process, which verifies tree connectivity by maintaining the server name, address, and replicas. This involves verifying and fixing the server name and server address if it changes.
LOCKING (LOCKS)	Enables messages related to NDS database record locking information.
MERGE	Displays messages when objects are being merged.
MIN	Enables debug messages at the minimum debug level. (To use this, first type **SET DSTRACE=NODEBUG**, then **SET DSTRACE=+MIN**.)
MISC	Enables information from miscellaneous processes.
OUT	Displays messages related to outbound synchronization traffic.

Continued

DSTRACE Filters (continued)

DSTRACE FILTER	DESCRIPTION
PART	Displays messages related to partitioning operations. This trace filter may be useful for tracking partition operations as they proceed.
RECMAN	Displays messages related to the record manager to track name base transactions, such as rebuilding and verifying the internal hash table and iteration state handling.
REPAIR	Enables messages from the repair process. This filter is rarely used.
RESNAME (RN)	Displays messages related to resolve name requests (tree walking). Resolve name resolves the name maps and object names to an ID on a particular server.
SAP	Enables messages related to Service Advertising Protocol (SAP) when the tree name is sent via SAP.
SCHEMA	Enables messages related to the schema being modified or synchronized across the network to the other servers.
SKULKER (SYNC, S)	Enables messages related to the synchronization process, which is responsible for synchronizing replicas on the servers with the other replicas on other servers. This is one of the most useful trace flags available.
STREAMS	Enables messages related to the stream attributes information.
TIMEVECTOR (TV)	Enables messages related to the synchronization or exchange of the time stamps between replicas. These messages display local and remote synchronized up to vectors, which contain the time stamps for the replica.
VCLIENT (VC)	Enables messages related to the virtual client, which handles the outbound server connections needed to pass NDS information.

Listed in Table 7.3 are the various NDS background processes (ones that have an asterisk in their names) and NDS tuning parameters (ones that have an exclamation mark in their names) that can be manipulated using DSTRACE SET commands. You can force a specific NDS background process, such as schema synchronization, to run by using SET DSTRACE=*SS. Should you have a specific reason to change the default time intervals for an NDS process, you can use the SET DSTRACE=!parameter command.

T A B L E   7 . 3

NDS Background Processes
and Tuning Parameters

DSTRACE PROCESS OR PARAMETER	DEFAULT VALUE	RANGE	DESCRIPTION
*.	n/a	n/a	Unloads and reloads DS.NLM from the SYS:SYSTEM directory. The old copy of DS.NLM in memory is renamed to DSOLD.NLM, the new copy of DS.NLM loaded and then DSOLD.NLM unloaded; therefore, for a short period of time, both DS.NLM and DSOLD.NLM will be loaded. This command is extremely useful when you are updating a version of DS.NLM without having to restart the server. You can perform this operation during normal business hours without disrupting users on that server.
*B	n/a	n/a	Forces the backlink process to begin running. Be aware that the backlink process can be traffic intensive, and you should probably wait until a slow time on the network before executing this command.
!B time	1,500	2–10,080	Sets the backlink process interval used by NDS (in minutes) to check the backlink consistency. This command is the same as the NDS SET NDS Backlink Interval command.
*C	n/a	n/a	Shows connection table statistics for outbound connection caching or vclients. Not supported on NetWare 5.
*CI	n/a	n/a	Shows connection table statistics for vclients, including idle time information. Not supported on NetWare 5.
*CR	n/a	n/a	Shows connection table statistics for vclients, including routing table packets. Not supported on NetWare 5.
*CT	n/a	n/a	Shows connection table statistics for vclients, including which servers this server is connected to. Not supported on NetWare 5.
*C0 (C-zero)	n/a	n/a	Resets the display of connection table statistics for vclients. Same effect as reloading DS.NLM. Not supported on NetWare 5.

Continued

TABLE 7.3

*NDS Background Processes
and Tuning Parameters
(continued)*

DSTRACE PROCESS OR PARAMETER	DEFAULT VALUE	RANGE	DESCRIPTION
!C number	75	25–100	Sets the maximum sockets threshold, which is the percentage of sockets to use on the server before they're recycled. Not supported on NetWare 5.
!CE time	135	10–1,440	Specifies the connection expiration time-out value in minutes. Not supported on NetWare 5.
*D rootEntry ID	n/a	n/a	Aborts the send all updates or *I for a given replica (as identified by the rootEntryID). This command is used only when a send all updates or *I can't complete and is therefore endlessly trying to send the objects to all replicas. This situation usually occurs because one of the servers is inaccessible.
!D time	24	1–10,080	Disables both inbound and outbound synchronization for the specified number of hours.
!DI time	24	1–10,080	Disables inbound synchronization for the specified number of hours.
!DO time	24	1–10,080	Disables outbound synchronization for the specified number of hours.
*E	n/a	n/a	Checks entry cache. Locks the NDS database, verifies the entry cache is okay, then reopens the database.
!E	n/a	n/a	Enables both inbound and outbound synchronization.
!EI	n/a	n/a	Enables inbound synchronization.
!EO	n/a	n/a	Enables outbound synchronization.
*F	n/a	n/a	Forces the flat cleaner process, (part of the janitor process) to run. The flat cleaner purges or removes the objects marked for deletion in NDS.
!F time	60	1–10,080	Sets how often (in minutes) the flat cleaner process runs. The flat cleaner process purges or removes the deleted objects and attributes from NDS.
*G	n/a	n/a	Gives up on a server when there are too many requests being processed. The process gives up on the server and sets the server status to down.

DSTRACE PROCESS OR PARAMETER	DEFAULT VALUE	RANGE	DESCRIPTION
!G ticks	1,000	0–200,000	Changes the amount of time (in ticks) to wait before giving up when outstanding requests in process are not answered.
*H	n/a	n/a	Forces the heartbeat process to start. This flag starts immediate communication to exchange time stamps with all servers in replica lists. This command is useful for force starting the synchronization between servers so that you can observe the status.
!H time	30	2–1,440	Sets the heartbeat process interval (in minutes). This parameter changes how often the heartbeat process begins.
*I rootEntryID	n/a	n/a	Forces the replica (as indicated by the rootEntryID) on the server where the command is issued to send a copy of all its objects to all other servers in the replica list. This command is the same as send all objects in DSREPAIR.
!I time	30	2–1,440	Sets the heartbeat for the base schema synchronization interval (in minutes).
!J time	2	1–10,080	Sets the janitor process interval (in minutes). This parameter changes how often janitor process executes.
*L	n/a	n/a	Starts the limber process, which checks the server name, server address, and tree connectivity of each replica.
*M hex_number	n/a	10,000–10,000,000	Sets the maximum size of the trace file in bytes. TTF must be off first before you can set the file size.
*P	n/a	n/a	Displays the tunable parameters and their default settings on the trace screen.
*R	n/a	n/a	Resets the SYS:SYSTEM\DSTRACE.DBG file. This command is the same as the SET NDS Trace File Length Set to Zero console command.
!R number	10	1–10,000	Sets the maximum number of times the server's disk can be accessed by DS before it yields. Not supported on NetWare 5.
*SS	n/a	n/a	Forces immediate schema synchronization.

Continued

TABLE 7.3

*NDS Background Processes
and Tuning Parameters
(continued)*

DSTRACE PROCESS OR PARAMETER	DEFAULT VALUE	RANGE	DESCRIPTION
!S number	1	0–1	Enables (1) or disables (0) schema synchronization.
!SI	n/a	n/a	Enables inbound schema synchronization.
!SO	n/a	n/a	Enables outbound schema synchronization.
!T time	30	1–720	This flag changes the server state threshold, which is the time interval (in minutes) at which the server state is checked.
*U [number]	n/a	n/a	Forces the server state to up and resets the communication status list. If no server ID is specified, all servers in replica lists are set to up. This command performs the same function as the SET NDS Server Status = UP console command.
!V	n/a	n/a	Lists any restricted versions of the DS. If there are no versions listed in the return, there are no restrictions.
!W ticks	15	1–2000	Changes the IPX request in process delay. This is the length of time (in ticks) to wait after getting an IPX time-out before resending the request.
!X number	3	1–50	Specifies the number of IPX retries for the DS (server-to-server) client. After the retry count has been exceeded, an NDS error -625 is displayed.
!Y number	2	0–530	Changes the IPX time-out scaling factor (Y) used for the estimated trip delay used in the equation: IPX Time-out = $(T * Y) + Z$ where T is equal to the ticks required to get to the destination server.
!Z number	4	0–500	Adds additional delay (Z) for the IPX time out. To increase the time out, change this parameter first. It is used in the equation: IPX time-out = $(T \times Y) + Z$, where T is equal to the ticks required to get to the destination server.

Some of the tuning parameters can also be changed using **NDS SET** commands in **SERVMAN.NLM or MONITOR.NLM.**

NOTE

There is a known cosmetic bug with NetWare 4.11's **DSTRACE** command: if you enter this **DSTRACE** command twice, back-to-back, it doesn't take effect. For example: **SET DSTRACE=*H** followed immediately by another **SET DSTRACE=*H** (because you didn't catch the displayed info and wish to see it again) will give the message "**DSTRACE is ALREADY** set to *H". In order for a given command to be issued twice you must set another (different) command after the first one and then reissue the first command. For example: **SET DSTRACE=*H,** followed by **SET DSTRACE=*U,** then **SET DSTRACE=*H** again.

TIP

DSVIEW

If you had the misfortune of requiring Novell Technical Support to dial in to your network to fix your NDS problems, you'd have seen them use the DSDUMP NLM utility to directly edit your NDS database files. DSVIEW is the read-only version of DSDUMP. You can use it to get a server-centric view of your NDS data, including information (such as when an object or attribute of an object was last modified — alas, not by whom, because that information is not recorded in the NDS unless auditing is enabled) that is not reported by standard management utilities, such as NWAdmin.

Versions of the **DSVIEW NLM** have been made available for NetWare 4.10 and 4.11 as part of the **DS.NLM** update files. At the time of this writing, a version of **DSVIEW** does not exist for NetWare 5, but it is said to be under development. Check http://support.novell.com to see if a version is available for download.

NOTE

DSVIEW can display the following six information categories from the main menu:

▶ **Entry Information**. Use this option to view the information about the entries themselves; in DSVIEW's vocabulary, an entry can be the local object ID, a base class, creation time, an attribute, an attribute's value, and so on.

▸ **Partition Information**. Displays information about the partitions located on the server. The partitions in reference here include all NDS partitions, such as the schema and external references.

▸ **Tree (Start at [Root])**. Displays the entries, beginning at [Root]. This is a quick way to "walk the tree" in a top-down manner.

▸ **Attribute Definitions**. Displays the attributes defined by the schema.

▸ **Class Definitions**. Displays the classes defined by the schema.

▸ **Display Server Information**. Displays the tree name the server belongs to and the total size of the local NDS database.

DSVIEW navigates through the entries using the tree model: you go from parent (container) to child (container) or from sibling (object) to sibling (object) within the same container. When you are viewing the entry information, DSVIEW displays at the bottom of the screen whether the current object has any siblings (other objects at the same NDS context level) or not. For example, the following sample DSVIEW output shows that the entry being viewed is OU=Toronto.O=DreamLAN in the WEBSITE_FOR_NETWARE tree. It is an Organizational Unit (OU) that has 26 objects within that container (subordinate count: 26) and has siblings, that *is*, other OUs and leaf objects at the same level (O=DreamLAN):

```
Key<Action> 1<Parent> 2<Child> 3<Sibling> 4<Go To Another
Entry>

                5<Attribute list> 6<Backup To Previous Entry>

                7<View Partition Entry> 8<Find Sibling>

                9<Toggle Display Mode> ESC<Return to Main Menu>



     ********—   Entry Information   —********
```

```
Entry ID: 010000B8      "OU=Toronto"
.O=DreamLAN.WEBSITE_FOR_NETWARE


Partition ID: 00000004

Partition Type: User Created   Name: "WEBSITE_FOR_NETWARE"

Parent ID: 010000B7   "O=DreamLAN"

Class Name: "Organizational Unit"

Subordinate Count: 26

Flags:   Present

Creation      TimeStamp: 96/11/09 05:16:41; rep# = 0001;
event = 000B

Modification TimeStamp: 98/05/27 18:30:06; rep# = 0001;
event = 0014



Siblings: Yes
```

You navigate using the number corresponding to the desired action, such as 3 for moving to the next sibling (the next object in the same container); however, you can also use the first letter in the action as well. So, in the example, you can either press 3 or press the letter s to move to the next sibling. If, however, more than one command has the same first letter, such as next attribute and next value, use the first letter of the second word (a and v) instead.

When browsing through the data, you'll find the entries listed are not in any logical order, such as by creation or modification date or even alphabetical. Because DSVIEW actually reads from the local NDS data files, the entries are listed in the order in which the entry's data record is found in the database.

One of the most powerful features of DSVIEW is its capability to display the attributes and their data of any object. In the example shown in Figure 7.7, you can see that the user Admin can change its password, because the Password Allow Change attribute is true. You can also see that this attribute is single-valued, because the more attribute values indicator is No.

DSVIEW is a very powerful tool for learning about and for finding out about various NDS tidbits that the standard utilities don't and can't provide. DSVIEW can be an indispensable tool for NDS-aware application programmers who need to look up attribute syntax and attribute names — the attribute names we see in NWAdmin, for example, do not truly reflect the names used in the schema and, therefore, if you use the attribute name listed in NWAdmin, your program will not find that attribute. To illustrate the point, shown in Table 7.4 is a comparison table of ACL attribute names defined for a user object in the NetWare 4.11 schema and the ACL attribute names used in NWAdmn32; the entries that are different are shown in italics.

FIGURE 7.7

Viewing an object's attributes and attribute values using DSVIEW

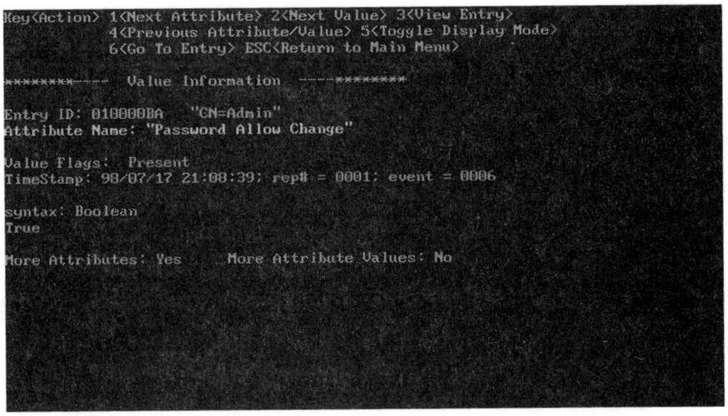

> It is interesting that **NETADMIN, the DOS** version of **NWAdmin** shipped with NetWare 4, uses the same **ACL** attribute names as those used to define the schema.
>
> NOTE

T A B L E 7 . 4

ACL Attribute Names

USER OBJECT ACL ATTRIBUTE NAMES DEFINED IN SCHEMA	USER OBJECT ACL ATTRIBUTE NAMES USED BY NWADMN32
[All Attributes Rights]	*Property rights: All properties*
[Entry Rights]	*Object rights*
Account Balance	Account Balance
ACL	*Object Trustees (ACL)*
Aliased Object Name	Aliased Object Name
Allow Unlimited Credit	Allow Unlimited Credit
App Blurb	App Blurb
App Contacts	App Contacts
App Drive Mappings	App Drive Mappings
App Flags	App Flags
App Icon	App Icon
App Parameters	App Parameters
App Path	App Path
App Printer Ports	App Printer Ports
App Shutdown Script	App Shutdown Script
App Startup Script	App Startup Script
App Working Directory	App Working Directory
App:Administrator Notes	App:Administrator Notes
App:Alt Back Link	App:Alt Back Link
App:Associations	App:Associations
App:Back Link	App:Back Link
App:Caption	App:Caption
App:Contacts	App:Contacts
App:Copy Files	App:Copy Files
App:Description	App:Description

Continued

TABLE 7.4

ACL Attribute Names
(continued)

USER OBJECT ACL ATTRIBUTE NAMES DEFINED IN SCHEMA	USER OBJECT ACL ATTRIBUTE NAMES USED BY NWADMN32
App:Drive Mappings	App:Drive Mappings
App:Error Log Path	App:Error Log Path
App:Fault Tolerance	App:Fault Tolerance
App:Flags	App:Flags
App:GUID	App:GUID
App:Icon	App:Icon
App:INI Settings	App:INI Settings
App:Inventory	App:Inventory
App:Launcher Config	App:Launcher Config
App:Load Balancing	App:Load Balancing
App:Macros	App:Macros
App:Monitor Module	App:Monitor Module
App:NLSFlags	App:NLSFlags
App:NLSProductContainer	App:NLSProductContainer
App:Parameters	App:Parameters
App:Path	App:Path
App:Platform	App:Platform
App:Printer Ports	App:Printer Ports
App:Program Groups	App:Program Groups
App:Registry Settings	App:Registry Settings
App:Schedule	App:Schedule
App:Shutdown Script	App:Shutdown Script
App:Startup Script	App:Startup Script
App:Text Files	App:Text Files
App:Version String	App:Version String
App:Working Directory	App:Working Directory

USER OBJECT ACL ATTRIBUTE NAMES DEFINED IN SCHEMA	USER OBJECT ACL ATTRIBUTE NAMES USED BY NWADMN32
Audit:A Encryption Key	Audit:A Encryption Key
Audit:B Encryption Key	Audit:B Encryption Key
Audit:Contents	Audit:Contents
Audit:Current Encryption Key	Audit:Current Encryption Key
Audit:File Link	Audit:File Link
Audit:Link List	Audit:Link List
Audit:Path	Audit:Path
Audit:Policy	Audit:Policy
Audit:Type	Audit:Type
Authority Revocation	Authority Revocation
Auto Start	Auto Start
Back Link	Back Link
Bindery Object Restriction	Bindery Object Restriction
Bindery Property	Bindery Property
Bindery Restriction Level	Bindery Restriction Level
Bindery Type	Bindery Type
C	Country Name
CA Public Key	CA Public Key
Cartridge	Cartridge
Certificate Revocation	Certificate Revocation
Certificate Validity Interval	Certificate Validity Interval
CN	Name
CommonCertificate	CommonCertificate
Convergence	Convergence
Cross Certificate Pair	Default Queue
Description	Description
Desktop	Desktop

Continued

TABLE 7.4

ACL Attribute Names
(continued)

USER OBJECT ACL ATTRIBUTE NAMES DEFINED IN SCHEMA	USER OBJECT ACL ATTRIBUTE NAMES USED BY NWADMN32
Detect Intruder	Detect Intruder
Device	Device
DS Revision	DS Revision
EMail Address	EMail Address
Equivalent To Me	*Security Equal To Me*
External Name	External Name
External Synchronizer	External Synchronizer
Facsimile Telephone Number	*Fax Number*
Full Name	Full Name
Generational Qualifier	Generational Qualifier
GID	GID
Given Name	Given Name
Group Membership	Group Membership
High Convergence Sync Interval	High Convergence Sync Interval
Higher Privileges	Higher Privileges
Home Directory	Home Directory
Home Directory Rights	Home Directory Rights
Host Device	Host Device
Host Resource Name	*Volume*
Host Server	Host Server
Inherited ACL	Inherited ACL
Initials	Initials
Intruder Attempt Reset Interval	Intruder Attempt Reset Interval
Intruder Lockout Reset Interval	Intruder Lockout Reset Interval
L	*Location*
Language	Language

USER OBJECT ACL ATTRIBUTE NAMES DEFINED IN SCHEMA	USER OBJECT ACL ATTRIBUTE NAMES USED BY NWADMN32
Last Login Time	Last Login Time
Last Referenced Time	Last Referenced Time
Launcher Config	Launcher Config
License Database	License Database
LicenseID	LicenseID
Locked By Intruder	Account Locked
Lockout After Detection	Lockout After Detection
Login Allowed Time Map	Login Time Restrictions
Login Disabled	Account Disabled
Login Expiration Time	Account Has Expiration Date
Login Grace Limit	Grace Logins Allowed
Login Grace Remaining	Remaining Grace Logins
Login Intruder Address	Last Intruder Address
Login Intruder Attempts	Incorrect Login Attempts
Login Intruder Limit	Incorrect Login Count
Login Intruder Reset Time	Account Reset Time
Login Maximum Simultaneous	Maximum Connections
Login Script	Login Script
Login Time	Login Time
Low Convergence Reset Time	Low Convergence Reset Time
Low Convergence Sync Interval	Low Convergence Sync Interval
Mailbox ID	Mailbox ID
Mailbox Location	Mailbox Location
Member	Members
Members Of Template	Members Of Template
Memory	Memory
Message Routing Group	Message Routing Group

Continued

. . . . .

T A B L E 7.4

ACL Attribute Names
(continued)

USER OBJECT ACL ATTRIBUTE NAMES DEFINED IN SCHEMA	USER OBJECT ACL ATTRIBUTE NAMES USED BY NWADMN32
Message Server	Default Server
Messaging Database Location	Message Database Location
Messaging Server	Messaging Server
Messaging Server Type	Messaging Server Type
Minimum Account Balance	Low Balance Limit
NetWare Mobile: DIS Name	NetWare Mobile: DIS Name
NetWare Mobile: DIS Phone	NetWare Mobile: DIS Phone
NetWare Mobile: DIS Properties	NetWare Mobile: DIS Properties
NetWare Mobile: DIS Properties 2	NetWare Mobile: DIS Properties 2
NetWare Mobile: DIS Type	NetWare Mobile: DIS Type
NetWare Mobile: DIS Version	NetWare Mobile: DIS Version
NetWare Mobile: DIS Writer	NetWare Mobile: DIS Writer
Network Address	Network Address
Network Address Restriction	Network Address Restriction
New Object's DS Rights	New Object's DS Rights
New Object's FS Rights	New Object's FS Rights
New Object's Self Rights	New Object's Self Rights
NLS:Current Installed	NLS:Current Installed
NLS:Current Peak Installed	NLS:Current Peak Installed
NLS:Current Peak Used	NLS:Current Peak Used
NLS:Current Used	NLS:Current Used
NLS:Hourly Data Size	NLS:Hourly Data Size
NLS:Peak Installed Data	NLS:Peak Installed Data
NLS:Peak Used Data	NLS:Peak Used Data
NLS:Summary Update Time	NLS:Summary Update Time
NLS:Summary Version	NLS:Summary Version

USER OBJECT ACL ATTRIBUTE NAMES DEFINED IN SCHEMA	USER OBJECT ACL ATTRIBUTE NAMES USED BY NWADMN32
NNS Domain	NNS Domain
Notify	*Notification*
NRD:Registry Data	NRD:Registry Data
NRD:Registry Index	NRD:Registry Index
NWCLPROV:WIN95PNP CONTROL	NWCLPROV:WIN95PNP CONTROL
NWCLPROV:WIN95PNP DATA	NWCLPROV:WIN95PNP DATA
NWCLPROV:WINNT4PNP CONTROL V1 V1	NWCLPROV:WINNT4PNP CONTROL
NWCLPROV:WINNT4PNP DATA V1	NWCLPROV:WINNT4PNP DATA V1
O	O
Object Class	Object Class
Operator	Operator
OU	*Organization*
Owner	Owner
Page Description Language	Page Description Language
Partition Control	Partition Control
Partition Creation Time	Partition Creation Time
Partition Status	Partition Status
Password Allow Change	*Allow User To Change Password*
Password Expiration Interval	*Days Between Forced Changes*
Password Expiration Time	*Date Password Expires*
Password Minimum Length	*Minimum Password Length*
Password Required	*Require a Password*
Password Unique Required	*Require Unique Passwords*
Path	Path
Permanent Config Parms	Permanent Config Parms
Physical Delivery Office Name	*City*

Continued

TABLE 7.4

ACL Attribute Names
(continued)

USER OBJECT ACL ATTRIBUTE NAMES DEFINED IN SCHEMA	USER OBJECT ACL ATTRIBUTE NAMES USED BY NWADMN32
Postal Address	Postal Address
Postal Code	*Postal (Zip) Code*
Postal Office Box	Postal Office Box
Postmaster	Postmaster
Print Job Configuration	*Print Job Configuration (Non NDPS)*
Print Server	Print Server
Printer	Printer
Printer Configuration	Printer Configuration
Printer Control	Printer Control
Product	Product
Profile	Profile
Profile Membership	Profile Membership
Public Key	Public Key
Publisher	Publisher
Queue	*Print Queue*
Queue Directory	Queue Directory
Received Up To	Received Up To
Replica	Replica
Replica Up To	Replica Up To
Resource	Resource
Revision	Revision
Role Occupant	Occupant
Run Setup Script	Run Setup Script
S	*State or Province*
SA	*Street*
SAP Name	SAP Name

USER OBJECT ACL ATTRIBUTE NAMES DEFINED IN SCHEMA	USER OBJECT ACL ATTRIBUTE NAMES USED BY NWADMN32
Security Equals	*Security Equal To*
Security Flags	Security Flags
See Also	See Also
Serial Number	Serial Number
Server	Server
Server Holds	Server Holds
Set Password After Create	Set Password After Create
Setup Script	Setup Script
Status	Status
Supported Connections	Supported Connections
Supported Gateway	Supported Gateway
Supported Services	Supported Services
Supported Typefaces	Supported Typefaces
Surname	*Last Name*
Synchronized Up To	Synchronized Up To
Telephone Number	Telephone Number
Timezone	Timezone
Title	Title
Transaction Database	Transaction Database
Transaction Log Name	Transaction Log Name
Transaction Log Size	Transaction Log Size
Transitive Vector	Transitive Vector
Trustees Of New Object	Trustees Of New Object
Type Creator Map	Type Creator Map
UID	UID
Unknown	Unknown
Unknown Base Class	Unknown Base Class

Continued

TABLE 7.4	
ACL Attribute Names (continued)	
USER OBJECT ACL ATTRIBUTE NAMES DEFINED IN SCHEMA	**USER OBJECT ACL ATTRIBUTE NAMES USED BY NWADMN32**
User	Users
Version	Version
Volume Space Restrictions	Volume Space Restrictions

For speed and simplicity, DSVIEW is not designed with a fancy user interface, nor does it even have any online help; however, if you can spend perhaps 30 minutes working with it, you'll find it easy to use and understand.

WARNING

There has been some reports that on a NDS tree that has mixed NetWare 4 and NetWare 5 servers, DSVIEW v1.05 (which is the latest available version as of this writing) may cause a server ABEND.

DSDIAG

DSDIAG, a DS diagnostics NLM, was first introduced by Novell in March of 1997 during the BrainShare Conference in Salt Lake City, Utah, as a nonsupported utility. DSDIAG gathers NDS diagnostics information for an entire tree, rather than on a partition-by-partition or server-by-server basis.

NOTE

DSDIAG is shipped with NetWare 5. For NetWare 4.11 networks, you can download DSDIAG1.EXE from the file finder area at http://support.novell.com.

The functions within DSDIAG are divided into two sections: the tool manager section and the reports section. The tool manager section of DSDIAG collects data about servers, partitions, and replica rings. Tool manager establishes a baseline of how data is collected and included in the reports that are produced. After tool manager has collected the information, the reports section, which contains several types of reports, is used to compile and display the data.

DSDIAG's main menu offers a general report and preferences selection. The preferences menu establishes points of reference in the NDS tree and includes the following settings:

▸ **Manage Naming Conventions.** This option allows you to set the NDS context and base Distinguished Name (DN) for reading and reporting purposes:

  • The idea behind the separate input context and file output contexts and the base DN is flexibility in reporting. For example, output context can be different from input if you want output to be in a standardized format with fully qualified names but don't want to input that much text when specifying the input.

  • The DN option sets the base DN for the object where you want to set the context. For example, if you set the input context to Toronto.North_America, then all relative distinguished names (RDNs) input are assumed to be in the Toronto.North_America container. This name is used to fully qualify relative names and to reduce the size of displayed names.

▸ **Managing Identities.** This option allows you to enter a new NDS object name (referred to as *identity* within DSDIAG). You can use different object names and their associated browse rights to gain more (or less) access to information in your network.

NOTE

The identity must be entered using the DN syntax (relative to [Root]), and may optionally include the tree name of the object name you want to use, for example, peter.toronto.acme_company. To specify a different tree, add the tree name to the end of the name, for example, peter.toronto.acme_company.netware5_tree. Note that you must include a period after the tree name to denote that it is an NDS tree name and not part of the context.

TIP

By specifying a NetWare 4 tree name in the identity, you can use DSDIAG running on a NetWare 5 server to retrieve NDS diagnostic information from a NetWare 4 tree. Ensure you change the base DN name to match the name of your new tree name, or else DSDIAG will return an error indicating "wrong tree."

▶ **Preferences**. Use this option to configure how you want to display and format values in your reports. For example, you can select to display values in hexadecimal or decimal. Flag formats can be displayed in hexadecimal or in a translated string. You can also specify how time is to be displayed (that is, local, UTC, or in hexadecimal).

DSDIAG includes six built-in reports. The first four reports can be considered as documentation-type reports and the last two reports provide diagnosis data.

▶ **Check NDS Versions**. It provides information about servers as it may relate to NDS. The data provided by this report includes NDS version, server name, server address, and replica depth. The following is a sample NDS versions report:

```
Report Title: DSD NDS Versions Report

Report Version: 1.0

Base DN: .NETWARE5.

Identity: .[Public].

Start Date: Feb 14, 1999    6:42:02 pm EST

Retrieved Servers From: NDS

     Search Context:

     Type: Readable

     Depth:   Subtree

NDS Version:

Status   Warni   Address          Repl   Obje   NDS    Server's NDS Name

                                  Dept   Vers   Vers
```

0	00402418	0	709	709	CN=NETWARE5-A.O=dreamlan
0	0000005B	-1	709	709	CN=NETWARE5-B.O=dreamlan
0	0000005B	0	709	724	CN=NETWARE5-C.O=dreamlan
0	0000005B	0	723	723	CN=NETWARE5-D.O=dreamlan

Contacted 4 server(s) out of 4 attempted.

End Date: Feb 14, 1999   6:42:02 pm EST

****

▸ **Check Partition Status.** This report provides information about servers and their partitions, such as partition status, number of readable replica rings, and the subordinate references in each ring. The following is a sample check partition status report:

Report Title: DSD Partition Sync. Status

Report Version: 1.0

Base DN: .dreamlan.

Identity: CN=admin.O=North_America

Start Date: Feb 14, 1999   8:22:43 pm EST

Retrieved Partition Roots Form: NDS

    Search Context:

    Type: Readable

    Depth: Subtree

Retrieved replica ring from: Ring

Replica Synchronization Summary:

TROUBLESHOOT AND RESOLVE THE PROBLEM

```
        Status   Warni   Tota   OK      Acce    Repl    Repl    Most-Recent Complete
Partition

                         Repl   Repl    Erro    Erro    Unkn    Synchronization
Time            Name

            0        R     2     2        0       0       0     Feb 14, 1999
8:34:54 pm EST

            0        R     2     2        0       0       0     Feb 14, 1999
8:27:09 pm EST    O=Europe

            0        R     2     2        0       0       0     Feb 14, 1999
8:09:43 pm EST    O=DreamLAN

            0        R     2     2        0       0       0     Feb 14, 1999
8:09:43 pm EST    O=Empty

            0        R     2     2        0       0       0     Feb 14, 1999
8:09:43 pm EST    O=DreamLAN2

            0        R     2     2        0       0       0     Feb 14, 1999
8:09:43 pm EST    OU=BRAM.O=CTC

            0        R     2     2        0       0       0     Feb 14, 1999
8:09:43 pm EST    OU=Toronto.O=North_America

Replica Synchronization Total:

Status   Warni   Tota   OK      Acce    Repl    Repl    Most-Recent Complete
                 Repl   Repl    Erro    Erro    Unkn    Synchronization Time
    0        R    14     14       0       0       0     Feb 14, 1999   8:09:43
pm EST

Report Synchronization Total:

Status   Warni   Tota   OK      Acce    Part    Part    Most-Recent Complete
                 Part   Part    Erro    Erro    Unkn    Synchronization Time
    0        R     7      7       0       0       0     Feb 14, 1999   8:09:43
pm EST


Replicas found: 14

Partitions found: 7

Servers contacted with Partitions and Replicas: 2
```

```
Count    Warning    Message

   14          R     Fewer than the minimum readable replicas found.



End Date: Feb 14, 1999    8:22:43 pm EST

********************
```

> ▶ **List Replica Rings.** This provides a logical view of your NDS partitions. The report can be used to document the replica rings (as it gives you a breakdown of what replicas are located on what servers and of the replica types) and will show you partition roots by NDS or servers. The following is a sample list replica rings report:

```
Report Title: DSD List Replica Rings

Report Version: 1.0

Base DN: .dreamlan.

Identity: CN=admin.O=North_America

Start Date: Feb 14, 1999    8:33:19 pm EST

Retrieved Partition Roots Form: NDS

     Search Context:

     Type: Readable

     Depth:  Subtree

Retrieved replica ring from: Single


Name:

Server Name: CN=dreamlan.OU=Toronto.O=North_America

Server's Address: 000f411a

Entry:

         Status    Warni    Entry ID    Repl    Entry

                                         Type    Name
```

```
              0            010000B4    M

Replica:

       Status    Warni    Repl    Repl    Replica    Replica    Server
Address

                          Numb    Type    State      Root ID    Name
              0        R     3      M       On         010000B4
CN=dreamlan.OU=Toronto.O=North_America    000F411A

              0        R     1      RW      On         010000B4
CN=NW411B.OU=Consulting.OU=Toronto.O=North_America    0000411B


Name: O=Europe

Server Name: CN=dreamlan.OU=Toronto.O=North_America

Server's Address: 000f411a

Entry:

       Status    Warni    Entry ID    Repl    Entry

                                      Type    Name
              0            010000CE    M       O=Europe

Replica:

       Status    Warni    Repl    Repl    Replica    Replica    Server
Address

                          Numb    Type    State      Root ID    Name
              0        R     1      M       On         010000CE
CN=dreamlan.OU=Toronto.O=North_America    000F411A

              0        R     2      RW      On         03000174
CN=NW411B.OU=Consulting.OU=Toronto.O=North_America    0000411B


Name: O=DreamLAN

Server Name: CN=dreamlan.OU=Toronto.O=North_America

Server's Address: 000f411a

Entry:
```

Status	Warni	Entry ID	Repl Type	Entry Name
0		0A0000C3	M	O=DreamLAN

Replica:

Status	Warni	Repl Numb	Repl Type	Replica State	Replica Root ID	Server Name
0	R	1	M	On	0A0000C3	

CN=dreamlan.OU=Toronto.O=North_America   000F411A

| 0 | R | 2 | RW | On | 01000124 | |

CN=NW411B.OU=Consulting.OU=Toronto.O=North_America   0000411B

Name: O=Empty

Server Name: CN=dreamlan.OU=Toronto.O=North_America

Server's Address: 000f411a

Entry:

Status	Warni	Entry ID	Repl Type	Entry Name
0		010001C1	M	O=Empty

Replica:

Status	Warni	Repl Numb	Repl Type	Replica State	Replica Root ID	Server Name
0	R	1	M	On	010001C1	

CN=dreamlan.OU=Toronto.O=North_America   000F411A

| 0 | R | 2 | SR | On | 010001C1 | |

CN=NW411B.OU=Consulting.OU=Toronto.O=North_America   0000411B

Name: O=DreamLAN2

Server Name: CN=NW411B.OU=Consulting.OU=Toronto.O=North_America

Server's Address: 0000411b

Entry:

Status	Warni	Entry ID	Repl Type	Entry Name
0		010001A6	M	O=DreamLAN2

Replica:

Status	Warni	Repl Numb	Repl Type	Replica State	Replica Root ID	Server Name	Address
0	R	2	M	On	010001A6	CN=NW411B.OU=Consulting.OU=Toronto.O=North_America	0000411B
0	R	1	SR	On	020001A6	CN=dreamlan.OU=Toronto.O=North_America	000F411A

Name: OU=BRAM.O=CTC

Server Name: CN=dreamlan.OU=Toronto.O=North_America

Server's Address: 000f411a

Entry:

Status	Warni	Entry ID	Repl Type	Entry Name
0		010001A0	RW	OU=BRAM.O=CTC

Replica:

Status	Warni	Repl Numb	Repl Type	Replica State	Replica Root ID	Server Name	Address
0	R	2	M	On	010001A0	CN=NW411B.OU=Consulting.OU=Toronto.O=North_America	0000411B
0	R	3	RW	On	010001A0	CN=dreamlan.OU=Toronto.O=North_America	000F411A

```
Name: OU=Toronto.O=North_America

Server Name: CN=dreamlan.OU=Toronto.O=North_America

Server's Address: 000f411a

Entry:

        Status   Warni    Entry ID    Repl     Entry

                                       Type     Name

            0               010000B6    M          OU=Toronto.O=North_America
Replica:

        Status   Warni    Repl    Repl    Replica    Replica     Server
Address

                          Numb    Type    State      Root ID     Name

            0        R      1      M       On         010000B6
CN=dreamlan.OU=Toronto.O=North_America    000F411A

            0        R      2      RW      On         010000B6
CN=NW411B.OU=Consulting.OU=Toronto.O=North_America    0000411B



Replicas found: 7

Partitions found: 7

Servers contacted with Partitions and Replicas: 2




Count    Warning    Message

    7         R    Fewer than the minimum readable replicas found.


End Date: Feb 14, 1999   8:33:19 pm EST

********************
```

▶ **List Server's Partition Table.** This report documents the relationship of the servers and their partitions. It provides a physical view of the logical NDS world. The data provided by this report includes a list of the server's replicas and their state and type. The following is a sample list server partition table report:

```
Report Title: DSD Server Partition Table

Report Version: 1.0

Base DN: .dreamlan.

Identity: CN=admin.O=North_America

Start Date: Feb 14, 1999   8:40:12 pm EST

Retrieved Servers From: NDS

    Search Context:

    Type: Readable

    Depth:  Subtree

    Type: All

    Type: Read/Write



Server Name: CN=dreamlan.OU=Toronto.O=North_America

Server's Address: 000f411a

Server Partition Table:
```

Status	Warni	Repl Type	Replica State	Repl Numb	Part Busy	Partition Name
0		M	On	3	No	
0		M	On	1	No	O=Europe
0		M	On	1	No	

```
OU=Toronto.O=North_America
```

Status	Warni	Repl Type	Replica State	Repl Numb	Part Busy	Partition Name
0		M	On	1	No	O=DreamLAN
0		M	On	1	No	O=Empty
0		SR	On	1	No	O=DreamLAN2
0		RW	On	3	No	OU=BRAM.O=CTC

```
7 Replica(s) Found
```

Server Name: CN=NW410B.OU=Consulting.OU=Toronto.O=North_America

Server's Address: 0000411b

Server Partition Table:

Status	Warni	Repl Type	Replica State	Repl Numb	Part Busy	Partition Name
0		RW	On	2	No	O=Europe
0		RW	On	2	No	
OU=Toronto.O=North_America						
0		RW	On	1	No	
0		RW	On	2	No	O=DreamLAN
0		SR	On	2	No	O=Empty
0		M	On	2	No	O=DreamLAN2
0		M	On	2	No	OU=BRAM.O=CTC

7 Replica(s) Found

Server Name: CN=LOUVRE.OU=Paris.O=Europe

Server's Address: 0000a11a

Server Status: -625

Warnings:

Contacted 2 server(s) out of 3 attempted.

Count	Error Numbers		Message
1	-625	FFFFFD8F	transport failure

End Date: Feb 14, 1999   8:40:13 pm EST

****

NOTE

Because the report's information is generated using real-time data, any network errors could result in incomplete reports.

▸ **Check NDS Background Process Status.** This selection lists the status of the various NDS background processes (discussed in Chapter 6) for each server found either via NDS, SAP, or a specific address (IPX or IP), depending on your selection (see Figure 7.8).

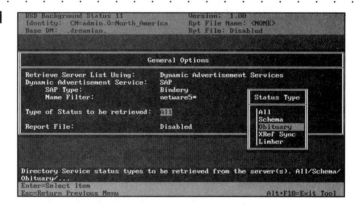

▸ **Compare Replica Rings.** This option allows you to generate a report to compare replica rings for each partition found with other replicas in the ring. The following is a sample compare replica rings report:

Report Title: DSD Replica Ring Compare

Report Version: 1.0

Base DN: .dreamlan.

Identity: CN=admin.O=North_America

Start Date: Feb 14, 1999   9:17:20 pm EST

Retrieved Partition Roots Form: NDS

Search Context:

Type: Readable

Depth: Subtree

Retrieved replica ring from: Ring

Replica Comparison Summary:

Status	Warni Repl	Tota Repl	Equa Repl	Acce Erro	Not Repl	Partition Name
0	R	2	2	0	0	
0	R	2	2	0	0	O=Europe
0	R	2	2	0	0	O=DreamLAN
0	R	2	2	0	0	O=Empty
0	R	2	2	0	0	O=DreamLAN2
0	R	2	2	0	0	OU=BRAM.O=CTC
0	R	2	2	0	0	OU=Toronto.O=North_America

Replica Comparison Total:

Status	Warni Repl	Tota Repl	Equa Repl	Acce Erro	Not Repl
0	R	14	14	0	0

Report Comparison Total:

Status	Warni Part	Tota Part	Equa Part	Acce Erro	Part NEQ
0	R	7	7	0	0

Replicas found: 14

Partitions found: 7

```
Servers contacted with Partitions and Replicas: 2



Count    Warning    Message

  14          R      Fewer than the minimum readable replicas found.



End Date: Feb 14, 1999    9:17:21 pm EST

*********************
```

Because Novell recommends that you should have at least three copies of any partition for fault tolerance, DSDIAG will show a warning message if it finds fewer than three replicas of any partition.

NOTE

The DSDIAG NLM offers a fairly convenient way of collecting data about servers, partitions, and replica rings from a single server, regardless of how many NDS trees you have on your network.

Third-Party Utilities

There are a number of third-party NLM products on the market that can help you manage and monitor the status of your NDS tree. Perhaps the most well known one is DS Expert, from NetPro, Inc.

DSExpert

DS Expert is a proactive NDS monitoring and troubleshooting tool featuring NDS subtree monitoring, duplexing, and new remote access to alert reports through most Web browsers:

- ▸ Earlier versions of DS Expert monitored the entire corporate tree while the current version of DS Expert (2.6 and higher) features a subtree option that enables administrators to compartmentalize portions of their trees for individual monitoring.

- ▸ DS Expert version 2.6 and higher also features enhanced off-site monitoring, which allows support personal to use Web browsers to view alert data via HTML reports.

▸ Also featured is duplexed monitors, which enable one monitor station to back up the other, increasing their capability to maintain user service level agreements through constant, proactive monitoring.

▸ DS Expert sends alerts directly to a dedicated monitor and can also forward the alerts to third party paging products and management consoles via Simple Network Management Protocol (SNMP).

DS Expert constantly monitors for NDS problems so that small issues do not escalate into network-wide crises. It checks server availability, time synchronization and replica and partition synchronization on a continuous basis, flagging trouble and notifying you in time to forestall serious network problems.

You can request an evaluation copy of DS Expert by visiting the NetPro Web site at `http://www.netpro.com` **or by calling 602-941-3600.**

NOTE

DS Analyzer

One of the challenges in diagnosing a problem is to answer the question: "Is what I'm seeing normal?" In order to know what's normal, you need to first have a baseline, a measurement of some quantifiable variables when everything is running well and no users are complaining (too loudly). At the time of this writing, there are no applications on the market that can provide NDS performance information; however, NetPro is beta testing DS Analyzer for NDS.

The DS Analyzer for NDS can trend, analyze, and report on all NDS traffic to pinpoint structural problems in an NDS implementation. The product displays a graphical view of directory traffic, enabling you to readily identify where configuration changes and resource allocation would enhance NDS' scalability and reliability; furthermore, DS Analyzer enables you to analyze and optimize NDS by capturing baseline information for comparison purposes to accurately trend specific NDS behavior over time.

For information on other NDS-related utilities, visit the Novell Partner and Product Search webpage at `http://developer.novell.com/npp`.

TIP

Workstation Tools

There will be times that you don't have ready access to the server console in order to run any of the server-based tools mentioned in the previous section. This section describes how you can use workstation-based applications to accomplish similar, if not the same goals, as those server-based utilities.

NOTE

The functionality and number of objects you see using workstation-based utilities is determined by the NDS rights of the user object that you're logged in with.

TIP

When using workstation-based applications, the NDS information is read from your current default server. For example, if you have a drive (F:) mapped to server NETWARE5-A and another drive (G:) mapped to NETWARE5-B, you'll be reading NDS data from NETWARE5-A if your current drive is F:, otherwise the data will be retrieved from NETWARE5-B. When working from the Windows desktop, such as Windows NT, and using Client32 you can easily change your default server: right-click Network Neighborhood, select NetWare Connections from the context menu, select the server that you wish to be your default server, and click Set Primary.

NDS Manager

The NDS Manager utility provides you with the capability to perform partitioning and replication operations for the NDS database from a workstation. It also provides repair capabilities for repairing the database from a client workstation, which alleviates your dependence on either having to work at the server console or through remote console access using a text-based interface. NDS Manager offers a graphical look of your replica placements, either by containers (known as the tree view; see Figure 7.9) or by partitions and servers (see Figure 7.10).

FIGURE 7.9

NDS Manager's tree view

In the tree view, the left panel displays your NDS containers in much the same way as NW Admin does; however, only containers are shown. A jigsaw puzzle icon to the left of any container indicates it is a partition. For example, [Root], O=DreamLAN, and O=Europe are partitions. When you click one of these entries in the left panel, the servers holding replicas of this partition are displayed on the right panel, together with the replica type (such as master or read/write) and replica status (such as on or transition on). When you click a container that is not a replica root, the right panel shows blank.

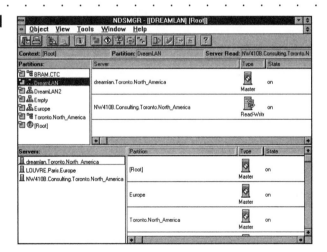

FIGURE 7.10

NDS Manager's partitions and servers view

In the partitions and servers view, the screen is divided into two parts: the partitions screen at the top and the servers screen at the bottom. The partitions screen is similar to the tree view screen except only partitions are shown. The servers screen serves a similar function as the partitions screen: clicking on a server in the left panel will show you what partitions are stored on that server, along with the replica type and replica status.

Other than displaying replica placement information, NDS Manager also offers the following functionalities:

▸ NDS version update capability so that NetWare 4 and NetWare 5 servers in a network can be updated to a newer version of DS.NLM, without you having to manually copy the necessary files to each and every server in the tree. This is further discussed in Chapter 13.

▸ Capability to print a list of partitions in the directory tree, the partition replica list (the replica ring), and server data, and information about replicas (such as network address and NDS version number). The following is an example of server and replica data and server information printout:

```
NDS Manger - Server Information                        02/09/99
08:46:22 pm



Server Name:            NETWARE5-F.Consulting.Toronto
```

Replicas on Server	Type	State
DreamLAN	Master	on
Europe	Read-Write	on
[Root]	Read-Write	on
Toronto.ACME_Company	Master	on
Testing	Subordinate Reference	on

The following is an example of server information printout:

```
NDS Manger - Server Information        02/09/99 08:47:04 pm
```

```
Server Name:        NETWARE5-F.Consulting.Toronto

Full Name:

Server version:     Novell NetWare 5.0[DS]

NDS version:        724

Time in sync:       02/09/99 08:47:04 pm (EDT)

Replicas on server: 5

Network address:    IPX: 00001234:000000000001:0451
```

▸ Diagnostic features (such as partition continuity check) enable you to get a sense of the general condition of the whole directory tree from a central workstation.

NDS Manager replaces the partition manager utility that existed under the Tools menu in the NetWare Administrator (NWAdmin) utility in NetWare 4.10 and prior. NDS Manager is now the standard workstation-based partition management utility for NetWare 4.11 and higher.

Included with NetWare 4 (including NetWare 4.11) was PARTMGR.EXE, a DOS-based partition management application, but it is not included with NetWare 5. Although you can use PARTMGR with NetWare 5 trees, it is recommended that you use NDS Manager instead, because the latter is much more full-featured and performs comprehensive health checks prior to partitioning and replication operations.

You'll learn more about using NDS Manager's diagnostic and management operations in later chapters.

NWAdmin

It is not often considered by network administrators that NWAdmin, mainly a management application, can be used as a crude diagnostic tool. When you don't have ready access to utilities such as DSVIEW and need to check the data consistency or synchronization between servers in a replica ring, you can use NWAdmin. Suppose you suspect there's something wrong with the synchronization between the replicas of a given partition, use the following steps to see if NDS changes are being sent from one replica to another:

1. Identify the servers that have a replica of the partition in question.

2. Ensure you're only logged into the server holding the master replica.

3. Use NWAdmin to change an attribute value of one of the objects in this partition. For example, the Location attribute of an user object.

4. At the server console of this server, issue the SET DSTRACE=*H command to force an immediate synchronization; otherwise, the change you just made may not be synchronized for some time (as it is not a Sync Immediate attribute).

NOTE

NDS attributes are classified either as sync immediate (or fast sync, as it is sometimes known as) or not. Security-sensitive attributes, such as user passwords, are immediately synchronized; otherwise, the changes are queued up and are sent later (they could be delayed by up to 30 minutes).

5. Log into each server in the replica ring separately (using LOGIN servername/username if logging in from DOS or specifying the server name in the server field in the GUI login dialog box), and use NWAdmin to check if the changed attribute value has been propagated correctly to the server.

You can also use the same technique (logging into each server in turn) and look for unknown objects (because of schema inconsistency or corruption) or missing objects (perhaps due to obituaries). The key to this exercise is to only log into one server at a time or ensure you correctly set your default server so you know from which server you're retrieving the data.

TIP

In NWAdmn3X, there is a Use Master = True INI file parameter so that when you create a user in NWAdmin, the master replica is used. The same setting is available in Windows 95 and NT via the registry key. The key that governs this Use Master situation is HKEY_CURRENT_USER\Software\NetWare\Parameters\NetWare

Administrator\UserCreation\Use Master. If you know you have an inconsistent replica ring but NWAdmin isn't showing any differences when you log into specific servers, check to see if this setting is enabled.

ODBC Driver for NDS

With the popularity of the Open Database Connectivity (ODBC) technology, many data applications (including spreadsheet programs, such as Excel) provide an ODBC interface for connecting to an ODBC data source. And because NDS is a database, you can use the Novell ODBC Driver for NDS to easily query, retrieve directory data, and generate reports either for management or diagnosis needs.

Though NWAdmin provides a convenient interface for NDS management, it is not the best application when it comes to generating reports. This NDS ODBC driver serves as an independent interface for extracting and reporting specified NDS information for use in the applications that you use everyday. It allows you to populate reports, import data into your custom programs, or view within a spreadsheet.

The architecture behind the Novell ODBC Driver for NDS consists of the application, the ODBC.DLL Driver Manager, the Novell ODBCNDS.DLL driver, the network, and NDS itself. The driver employs the ODBCNDS.DLL to abstract the directory tree into accessible relational database tables, which hides the complexity of the underlying directory syntax. Information is selected and ordered from the relational tables using standard Structured Query Language (SQL) statements embedded into the application.

Using embedded SQL statements or ODBC functions, you can set queries and sort NDS information. For example, you can access the account information for each user. You can also set search conditions and sort directory entries to return specified entry attributes, such as the user name, user description, telephone number, address, or other user-specific types of information. These retrieved user data can then be viewed in a report or used in programs. Shown in Figure 7.11 is a Visual Basic program that uses the Novell ODBC Driver for NDS to access NDS information.

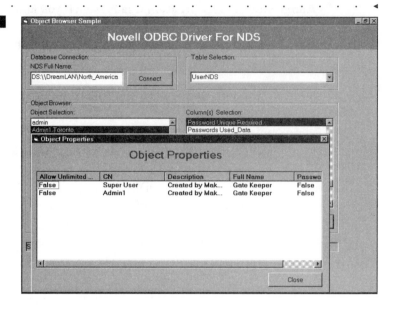

Access the Novell ODBC driver for NDS from a sample Visual Basic program.

NOTE

At the time of this writing, the Novell ODBC Driver for NDS is read-only, so it uses only a subset of the SQL statements to query information. You cannot use requests that delete or update information in the directory. In most cases, you will only use simple SELECT and FROM statements to browse the directory and populate directory reports.

Schema Manager

Schema Manager is a Windows-based application that allows users with supervisor rights to a tree (the [Root] object) to customize the schema of that tree. It is implemented as an enhancement to NDS Manager, meaning you need to access it through NDS Manager. After you select a partition or a server from the left panel in NDS Manager, Schema Manager is available from the Object menu, otherwise the option is grayed out. You can use Schema Manager to perform the following functions:

▸ View a list of all classes and attributes in the schema (see Figure 7.12). An icon that is a question mark with a right-pointing arrow on the left is assigned to all classes that are extensions to the base schema, such as is the case with the DNIP:DHCP server class.

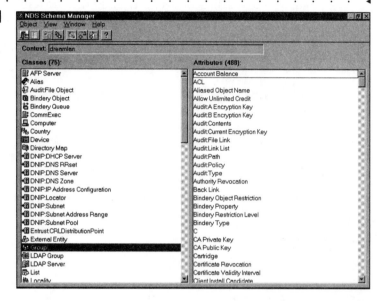

F I G U R E   7.12

Viewing a tree's schema classes and attributes using Schema Manager

▸ View information on an attribute such as its syntax and flags.

▸ Extend the schema by adding a class or an attribute to the existing schema; you need to have supervisor rights to [Root] for this operation.

▸ Create a new class by naming it and specifying applicable attributes, flags, containers to which it can be added and parent classes from which it can inherit attributes.

▸ Create an attribute by naming it and specifying its syntax and flags.

WARNING

Any attributes added to a base class (that is, one that is part of the base schema, such as the user) cannot be removed at a later time.

▸ Add an attribute to an existing class.

▸ Compare the schemas of two trees and print the results. Shown in Table 7.5 is a schema comparison between a NetWare 5 tree (Z.E.N.works has not been installed on this tree yet; therefore, the NAL objects are not present) and a NetWare 4.11 tree.

▸ View or print a report on a selected class, attribute, or the entire schema.

▸ View or print the extensions to the schema.

▸ Delete a class that is not in use or that has become obsolete.

WARNING

You can't remove a class definition that's part of the base schema.

▸ Delete an attribute that is not in use or that has become obsolete.

WARNING

You can't remove an attribute definition from a base schema class, even if this attribute was added as an extension. For example, if you added a nickname attribute to the user object, you can't remove this attribute, because user is part of the base schema.

Table 7.5 is a comparison table showing the classes defined in NetWare 5 versus those defined in NetWare 4.11. Notice that more new classes have been introduced in NetWare 5.

TABLE 7.5 *Comparison of NetWare 5 Classes with NetWare 4.11 Classes*	CLASSES DEFINED IN A NETWARE 5 TREE	CLASSES DEFINED IN A NETWARE 4.11 TREE
	AFP Server	AFP Server
	Alias	Alias
		App:Application

TABLE 7.5	CLASSES DEFINED IN A NETWARE 5 TREE	CLASSES DEFINED IN A NETWARE 4.11 TREE
Comparison of NetWare 5 Classes with NetWare 4.11 Classes (continued)		Application
		Application (DOS)
		Application (Windows 3.x)
		Application (Windows 95)
		Application (Windows NT)
	Audit:File Object	Audit:File Object
	Bindery Object	Bindery Object
	Bindery Queue	Bindery Queue
	CommExec	CommExec
	Computer	Computer
	Country	Country
	Device	Device
	Directory Map	Directory Map
	DNIP:DHCP Server	
	DNIP:DNS RRset	
	DNIP:DNS Server	
	DNIP:DNS Zone	
	DNIP:IP Address Configuration	
	DNIP:Locator	
	DNIP:Subnet	
	DNIP:Subnet Address Range	
	DNIP:Subnet Pool	
	Entrust:CRLDistributionPoint	
	External Entity	External Entity
	Group	GroupLDAP Group
	LDAP Server	
	List	List
	Locality	Locality

Continued

TABLE 7.5	CLASSES DEFINED IN A NETWARE 5 TREE	CLASSES DEFINED IN A NETWARE 4.11 TREE
Comparison of NetWare 5 Classes with NetWare 4.11 Classes (continued)	MASV:Security Policy	
	Message Routing Group	Message Routing Group
	Messaging Server	Messaging Server
	NCP Server	NCP Server
	NDPS Broker	
	NDPS Manager	
	NDPS Printer	
	NDSCat:Catalog	
	NDSCat:Master Catalog	
	NDSCat:Slave Catalog	
	NDSPKI:Certificate Authority	
	NDSPKI:Key Material	
	NetSvc	
		NetWare Mobile: Dial-in Service
		NLS License Server
	NLS:License Certificate	
	NLS:License Server	
	NLS:Product Container	
		NLS LicenseCertificate
		NLS Product
	NSCP:groupOfUniqueNames5	
	NSCP:mailGroup5	
	NSCP:NetscapeMailServer5	
	NSCP:NetscapeServer5	
	NSCP:Nginfo	
	NSCP:Nginfo2	
	Organization	Organization
	Organizational Person	Organizational Person
	Organizational Role	Organizational Role

TABLE 7.5

*Comparison of NetWare 5
Classes with NetWare 4.11
Classes (continued)*

CLASSES DEFINED IN A NETWARE 5 TREE	CLASSES DEFINED IN A NETWARE 4.11 TREE
Organizational Unit	Organizational Unit
Partition	Partition
Person	Person
Print Server	Print Server
Printer	Printer
Profile	Profile
Queue	Queue
Resource	Resource
SAS:Security	
SAS:Service	
Server	Server
SLP Directory Agent	
SLP Scope Unit	
SLP Service	
SMS SMDR Class	
Template	Template
Top	Top
Tree Root	
Unknown	Unknown
User	User
Volume	Volume
WANMAN:LAN Area	
[Anything]	
[Nothing]	

It is interesting to point out here that the name of the class definitions for Novell Licensing Services (NLS) changed between NetWare 4.11 and NetWare 5.

NOTE

Keep in mind that standard Novell-supplied management utilities, such as NWAdmin, cannot manage objects (such as create or update) that use extended schemas definitions unless you have a snap-in for NWAdmin or custom applications that know about the extensions. Further discussions about NWAdmin snap-ins and a utility called ScheMax, (from Netoria) that allows you to extend the schema and create your own snap-ins, can be found in Chapter 13.

Other Tools

As mentioned in a previous section, DSVIEW NLM isn't available for NetWare 5 at the time of this writing; therefore, if you need to view your NetWare 5's NDS in a similar manner, you can use the workstation-based DSVIEW as an alternative. It is by no means as powerful as the NLM version, but it is a lot easier to use. For example, you can view only the data, but the utility will not show you the additional information, such as syntax, which the NLM version does (see Figure 7.13).

The workstation-based DSVIEW is available as both a 16-bit and 32-bit version, you can download them from the Novell Consulting Web site at `http://consulting.novell.com/toolkit/iw_tools.html`.

DSVIEW16/32 is written by Novell Developer Support to illustrate how to use the various APIs to browse the NDS tree. It is not officially supported by Novell Technical Support.

NOTE

What do you do when an NDS-aware application worked on one NDS tree but doesn't on another? Or when you're encountering -625 communication errors, where are you going to start looking? Our favorite tool for diagnosing such problems is a *protocol analyzer*. A protocol analyzer is a combination of hardware and software that can capture and analyze individual packets on your network. Some protocol analyzer manufacturers require you to use their specific hardware while others are software-only and can be used with a variety of network cards that can operate in the promiscuous mode.

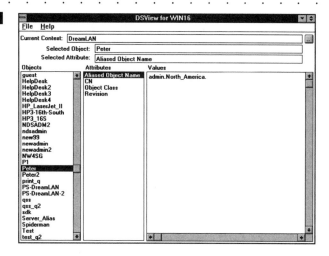

F I G U R E   7 . 1 3

*Browsing the NDS using
DSVIEW16*

NOTE

Promiscuous mode operation is the capability of a network adapter (or network interface card, NIC) to make a copy of the packets that are not addressed to it. Not all NICs can operate in this mode, therefore, you should check with your NIC's vendor if you're unsure.

Novell's LANalyzer for Windows is a software-only protocol analyzer that can monitor, capture, and analyze both Ethernet and Token Ring data frames. It can decode all NetWare, AppleTalk, and TCP/IP protocol suites; for protocols it doesn't support, you're presented with the hexadecimal dump of the contents. To use a protocol analyzer effectively, you need to be versed with the protocols in order to understand what you're seeing. The analyzer will tell you what it sees on the wire, but it's up to you, the user, to interpret the presented data and take appropriate action. Here's an example on how you can use LANalyzer for Windows to diagnose your NDS problems: the -625 error.

You learned in Chapter 5 that this error is due to failure somewhere in the LAN/WAN infrastructure or it could be the target server that is unavailable. How do you tell? In an IPX/SPX environment, each NetWare server will broadcast its presence to the network once every 60 seconds using the Service Advertising Protocol (SAP). So you can use LANalyzer for Windows to capture SAP packets and see if the target server is broadcasting (see Figure 7.14); Furthermore, check the Routing Information Protocol (RIP) packets to see if the internal IPX number of the target server is being broadcast. A -625 error can be a result of RIP/SAP filtering on a network and not due to any network failures.

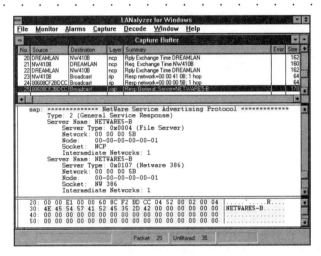

F I G U R E   7 . 1 4

Capturing and decoding SAP
packets using LANalyzer for
Windows

**An excellent reference on NetWare protocols is *Novell's Guide to
LAN/WAN Analysis: IPX/SPX*, by Laura A. Chappell, from Novell Press.**

NOTE

One last utility we'd like to discuss in this section is NLIST. Because it is a DOS-based application, NLIST is often overlooked as a useful tool in this GUI-centric environment. Consider this: How do you compare the group membership of a group object in a replica ring? You can use NWAdmin to call up the group membership list using the technique discussed in the NWAdmin section earlier. But using NWAdmin, there isn't an easy way to either export the necessary information to a text file or print out just the group membership list. You can, however, easily do this using NLIST:

```
nlist group=group_name show member > filename
```

The following is a sample output from a group membership listing:

```
nlist group = ndsadmin show "member"

Object Class: Group
```

```
Current context: DreamLAN

Name: ndsadmin

        Member: sdk

        Member: admin.North_America.

One Group object was found in this context.


One Group object was found.
```

Information Tools

Oftentimes, the amount of useful information provided by the various utilities we've discussed in this chapter is limited, because the tools assume you know what you're looking for in the first place, which is often not the case. Also, knowing the cause of the error or understanding the error code doesn't not always automatically tell you what the solution is; therefore, you need to combine the diagnosis of your problem with some type of knowledge base in order to formulate an action plan to fix your NDS problem. This section introduces a number of information tools that can assist you in the task:

▶ LogicSource for NDS

▶ Novell's technical support knowledgebase

▶ Internet newsgroups

▶ Help files

LogicSource for NDS

In March of 1998, during Novell's annual BrainShare Conference in Salt Lake City, Utah, Novell released an electronic document called "Understanding, Identifying and Resolving NDS Issues" (code named the Phoenix Document) that offered in-depth explanations of the concepts, processes, and operations of NDS. In mid-1998, the product was enhanced with more information, and searching for data was made easier. The document is now known as the LogicSource for NDS.

Designed to help you manage and support NDS in NetWare 4 and NetWare 5 environments, LogicSource for NDS includes descriptions of common error codes to help you learn why they occur and learn how to avoid them. LogicSource for NDS contains more than 1,500 pages of detailed information (perhaps more than you ever cared to know!) about the various NDS processes and steps for setting up directory trees.

The information included in LogicSource for NDS covers the following subjects:

▶ Understanding Novell Directory Services

▶ Novell Directory Services Background Processes

▶ Novell Directory Services Background Process Requests

▶ Novell Directory Services Partition and Object Operations

▶ Resources for Supporting Novell Directory Services for NetWare and intraNetWare

▶ Identifying and Resolving Novell Directory Services Issues

▶ Novell Directory Services Error Codes

▶ NetWare Client, Operating System, and Other Error Codes

For more information about and purchasing LogicSource for NDS, **visit** http://support.novell.com/logicsource/nds/.

NOTE

Novell's Technical Support Knowledgebase

Over the years, Novell Technical Support (NTS) has collected and published reported issues and resolutions for all Novell products, including the NetWare operating system and its components. The information is available in the form of

Technical Information Documents (TIDs). You can access these TIDs, free of charge, 24 hours a day, 7 days a week over the Internet from Novell Technical Support's Web site at `http://support.novell.com/search/kb_index.htm`. The TIDs are stored in a searchable database, and you can search using a single word, a phrase, or a TID number; and you can combine multiple words together using Boolean operators (see Figure 7.15).

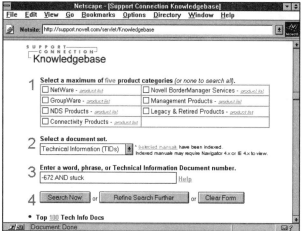

Novell technical support knowledgebase website

The resulting hit list is graded by relevance. The better a TID matches your search criteria, the higher is the assigned percentage. From the same website `http://support.novell.com`, you can find and download the latest patches and file updates relevant to your problem.

The online knowledgebase is easy to use and readily available — if you have a reliable Internet connection. Have you ever been at a client site at two in the morning and needed the latest NetWare 4.11's DS.NLM update so you can install a NetWare 5 server into an existing NetWare 4 tree and there's not a RJ-11 jack in sight? Or have you been in the situation that you needed to download NetWare 5's Service Pack 1 to get the new DS.NLM update to address an NDS error you have encountered and only to find your Internet connection is slower than molasses in winter because everyone is checking the Super Bowl Web site and eating up all available bandwidth? Yes, you can easily find and download these patches from the Internet, if you have a fast (T1 or better) link, because the files are very large. (For example, NW5SP1.EXE is 60MB!)

But sometimes you simply can't wait an hour for a file to be downloaded. The alternate solution is the Novell Support Connection CD.

Other than LogicSource for NDS, NTS also makes the TIDs and patch files available on a set of CDs, known as the Novell Support Connection (NSC) CD. The Novell Support Connection CD provides fast and easy access to the specific information you need, and enables you to do on-site troubleshooting, acting as an immediate first point of reference for technical information.

The NSC CD is usable on any Windows desktop. No network access is required to fully use the monthly updates.

NOTE

Distributed in a compact, two-ring binder, the Novell Support Connection CD includes four tabs: Monthly Updates, Special Editions, Novell Products, and Miscellaneous. With a subscription to the Novell Support Connection CD, you receive two update CDs each month with Novell technical information in a searchable format. Besides the monthly updates, additional CDs containing a wide range of network support content are sent periodically and can be inserted into your binder behind the appropriate tab. The following additional CDs have been shipped to NSC CD subscribers:

- Technical Resource CD from the Institute for Network Professionals Association (NPA)

- intraNetWare Client CD

- Support On Site for Networks demo version from Ziff-Davis Support Publishing

If you have Internet access, the NSC CD also contains links that take you to the World Wide Web (WWW) for further information; therefore, you have the best of both worlds. The Novell Support Connection CD includes the following:

- More than 40,000 TIDs

- Over 1,200 files containing software updates, patches, and third-party drivers

▸ More than 200 product documentation manuals

▸ The entire collection of Novell Application Notes (AppNotes)

▸ Novell Developer Notes (DevNotes) since January 1996

▸ Up-to-date Novell Labs certification (yes, it runs on NetWare) bulletins

The one disadvantage of NSC CD versus the on-line knowledgebase is that the CD is generally six weeks behind what's available on the WWW, due to lead time needed to produce and ship the product.

For more information about the Novell Support Connection CD, visit `http://support.novell.com/additional/nsc-prodinfo.htm.`

NOTE

Internet Newsgroups

We all know from history lessons that not all knowledge is passed on in writing — some is simply passed verbally as whispered wisdom, while others are gained from hands-on experience. Knowledgebases are wonderful tools, but they are only as complete as the number of issues reported to Novell Technical Support. For every reported problem, there's probably five that are not reported.

To facilitate Novell customers around the world to share their experiences, tips, and tricks for dealing with problems, Novell operates a set of newsgroups, known as the Novell Support Connection forums. The main purpose of these message forums is to offer a place to discuss and obtain technical support with regard to released Novell products. Within these newsgroups, you're free to ask questions, respond to any forum message that interests you, or tell others about your latest adventure with your Novell product. If you can assist a fellow user, feel free to jump into the conversation as peer-to-peer support is highly encouraged.

You may have used the NSC forums in its previous incarnation. Prior to being on the Internet, Novell sponsored a set of messaging forums on CompuServe Information Service (CIS; now part of America Online), known as NetWire. In 1997, Novell moved off CIS and implemented the current Internet newsgroups infrastructure.

NOTE

You can access the NSC forums either via the Web interface using your favorite browser or via an NNTP (Internet news protocol) newsreader. For more information, visit `http://support.novell.com/forums/`.

Help Files

Other than the various knowledge sources discussed here, many people often overlook the wealth of information available in the online help files that are included with many of the utilities. For example, NDS Manager includes context-sensitive help and can offer you information about a reported DS error code (see Figure 7.16), such as possible cause and corrective actions. Also included with the NDS Manager help file is a list of NDS and server error codes that you may find useful.

F I G U R E   7.16

NDS Manager online help

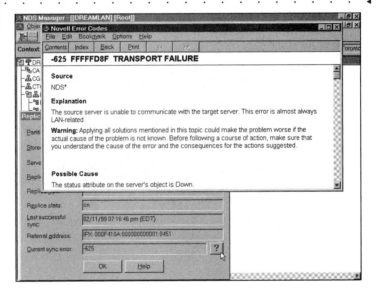

Frequently, by combining the help information offered by the utilities and the TIDs available from Novell, you'll have a good starting point for your troubleshooting efforts.

Summary

This chapter introduced you to the various server- and workstation-based diagnosis tools and utilities included with the NetWare 4 and NetWare 5 operating systems, such as DSREPAIR and NDS Manager, and a number of additional applications available from either Novell (such as LANalyzer for Windows and DSVIEW) or third parties (such as DS Analyzer for NDS). In the Chapter 8, you'll read about a number of NDS data recovery tools.

NDS Recovery Tools

Chapter 7 discussed various utilities that can assist you in diagnosing and understanding NDS issues. In this chapter, you'll learn about tools that will help you in protecting and recovering lost NDS information, such as a User object (such as Admin) that has been deleted by mistake or a corrupted container login script that needs to be restored.

X-REF

The information presented in this chapter compliments the material found in Chapter 11. This chapter covers recovery tools in general and offers some one-step solutions to simple NDS recovery needs, while Chapter 11 presents some specific NDS issue examples in detail.

The following topics are discussed in this chapter:

▸ Backing up and restoring NDS with Storage Management Services (SMS)

▸ Exporting data from and importing information into NDS

▸ Recovering lost passwords and Admin users

▸ Detecting and gaining objects that are blocked by Inherited Rights Filters (IRFs)

▸ Creating Server Specific Information (SSI) data for server recovery purposes

SMS Backup and Restore

Storage Management Services (SMS), developed by Novell, provides a standard for data, devices, media, and storage management interfaces. With the appropriate agents, SMS can be configured to service different targets, such as NetWare, NDS, Windows NT and so on, from a single backup engine. To fully understand the terminology and appreciate why you need an SMS-compliant backup solution for your NetWare network, the following sections offers a brief architectural overview of SMS and some example SMS backup implementations.

SMS Architecture

SMS divides the storage management function into four areas of responsibility:

▸ Transparent communications interface

▸ Target-specific agent

▸ Storage engine

▸ Device interface

They are incorporated into four modules or applications, as shown in Figure 8.1.

The Storage Management Data Requester (SMDR) provides transparent local and Remote Procedure Call (RPC) links between the SMS modules running on the storage engine and the SMS modules running on the target. For example, when you're running an SMS-compliant tape backup software on a NetWare server that is backing up a remote NetWare server, SMDR.NLM must be running on both servers to facilitate the communication.

NOTE

SMDR versions prior to 5.00 depend on SPX and, thus, IPX; however, starting with SMDR 5.00 (shipped with NetWare 5), it is protocol independent. For NetWare 5, this requester can use TCP/IP to communicate with other SMDRs. Although SMDR 5.00 can be configured to support TCP/IP and SPX/IPX or TCP/IP and SPX/IPX; both protocols are supported by default. The SPX protocol is used with SMDR versions prior to 5.00.

The ability to back up data from a specific operation system platform is provided through the Target Service Agent (TSA), which runs on the *target*. In SMS parlance, a SMS target is what you want to back up (the source of your data). The TSA is SMS' access road to a target's data. Through a set of generic Target Service APIs, SMS can read from, write to, and scan the target. All of SMS, except the TSA, treats the target's data as *"black box data"* — only the TSA knows the target's data structure. Generally, one TSA is required for each target. For example, to back up NDS data, you need TSANDS.NLM; to back up a NetWare 4.11 server's file system, you need TSA410.NLM; and to back up the file system of a NetWare 5 server, you need TSA500.NLM. TSA500 supports both the traditional NetWare file system and the new Novell Storage Services (NSS) released with NetWare 5; however, the initial release of TSA500 does not support NSS mounted DOS FAT file systems. If you need to back up a DOS partition, use TSADOSP.NLM instead.

NOTE

The file system TSA for NetWare 4.10 and NetWare 4.11 are both called TSA410.NLM; there is no TSA411.NLM.

Storage Management Engine (SME) is the heart of an SMS-compliant backup system. Its main task is to retrieve and dispense data. It is in this module where third-party vendors provide value-added features, such as maintaining a database of backed up files and management of tapes.

Instead of directly communicating with the various types of storage devices, SMS communicates with them via the Storage Device Interface (SDI) module. With the assistance of Media Manager, SDI provides SMS a logical view of the media and storage devices; therefore, any applications using SDI can use all SMS-compatible devices without making any changes. In essence, SDI is a *storage device abstraction layer* within the SMS architecture, so the higher layers within SMS, such as the SME, don't need to know how to address a specific storage device for data retrieval or writing to it.

System Independent Data Format

SMS' capability to work with many different types of targets or services (such as NetWare file systems, NDS, Windows NT, and so on) whose data structures are varied is due to the System Independent Data Format (SIDF). SIDF specifies how a target's data is formatted, who does the formatting, how a session is placed on the media, and so on. The TSA is responsible for formatting and deformatting the target's data set (such as file data and name-space information) according to the specification, and the SME simply writes the SIDF-formatted data to the storage media; therefore, in concept, SMS' use of SIDF is very similar to the use of XDR (External Data Representation) in NFS (Network File System) developed by Sun Microsystems, except the receiving side (the SME) does not deformat the data before recording it.

SMS Backup Session Example

The interactions between the various SMS modules are complex. The following example offers you a high-level look at how an SMS backup session works and gives you some insights into how and why SMS-compliant software functions the way it does. The example assumes that the SMS engine (SME, SDI, and SMDR) are running on a NetWare 5 server and it is backing up the SYS volume of another NetWare 5 server, which has a TSA and SMDR running (see Figure 8.2).

1. The user selects the backup media to use. This connects the SME to SDI.

2. The user selects NETWARE5-B as the target. During this process the SMDRs on each server connect to each other; this is transparent to the user as well as the SME programmer. Through the SMDR connection, the SME running on NETWARE5-A connects to the TSA running on NETWARE5-B.

If the SME is backing up local data, the SMDR is bypassed so that all communication between the SME and TSA is direct.

NOTE

FIGURE 8.2

SMDR.NLM
SME+SDI+tape driver

SMDR.NLM
TSA500.NLM

The SYS volume of NETWARE5-B server is being backed up across the wire by NETWARE5-A.

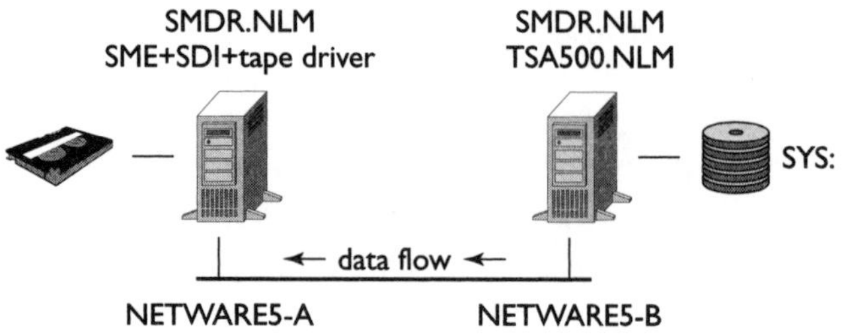

SYS:

← data flow ←

NETWARE5-A   NETWARE5-B

3. The SME asks the TSA to provide a list of resources or data sets the user can choose to back up. The SME presents this list to the user for selection.

4. The user selects the SYS volume and specifies that the file system trustees are to be backed up as well.

5. The SME sends the user selections back to the TSA.

6. The TSA then scans (searches) NETWARE5-B for the specified data sets (resources).

7. Upon finding a data set that matches the selection criteria, the TSA formats the data set (which includes file attributes, file names, name space information, and so on) according to SIDF specifications and sends it to the SME.

8. File system trustee assignments are backed up as follows:

   a. For each given file or directory, the TSA reads the Directory Entry Table (DET) to determine if any trustees are assigned.

   b. If a trustee assignment is found, TSA reads the trustee — this is stored as an object ID and not an NDS object name.

   c. The object ID is then translated into a full NDS object name.

   d. The TSA formats the data according to SIDF specifications and sends it to the SME.

9. The SME sends the received data to SDI, through Media Manager and device-specific driver, for storage on the (selected) media.

10. Steps 6 through 9 are repeated until all data sets matching the user selection criteria are found and stored.

You can use a non-SMS solution to back up your file system provided it is NetWare-aware (so file system trustee information is properly backed up); however, because it doesn't make use of TSA, it cannot back up the NDS — some of the NDS files are kept open by DS.NLM and thus can't be backed up or copied by conventional means.

SBackup

Included with NetWare (from NetWare 3.0 and up) is an SMS-compliant backup utility called SBackup. It is an NLM-based tape backup program. Shipped with NetWare 5 is an enhanced version of this backup engine. It contains all the functionality provided by earlier versions of SBackup and has the following enhancements:

▸ Autoloader support

▸ Enhanced user interface (SBCon)

▸ Win95/NT workstation graphical interface (NWBack32)

▸ Multiple and repeatable job scheduling

▸ Concurrent jobs can run on multiple devices (but not on same device)

▸ Compatible with SBACKUP 4.20

▸ Runs on NetWare 4.1x and NetWare 5 and is compatible with all TSAs

▸ Runs in an IP-only environment if preferred

If multiple backup and restore jobs are submitted to run at the same time *on the same device*, the second and subsequent jobs will receive an error because the device (tape drive or other) is busy servicing the current job. The error message does not make it sufficiently clear that the problem is simply that the device is in use. To avoid this conflict, set the execution time for subsequent jobs to run sometime after prior jobs are completed or submit concurrent jobs to different devices.

NOTE

This section outlines the necessary steps for backing up and restoring your NDS using SBackup; however, before learning that, you need to know how to correctly set up and configure SMS for your NDS environment.

Configuring SMDR and QMAN

As mentioned earlier in this chapter, SMS-compliant applications make use of SMDR, and SBackup is no exception. Unlike previous versions of SMDR that use Service Advertising Protocol (SAP) to locate other SMDRs on the network, the new SMDR uses NDS. Older versions of SMDR advertised the server name where it was loaded using SAP type 0x23F. This mechanism worked well in small LAN environments, but did not scale well in large environments and does not work at all in a pure IP environment. In a pure IP environment, SMDR uses NDS as a service locator instead of SAPs.

Each server that will be running an SMS-compliant software needs to have its own SMDR object.

NOTE

You need to install and configure SMDR and QMAN (SMS Queue Manager) before you can use any SMS applications, such as SBackup. Some third-party SMS applications may include their own queue manager instead of using the SMS Queue Manager. This can be done during the server installation by choosing to install SMS or you can add this service at a later time using NWConfig. If SMDR fails to load or if the SMDR object is corrupted, you can restore it to the state when the server was first installed and before it was configured. You need to delete two configuration files and two NDS objects to do so. The procedure is as follows:

1. Login to the server as a user that has Admin rights.

2. Make your working directory SYS:ETC\SMS.

3. There are two files within this directory, SMDR.CFG and SBACKUP.CFG. Both of these files are text based and can be viewed with any text editor. Either delete or rename the files.

4. Use NWAdmin to locate the two SMS-related objects in the tree. Usually these two objects are in the container where the server object is located. If the objects are not there, look through the tree for them. Once they are found, delete them. The default names of the objects are "SMS SMDR Group" and "SERVER NAME Backup Queue." For example, for a server named "NETWARE5-A," the object names are "SMS SMDR Group" and "NETWARE5-A Backup Queue."

5. At the server console prompt, type **LOAD SMDR NEW**. The new switch brings up the SMDR Configuration Screen (see Figure 8.3), and you're asked for three pieces of information:

  a. The default context for the SMDR group: enter the desired context (such as OU=Servers.O=Company) or press Enter to use the default context.

  b. The default SMDR context: enter the desired context (such as OU=Servers.O=Company) or press Enter to use the default context.

  c. The name and password of the user that has managing rights to the object that will be created in the specified context: An example of a user name is given. When entering the user name, use *absolute fully distinguished naming* such as .CN=Admin.OU=Servers.O=Company.

▶ • ◀

FIGURE 8.3

The SMDR Configuration Screen

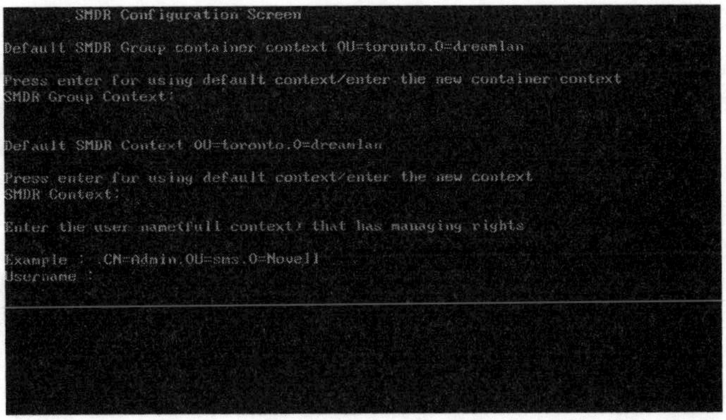

The previous steps create a new SYS:ETC\SMS\SMDR.CFG configuration file that looks similar to this:

```
#This is SMDR default configuration file
#Lines beginning with # are treated as comment




SMDR Context: OU=toronto.O=dreamlan


SMDR Group Context: OU=toronto.O=dreamlan


#Both the protocols are enabled
```

d. At the server console prompt, type **LOAD QMAN NEW**. The NEW switch brings up the SMS Queue Manager Configuration Screen (see Figure 8.4). Similar to configuring SMDR, you'll be asked to specify the context and the name of the SMS Job Queue. After the job queue name is created, the name of the user who has managing rights is requested. This time, however, an example of the user name is not given. Follow the previous step's suggestion for the user naming. It is suggested that the same user be given rights to the queue object as the SMS group object.

▶ · ◀

F I G U R E 8.4

The SMS Queue Manager configuration screen

If everything is entered correctly, the configuration screen disappears and a console message similar to the following is displayed:

```
Started service the job queue .CN=NETWARE5-A Backup Job
Queue.OU=toronto.O=dreamlan

Using transfer buffer size 65536 bytes.
```

Also, the previous steps create a new SYS:ETC\SMS\SBACKUP.CFG configuration file that looks similar to this:

```
# This is QMANAGER Configuration file

# Lines beginning with # are treated as comment.

# QMAN.NLM reads the information from this file when
loaded

Sbackup Job Queue: .CN=NETWARE5-A Backup Job
Queue.OU=toronto.O=dreamlan

# Default Transfer buffer size

# Transfer Buffer Size: 64000
```

Now you're ready to run SBackup.

Backing Up NDS

In NetWare 5, the SBackup NLM has been renamed to SBCON.NLM (NetWare Storage Management Console) and has a slightly different look than previous versions of SBackup (see Figure 8.5). The main difference is the Job Administration option, which enables you to create, submit, and administrate jobs in an NDS queue.

WARNING

You should be aware that NDS partition boundary information is not backed up; therefore, you should keep a written record of your NDS tree partition placement. If no partition information exists when a restore is performed (for instance, after a total loss of an NDS tree), the entire tree structure is placed into one partition ([Root]). You must then manually recreate the partitions and replicas.

The following steps outline how you can use SBCon to back up your NDS tree (it is assumed that you have already correctly installed and configured your tape device):

1. Load TSANDS.NLM on one of your NetWare 5 servers. (SMDR be auto-loaded if not already loaded.)

For best performance, you should load TSANDS.NLM and SBCON.NLM on the server holding the most replicas. This reduces the amount of tree-walking required during the backing up of the whole NDS tree.

TIP

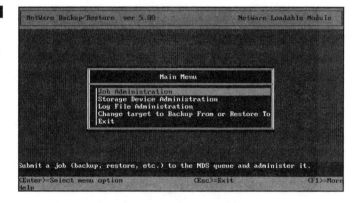

F I G U R E 8.5

The version of SBackup shipped with NetWare 5 is now called the NetWare Storage Management Console (SBCon).

If you see the "SMDR Group Context is invalid" message displayed when SMDR is loading, this means you have not completely configured the SMDR object. Refer to the previous section, "Configuring SMDR and QMAN," to (re)configure SMDR.

NOTE

2. On the server with the tape device, load QMAN.NLM and then load SBCON.NLM.

3. From the Main Menu, select Storage Device Administration.

4. From the Select a Device menu, highlight the device you wish to use (see Figure 8.6). If the device is an autoloader, press Enter to display a list of loaded media.

TIP

If SBCon can't communicate with the tape drive, or if the console List Devices command shows the device in an Unbound state, ensure NWTAPE.CDM is loaded. If the LIST DEVICES console command sees the tape device properly, but SBCon does not recognize the device, it's possible that SBCon does not support the tape device. A list of SBCon-supported tape devices can be found in Table 8.1.

5. Highlight the media you wish to use and press Enter to select it.

6. Press Esc to return to the Main Menu.

FIGURE 8.6

Select the backup device and media using the Select a Device menu.

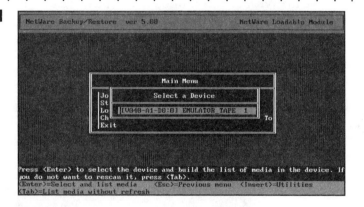

NOTE

Steps three through six are not absolutely necessary; however, these steps do help you to ascertain if the job will be able to access the tape device or not before you submit the job.

7. Select Job Administration.

8. Select Backup from the Select Job menu.

9. Use the Target Service option of the Backup Options menu (see Figure 8.7) to select the target server. If the selected target server has multiple TSAs, such as TSANDS and TSA500, running, you also need to select the appropriate service. The name of the NDS service is SERVER NAME. Novell Directory (for example, NETWARE5-A.Novell Directory).

10. You're then prompted for a username and password that has sufficient NDS rights to back up the tree; use the .username.org naming syntax. Upon successful login, a message similar to "You are connected to target service . . . <Press ENTER to continue>" is displayed. In the Target Service option, you'll now see the NDS tree name listed.

11. Use the What to Back Up? option if you're backing up the whole Directory tree, the schema, objects, or a branch of the tree (see Figure 8.8). After selecting the option, the List Resources menu is displayed.

▶ . . . . ◀

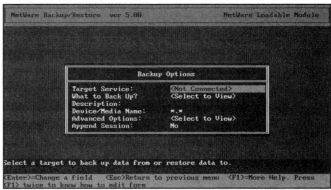

FIGURE 8.7

Use the Backup Options menu to select your targets and configure backup options.

▶ · ◀

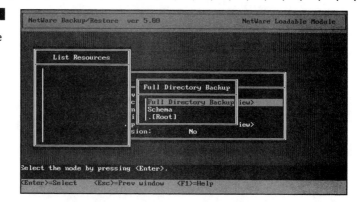

FIGURE 8.8

You can back up the whole tree, the schema, the selected objects, or the selected branches of the tree.

12. Press Insert to bring up a list of NDS resources that you can select for backup. To back up the schema, for example, highlight Schema in the Full Directory Backup menu, press Enter and the Schema menu is displayed; you'll see "[..]" in the menu. Press Esc and the word *Schema* is now shown in the List Resources menu indicating it will be backed up.

NOTE

Selecting Full Directory Backup will back up all objects in the tree, including schema. Selecting SYS volume backup will also back up Server Specific Information (SSI) data, which is important when restoring a crashed server (see the section "Creating Server Specific Information Data" for more details.)

TIP

To make it easier to back up portions of the NDS tree, you can create a TSANDS.CFG file, which enables you to specify the names of containers where you want backups to begin. TSANDS.CFG is simply a text file that contains a list of NDS contexts (one per line). It is to be placed in the SYS:SYSTEM\TSA directory on the server that TSANDS.NLM is loaded on. With this file present, SBackup lists the additional contexts as available resources that you can select for backup. Note that not all backup programs support the additional resources made available by TSANDS.CFG.

13. Repeat Step 12 to select any other NDS resources you want to back up.

14. Enter a description (up to 23 characters), such as NETWARE 5 tree backup, in the Description field.

15. Use the Device/Media Name field to select the tape device that will be used.

16. Use the Advanced Backup Options menu to schedule when the job will run (see Figure 8.9) and to designate if it's a repeating job (see Figure 8.10).

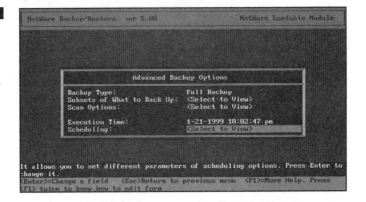

Use the Advanced Backup Options menu to further control what data to back up and to schedule the job.

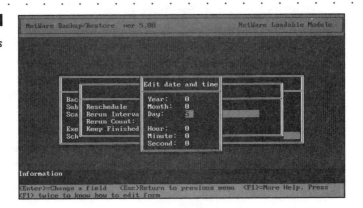

You can schedule the job as a run-once or as a recurring job.

17. Finally, use the Append Session option to specify if the data on the tape is to be appended or overwritten.

18. Press Esc and select Yes in response to the Do you want to submit a job? prompt. You're then returned to the Select Job menu.

TABLE 8.1

List of Tape Device Architectures Supported by SBCon

VENDOR	TAPE DEVICE ARCHITECTURES
Archive	ANCDA $\frac{1}{4}$ inch, PYTHON DAT, IBM4326 DAT, VIPER 150 $\frac{1}{4}$ inch, VIPER 2525 $\frac{1}{4}$ inch
Cipher	T826S DLT, T860S DLT
Compaq	15–30 GB DLT, 4–8 GB DAT, 2–8 GB DAT, 2–4 GB DAT
Conner	CTMS 3200 $\frac{1}{4}$ inch, CTT8000-S $\frac{1}{4}$ inch
DEC	DLT2000, TLZ06 DLT, TZ89 DLT
Exabyte	CTS-8510 8mm, EXB-8500 8mm, EXB8500C 8mm, EXB-8505 8mm, IBM-8505 8mm
HP	C1533A DAT, C1537A DAT, C5683A DAT, C1553A DAT Magazine, C1557A DAT Magazine, C5713A DAT Magazine, HP35450A DAT, HP35470A DAT, HP35480A DAT
Quantum	DLT4000 DLT
Seagate	AIT AIT, AIT-LDR AIT Magazine, DAT 02779, DAT 04106, STT8000 $\frac{1}{4}$ inch
Sony	SDT-1000 DAT, SDT-4000 DAT, SDT-5000 DAT, SDT-9000 DAT, SDX-300 AIT, TSL-A300C AIT Magazine
Tandberg	MLR1 $\frac{1}{4}$ inch, MLR3 $\frac{1}{4}$ inch, SLR5 4–8 GB $\frac{1}{4}$ inch, SLR6 $\frac{1}{4}$ inch, TDC 3800 $\frac{1}{4}$ inch, TDC 4100 $\frac{1}{4}$ inch, TDC 4120 $\frac{1}{4}$ inch, TDC 4200 $\frac{1}{4}$ inch, TDC 4220 $\frac{1}{4}$ inch, TDC 4222 $\frac{1}{4}$ inch
WangDat	1300 DAT, 3100 DAT, 3200 DAT, 3400DX DAT
Wangtek	5150ES $\frac{1}{4}$ inch, 5525ES $\frac{1}{4}$ inch, 6130 DAT, 9500 $\frac{1}{4}$ inch

The HP C1556B has been found to work with SBCon and NWTAPE.CDM but is not yet certified by Novell.

The job will execute automatically at the scheduled time. You can use the Current Job List option to manage the submitted jobs: from the Main Menu, select Job Administration ⇨ Current Job List. A list of queued jobs is displayed in the Queue Job menu. Similar to managing print jobs, you can put a backup job on hold and change its execution time and scheduling (see Figure 8.11).

You can monitor the runtime status of an executing job by first highlighting the job in the Queue Job menu and then pressing Insert. A real-time display similar to the one you're familiar with in previous versions of SBackup is shown (see Figure 8.12). From this menu, you can delete or stop the job by pressing Delete.

▶ . . . . ◀

F I G U R E   8.11

Use the Current Job List to manage submitted SBackup jobs.

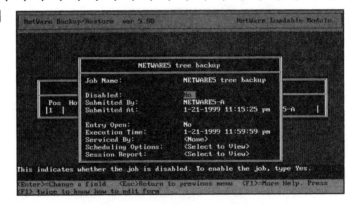

You can also check the execution status of a job using SBCon's status screen. SBCon creates two NLM screens; one is the user menu screen and the other a SMS Activity Log screen (see Figure 8.13). The information displayed in the SMS Activity Log screen is available for review at a later time, because it is recorded in the SYS:SYSTEM\TSA\LOG\ACTIVITY.LOG file. Alternatively, you can use SBCon's log files to determine what resources were backed up and if there were any errors. You can access the run log from the main menu: Log File Administration ⇨ View a log file; to access the error log, use Log File Administration ⇨ View an error file. By default, these files are stored in the SYS:SYSTEM\TSA\LOG directory.

FIGURE 8.12

Real-time status of a
currently executing job

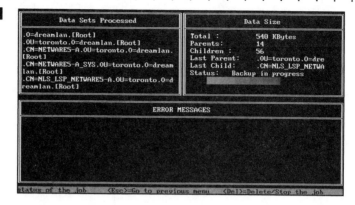

FIGURE 8.13

QMAN reports the success
or failure of a given job
using the SMS Activity Log
screen.

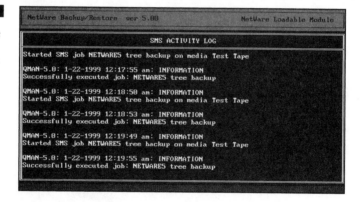

**SME.NLM is autoloaded when the backup job starts and is unloaded
after the job finishes.**

NOTE

Using NWBACK32

If you prefer to work using a GUI instead of the text-based menu of SBCON, you
can use NWBACK32.EXE instead; it is located in the SYS:PUBLIC directory. This
32-bit application runs on both Windows 9x and Windows NT workstations. The
following steps outline how you can use NWBACK32 to back up your NDS tree:

I. Start NWBack32 from the SYS:PUBLIC directory. The first time you run NWBackup you'll be asked to select the NDS tree and the SMDR context settings (see Figure 8.14).

2. Select Backup from the Quick Access dialog box (see Figure 8.15).

▶ · ◀

FIGURE 8.14

The first time you run NWBack32, you need to configure the SMDR settings.

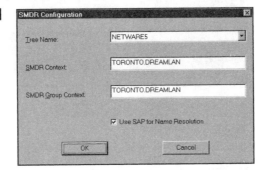

▶ · ◀

FIGURE 8.15

The Quick Access dialog box can be accessed using File ⇨ Quick Access Dialog.

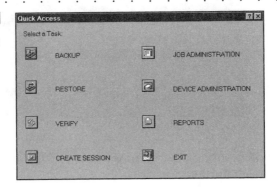

3. Double-click WHAT TO BACK UP to select the target to back up.

   a. Double-click NDS to display a list of servers running TSANDS.

   b. Double-click the desired server to display the name of the NDS tree.

4. Double-click the NDS tree name and authenticate to the server. Use the .username.org naming syntax. Upon successful server authentication, you'll have three selections (see Figure 8.16): Full Directory Backup, Schema, and [Root]. Check the resources you want to back up; to back up a branch of the tree, double-click [Root] to expand the tree before making your selection.

F I G U R E   8.16

Select the NDS resource you want to back up.

5. Double-click WHERE TO BACK UP to select the tape device.

a. Select the context. You can change the context at the toolbar using the first button on the second toolbar. If no job queues are displayed after you double-clicked on the context, click the Change Context button on the toolbar and authenticate to the tree. After successful authentication, all the queues under the context are visible. (Use the username.org naming syntax; don't specify a leading period as was the case for NDS.)

NOTE

The context specifies the starting container from which the queues will be displayed. All queue types, regardless if it's a print queue or a job queue, will be listed; therefore, you should use meaningful names for the queues.

    b. Select the queue for which QMAN is configured at the NetWare server.

    c. Right-click and then select Submit the Job. In this case, any servers you select that use the queue will service the job.

TIP

You can double-click the selected queue to expand it and show a list of servers using the queue. Then select the server on which you want to submit the job (right-click and then select Submit the Job). You can further expand the server to obtain the list of devices attached to the server (if there is more than one tape device attached). If you continue to expand the devices, the media will appear where the job is to be submitted (right-click and then select Submit the Job).

  6. Choose the backup type from the dialog box and click Next.

  7. Select the subset of what you are backing up. Here, you can specify the objects you want to include or exclude from the backup set selected earlier. Click Next to continue.

  8. Set any Filtering Options as desired and then click Next.

  9. Schedule the backup job. Click the pull-down icon to select from the calendar and click Next.

 10. Specify the rerun interval and click Next.

 11. Enter the required information (such as a description of the job) in the dialog box (see Figure 8.17) and click Finish.

▶ • ◀

F I G U R E   8 . 1 7

*The final job submission
dialog box*

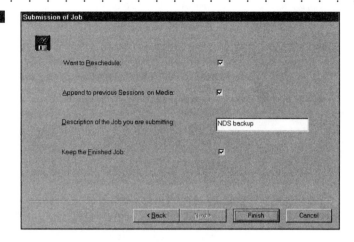

12. Click OK to confirm submission of the job.

After you have submitted the job using NWBack32, you can view the results of the verification using Dynamic Status as follows:

1. Click Job Administration.

2. Double-click the queue in which the job is getting serviced, and the list of jobs appears. The job currently active has a green icon.

3. Right-click and select Dynamic Properties. A screen appears with the results of the verified job.

Restoring NDS

The mechanics for restoring NDS using SBCon is very much similar to that of the backing up of NDS except that now your source is the tape instead of TSANDS. You can restore a single object, a branch of the tree, or the whole Directory tree. The following steps outline how you use SBCon to restore your NDS (we assume that you have already correctly installed and configured your tape device):

1. Load TSANDS.NLM on one of your NetWare 5 servers. (SMDR will be auto-loaded if not already loaded.)

2. On the server with the tape device, load QMAN.NLM and then load SBCON.NLM.

3. Select Job Administration.

4. Select Restore from the Select Job menu to bring up the Restore Options menu (see Figure 8.18).

5. Select the Target Service to select the server to which you wish to restore NDS. Press Enter to bring up a list of servers running TSAs. If the selected server has multiple TSAs running, such as TSANDS and TSA500, you also need to select the appropriate service. The name of the NDS service is SERVER NAME.Novell Directory (for example, NETWARE5-A.Novell Directory).

6. You're then prompted for a username and password that has sufficient NDS rights to the tree; use the .username.org naming syntax. Upon successful login, a message similar to "You are connected to target service . . . <Press ENTER to continue>" is displayed. In the Target Service option, you'll now see the NDS tree name listed.

▶ • ◀

F I G U R E 8.18

Configure your restore options using this menu.

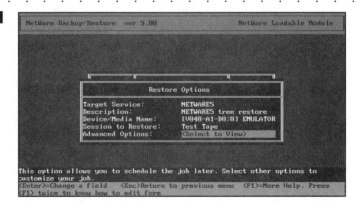

7. Enter a description to identify the job in the Description field.

8. Select the device and media on which NDS data is stored.

9. Select the correct session on the media containing the NDS data that you wish to restore.

10. Use Advanced Options to set any filters desired in restoring the NDS, if any existing objects should be overwritten, and configure the execution time and run schedules (see Figure 8.19).

WARNING

You should be careful when choosing the overwrite option, because any recent NDS-related changes (this does not include file system trustee assignments, because they are not stored in NDS) to the object, including password, will revert back to whatever they were at the time of the backup.

11. Press Esc and then select Yes in response to the Do you want to submit a job? prompt. You're then returned to the Select Job menu.

As previously mentioned, your job will execute automatically at the scheduled time. You can manage and monitor your restore jobs through the Current Job List option.

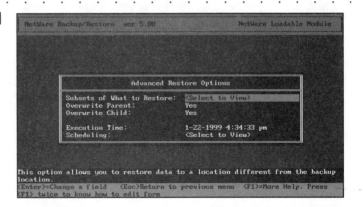

FIGURE 8.19

The Advanced Restore Options menu

Backing Up and Restoring Schema Extensions

During an NDS backup, the TSANDS.NLM sends every object — those defined by both native (base) and extended schemas — to the backup program for back up; however, versions of TSANDS.NLM prior to v4.14 do not send the definitions of the object types you have added to the NDS database; consequently, the resulting backup of NDS contains information for objects defined in an extended schema, but *not* the extended schema data that defined those objects. This means that before you restore these NDS objects, you have to first re-extend the schema so that the definitions for extended objects would exist in the tree during the restore; otherwise, NDS would contain restored objects that it didn't know how to use and would display them as Unknown objects.

The version of TSANDS.NLM shipped with NetWare 4.11 and NetWare 5, and the updated TSANDS.NLM included in SMSUP6.EXE (or higher) for NetWare 4.10, backs up and restores any schema extensions by default. You no longer have to re-extend the schema before NDS can recognize restored objects defined by an extended schema.

Third Party SMS-Compliant Backup Solutions

Other than SBCon from Novell, there are a number of third party SMS-compliant tape backup solutions available for NetWare 5. The following are some of the more popular choices:

- **Seagate Backup Exec for NetWare** Version 8. Seagate's Backup Exec is the first NetWare 5-certified data protection solution. Because NetWare 5 can be configured to run in a pure IP environment, Backup Exec for NetWare Version 8 fully supports IP and IPX protocols, ensuring your data protection no matter how you configure the network. As a fully SMS-compliant backup application, Backup Exec protects any size Novell Storage Services (NSS) volume by utilizing Novell (or Seagate Software-developed) Target Service Agents — even terabyte size volumes. In addition, Backup Exec's NDS protection includes all objects, containers, and extended schema, plus additional client network information that has been added in NetWare 5. For more information about Seagate Backup Exec for NetWare, visit http://www.seagatesoftware.com/benw/.

▸ **ARCserveIT 6.6 for NetWare**, from Cheyenne/Computer Associates, is an enterprise-wide storage management software product that enables you to back up and restore data on NetWare servers and all workstations attached to those servers. Similar to Backup Exec, ARCserveIT is a fully SMS-compliant backup solution that supports NSS volumes and works over both IPX and IP. For more information about ARCserveIT 6.6 for NetWare, visit `http://www.cai.com/arcserveit/`.

WARNING

ARCserve 6.x is not certified for NetWare 5 and can ABEND your NetWare 5 server; note the difference between ARCserve and ARCserveIT.

▸ **Tivoli Storage Management** (formerly **ADSTAR Distributed Storage Manager;** ADSM) Ver. 3 Release 1 Lev 0.6. If you have a mainframe, you may want to consider IBM's ADSM as a possible enterprise storage management solution for your NetWare network. ADSM provides automated, unattended backup and long-term data archives. ADSM uses Novell's SMS to enable the backup and restoration of NetWare servers and NDS over the LAN to a variety of hosts, including AIX, MVS, OS/2, VM, Windows NT, Sun Solaris, HP-UX, AS/400, and VSE/ESA. In addition to the support for IPX/SPX and TCP/IP, ADSM hosts can also communicate with NetWare servers using APPC (LU6.2), through NetWare for SAA gateway servers. For more information about ADSM, visit `http://www.storage.ibm.com/software/adsm/`.

WARNING

ADSM versions prior to Ver. 3 Release 1 Lev 0.6 are *not* NetWare 5-certified.

From our experience, the major data backup solutions players for the Intel platform are ARCserve and Backup Exec; many large sites that have mainframes use a combination of ARCserve and Backup Exec along with ASDM or similar mainframe-based backup solutions for their enterprise-wide backup strategies. For a complete and up-to-date list of Novell-certified SMS-compliant backup solutions, consult Novell's YES! Bulletin listings at `http://developer.novell.com/npp`.

Importing User Objects with UIMPORT

UIMPORT (User Import) is a Novell-supplied utility shipped with NetWare 4 and NetWare 5. Its function is the same as the MakeUser application included with NetWare 2 and NetWare 3 — to create users in a batch mode. Even though UIMPORT may also be used to update various User object attributes, not many administrators have considered using UIMPORT as a data recovery tool when NDS data, such as Location information, for User objects is lost.

How UIMPORT Works

UIMPORT uses two text files for input: a control file containing keywords that specify how the objects are to be created and how the data file is formatted and an ASCII data file containing user object information. Table 8.2 is a list of valid keywords and their default values.

TIP

DS changes from NetWare 4.10 to 4.11 (and NetWare 5) included a change for the user template. In NetWare 4.10, the user template was simply a user object called USER_TEMPLATE; in NetWare 4.11 and higher, it is a separate object (of the Template class) and you can have multiple User Templates in a container, whereas in NetWare 4.10 you could only have one. Unfortunately, UIMPORT was not updated to include the new template class, therefore the Template option does not work for UIMPORT, but you can still create a User object called USER_TEMPLATE and UIMPORT will take settings from it when creating new users.

TABLE 8.2

Valid UIMPORT Keywords and Their Settings

KEYWORD	DEFAULT SETTING	ALLOWED SETTINGS	DESCRIPTION
CREATE HOME DIRECTORY	N	Y or N	Specifies whether a home directory is created for the user.
DELETE MAILBOX DIRS	N	Y or N	Determines whether the user's current mailbox directories are deleted when you change a user's mailbox location.
DELETE PROPERTY	\<No Default\>	Any character pattern	If you wish UIMPORT to delete property values, use this option to define a DELETE PROPERTY character pattern (such as #REMOVE). Include this character pattern in your data file in the field position that corresponds to the value you want to delete.
HOME DIRECTORY PATH	\<No Default\>	Any path name	If CREATE HOME DIRECTORY is set to Y, use this to specify the directory path that the user's home directory should be created under. Enclose the path name in quotes and don't include the volume name.
HOME DIRECTORY VOLUME	\<No Default\>	Any volume name	If CREATE HOME DIRECTORY is set to Y, use this to specify the volume that the user's home directory should be created on. Enclose the full NDS Volume object name in quotes and don't include the path name.
IMPORT MODE	B	C, B, R, or U	Specifies UIMPORT's action: C = create new user objects; B = create new user objects or update existing objects; U = update existing objects; R = remove user objects.
MAXIMUM DIRECTORY RETRIES	5	Any numeric value	Determines how many times UIMPORT tries to get the User object's ID number on a server.
NAME CONTEXT	*Current context*	Any context name	Specifies the Directory tree context that you want the new User objects to be created in, or where UIMPORT is to locate the objects to be updated. Enclose the full context in quotes.

Continued

T A B L E 8 . 2

Valid UIMPORT Keywords and Their Settings (continued)

KEYWORD	DEFAULT SETTING	ALLOWED SETTINGS	DESCRIPTION
QUOTE	"	Any character	UIMPORT requires that field data be enclosed in quotation marks if it contains embedded spaces, tabs, or carriage returns. You can, however, specify a different character in place of the quotation mark.
REPLACE VALUE	N	Y or N	Determines whether the values that you specify in the data file replace existing values in the NDS. If the attribute is multivalued, setting this option to N will append the new value to the list or else it will overwrite the existing values.
SEPARATOR	,	Any character	By default, field values must be separated by commas. Use this option to specify an alternate separator character.
USER TEMPLATE	N	Y or N	Specifies whether UIMPORT should use the settings of the User Template object when creating User objects.

The following User object attributes are supported by UIMPORT. Note that Name and Last Name are mandatory User attributes while the rest are optional. Also note that the UIMPORT keywords and attributes are not case-sensitive.

Name	Last Name
Account Balance	Account Disabled
Account Has Expiration Date	Allow Unlimited Credit
Allow User to Change Password	City
Date Password Expires	Days Between Forced Changes
Default Server	Department
Description	Email Address
Fax Number	Facsimile Telephone Number
Full Name	Foreign Email Address
Foreign Email Alias	Generational Qualifier
Given Name	Grace Logins Allowed
Group Membership	Home Directory
Initials	Location
Language	Login Disabled
Login Expiration Time	Login Grace Limit
Login Grace Remaining	Login Maximum Simultaneous
Login Script	Low Balance Limit
Mailbox ID	Mailbox Location
Mailing Label Information	Maximum Connections
Middle Initial	Minimum Account Balance
Minimum Password Length	Other Names
Password	Password Allow Change
Password Expiration Interval	Password Expiration Time
Password Minimum Length	Password Required
Password Unique Required	Postal Address
Postal (Zip) Code	Post Office Box
Profile Remaining Grace Logins	Require a Password
Require Unique Passwords	Security Equal to
Security Equals	See Also
State or Province	Street Address
Skip	Telephone
Telephone Number	Title
Volume Restrictions	

UIMPORT can't be used to change a user's password.

NOTE

The following is a sample control file for UIMPORT, using the keywords listed in Table 8.2 and some of the available attributes.

```
IMPORT CONTROL

    CREATE HOME DIRECTORY = Y

    DELETE PROPERTY = #REMOVE

    HOME DIRECTORY PATH = "\USERS"

    HOME DIRECTORY VOLUME = "NETWARE5-
B_VOL1.TORONTO.ACME_COMPANY"

    IMPORT MODE = C

    NAME CONTEXT = "TORONTO.ACME_COMPANY"

    QUOTE = '

    REPLACE VALUE = N

    SEPARATOR = ;

    USER TEMPLATE = N

FIELDS

    NAME

    LAST NAME

    GROUP MEMBERSHIP

    PASSWORD REQUIRED

    MINIMUM PASSWORD LENGTH

    PASSWORD EXPIRATION INTERVAL
```

Note that the IMPORT CONTROL and FIELD headings are required. The following is a sample data file that corresponds to the previous control file specifications:

```
Peter; Kuo; Admin.Toronto.ACME_Company; y; 6; 45

Jim; Henderson; Admin.SLC.ACME_Company; y; 12; 45

Test1; 'Test User #1'; Staff.Toronto.ACME_COMPANY; y; 6; 90

Test2; 'Test User #2'; Staff.SLC.ACME_COMPANY; y; 6; 90
```

After building the control and data files, run UIMPORT as follows:

```
uimport demo.ctl demo.dat
```

You should have at least 500K of free memory for UIMPORT to run correctly.

Using UIMPORT to Recover Lost NDS Data

This section explains how UIMPORT can be used to recover lost NDS information. When a volume is deleted and then later recreated, and the data restored from backup, all information is restored but the volume ID is changed; consequently, the users still have file system rights to their home directory, but in NW Admin under the environment tab for the user, the home directory path is not listed. This is because the HOME_DIRECTORY attribute is tied to the volume object ID, and when the old ID is lost or changed, the HOME_DIRECTORY attribute's value is cleared.

If you're not using this attribute, there's nothing to worry about; however, often times, administrators use this to map a user's home directory in the login script:

```
MAP H:=%HOME_DIRECTORY
```

Losing this information is a major issue. You have a number of options when this happens. You can manually reset the HOME_DIRECTORY setting for each user, one at a time, or you can use UIMPORT and the method following to add the value back for the user:

1. Create a UIMPORT control file (for example, CONTROL.CTL) with the following settings:

```
Import control

    Name context=container_name

    User template=n
```

```
        Create home directory=n

        Import Mode = U

    Fields

        name

        last name

        home directory
```

2. Create a data file (*for example,* DATA.DAT) with the users' Login Name, Last Name, and home directory path information in it; the Login Name and Last Name fields are mandatory. The following are examples:

```
Peter, Kuo, Server1_VOL1.Toronto.ACME_Company:users\peter

Jim, Henderson, Server1_VOL1.Toronto.ACME_Company:users\jim
```

3. Execute UIMPORT, using CONTROL.CTL and DATA.DAT (*for example,* UIMPORT CONTROL.CTL DATA.DAT), to update the Home Directory attribute for the users.

When you need to repopulate the Home Directory field for many users, it can be quite time consuming and subject to human error. In Chapter 10 you'll find an AWK script that will help you to create this data file quickly and error free.

TIP

If you plan to use UIMPORT on a regular basis, create a data template file containing, on each line, the username and its last name using the following as an example:

```
Peter, Kuo, *****

Jim, Henderson, *****

Kim, Groneman, *****
```

Using a text editor you can easily make global changes to the file for whatever your UIMPORT needs are. For example, by globally replacing ***** for *English, Server1.Toronto.ACME_Company* you create a data file for populating or changing Language and Default Server settings.

Importing and Exporting Object Information

UIMPORT is a great tool for creating and making changes to User objects in batch mode; however, its strength is also its limitation — UIMPORT can only deal with Users and not with other NDS object types. If you need a batch alternative to the NWADMIN and NETADMIN utilities for creating and administrating NDS objects of any type, OImport can help you.

OImport enables you to create, update, or delete any object contained in a NetWare 4 and NetWare 5 NDS tree via a text file. Following is a summary of OImport features:

▶ Create, update, and delete any NDS object, including nonstandard NDS objects created by third-party NDS-aware applications.

▶ Use special import rules to create sequence (order) in which objects will be created in the tree.

NOTE

NDS objects are interdependent and great care must be taken to create objects in the proper sequence. For example, a container must be created before the leaf objects it will contain (hierarchical relation); a NCP server must be created before its volumes (server-device relation); an Alias must be created after its aliased object (shadow relation) and so on. OImport has a set of built-in rules to handle these relations. An optional rule file can be created to modify or update the built-in rules to change the import sequence.

▶ Use rules to create *class filters*. From a large input file, you may wish to import only a specific type of objects (according to their class).

▶ Use rules to create *attribute filters*. An object has a set of attributes, from which you may want only some of them to be imported. You can create global attribute filters (the Description attribute will not be imported for any object having this attribute) or class specific attribute filters (the Description attribute will not be imported for objects of class NCP Server, Organization, and Queue but will be imported for all other classes.)

▸ Create *cross reference rules*. A cross reference rule lets you automatically create one attribute in an object A referenced by an attribute of an object B being created, even when A does not yet exist at the time B is created. For example, when creating User object Peter, you can set OImport to create a reference to Peter in Group object Sales, even if the Group object does not exist.

▸ Generate an NDS schema description file for reference.

▸ Import login script files from a global script database. Rather than creating a separate file for each login script you want to import, you can store all the scripts in the same text file. OImport will extract the script of your choice for each object (Users, Profiles, and OUs) you want to create in the NDS tree.

▸ Import binary data. Object attributes such as Print Job Configuration or Printer Control are stream attributes (a series of data bytes).

▸ Create User passwords.

▸ Create file system rights (trustees) for any object.

The following is a sample OImport data file that accomplishes the same function (while also assigning user passwords) as the UIMPORT example presented earlier in this chapter:

```
[User=Peter, CREATE, ".OU=Toronto.O=ACME_Company"]

Surname=Kuo

!Password=HELLO

Group Membership=Admin.Toronto.ACME_Company

Password Required=1

Password Minimum Length=6

Password Expiration Interval=45 0 0 0

#

[User=Jim, CREATE, ".OU=Toronto.O=ACME_Company"]
```

```
Surname=Henderson

!Password=HELLO

Group Membership=Admin.SLC.ACME_Company

Password Required=1

Password Minimum Length=6

Password Expiration Interval=45 0 0 0

#

[User=Tes1, CREATE, ".OU=Toronto.O=ACME_Company"]

Surname=Test User #1

!Password=HELLO

Group Membership=Staff.Toronto.ACME_Company

Password Required=1

Password Minimum Length=6

Password Expiration Interval=90 0 0 0

#

[User=Test2, CREATE, ".OU=Toronto.O=ACME_Company"]

Surname=Test User #2

!Password=HELLO

Group Membership=Staff.SLC.ACME_Company

Password Required=1

Password Minimum Length=6

Password Expiration Interval=90 0 0 0
```

The Password Expiration Interval is given in *#-of-days #-of-hours #-of-minutes #-of-seconds*; 45 days is given as 45 0 0 0. The Password Required attribute is a Boolean field, so a 1 corresponds to True.

NOTE

OImport has a companion utility called OExport. Using OExport, you can export NDS object information into a text file that can be later read by OImport. In Chapters 13 and 14 you'll find out more on how to use OExport and OImport to manage your NDS tree.

NOTE The OImport and OExport utilities are being developed by Novell Consulting Services. For the latest product and pricing information, see `http://consulting.novell.com/products/oimport/index.html`.

Third-Party Utilities

As NDS and NDS software development tools have been available for many years, a number of third-party NDS-specific utilities are available to help you manage your NDS trees more easily and effectively as well as to recover lost NDS data. The following sections introduce you to some third party tools that can help you to recover lost NDS data, and, in Chapter 13, you'll find a discussion of some third-party NDS management applications.

Recovering Lost Passwords

It is not uncommon to forget a password, especially one that's considered to be a good, secure password. What can you do if the Admin password is lost, either due to human error or NDS data corruption? If you have a backup Admin user that has Write rights to Admin's Access Control List (ACL) attribute then you can simply use it to reset Admin's password. What if you don't have a user that can reset Admin's password? There are a few solutions that you can try.

TIP It is generally recommended that a password should not be a common (single) word that is easily guessed; however, instead of using a meaningless word for your password, such as *435ggerpwe*, combine a few meaningful (thus easily remembered) words together into a password, such as *try2guessthispassword*.

The first technique is to make use of Bindery Services. If you have a server that holds a writable replica (Master or Read/Write) of the partition containing the Admin object, you can use one of the two following methods:

▸ Log into that server using the bindery Supervisor id, and use SYSCON to change Admin's password. (You can download a copy of SYSCON from Novell's Consulting site at `http://consulting.novell.com/toolkit/iw_tools.html`.)

▸ If you don't know the bindery Supervisor's password, you can use one of the NLM tools (such as SetPwd), available on the Internet, to reset the Admin password.

WARNING

There are NLMs easily available on the Internet that can be used to change Admin's password. Because these NLMs require server console access, you need to take appropriate steps and care to secure your server console from both physical and remote (*for example*, RConsole) unauthorized access. Third party utilities, such as DreamLAN Network Consulting's SSLock for NDS and Protocom Development Systems' SecureConsole can enhance your server console security. See Chapter 15 for additional information.

If you don't have a server that holds a writable replica (Master or Read/Write) of the partition containing the Admin object, you can consider the following solutions instead:

▸ Open an incident call with Novell Technical Support (consult `http://support.novell.com/additional/telephone.htm` for a list of telephone numbers for your region). After verifying your serial number and completing nondisclosure agreements, NTS will provide you with a single-use NLM that can reset passwords in NDS mode.

▸ DreamLAN Networking Consulting has a DSPass NLM that can reset an NDS User object password without Bindery Services or reset a bindery password if Bindery Services is enabled. Visit `http://www.dreamlan.com/dspass.htm` for more information.

Recovering a Lost Admin User

If you have administered NetWare networks prior to NetWare 4.0, you'd likely know that the user Supervisor can't be deleted (at least not by accident and not through standard management tools such as Syscon); however, with NetWare 4 and higher it is possible for you to (accidentally) remove the Admin user and leave yourself with an unmanageable NDS tree! Chapter 15 contains information on how to safeguard your administrative accounts so you'll never have an unmanageable tree. In the unpleasant event that you've lost your Admin user, here are some solutions:

▶ If it is a single-server test tree or a tree that can easily be recreated, you can use the following steps to recreate a new Admin user:

1. Remove NDS by loading the NWConfig or Install NLM with the -DSREMOVE command-line switch (for example, LOAD NWCONFIG -DSREMOVE).

2. Select Directory Options.

3. Select Remove Directory Services from the server.

4. Press Enter after reading the warning message.

5. Select Yes to the Remove Directory Services? prompt.

6. Press Esc when prompted for the Admin user and password.

7. Select Yes to the Remove the Directory without logging in recommended? prompt.

8. After the NDS has been removed, exit NWConfig then reload NWConfig without the -DSREMOVE switch.

9. Use the Directory Options to reinstall NDS. You'll be asked to create the Admin user.

WARNING

These steps described will destroy your current NDS tree! The file system will not be touched, however.

▸ Open an incident call with Novell Technical Support (visit `http://support.novell.com/additional/telephone.htm` for a list of telephone numbers for your region). After verifying your serial number and completing nondisclosure agreements, NTS will provide you with a single-use NLM that can create a user with Supervisor rights to [Root]and, thus, admin rights to your tree.

▸ DreamLAN Networking Consulting has a MakeSU (Make SuperUser) NLM that can create an NDS User object that has Supervisor rights to [Root]. Visit `http://www.dreamlan.com/makesu.htm` for more information.

Unlike the first option, the last two options will create an Admin user in a nondestructive manner.

Detecting and Gaining Access to IRF-Blocked Objects

Similar to NetWare file system's Inheritance Rights Filters (IRFs), NDS administrators can apply IRFs to NDS objects so they are not accessible by other users except those that have trustee assignments. The one main difference between file system IRFs and NDS IRFs is that you can use an IRF to block Supervisor access to NDS objects while you can't do this in file systems; therefore, it is not uncommon for security-conscious NDS administrators to protect administrative accounts, such as Admin and admin-equivalent user objects, using IRFs. For details on how to protect NDS objects from tampering, see Chapter 15. The following section deals with what to do if you need access to IRF-blocked objects.

IRF-blocked objects can be categorized into three types: visible but unmanageable (you can't delete or modify them), invisible but manageable, and invisible and unmanageable. The invisible objects are generally referred to as *stealth* objects. You can't see stealth objects easily using the standard management utilities, such as NWAdmin, because the IRF blocked the Browse right to the object. They can be detected, however, using certain techniques (if they leave a "footprint" via ACL assignments, for example) and using specialized utilities. You'll find a discussion of one of the utilities, Hidden Object Locator from Novell Consulting, in Chapter 14.

NOTE

Another stealth object detector is the **NDSTree utility, available from DreamLAN Network Consulting. For more information, see** http://www.dreamlan.com/ndstree.htm.

Once the unmanageable object names are determined, you can regain access to them using one of the following methods:

▶ Open an incident call with Novell Technical Support. After verifying your serial number and completing nondisclosure agreements, NTS will provide you with a single-use NLM that can create a user with full NDS rights to the stealth or unmanageable object, giving you admin rights (including Browse so you can see it) to this object.

▶ The MakeSU NLM from DreamLAN Network Consulting can also be used to create an NDS User object or grant an existing user object full NDS right to the stealth or unmanageable object.

Creating Server-Specific Information Data

In NetWare 4.11, Novell introduced some enhancements to TSA modules to provide more efficient backup and restore capabilities for NDS, as well as more efficient server recovery after a failure. In a network environment, the most likely failure scenario is the loss of a single server or its hard drive. To simplify the complex recovery procedure necessary in previous versions of NetWare, the new enhancements made to the file system TSA module (TSA410.NLM for NetWare 4.1x) helped to facilitate server recovery in this scenario; the same improvements are carried into TSA500.NLM for NetWare 5.

NOTE

For NetWare 4.10, you need to use TSA410.NLM dated July 23, 1996, or later (*for example,* v4.14 or higher) to receive the same functionality as the version of TSA410.NLM shipped with NetWare 4.11. The updated TSA410 can be found in SMSUP6.EXE (or newer) available from the Novell Support Connection Web site at http://support.novell.com.

The enhanced file system TSA provides a new major SMS resource called *Server Specific Info* (SSI), which appears in the list of Resources displayed by SMS-based backup applications, along with the SYS volume and other mounted volumes (see

Figure 8.20). The Server Specific Info resource should be backed up on a regular basis as it plays an important role in server recovery. Selecting Server Specific Info stores critical server information into five files that can later be used for recovery purposes:

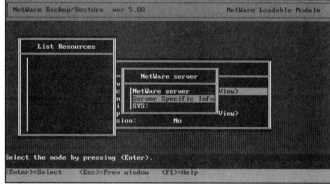

F I G U R E   8 . 2 0

The Server Specific Info resource

▸ **SERVDATA.NDS**. This (binary) file contains server-specific NDS information, such as the schema information and server-centric object IDs. The information is used by Install/NWConfig to recover from a SYS volume drive failure. You'll find out in Chapter 11 how to use this file to recover from a SYS volume crash in a multiserver environment where replicas exist on other servers.

▸ **___DSMISC.LOG**. This is a text file containing a list of replicas, including replica types, which the backed up server held at the time of backup. It also provides a list of the other servers that were in the failed server's replica ring. Use this information to reestablish replicas on the server. The following is an example DSMISC.LOG file:

```
Sunday, January 31, 1999     8:26:56 pm

Backing up server-specific NDS data

Current partition/replica list
```

```
Partition .[Root]., current replica list:
    .NETWARE5-A.toronto.dreamlan, type master
    .NETWARE5-C.toronto.dreamlan, type read/write
```

▸ **VOLSINFO.TXT.** This text file contains needed information about the server's volumes, including name space, compression, and data migration information, at the time of backup. Use this file as a guide to recreate the lost volumes during the recovery process. The following is an example VOLSINFO.TXT file — note that the SHARED volume doesn't have compression enabled:

```
NETWARE5-A

Sunday, January 31, 1999      8:26:56 pm


SYS:
    Supported Name Spaces:
        DOS
        LONG
    Extended File Formats:
        Compression is enabled.


SHARED:
    Supported Name Spaces:
        DOS
        NFS
        LONG
```

▸ **STARTUP.NCF**. This is a copy of the server's STARTUP.NCF file.

▸ **AUTOEXEC.NCF**. This is a copy of the server's AUTOEXEC.NCF file.There are two ways to back up this SSI data using your SMS-based application: The first way is to select Server Specific Info from the list of available resources when doing a file system backup. The second way is to simply select a full file system backup of the *entire* NetWare server — the SSI data is included by default.

If your backup software doesn't show SSI as an available resource, check with the vendor before assuming that these files are being included in a full system backup.

NOTE

If your backup program doesn't support SSI, you can create the SSI files using SBackup. Use SBCon to schedule a job that executes daily (or frequently so you have up-to-date SSI files) and that backs up *and* restores the SSI data. The restore step is to create the actual SSI files on the SYS volume so your backup program can then back up these files to tape; the backup process simply creates these files in server memory and then writes to tape directly. The downside of this method is that the same tape is to be used by SBackup and your backup software, which is sometimes not possible due to formatting requirements, unless you have two tape drives on your server.

An alternative to the previous method is to use the MakeSSI NLM from DreamLAN Network Consulting. This NLM is specifically designed to create the previously mentioned SSI data files. Run the NLM just prior to your backup schedule so you can back up the SSI files to tape, ensuring you have a set of SSI files that matches the data backed up on tape. See `http://www.dreamlan.com/makessi.htm` for more information on the MakeSSI utility.

You'll find detailed procedures on how to use the SSI files when recovering from a server or SYS volume failure in Chapter 11.

Write Your Own

There are a large number of utilities available to assist you in data recovery; however, because every network is unique, you may have specific requirements that the available utilities do not address. If you have some programming background or have access to a programmer, coding your own recovery utility is an option. A wide variety of tools that interface with network services and NDS is available for your choosing. You're not limited to using the C programming language, as was the case in the past when programming for NetWare. Novell and third party vendors offer class libraries, JavaBeans, scripting languages (such as Visual Basic, JavaScript, and Perl), and C/C++ APIs to support the widest range of developer participation and opportunity. Chapter 10 offers some examples on how you can "roll your own" data recovery utilities.

Summary

This chapter covered a number of tools that can help you in protecting and recovering lost NDS information and help you restore a corrupted container login script. The following topics were discussed:

- ▶ Storage Management Services (SMS)

- ▶ Exporting data from and importing information into NDS

- ▶ Recovering lost passwords and users

- ▶ Detecting and gaining access to objects that are blocked by Inherited Rights Filters (IRFs)

- ▶ Creating Server Specific Information (SSI) data for server recovery purposes

In the next chapter you learn how to apply the various tools we have discussed up to this point in real-world situations.

## CHAPTER 9

Diagnosis and Recovery Techniques

Now that we have discussed the different tools available and the information necessary to diagnose problems with your NDS tree, we need to look at some of the different ways of using this information. In this chapter, we will look at some techniques for combining the different tools available to maximize your ability to resolve issues with your tree.

The combination of the different tools available is a powerful way to enhance your ability to diagnose problems and resolve them.

Using Diagnosis Tools with Other Diagnosis Tools

The first combination of tools we will look at is diagnosis tools with other diagnosis tools. Being able to combine information from multiple tools gives you a better idea of what is really happening. As we have discussed before, having as much information available as possible increases your chances for correctly identifying the source of a problem, and correctly identifying the source of a problem is as important as resolving the problem.

In Chapter 7, we examined a number of different tools from Novell for diagnosing problems:

- DSREPAIR

- DSTRACE

- DSVIEW

- DSDIAG

- NDS Manager

- NetWare Administrator

- Schema Manager

We also examined four tools for looking up and providing general NDS information and information on the tree:

- LogicSource for NDS

- Online and CD-ROM-based knowledgebases

- Help files

- NLIST

Individually, these tools provide a number of useful functions, but when combined, the usefulness of these tools increases significantly.

One combination of these tools that you are probably already familiar with a diagnosis tool used to determine an error condition followed by the use of an information tool to define an error message. For example, you probably have used DSREPAIR to determine that there was an error -625 in the NDS synchronization process and then used the help files, knowledgebases, LogicSource for NDS, or this book to look up what an error -625 was. This is a very simple example, but it is intuitive and something you probably do on a day-to-day basis.

Combining tools needs to become as second nature to you as using an information resource to look up an error code. When you are attempting to determine if a problem exists, it is important to look at the problem from multiple angles — and this frequently involves using multiple tools.

The diagnostic tools listed previously are good at specific things; in cases where there is overlap in functionality between the two tools — for example, between NDS Manager and DSREPAIR — using both tools to validate a problem still is recommended. Doing this enables you to see two different views of the same problem — even to the extent of giving you different views of the same error conditions.

Suppose that during a routine check of synchronization status with NDS Manager, you find a partition that is out of synchronization. You can use the features in NDS Manager to isolate the server that is having the problem and isolate the error code itself. The easiest way to do this is to switch to the list view, shown in Figure 9.1, and report synchronization status on all partitions. This gives you the ability to see errors that all servers agree exist.

F I G U R E   9.1

Checking synchronization status with NDS Manager

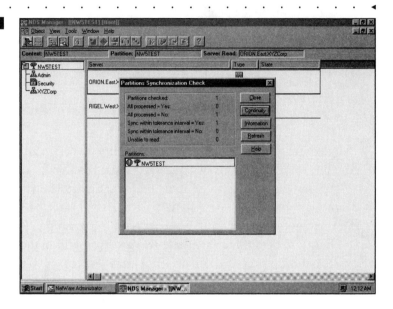

NOTE

You should recall from the discussion about NDS Manager in Chapter 7 that the Check Synchronization Status option in NDS Manager gives you a quick overview but only reads one server in each replica ring. Just because NDS Manager shows everything is running okay does not necessarily mean that synchronization is running correctly across all servers. This should be treated as a quick check diagnostic.

NDS Manager shows one partition out of synchronization — using the Partition Continuity option on the partition that is not synchronized isolates the problem to a specific server. This is shown in Figure 9.2.

Now suppose the error is something more complex than a -625 error, for example, a -694 error (ERR_ENTRY_LOST). As discussed earlier, the error type displayed is found by right-clicking the server reporting the error and selecting the information item. This is shown in Figure 9.3.

F I G U R E   9 . 2

Viewing the partition continuity screen to determine where an error is

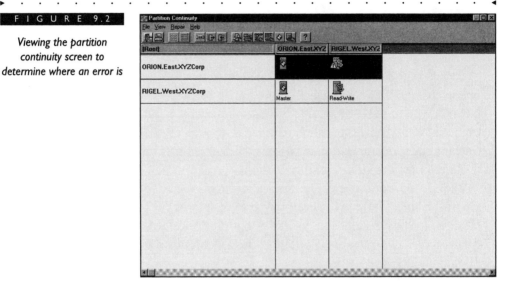

F I G U R E   9 . 3

Finding the error code in the partition continuity screen

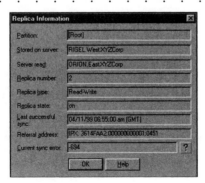

At this point, in order to isolate the object that the -694 error is being reported on, you need to switch to a different tool This can be done in two different ways:

▸ Use DSTRACE to watch the synchronization take place and observe the error.

▸ Use DSREPAIR to check the synchronization status from the server reporting the problem.

Either method is appropriate, depending on the circumstances. The first option, using DSTRACE, is not a bad choice because it's a good starting point; however, you need to know the source server — which you have already obtained from the NDS Manager partition continuity report — but DSTRACE also requires catching the synchronization in progress. If the server is low on memory, though, this option requires fewer resources on the server.

The second option, DSREPAIR, is a nonimpact way to check the status and report the object the error is occurring on. As options go, this is a very good one. Most servers have sufficient memory to load DSREPAIR, and locking the DS database files is not required to report the synchronization status on a partition. Additionally, DSREPAIR reports specifically where the problem exists and what the error code is. This is shown in Figure 9.4.

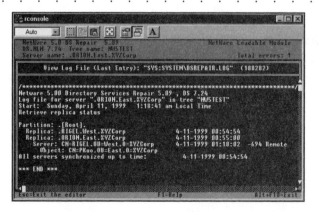

FIGURE 9.4

Report synchronization status showing a DS error during synchronization

This combination of diagnosis tools is frequently necessary to completely diagnose a problem. Remember that the better you diagnose the problem, the better your chances are for resolving the issue and returning to normal operation.

Using Recovery Tools with Other Recovery Tools

Once a problem is diagnosed, it is necessary to work towards resolution of the problem. Sometimes, though, complete recovery involves the use of multiple recovery tools, because a single tool does not have the complete capability you need to resolve the issue.

In Chapter 8, we examined a number of different recovery tools, including:

- UIMPORT

- SMS Backup and Restore

- OIMPORT and OEXPORT

In addition to these four tools, a number of the diagnosis tools listed in the previous section can be used for recovery as well:

- DSREPAIR

- DSDIAG

- NetWare Administrator

- NDS Manager

TIP

The last of these additional recovery tools — NDS Manager — does not actually contain much in repair functionality; it does, however, have the capability to launch DSREPAIRDSREPAIR remotely to perform repair operations. If you are more comfortable working with a graphical user interface (GUI), there may be a benefit for you

to perform repair operations under NDS Manager when working through a crisis situation.

You might have noticed that the recovery tools overlap significantly with the management tools—this is not accidental. By working with these tools on a day-to-day basis, you will become familiar enough with them to understand how they can help you during a recovery situation. Having a separate set of tools to work with for recovery makes life more difficult because you need to learn more; it requires knowledge on how to use the recovery tools, and puts you in a different environment only during recovery operations.

In Chapter 11, there are examples where combining recovery tools results in a faster solution than if a single recovery tool were used. Remember that in a disaster situation, once you have a diagnosis, you want to work as quickly as possible to resolve the problem.

Working with a combination of recovery tools requires a good knowledge of the tools themselves. If you do not know for certain what a tool does or how it can help in a problem resolution, you might end up using a tool that will get you most of the way to a complete resolution but will not let you finish the job. Continuing with the previous example of a -694 error in synchronization, we now know the object the synchronization is having problems with. Now we need to work to resolve the issue.

The first thing you should do is verify that the object is good on the server that holds the master replica—if it is, you can recover the object without deleting it. To check this, start by using DSREPAIR to lock the database on each server that holds a replica of the partition in question. This is done by initiating a local database repair and leaving it at the prompt at the end of the repair that asks if you want to save the database, view the log file, or abort the repair by not saving the repaired database.

Now that DSREPAIR has locked each replica of the partition, unlock the server with the master replica and examine the object with NetWare Administrator. If, on examination, the object appears to be fine, run a DSREPAIR on the server that is reporting that it lost the entry. Either an unattended full repair of the database or a repair of the local database from the advanced options menu is good. This is done to ensure the database is consistent locally.

The best way to proceed is to force an outbound synchronization of all objects. This can be most effectively done in one of two ways:

▸ Delete the partition from the server reporting the error, and recreate it when the replica ring reports that everything is done with the removal. If you have attempted a send all or receive all from NDS Manager, this option may not work because there may already be a partition operation in progress.

▸ Use the repair time stamps option. Note that this does essentially the same thing as the first option, except that it recreates the replicas on all nonmaster servers. This option issues new time stamps for everything and forces all objects to be resent to the target servers. This option also handles situations when a previously initiated partition operation cannot be aborted and the replica cannot be removed from the problem server because of a previous partition operation in progress.

NOTE

Looking over the options in NDS Manager, you may notice options that say "send all objects" or "receive all objects". These options may at first appear as if they would do what you want; however, if you attempt one of them, you will see that they only perform an outbound synchronization and may not resynchronize the object that has been reported as missing in the target replica.

Using Diagnosis Tools with Recovery Tools

In this chapter, we have discussed combining the use of diagnosis tools with recovery tools in order to resolve an issue with a -694 error in synchronization. The technique for combining diagnosis tools and recovery tools is really no different than combining any of the tools.

Using diagnosis tools and recovery tools together in the recovery phase of the troubleshooting process provides more flexibility than categorizing each of the tools and using them only during specific phases of the process. Troubleshooting is an iterative process that sometimes involves many trips through the process of examining the problem, making a change, looking at the result, and reexamining the problem to see if it has been resolved.

As with other combinations of tools, knowing the features and functionality of each tool is critical. If you are using tools that produce output or take input, knowing what the formats are and how to convert them is also a significant part of getting the tools to work together. In Chapter 11, we examine a situation that calls for the combination of NLIST and UIMPORT to recover lost group membership information.

This idea of combining tools is central to resolving critical NDS issues. Without effectively using the tools you have at hand, your troubleshooting method is more likely to be disorganized, resulting in lost time.

Bridging Techniques

In discussing how to combine tools, we have not yet touched on how to bridge the gaps between tools. In the last section, we mentioned an example in the Chapter 11 where we combine NLIST and UIMPORT to resolve an issue with lost group memberships. At first glance, these tools may not appear useful for recovery purposes: On the one hand, we have NLIST — a utility that is very powerful but clumsy to use because it has a complex command line interface and output that is intended to be human-readable. On the other hand, we have UIMPORT, a utility designed to take machine-readable input and fill values in for existing user objects or to take the data and create a new object from it.

There are a few ways to bridge utilities together. You could take the output from one, read it into a spreadsheet, and use complex formulas to extract the information you need. If the information is limited in scope, you could even use the DOS-based Edit utility and its primitive search-and-replace capability to remove excess information.

However you choose to manipulate the data, the key in bridging the different utilities is that you learn how to manipulate data using whatever tools you are comfortable with. If you are not a programmer, pick up an introductory programming book and learn how to program. The language doesn't matter; it's the programming skills that are important. You will find that the combination of programming skills along with network administration is a very strong combination that can carry you far in your understanding of how computers work.

Summary

In this chapter, we looked at a number of techniques to combine tools for troubleshooting purposes. Through various combinations of diagnosis tools and recovery tools, you can effectively handle many critical situations that may arise in your NDS implementation.

In Chapter 10, we introduce some programming concepts that can help you in a troubleshooting situation.

Programming for NDS Disaster Recovery

In previous chapters, you've learned how to apply a number of Novell-supplied and third-party NDS data recovery applications. However, because every network environment is unique in its own way, no one off-the-shelf utility will totally fulfill your requirements. If you have some basic programming background, this chapter offers you an overview of how you may develop some rather complex data recovery tools for your own network — this chapter does not discuss programming in detail.

NOTE

If you are interested in NDS programming, we suggest you take a look at *Novell's NDS Developer's Guide* (Novell Press, 1999).

awk

Programming for NDS disaster recovery need not always involve the Novell Developer Kit (NDK) or any form of NDS or NetWare API set. Some of the most effective programming techniques available are nothing more than text file manipulations. This type of manipulation is good for data conversions such as converting NList output to a format suitable for UImport to use for input.

There are several programming languages available that include text (or *string*) manipulation. BASIC, C, Pascal, and even Assembly include interfaces and libraries for performing string manipulation. One of the best languages for this sort of work, however, is a programming language called *awk*.

The awk language was developed in 1977 by Alfred Aho, Brian Kernighan, and Peter Weinberger at AT&T Bell Labs — the name of the language comes from the last initials of the three authors. The original development of awk was done in a Unix environment, and because of this, many of the concepts are familiar if you have had exposure to utilities such as grep or sed.

Awk is an interpreted scripting language; this means that there is no compiler or means to turn an awk program into a self-sufficient executable program as you would a C or Pascal program.

NOTE **The examples in this book are all interpreted using the GNU version of awk (called Gawk), available from the Free Software Foundation. The version used in this chapter is 3.0.3, available from the Simtel software repository at** `ftp://ftp.simtel.net/pub/simtelnet/ gnu/djgpp/v2gnu/gwk303d.zip.` **An updated list of sites maintaining awk source code and binaries is available from the comp.lang.awk FAQ at** `ftp://rtfm.mit.edu/pub/usenet/comp.lang.awk/faq.`

Why awk?

You may be wondering why awk is recommended for this sort of operation. There are several languages out there that are very good at text manipulations — Perl, Visual Basic, BASIC, Pascal, and even C all handle strings fairly well.

There are several reasons why awk might be a better choice for the sort of rapid development that may be necessary in a disaster situation:

▸ Awk interpreters are available for any DOS-based platform, as well as Unix platforms.

▸ Awk interpreters do not require any sort of special memory manager. Many Intel-platform Perl interpreters require a DOS extender of some sort.

▸ Awk is not a compiled language.

▸ The interpreter is very small (typically around 30K or so), and it can be put on a diskette along with a number of standard scripts for disaster recovery purposes.

▸ Unlike C or C++, awk does not require that you understand pointers when manipulating strings.

▸ The user interface is very straightforward. If you are recovering from a very serious disaster, a minimal workstation configuration can be used — DOS 6.22 with a NetWare Client installed is sufficient to start parsing NList outputs.

▶ The regular expression parsing capabilities exceed many of the capabilities of traditional programming languages such as C and Pascal.

How Does awk Work?

An awk program takes input a line at a time, parses and processes it, and produces an output file. This is usually done through command-line *pipes* or *redirection*. Normal usage involves the use of three files: an awk script, an input file, and an output file.

The awk script itself is a set of rules for processing lines of text from the input file. These rules are written using a pattern matching technique common in the Unix world called a *regular expression*, or *regex*. Regex pattern matching enables you to specify the format of a line of text in the input file; if a line matches the regex, the text is processed in a manner described by that portion of the script.

Regex pattern matching uses the basic format:

```
/pattern/
```

Where *pattern* is replaced by a string that represents an input format. Table 10.1 shows special sequences of characters that can be used in the pattern.

TABLE 10.1

Sample Regular Expressions

SAMPLE	MEANING	EXAMPLE MATCHES
/User:/	Match lines containing the case-sensitive string *User:*	User: Jim
/L* Name:/	Match lines containing a string with *L*, any other characters, and the string *Name:*	Last Name: Henderson
/[JK][iu][mo]/	Match lines containing the letter *J* or *K*, then the letter *i* or *u*, and then the letter *m* or *o*.	Jim, Kuo, Juo, Kim, Jio
/[Jj][Ii][Mm]/	Match lines containing *J* or *j*, *I* or *i*, and *M* or *m*.	Jim, jIm, Jlm, jIM
/^$/	Match blank lines	
/^Jim[0-9][0-9]/	Match lines starting with *Jim* followed by a two digit number.	Jim00, Jim01, Jim90, Jim42

For example, if you execute the command **NLIST USER SHOW Name /S /R /C > OUTPUT.TXT** and use the file OUTPUT.TXT as the input file to the script

```
/User:/ { print "Found a user ID" }
```

awk searches the input file for the case-sensitive string User: and — if this text is found, it prints the string Found a user ID.

Awk supports two special patterns: BEGIN and END. These are not really patterns but are used to include special instructions — such as variable initialization and final output options — in the script.

```
BEGIN { count = 0 }
```

```
/User:/ { count++ }
```

```
END { printf("Total users found:  %d\n", count) }
```

This script searches for instances of the case-sensitive string User: (as in the previous example) but rather than print a string out, it increments the variable count, and when completed, prints a total count of the user objects listed in the input file.

An awk script parses the input line based on a *field separator*. By default, the field separator is whitespace. Whitespace includes any number of spaces or tabs between the data. The line is then split out into internal variables based on the field separator found.

For example, the line

```
Full Name:   Jim Henderson
```

consists of a total of four fields. These fields are referred to by the names $1, $2, $3, and $4, with the values shown in Table 10.2.

TABLE 10.2	FIELD	VALUE
Field Names and Corresponding Values	$1	Full
	$2	Name:
	$3	Jim
	$4	Henderson

The entire line of text is referred to by the variable $0. This variable always represents the entire line up to the *record separator*, which is typically a carriage return.

TIP

Another special value is the NF value. This value reports the number of fields in the line. If you are uncertain of the number of fields but need the last value from the line, you can reference this as $NF. In Table 10.2, $4 has the value Henderson, as does $NF; therefore, NF would have a value of 4.

The defaults for the field separator and record separator can be changed. For example, if you have a tab-delimited file, you would want the field separator to be the tab character rather than a space. This is changed typically in the beginning of the script in the BEGIN segment:

```
BEGIN { FS = "\t" }
```

NOTE

As with the C, C++, and other programming languages, awk uses escaped characters for nonprintable characters. The \t sequence refers to the tab character, the \n sequence refers to the newline character, and so on.

The record separator can also be changed using the RS variable. Typically you will not want to change this, but there are circumstances where it might make sense to do so.

There are also a number of string manipulation functions in awk. Table 10.3 shows the functions available and what they can be used for.

In addition to string manipulation, numeric manipulation can also be done. This type of manipulation of data is done in the same manner as C or C++ numeric manipulation. If you need to manipulate a number with an initial value, you can initialize it in the BEGIN section of the script.

When scanning a line and breaking it into the initial subcomponents ($1 through $NF), or when breaking it down using the split()function, if a numeric value is found, it is automatically treated as a number; however, if you need to perform string manipulations on it, you are also able to do this. In this respect, awk provides greater flexibility than most programming languages.

TABLE 10.3

Awk String Manipulation Functions

FUNCTION	USE	RETURN VALUE
gsub (SearchFor, Replace)	Replace all occurrences of SearchFor with Replace in $0 (the input line)	Number of replacements made
gsub (SearchFor, Replace, SearchIn)	Replace all occurrences of SearchFor with Replace in SearchIn	Number of replacements made
index (String, Text)	Locate the first occurrence of String in Text	Offset in the string where the occurrence is; if not found, returns 0
length (String)	Determine the length (in characters) of String	Number of characters in String
match (String, Text)	Locate the first occurrence of String in Text	Offset in the string where the occurrence is; if not found, returns 0. This function also sets the variables RSTART and RLENGTH, which are the start index and length of the substring.
split (String, Array)	Breaks String into array Array on the default field separator (specified by FS)	Number of fields. Values in the array can be referred to with a subscript—if the array name is A, the first element is A[1], the second is A[2], and so on.
split (String, Array, FieldSeparator)	Breaks String into array Array on the specified field separator, FieldSeparator	Number of fields
sprintf (format, expressionlist)	Print output using a specified output format. This is similar to the C function sprintf(), except that the output is on the left-hand side of the equals sign instead of inside the parenthesis.	The value returned is the formatted string.
sub (Replace, String)	Substitute the first instance of Replace with String in $0	Number of replacements made (should always be 1)

(Continued)

TABLE 10.3

Awk String Manipulation Functions (continued)

FUNCTION	USE	RETURN VALUE
sub (Replace, String, Input)	Substitute the first instance of Replace with String in the input Input	Number of replacements made (should always be 1)
substr (String, Position)	Return the suffix of string String starting at position Position	String value with the result
substr (String, Position, Length)	Return the suffix of String starting at Position of Length	String value with the result

Awk also supports the use of several other statements and structures. Table 10.4 lists the more common of these.

TABLE 10.4	ACTION	EXAMPLE/FUNCTION
Awk Language Actions	assignment	x = 25
	print	print The user name is username
	printf (format, expression list)	printf ("The user name is %s\n", username)
	if (expression) statement	if (username == "Jim") print "Found Jim!"
	if (expression) statement else	if (username == "Jim") print "Found Jim!" else print "Found someone else"
	while (expression) statement	while (NF > 10) printf("Too many fields, line %d, %d fields\n", NR, NF)
	for (initialization; while expression; initialization variable modification) statement	for (x=0;x<10;x++) print x
	exit	Exits the interpreter
	break	Breaks out of the current for/while/do loop

An additional feature of the language that is occasionally useful is the capability to create specialized functions for repeated operations. If you are coding an involved script, you are able to package the code so you can minimize your coding time; however, in disaster recovery situations, you will generally find that the scripts you write will perform very specific manipulations, and as a general rule, you do not need to reuse code within the script.

Creating functions within awk is a simple matter. For example, a function to return the minimum value of two passed-in parameters would be:

```
function min(a, b){

  if (a < b)

    return a

  else

    return b

}
```

As awk supports the abbreviated *if* structure that C provides, this can also be coded

```
function min(a, b){

  return a < b ? a : b

}
```

This code sample provides the same functionality as the previous sample.

Once you have your awk script written, you need to give it an input file. Using the gawk interpreter, this is done using a command in the format of

```
gawk awkfile.awk < inputfile [> outputfile]
```

This tells gawk to use awkfile.awk as the script and to pipe the contents of inputfile into the script. The input file can be left out, but doing so means that you must type the input file in by hand. The output file contains the results of the script if an output file is specified; if it is not specified, the output is written to the screen.

TIP

Writing the output to the screen can be very useful during the development process. By exiting the script with the exit command after processing the first line of text, you can get an idea as to whether or not the program is working close to how you want it to be working without going through and processing the entire input file.

In a disaster recovery situation, it is not absolutely necessary that the script work *completely correctly* when you finish it. Instead of spending time correcting it, using awk with a combination of other tools may get you through your problem more quickly. Suppose you have a script that outputs a UIMPORT file containing group membership information. The file is missing part of one group name because of an embedded space, but the affected group has only ten users. Instead of trying to perfect the script to handle that small number of exceptions, use your favorite text editor to either remove those entries from the file or to make the correction using a search-and-replace function.

Example

The following example shows a full awk program designed to take the output from the NLIST command and convert it into a format suitable for importing into a spreadsheet or database program. For simplicity, we limit the scope of this example to a single context (in Chapter 11, we examine a case study that builds a UIMPORT file based on information from the entire tree.)

For this example, the input file is generated using the command

```
NLIST USER SHOW SURNAME, "FULL NAME", "GIVEN NAME" >
USERS.TXT
```

The output file USERS.TXT contains the same information you would normally see on the screen. The contents of the file in this example are as follows:

```
Object Class: User

Current context: east.xyzcorp

User: JimH

    Last Name: Henderson

    Full Name: Jim Henderson
```

```
     Given Name: Jim

User: PeterK

     Last Name: Kuo

     Full Name: Peter Kuo

     Given Name: Peter

User: PKuo

     Last Name: Kuo

     Full Name: Peter Kuo

     Given Name: Peter

User: JHenderson

     Full Name: Jim Henderson

     Given Name: Jim

     Last Name: Henderson

A total of 4 User objects was found in this context.


A total of 4 User objects was found.
```

From this information, we want to generate a comma-delimited file with the fields User ID, Context, First Name, Last Name, and Full Name. The output file also contains a header line with the field names in it.

This awk script performs the conversion to a comma delimited file.

```
BEGIN { flag = 0

        printf("\"User ID\",\"Context\",\"First
Name\",\"Last Name\",\"Full Name\"\n")

}


/User:/ {
```

```
    if (flag == 1) {
        printf("\"%s\",\"%s\",\"%s\",\"%s\",\"%s\"\n", user,
context, gn, ln, fn)
        gn = ""
        ln = ""
        fn = ""
    }
    user = $2
    flag = 1
}


/Full Name:/ { gsub(/Full Name: /,"")
               gsub(/\t/, "")
               fn = $0
}


/Last Name:/ { gsub(/Last Name: /,"")
               gsub(/\t/, "")
               ln = $0
}


/Given Name:/ { gsub(/Given Name: /,"")
                gsub(/\t/, "")
                gn = $0
}
```

```
/Current context:/ { gsub(/Current context: /, "")
                    context = $0
}


END { printf("\"%s\",\"%s\",\"%s\",\"%s\",\"%s\"\n", user,
context, gn, ln, fn)

}
```

To follow the flow of the script, we start with the BEGIN statement. This executes before any lines of the input file USERS.TXT are read. It sets a flag value to zero in order to avoid printing a blank first line. The headers are then printed to the output device.

Once this has completed, the first line is read. This line contains the object class information. Each line in the script that performs a pattern match on the data file is evaluated in order. First the line is checked for User:. However, this line does not contain that specific string, so the next pattern is evaluated. The line also does not contain the other strings (Full Name:, Last Name:, Given Name, or Current context:). As a result, the line is not processed and is not output.

The second line contains the string Current context:, so the code written to handle that is used to process the line. The first line of code (the gsub line) replaces the string Current context: with nothing, effectively removing it from the $0 variable. The variable *context* is then assigned to the string contained in the line, which contains the actual context. This variable is preserved from one line to the next and is printed each time a new user is read in and at the end of the script.

Once that line is processed, the next line is processed similarly. It contains a user ID and assigns the value. It also sets the flag variable to 1, but because the variable was 0 when the script started, the information gathered is not printed out. Now that flag is set to 1, each subsequent time a user ID is found, the previous user information will be printed, and all variables except *context* are reset to empty strings.

After the last line of the file is read, the last user's information is printed. This is done using the END clause, because there is no guarantee of the order in which the attributes are presented in the NLIST output—you want to make sure that you get the right information.

The result of this script with this input file is as follows:

```
"User ID","Context","First Name","Last Name","Full Name"

"JimH","east.xyzcorp","Jim","Henderson","Jim Henderson"

"PeterK","east.xyzcorp","Peter","Kuo","Peter Kuo"

"PKuo","east.xyzcorp","Peter","Kuo","Peter Kuo"

"JHenderson","east.xyzcorp","Jim","Henderson","Jim
Henderson"
```

▶ · ◀

Using C or C++

The C programming language has been, and still is, the programming language of choice for systems programming. It is, therefore, not a surprise that Novell's initial Software Developer Kit (SDK, now known as the Novell Developer Kit, or NDK) efforts were placed in C libraries. Even today, the NetWare Loadable Module (NLM) libraries are still C based, while workstation application developers now have more options in their choice of programming language (see the "Other Programming and Scripting Languages" section below).

When programming for NDS, there are a number of operations that your application must perform locally when accessing NDS information. The operations include

▶ Working with naming conventions

▶ Maintaining directory context data

▶ Initializing Unicode tables

▶ Managing local buffers

As mentioned previously, an NDS object may be referenced in multiple ways: using its Relative Distinguished Name (RDN) or its Distinguished Name (DN) in typeful or typeless naming syntax. Directory Services operates on *canonical* names only: names that include a full naming path with a type specification for each naming component — typeful DNs. Because it's not always convenient or practical to store or use canonical names, there are Application Programming Interfaces (APIs) that enable you to use partial names and enable the underlying library routines to handle the conversion.

Most NDS API calls that involve character data or interact with the NDS tree require additional information to be supplied. This is to indicate the default context and whether the character data should be translated to Unicode. This information is collectively held in a structure called the *directory context* and is used to pass the following details:

- ▶ Default context

- ▶ Whether alias objects should be dereferenced

- ▶ Whether character data should be translated to and from Unicode

- ▶ Whether object names should be given in canonical form

- ▶ Whether object names should be given in typeless form

When a directory context is created, the default context is the same as the workstation's current context, and the four action options listed previously are performed. The directory context should be freed once it is no longer needed (normally when the application terminates).

The information in a directory context can be read and modified. Care should be taken when changing the default context. This can be set to an arbitrary string, unlike the CX command-line utility which will not set the default context to an illegal value. If the default context is set to an illegal value then most API calls that rely on the directory context will fail.

The same naming conventions apply to the NDS API calls as to the NetWare command line utilities. That is, leading and trailing periods can be used to modify the default context and the type qualifiers such as CN and OU can be inserted into the name to override the default typing.

As suggested earlier, the Unicode conversion tables have to be loaded before an application can access NDS (this may not be necessary for NLMs), and should be released prior to an application terminating. These tables are used to convert character data between the general Unicode format used by the NDS and the local format used by the application. The Unicode tables are loaded by executing the Unicode API NWInitUnicodeTables(), specifying the local code page. The local code page can be obtained by executing the Internationalization Services APIs NWLsetlocale()and NWLlocaleconv().

NDS API functions use buffers for sending and receiving data between the application and the NDS. For example, a typical sequence in reading an object's attributes would be to initialize an input buffer, load the buffer with the list of desired attributes, execute the read object command, and unload the attribute values from an output buffer. Given that the output buffer is finite, it is sometimes necessary to call the read function repeatedly to get subsequent values. This protocol of using input and output buffers provides a general interface for transferring data.

Memory for directory buffers is allocated using an NDS API call. The suggested amount of memory to allocate is given by the constant DEFAULT_MESSAGE_LEN which is set to 4,096 bytes. This value is normally more than sufficient for any NDS application. The only exception under normal circumstances would be when there is a single attribute value that overflows the buffer. Directory buffers should be freed once they are no longer needed (normally when the application terminates); otherwise, memory leak results.

It is the directory buffer management tasks that make NDS-aware applications more complex than a bindery-based program; however, don't let that discourage you from developing NDS utilities, because it only looks harder than it really is.

The following is a sample C source code that enables you to change a user's telephone attribute from a command line. Error checking has been removed to simplify the example:

```
#include <stdio.h>

#include <stdlib.h>

#include <string.h>


#define N_PLAT_DOS

#include <nwcalls.h>
```

```
#include <nwnet.h>

#include <nwlocale.h>



void main (int argc, char *argv[])

{

        NWDSContextHandle       Cx;

        NWDS_BUFFER             *inBuf;

        LCONV                   lconvInfo;



        if ( argc < 4 ) {

                printf ("Usage: Newnumber objectname oldTnum
newTnum\n");

                exit (1);

        }



// Needed for workstation-based APIs only.


        NWCallsInit (NULL, NULL);



// Unicode table must be loaded in order to use DS calls.
```

```
        NWLlocaleconv (&lconvInfo);

        NWInitUnicodeTables (lconvInfo.country_id,
    lconvInfo.code_page);




    // Create directory context


        Cx = NWDSCreateContext ();




    // Allocate local buffers


        NWDSAllocBuf (DEFAULT_MESSAGE_LEN, &inBuf);

        NWDSInitBuf (Cx, DSV_MODIFY_ENTRY, inBuf);

        NWDSPutChange (Cx, inBuf, DS_REMOVE_VALUE, "Telephone
    Number");

        NWDSPutAttrVal (Cx, inBuf, SYN_CI_STRING, argv[2]);


        NWDSInitBuf (Cx, DSV_ADD_ENTRY, inBuf);

        NWDSPutChange (Cx, inBuf, DS_ADD_VALUE, "Telephone
    Number");

        NWDSPutAttrVal (Cx, inBuf, SYN_CI_STRING, argv[3]);
```

```
     if ( NWDSModifyObject (Cx, argv[1], NULL, (NWFLAGS)0,
inBuf) == 0 ) {

          printf ("%s's old telephone number [%s] has
been\n",

                    argv[1], argv[2]);

          printf ("replaced by a new number [%s]\n",
argv[3]);

     }

     else

          printf ("Unable to change telephone number.\n");



// Free allocated resources.


     NWDSFreeBuf (inBuf);

     NWDSFreeContext (Cx);

     NWFreeUnicodeTables ();



}
```

· ·

Other Programming and Scripting Languages

To help you quickly develop applications for NDS and NetWare without having to fully understand the underlying complexity, Novell Developer Support has several tools available. For example, you can build successful network-ready applications and utilities using your favorite Rapid Application Development

(RAD) Windows programming tool, such as Visual Basic. Novell Libraries for Visual Basic gives programmers full access to all of the low-level NetWare APIs that have traditionally been available only to C programmers. The Visual Basic libraries are a set of text files that contain the NetWare API definitions which can be copied into a Visual Basic project using the Visual Basic API Viewer Add-In.

Alternately, you can use Novell Controls for ActiveX which supports full access to NDS as well as administration capabilities for NetWare servers, print queues, and volumes. All of this functionality is packaged so it can be used quickly and easily in a Windows visual builder and other development tools, such as Visual Basic (see Figure 10.1), Delphi, PowerBuilder, Active Server Pages for Internet Information Server, Windows Scripting Host, and the Internet Explorer Web browser. Novell Controls for ActiveX contains the following controls:

- ▸ Application Administration (NWAppA)

- ▸ Bindery (NWBind)

- ▸ Client and Server Socket (NWCliSkt and NWSvrSkt)

- ▸ Directory (NWDir)

- ▸ Internet Directory (NWIDir)

- ▸ Print Queue Administration (NWPQA)

- ▸ Print Server Administration (NWPSA)

- ▸ Server Administration (NWSrvA)

- ▸ Session Management (NWSess)

- ▸ Volume Administration (NWVolA)

▶ · ◀

F I G U R E   10.1

*A sample Visual Basic (VB)
application that uses the
NWDir ActiveX control to
browse the NDS tree*

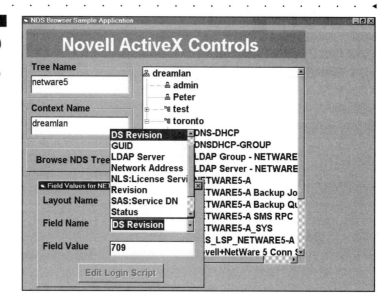

If you're a Java fan, there are JavaBeans available for you to use. Your Java applications can also access NDS through the Java Naming and Directory Interface (JNDI) APIs. If you're more comfortable with scripting languages, such as VB Script, Novell has support for them too. For example, using the Novell Script for NetWare, which is a Visual Basic Script compatible language for script automation and Web development on the NetScape FastTrack Server for NetWare platform, you can use Novell Script's prebuilt components to access NetWare and integrate NDS, Oracle, and Btrieve databases into your Web applications. Novell scripts can quickly and easily execute JavaBean components and regular Java classes.

If you're a more traditional Web page designer, Perl 5 for NetWare is an effective Web programming language suitable for use with the Netscape FastTrack Server for NetWare. Perl 5 support enables you to enhance and continue your investment in Perl scripts and Perl applications. At the time of this writing, Novell has not made available any NDS extensions for their Perl 5 implementation; however, there is a third-party Perl extension that offers NDS capability for your Perl scripts. Visit http://www.ahs.hist.no/distr/NDSm/ for more information.

TIP

By signing up as an electronic level member of DeveloperNet, you have no-charge, Web-based access to the Novell Developer Kit, DeveloperNet resources, support forums, and comarketing opportunities. Visit http://developer.novell.com/brochure **for more information about the DeveloperNet program.**

▶ · ◀

Summary

In this chapter, you've gotten a quick overview on how you can develop your own NDS disaster recovery and reporting utilities using various programming and scripting languages such as awk, C, and Perl.

In Chapter 11, you'll learn how to apply the various troubleshooting techniques and utilities discussed so far to some commonly encountered real-world scenarios.

Examples from the Real World

In this chapter, we bring together the concepts and various utilities that were discussed in previous chapters and apply them to some specific examples. The following case studies are examined:

- Bindery Services–related issues

- Unknown objects in NDS

- Schema problems

- Stuck obituaries

- Crashed SYS volume or server recovery

- Stealth objects

- Concurrent login restrictions

- NDS data recovery

- Replica ring inconsistency

- Time-stamp problems

Bindery Services Issues

Although NDS is backwards-compatible with the Bindery, there are a number of common issues that you need to be aware of when dealing with bindery-based applications in an NDS environment. NetWare bindery information is server-centric; therefore, when using Bindery Services in the NDS environment, the bindery data that you see is also server-centric. From our experience, there are four general areas of concern when using Bindery Services:

- The Supervisor user

- Mail directories and bindery-based queues

- Bindery clients

- Performance

The Bindery Supervisor User

The Supervisor user in the world of NDS is an odd creature. It is both an NDS object and a nonobject. It is a bindery object that exists on each and every NetWare 4 and NetWare 5 server, regardless of whether Bindery Services is enabled on that server or not. Similar to [Public], this bindery Supervisor user-object doesn't physically show up when you browse the NDS tree, but it is recognized and acted upon by the NetWare servers. You should be aware of the following:

- **The nature of Supervisor**. It is created as a pseudo-NDS object whose rights are restricted to a specific bindery context and *only* to that context. Supervisor does not have Admin-like rights in the NDS tree. Its rights within NDS are also restricted. If there are multiple servers within the server tree, the Supervisor can only traverse the portion specific to the bindery context it is restricted to.

  What this means is on initial installation, Supervisor has very restricted access to NDS but has full access to everything specific to the bindery context it was created for (including the file system). If Supervisor needs access to other objects (for example, servers) and those objects can be made part of the bindery context, then Supervisor is given access to them.

NOTE

If there is no bindery context set, which is normal for straight NetWare 4.*x* and NetWare 5 server installations, then Supervisor has no access.

- **Security Equivalences to Supervisor**. Depending on how you migrate the user information from a bindery server into NDS, you may have a security back door that you're not readily aware of. Any user that was Security Equivalent to Supervisor in the bindery will be made Security Equivalent (SE) to the server object (thus all volumes associated with that server object) which corresponds to the server that was used to import the bindery data. This means all users that were SE to Supervisor on the old server now have full rights to the new server.

▸ **NDS security implications**. Supervisor can, within the defined bindery contexts, perform administrational operations, such as changing a user's password and creating new users, regardless of NDS inheritance right filters; therefore, the Supervisor password should be closely guarded as you would with any other ids ID that has supervisory rights to the tree.

▸ **Safeguarding Supervisor's password**. This is one of the more confusing issues associated with Supervisor. The initial Supervisor password is the same as that of Admin's or that of the user's you used to authenticate the installation utility with—when you install the first NetWare server into the NDS tree, the passwords of Admin and the bindery Supervisor user are the same. Subsequent changes of the Admin password are *not* synchronized with the Supervisor password, and vice versa.

If you want to change the Supervisor password it must be done with a bindery utility such as SETPASS.EXE (shipped with NetWare 4 and NetWare 5) or SYSCON.EXE. It is important to keep in mind that the Supervisor password is not synchronized between servers; this means that when you change the Supervisor password, it applies only to the one server you are logged in to at the moment of change.

▸ **Unlocking MONITOR.NLM**. This is no longer an issue in NetWare 5 as the screen-saver and console-locking function have been removed from MONITOR.NLM and are placed into a separate NLM, SCRSAVER.NLM. NDS user objects are now used to unlock the console. For NetWare 4 servers, however, if you don't know the password that was used to lock the MONITOR.NLM or if the console was locked by pressing Enter twice at the Lock File Server Console option, you need the Supervisor password to unlock Monitor. The Admin password does not work unless it happens to be the same as the Supervisor password.

TIP

There are a few alternatives to this **MONITOR.NLM** issue. For example, SecureConsole for NetWare, which doesn't require a supervior, is available from Protocom Development Systems (`http://www.serversystems.com`). **If you don't need the complexity of SecureConsole, DreamLAN Network Consulting's SSLock for NDS** (`http://www.dreamlan.com/sslock.htm`) **is a good alternative (see Figure 11.1). Both of these products work on NetWare 4 and NetWare 5 servers.**

▶ · ◀

FIGURE 11.1

Depending on the group and the user's object rights, SSLock enables the user to either unlock the console or unload the NLM.

```
SSLock Version PK-4.61 (s/n: DLAN/981216-SSLockS-1585)
DreamLAN Network Consulting Ltd. (http://www.dreamlan.com)
Copyright (C) 1998. All Rights Reserved.
Licensed to Internal Testing and Use

        To UNLOCK the console, you must either belong to an appropriate
        SS_UNLOCK group or has [S] rights to this server's object.

        To UNLOAD SSLock, you must either belong to an appropriate
        UNLOAD_SS group or has [S] rights to this server's object.

NDS user's DN name (e.g. name.org_unit.org; 50 chars max)
-> .admin.dreamlan

Please enter password
-> ********
One moment please ... authenticating ... OK!

ESC to lock screen again; UNLOAD to Unload NLM; anything else will Unlock
-> unload
                                                                [4:07]
```

Mail Directories and Bindery Queues

Mail directories (created under SYS:MAIL) were an integral part of NetWare prior to version 4; however they are no longer required for use in the NDS environment, unless there are users that still run in bindery emulation. These bindery users create the need for mail directories to still exist on NetWare 5 and NetWare 4 servers.

Each mail directory is tied to its user through the user's hexadecimal object ID number—the name of the directory (located under the SYS:MAIL directory) is that of the hexadecimal number. There are times however, especially during a restore, where the ID of the user object is changed, and thus the link to the mail directory is broken. As a result, bindery users lose access to their personal login scripts, and any e-mail applications that make use of these directories fail to function correctly.

TIP

Novell has an NLM utility called RENMDR that restores the link between the users and their mail directories. This utility is to be run on the server to be fixed (because the mail directory naming is server-centric). You can find it on Novell's Support Connection Web site as RENMDR.EXE using the File Finder. There are instructions included on how to use the utility.

Queues suffer the same issue as user mail directories. The directory corresponding to a bindery queue is named after the queue object's hexadecimal ID number. Thus, if the object ID of a bindery queue object is changed, the link to its queue directory is broken. In such a case, you need to delete the queue object and recreate it so the proper linkage can be made. NDS queue objects do not fall under this category.

Bindery Clients

There may be times when you're unable to switch all your client workstations to use NDS-aware client software, such as Client32. Or your workstation platform may be such that you're unable to switch—for example, if you have old Macintosh workstations that can't be upgraded to the latest MacOS in order to use the NDS-aware client without great expense. In this situation, you need to bear in mind the difference between a Bindery Services and NDS connection:

▶ There's the matter of what NetWare Core Protocol (NCP) API calls the client can use. A bindery connection can't use any of the NDS NCPs. That means you can't run NWAdmin, NETADMIN, or perform administration of the tree.

▶ When logging in through Bindery Services, the container and profile login scripts are not read from the tree. The bindery client looks for a NET$LOG.DAT in the SYS:PUBLIC directory and a login script in the user's mail directory.

Performance Considerations

Frequently, administrators are not aware that NetWare 4 and NetWare 5 OS assign only one service process to service all bindery requests, regardless of the number of bindery connections to the server and the number of currently allocated service processes. Consequently, you'll notice a server that serves many bindery clients (workstations and/or printers) shows a higher utilization than one servicing NDS clients.

As a reference, a server servicing 300 bindery connections may show a CPU utilization of 35 percent while the same server servicing 300 NDS connections (doing the same type of work) shows a CPU utilization of only 10 percent.

Unknown Objects

NWAdmin uses two different icons to represent unknown objects in NDS: a yellow circled question mark and a white squared question mark, as illustrated in Figure 11.2.

From NWAdmin's perspective, there are two different types of unknown objects.

The cause for the white squared question mark is completely different from that of the yellow-circled question mark. The white squared question mark means that NWAdmin could not find the correct snap-in to associate the object with the necessary icon. Essentially, it is saying the object is perfectly legitimate in NDS, but the configuration of NWAdmin is not correct. On the other hand, the yellow-circled question mark is generally bad news.

The yellow circle question mark generally means that one or more of the mandatory attributes of the object are missing. When a mandatory attribute is missing from an object, NDS automatically marks the object as Unknown but leaves the name unchanged.

There are two conditions under which the presence of Unknown objects is normal and transitory. The first situation happens during replica synchronization, which is related to timing. The Unknowns can be caused by a new replica being added to a server or when objects are still being updated from one replica to another.

Some objects may start as Unknown objects (when viewed from NWAdmin, if the timing is right), but once the synchronization process is complete, the objects are updated with all the information they need and are turned into real objects. Depending on what you are doing, timing can make unknown objects go away.

The other situation under which Unknown objects appear is during an NDS restore. Because the objects are restored in the order in which they are backed up, some objects (such as a Volume object) may be restored before the object (such as the Server object) that defines their mandatory attribute (Host Server in the case of Volume objects) is restored; however, when all the objects are restored, the Unknowns should turn into known objects. For example, if a Group is restored but all its members (Users) do not yet exist in the tree, placeholder (Unknown) objects are created until the user objects are restored. At that time, the placeholder objects become real User objects and the User and Group objects are fully functional.

If you have not done any of the previously mentioned operations and you have an Unknown object, you can delete it and then recreate it if it is replaceable; however, before you do that, you should be familiar with the following repercussions:

▶ When the Unknown object is a volume, deleting the icon causes any user that has a Home Directory attribute pointing to this volume to lose its mapping — the Home Directory attribute value is cleared.

▶ When the Unknown object is a user, deleting the icon results in the user losing its specific trustee assignments (both file system and NDS).

▶ When the Unknown object is a server, deleting the icon causes the server to be deleted from the tree, and all DS references to this specific server is lost. This icon should not be deleted casually, because the action also can lead to inconsistent replica rings.

In most cases, an Unknown object can just be deleted and recreated; however, anytime a Server object or something of importance (such as the Admin User object) is turned into an Unknown object, you should consider your actions before taking them.

It has been observed that sometimes Directory Map (DM) and Print Server (PS) objects spontaneously mutate into Unknown objects for no apparent reason. This can be caused by one of three events:

1. The server hosting the volume the DM was pointing to, *at the creation time of the DM object*, has been deleted.

2. The server hosting the Print Server it was pointing to, *at the creation time of the PS object*, has been deleted.

3. The Volume object the DM is pointing to has been deleted.

The last situation is easy to understand; however, the first two are not. They are due to a bug in NWAdmin (it is also in NWADMN32 in NetWare 5) when dealing with DM and PS objects.

When changing the Path attribute of a DM object to point to a volume on a server different from the initial server (at the time the object was created) the Host Server attribute (which is not visible in NWAdmin) does not get updated. When the Server object referenced in the Host Server attribute gets deleted, the attribute disappears and the Directory Map turns into an Unknown object, because it loses its mandatory Host Server attribute. For example, when you create a DM object called TEST_DM and point it to NETWARE5-A_VOL1:HOME, the Host Server attribute points to NETWARE5-A (or whatever your current default server is). If later you change the DM to point to NETWARE5-B_SYS:DATA, the Host Server attribute of the DM remains pointing to NETWARE5-A. So, if at a later time you remove NETWARE5-A from the network, TEST_DM becomes an Unknown object. A similar problem exists with the Host Device attribute of Print Server objects.

NOTE

What's worse in the case of Print Servers is that the Host Device identifies where the print server's log file is to be kept, and when the print server is brought up, a licensed connection is made to the server identified by the Host Device, even if the log file option is not enabled. It can also cause performance issues or prevent the print server from being loaded if the Host Device happens to be across a WAN link or if the (remote) server or the link is down.

Although NWAdmin doesn't show the Host Server and Host Device attributes, you can easily look them up using DSView or using NList. The following NList command shows the Host Device setting of all Print Servers in the current context:

```
NLIST "PRINT SERVER" SHOW "HOST DEVICE"
```

and the output looks something like this:

```
Current context: test.dreamlan

Print Server: PS-test

        Host Device: NETWARE5-A.toronto.

-------------------------------


One Print Server object was found in this context.


One Print Server object was found.
```

To address these two problems, Novell has available the following (unsupported) solutions:

▶ Available from Novell's Developer Support Web site at
   `http://developer.novell.com/engsup/sample/areas/delphis.htm`
   is a sample application called MAPOBJCH contained in a file called
   D3MAPOBJ.EXE. MAPOBJCH includes an NDS browser to select what
   container you want to search and automatically changes the Host Server to
   that of the Volume object's, if they are not the same.

▶ There exists an Appware utility called HSTDEV that enables you to change
   the Host Device of a Print Server object. You can located this program by
   searching for HSTDEV.EXE using the file finder at Novell's Support
   Connection Web site at `http://support.novell.com/search/`
   `ff_index.htm`.

Generally when a normal object turns Unknown, the object name is unchanged; however, if your Unknown objects have names such as 1_2, 2_1, 3_5, (a number_ a number) and they keep coming back after you've deleted them, you have a synchronization problem.

These objects are called *renames*. These renames are caused by *name collisions* during synchronization. The collision occurs when the same object is found with different creation time stamps. The name collision problem happened mostly in a mixed NetWare 4.0x and NetWare 4.10 environment, which is a rare combination these days; however, it can also occur on a LAN/WAN where the communication is not stable. The following steps may fix the name collision problem:

1. Ensure time is in sync on the network and that each server in the replica ring is running the same or the latest compatible version of the DS.NLM. (All the servers in the tree should be running the latest version of DS.NLM.) Use the time synchronization option from DSRepair's main menu to check to see if time is in sync on the network and the versions of the DS.NLM.

2. Make sure that all the replicas for the partition in question are in the *on* state. Also make sure that the partition has a master replica and that the server holding that replica is accessible to the other servers. You can check them using DSRepair. It is suggested you do this on the server that holds the master replica of the partition.

3. Compare the replica ring information from the related servers in the ring. Resolve any conflicts if there are any found.

4. From the server that contains the master replica of the partition, issue the following console commands

```
SET DSTRACE=ON
SET DSTRACE=+SYNC
SET DSTRACE=*H
```

and see if the partition in question is synchronizing successfully or not.

If DSTrace reports "All Processed = Yes", try to delete the renamed or Unknown objects. They should remove from the tree without reappearing. If they persist, it's best to open a call with Novell Technical Support and have them dial in for a look.

Schema Problems

Before discussing schema issues, let's first review what an NDS schema is and how it may affect the network. The Directory Schema is the rules that define how the Directory tree is constructed. The schema defines specific types of information that dictate the way information is stored in the NDS database. The following information is defined by the schema:

▸ **Attribute information**. Describes what type of additional information an object can or must have associated with the object. Attribute types are defined within the schema by specific constraints and a specific syntax for their values.

▸ **Inheritance**. Determines which objects inherit the properties and rights of other objects.

▸ **Naming**. Determines the structure of the NDS tree, thus identifying and showing an object's reference name within NDS.

▸ **Subordination**. Determines the location of objects in the Directory tree, thus identifying and showing an object's location in the Directory tree.

The basis for all entries in an NDS database is a set of defined object classes referred to as the base schema. Object classes such as servers, Users, and Print Servers are some of the base object classes defined by the base schema. For a complete list of the base object classes, as well as attribute definitions, see Appendix C.

The NDS schema can be modified and expanded to suit the specific needs of your organization. Object class definitions can be added to and modified for the existing base schema. Such additions are called *schema extensions*.

There are generally two types of problems associated with the schema: NDS rights-related and timing-related (such as needing to wait for schema synchronization to complete between servers). NDS rights-related problems are easy to understand and address. In order to extend the NDS schema, you must have Supervisor rights to the [Root] object. Otherwise, you'll be unable to affect the changes. The timing-related problem requires some explaining. In large trees where schema extensions can take extended periods of time to be propagated to all servers, the very first installation of an application that requires schema extension, such as GroupWise, may fail to install a number of times before a successful installation. Let's assume this one application creates two custom NDS objects. During the first installation attempt, the application's install routine attempts to create a new NDS object using an extended class. NDS reports that this object class and the needed attributes do not exist in the schema and the setup program adds them to the schema. The installation fails, because the extension has not yet reached the server on which the object is to be created. Later (possibly 15 minutes or more in very large trees), the administrator attempts to install again. This time the installation finds the first needed object class but not the second one; therefore, the schema is once more extended but the setup program fails as the second class extension is not found on the target server. A third installation later is successful as all the necessary class extensions are already in the schema.

NOTE

The NDS schema is global. Each server stores a replica of the schema in its entirety. The schema replica is stored separately from the partitions that contain Directory objects (see Chapter 2 for more information about replica types.) Changes to any one schema replica are propagated to the other replicas and the server holding the master sends the changes to the other servers in the tree. You can perform modifications to the schema only through a server that stores a writable replica of [Root]. Servers storing read-only replicas of [Root] can read but not modify schema information. You need to have supervisory rights to the [Root] object in order to modify the schema.

If it becomes apparent that NDS had not yet propagated the schema extensions to the other servers, you can help to speed up the process. From the console of the server with the master of [Root], issue the following commands:

```
SET DSTRACE = ON

SET DSTRACE = +SCHEMA

SET DSTRACE = *SSA
```

```
SET DSTRACE = *H
```

(You can also use the DSTRACE SCMA SCREEN command if using DSTRACE.NLM.)

This forces the server to start an immediate outbound schema synchronization process. Switch to the DSTRACE screen, and wait for the message: "SCHEMA: All Processed = YES"; this may take several minutes depending on the number of servers in your network and link speeds. If DSTRACE says "NO", then there are most likely other issues preventing the synchronization.

If the setup program crashed in the middle of extending your schema, you may need to start over with a clean install. The only way to verify a clean install and extension on the NDS base schema is to completely remove all extended class objects (related to this one application you're trying to install) and reextend the schema. You can employ the following procedure:

1. Log out of all servers except the one you are installing the application onto.

2. Delete all related extended schema objects using NWAdmin, and remove all related file directories on the server volumes.

3. Use Schema Manager to delete all related extended schema class objects. If they do not all delete, verify that you are logged in to only one server.

4. Reinstall the application. It should notice that the schema is not properly extended and reextend the schema.

There are some known schema synchronization issues if you have a mixed NetWare 5 and NetWare 4.1x environment and the DS.NLM on the NetWare 4.1x servers are not up-to-date. See Chapter 12 for more information about DS.NLM requirements in a mixed NetWare 4 and NetWare 5 environment.

Stuck Obituaries

As we describe in Chapter 6, NDS makes extensive use of obituary notifications for object management, and any obituary flags are eventually cleared out when an object is removed. There are times, however, when an obituary gets stuck so that NDS can't finish the cleanup process. Most obituaries get stuck because a server was not notified that a change to objects has taken place. You learn if you have any stuck obituaries by using the latest available version of DSREPAIR and executing the Advanced options ⇨ Check external references option on the master replica of each partition (you need to load DSREPAIR with the -A command-line switch). This generates a list of all obituaries on the server. Review this list searching for any line with a Flags = 0 value. The server listed (the last entry on the backlink line) below this value has not been contacted. The following is a sample DSREPAIR log showing obituaries:

```
/***********************************************************************/

Netware 5.00 Directory Services Repair 5.07 , DS 7.09

Log file for server "NETWARE5-B.Test.DreamLAN" in tree "NETWARE5"

External Reference Check

Start: Thursday, March 3, 1999 2:14:25 pm Local Time


Found obituary at VID: 00054980, EID: 11000FE8, DN:
CN=User3.OU=Test.O=DreamLAN.NETWARE5

  TV: 1999/03/03 10:28:06 0004, Type = 0001 DEAD, Flags = 0000

Found obituary at VID: 00005C40, EID: 11000FE8, DN:
CN=User3.OU=Test.O=DreamLAN.NETWARE5

  TV: 1999/03/03 10:28:06 0004, Type = 0006 BACKLINK, Flags = 0000

  Backlink: Type = 00000001 DEAD, RemoteID = FFFFFFFF, ServerID = 010000BD,
CN=TEST-FS1.OU=Test.O=DreamLAN.NETWARE5

Found obituary at VID: 0000F800, EID: 11000FE8, DN:
CN=User3.OU=Test.O=DreamLAN.NETWARE5

  TV: 1999/03/03 10:28:06 0004, Type = 0006 BACKLINK, Flags = 0000
```

```
   Backlink: Type = 00000001 DEAD, RemoteID = FFFFFFFF, ServerID = 030010C3,
CN=TEST-FS2.OU=Test.O=DreamLAN.NETWARE5

Found obituary at VID: 00070C00, EID: 11000FE8, DN:
CN=User3.OU=Test.O=DreamLAN.NETWARE5

   TV: 1999/03/03 10:28:06 0004, Type = 0006 BACKLINK, Flags = 0000

   Backlink: Type = 00000001 DEAD, RemoteID = FFFFFFFF, ServerID = 03001101,
CN=TEST-FS3.OU=Test.O=DreamLAN.NETWARE5


*** END ***
```

The information presented in this DSREPAIR log is interpreted as follows:

► *VID* stands for value ID. This is a record number in the 1.NDS (or
  VALUE.NDS in NetWare 4) file that has been used as an Obituary
  attribute for the object identified by the EID.

► *EID* stands for entry ID. This is a record number in the 0.NDS (or
  ENTRY.NDS in NetWare 4) file that specifies the object that has the
  Obituary attribute assigned by the VID.

► *DN* stands for distinguished name. This is the full distinguished name of
  the object identified by the EID.

► *TV* stands for time vector. This is the time stamp that denotes when the
  Obituary attribute was created.

► *Type* indicates both a number and a text description. There are three
  categories of types: primary, secondary, and tracking. A primary obituary
  indicates an action on an object. A secondary obituary indicates the
  servers that must be contacted and informed of the primary obituary
  action. A tracking obituary is associated with certain primary obituaries.
  The following is a list of the valid obituary types:

  • Primary obituaries are 0000 Restored, 0001 Dead, 0002 Moved, 0005
    NEW_RDN (New Relative Distinguished Name), 0008
    Tree_NEW_RDN (Tree New Relative Distinguished Name — this does

not specify an NDS tree name but rather a partition root name), and 0009 Purge All.

- Secondary obituaries are 0006 Backlink—specifies a target server that needs to be contacted regarding an obituary, and 0010 Move Tree—this obituary is similar to the backlink obituary. There is one move tree obituary for every server that needs to be contacted regarding a Tree_NEW_RDN operation.

- Tracking obituaries are 0003 Inhibit Move, 0004 OLD_RDN (Old Relative Distinguished Name), and 0007 Tree_OLD_RDN (Tree Old Relative Distinguished Name—this does not specify an NDS tree name but rather a partition root name).

▶ *Flags* indicate the level or stage that the obituary is processed to. The following is a list of valid flags:

- 0000 ISSUED. This indicates the obituary has been issued and is ready for processing.

- 0001 NOTIFIED. This flag indicates that the obituary is at the notify stage, which essentially means that the servers identified in the backlink or tree move obituaries have been contacted and notified of the operation or action on an object.

- 0002 OK-TO-PURGE. This indicates that the obituary is being cleaned up on the local database of each server identified in the backlink or tree move obituaries. This clean up includes resolving all objects that reference the object with the obituary and informing them of the change (for example, deletion or move).

- 0004 PURGEABLE. This indicates that the obituary is ready to be purged. The purge process essentially recovers the value to the free chain and enables it to be reused.

Using this information, you can readily determined that the DSREPAIR log reports User3.Test.DreamLAN has been deleted but the obituary is temporarily stuck because server NETWARE5-B is waiting to pass that information to servers TEST-FS1, TEST-FS2, and TEST-FS3.

Armed with the necessary information provided by DSREPAIR, you can then begin to find the problem with that server. It could be that TTS is disabled, the server is down, SAP/RIP filtering may be causing a problem or the server may not even exist anymore but the Server object is still in the tree. By checking these issues almost all obituary problems can be resolved. With DS.NLM 5.95 or higher, you can use a SET DSTRACE=*ST command, and it reports back information in the DSTRACE screen on what servers are having the problems with obituaries.

One of the more commonly reported obituary-related NDS error is -637 (0xFD83), which is a Previous Move in Progress error. You may encounter it when trying to do any kind of partition operation, such as adding or moving a replica or even adding a user (after a replica move). In some cases, the -637 error can be resolved without Novell NDS Support group's intervention. In other cases, Novell would have to dial into your network to edit the NDS database in order to remove the stuck obituary that's causing the problem. For example, if the case is a server not able to communicate with one or more servers referencing the object being moved, you should be able to resolve the error without involving Novell; however, if a server referencing the object has actually been removed from the tree and the object move has still not completed, then you may need to contact Novell for additional help.

TIP

For many -637 errors, the cause is due to communication lost to a server holding an external reference of the object that's being moved from one container to another. Some times the cause is a server holding a subordinate reference of the replica that was taken offline, thus preventing the synchronization cycle from completing.

The actual -637 error is caused by the Type=0003 Inhibit_move obituary. This obituary is placed on the object that has been moved, in the container it has been moved to, to prevent another move from taking place on this object until the previous move has completed. In addition, two other obituary types may be involved: Type=0002 moved obituary, which is attached to the (original) object that has been moved from this container, and Type=0006 backlink obituary, which is attached to the object to point to another server holding an external reference of the object which must be notified when the object is modified (for example, deleted, renamed, or moved); and external reference, where a server must hold information about an object in a partition that the server does not hold a replica of. NDS stores this information in the server's database as an external reference, which is a placeholder containing information about the object that the server does not hold in a local replica. External references are updated periodically by servers holding a replica of the object via the backlink process, which point to the object on the server holding the external reference.

The following three steps can help you resolve most -637 errors without involving outside assistance:

1. You need to first locate the object with the Inhibit_move obituary as this is the culprit of the error. Go to the server holding the master replica of the partition reporting the -637 error and use DSREPAIR (with the -A switch) to perform an external reference check. Look for lines similar to this:

```
Found obituary VID... EID... RN
CN=Objectname.OU=Container.O=Container ...

TV: ... Type=0003 Inhibit_move Flags=0000
```

This is the object causing a -637 to be reported. Take note of the object's full name and context.

2. Locate the corresponding moved obituary. This is placed on the object that was moved from another container to the one with the Inhibit_move obituary. You need to find where this object was moved from. A server holding a replica of the partition where the object was moved from gives you this information. If you are lucky, the same server holding the Inhibit_move obituary also holds a replica of the partition where the object was moved from. If you are not lucky, you will have to run DSREPAIR (with the -A switch) on *every* server in the tree holding a master replica of a partition and look for the following error when checking external references:

```
Found obituary VID... EID... RN
CN=objectname.OU=Container.O=Container ...

TV: ... Type=0002 Moved Flags=0000
```

You are looking for the same CN name as the Inhibit_move obituary, only in a different container (remember that the -637 error is caused by moving

objects). A moved obituary is placed on the object that has been moved
until the move is completed. In this same DSREPAIR.LOG file, also look
for lines similar to the following:

```
Found obituary VID... EID... RN
CN=objectname.OU=Container.O=Container ...

TV: ... Type=0006 Backlink Flags=0000
```

Look for the same exact object as the moved obituary object. This object
has external references, held on other servers in the tree, that must be
notified of the move. A backlink obituary points to the server holding the
external reference, and a Flags=0000 tells us that the server holding the
external reference has not yet been notified of the move.

TIP

**If all Type=0006 backlink obituaries are at Flags=0000, verify that you
have a master replica of each partition in your tree — the master
replica is responsible for forwarding obituary states.**

3. Lastly, find out the status of the server(s) holding the external reference(s).
To find out which servers have external references to the moved object,
use DSVIEW. On the server reporting the moved and backlink obituaries,
use DSVIEW to locate the object and examine the value(s) of its Obituary
attribute. You should see information similar to this:

```
Type: Backlink

Flags: 0000

ServerID: ##...## CN=Servername
```

Once you find such entries, you have the names of the servers that are
holding up the process.

One you have the server names, determine if the servers are up. Are they
communicating properly (that is, no -625 errors)? Do the servers still exist? If the
servers are simply down (say, for maintenance), get them back up and running and
communicating as soon as possible. If they no longer exist, delete the server
objects from NDS using NDS Manager (or Partition Manager). Any external

references they were holding should clean up after the server obje
If the servers are up and communicating, you can try the follow
those servers:

1. Load DSREPAIR with the -XK3 switch. Select Advanced options menu ⇨
Repair local DS database and only set "Check local references" to Yes; set
the other options to No.

2. Perform the repair, save the repaired database, and exit DSREPAIR.

3. At the system console, enter the following commands:

```
SET DSTRACE = +BLINK

SET DSTRACE = *B

SET DSTRACE = *H
```

Or use the DSTRACE NLM, **DSTRACE SCREEN +BLNK**.

4. Toggle to the DSTRACE screen and watch for the line "BACKLINK:
Finished checking backlinks successfully." If the screen scrolls too fast for
you to catch the message, enter the following commands:

```
SET TTF = ON

SET DSTRACE = +BLINK

SET DSTRACE = *B

SET DSTRACE = *R

SET DSTRACE = *H

SET TTF = OFF
```

Then use EDIT.NLM, VIEW.NLM, or a text editor to examine the resulting
SYS:SYSTEM\DSTRACE.DBG file.

The backlink obituary should now have purged, which in turn enables the moved and then the Inhibit_move obituaries to process. You can check the flags of the obituaries using either DSVIEW or DSREPAIR, as described previously.

Give NDS some time for its various background processes to do their jobs. Wait for at least 15 to 30 minutes. It may take a while for this Inhibit_move obituary to purge based on how many replicas and objects are in the partition.

TIP

If this procedure doesn't work, or if the server no longer exists in the tree and the Server object has been deleted from out of NDS, call Novell's NDS Support group for assistance.

In some cases, there may be no corresponding moved obituary because the NDS obituary process was (somehow) abnormally interrupted. In such situations, you have to contact Novell Technical Services for assistance in cleaning up the orphaned Inhibit_move obituaries.

NOTE

To prevent this situation, run a DSRepair –A ⇨ Advanced options menu ⇨ Check external references, and look for any obituaries that have not completed processing (that is, not at Flags=0004 purgeable). Do this before removing a replica, bringing down a server permanently, or performing any other operation that may prevent communication to a server or its replica.

TIP

Recovering a Crashed SYS Volume or Server

One of the most asked question in any network is, "How do I correctly recover from a crashed server?" For those of you that have worked with NetWare 3, you know it's quite straightforward: install a new server, restore bindery from backup, and restore your file system. In the case of a single-server NDS network, the process is pretty much the same as that with NetWare 3: install a new server, restore NDS from backup, and restore your file system. With the distributed nature of NDS, however, things are a little more interesting when you have a multiserver NDS network.

To successfully recover from a lost server or a crashed SYS volume (which is the same as having a dead server, because your NDS is gone) in a multiserver environment, it is essential that you maintain a regular backup of the Server Specific Information (SSI) files for all your servers on your network. It would also be helpful if you have up-to-date documentation about your NDS tree, such as where Server and Volume objects are located. You should also have a record of the partitions, and a list of servers where the master and read/write replicas are stored. Lastly, you should have the correct license file(s) for the crashed server.

For more information about SSI files and their purposes, see Chapter 8.

X-REF

Following are steps to restore a crashed server or a SYS volume in a multiserver NetWare 4.11 and/or NetWare 5 network where NDS information is replicated:

These steps assume you have a current backup of the SSI data for the failed server.

WARNING

1. *Don't panic!*

2. Don't delete the Server or Volume objects for the failed server from the NDS. Leave them intact to preserve references that other objects (such as Directory Map objects) may have to these objects as well as any NDS trustee assignments made. If the Server or Volume objects are deleted and you had objects that depended on them, you'll need to reestablish the relationships through a selective NDS restore.

As discussed previously in this chapter, when an object is missing its mandatory attributes, it turns into an Unknown object. Because of this you need to pay special attention when doing a partial NDS restore so that any dependent object(s) are also restored; otherwise the restored object may not be functional.

NOTE

3. From your most recent tape backup of the failed server, restore the Server Specific Information files to another server. These SSI files (SERVDATA.NDS, DSMISC.LOG, VOLSINFO.TXT, STARTUP.NCF and

XEC.NCF) will be restored to a subdirectory (named after the

...iled server in the DOS 8.3 naming format) under SYS:SYSTEM. For
example, if the failed server was called TEST-NW5-A, the SSI files will be
restored to SYS:SYSTEM\TEST-NW5.-A.

4. If the failed server held a master replica of any partition, go to another
server in the replica ring that has either a read/write or read-only replica,
and use DSREPAIR to promote that replica to a master. (You can use the
information recorded in DSMISC.LOG to determine what replicas were
stored on the failed server and which servers are in the respective replica
rings.) Repeat this step for every master replica stored on the failed server.
You then need to clean up the replica rings to remove the downed server
from the lists. (See the "Replica Ring Inconsistency" section in this chapter
for details.)

**After your replica ring cleanup, you should spot-check the DSTrace
output on a number of servers to see if the replica rings are okay
and that everything is synchronizing correctly. You _do not_ want to
install a server into a tree that's not fully synchronized.**

TIP

**You can't use NDS Manager to perform the task in Step 4, because
NDS Manager requires that the master replica be up and all servers
in the replica ring be available. You _must_ use DSRepair for this step.**

NOTE

5. If the failed server contained any nonmaster replicas, you need to clean up
the replica rings following the procedures given in the "Replica Ring
Inconsistency" section of this chapter.

6. Install the new server hardware or new hard drive (if it was only the SYS
volume that had failed). _Do not yet connect the new server to your network_;
leave it in an isolated environment.

7. Install the NetWare OS on the new hardware following your standard
procedure to set up the LAN and disk driver and create the volumes. (Use
VOLSINFO.TXT to determine how many volumes you had on the crashed
server, their names, and if additional name spaces are required.)

When prompted for server name and server ID (in NetWare 5) or internal IPX network number (in NetWare 4), enter the same server name and addressing information. (Use the AUTOEXEC.NCF included with the SSI for these data.)

When you reach the point of installing NDS information, create a new (temporary) tree. This enables you to complete the OS reinstallation with the minimal amount of trouble.

The reason behind creating a temporary NDS tree at this point is that NetWare 5's GUI installation program doesn't have the option (that is available in NWCONFIG; and in INSTALL in NetWare 4) for you to restore NDS data using SSI information. You *could*, however, not create a temporary tree by aborting out of the GUI setup when prompted for NDS information, using NWCONFIG to restore the NDS data, and manually copy the server files. But it can get confusing and is a lot more extra work—something you don't need during a disaster recovery. Also, the upside of this technique is that you can build the server off site (or have a hot standby server prebuilt) and then bring it in to replace the crashed server.

8. After the server OS installation is complete, restart the server to ensure everything is working okay. Apply any server updates, such as Support Pack, that you have previously installed, and restart the server to ensure the updates haven't messed anything up.

   Log in from a workstation to test the server LAN card configuration, exercise the hard drives, and so on. After you're satisfied that the hardware is working correctly, create a directory off the root of your SYS volume and place the five SSI files there. The most important file is SERVDATA.NDS. Log out from the workstation after you've copied the files.

   If your new server's hardware configuration is different from the crashed server's, make a backup copy of the new STARTUP.NCF and AUTOEXEC.NCF files as they will be overwritten.

If your set of SSI files is small enough, you can place them on a diskette instead.

NOTE

9. At the server console, load NWCONFIG and use the Directory Options selection to remove NDS from this new server.

10. Connect the server to your production environment. Bring up your server and load NWCONFIG. Select the Install Directory Services onto this server option from the Directory Options menu.

11. At the screen to Select a Directory tree, press F5 (the option to restore NDS, as indicated at the bottom of the screen; see Figure 11.3). *Do not select a tree by pressing Enter.* A new window comes up with two options: A: (the default) or "Press <F3> to specify a different path."

FIGURE 11.3

Restore NDS data by pressing F5.

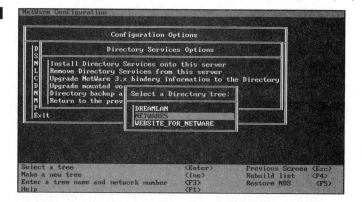

If your SSI files are on a diskette, insert the disk and continue with the restore; otherwise, press F3 and specify the path to where the SSI files were copied to in Step 8.

After you enter the path and press Enter, the SSI files will be copied to the SYS volume. DSMISC.LOG, VOLSINFO.TXT, and AUTOEXEC.NCF are copied to the SYS:SYSTEM directory, and STARTUP.NCF is copied to the

DOS partition. NDS information is also restored at this point, using the data contained in SERVDATA.NDS; unlike a traditional NDS restore using SMS, TSANDS.NLM is not required. Once this is complete, NDS is fully functional on the server, except that the partitions and replicas have not yet been reestablished.

12. You may also need to reestablish licensing information. For NetWare 5 servers, you can use NWAdmin to reassign or reinstall the proper license(s) to the new server. For NetWare 4, you reinstall the license(s) using INSTALL.NLM.

13. If the new server's hardware configuration is not identical to that of the old server's, you'll need to change the restored AUTOEXEC.NCF and STARTUP.NCF files to match the new settings, using the backup copies you made in Step 8. After making the changes, restart the server to ensure the changes are okay.

14. At this point, you can restore the file system from your most recent backup. You should be careful when restoring the SYS volume data so that you don't overwrite any new Support Pack files with older ones. If you've made modifications to your AUTOEXEC.NCF, you should ensure it is not overwritten by the older copy from your backup.

15. After the restore of the file system is complete, restart the server yet one more time to ensure the restore didn't overwrite any important system files. Perform a spot-check on some of the restored directories and files for trustee assignments, file ownership, and so on. Also spot-check NDS objects to ensure you don't have any Unknowns. Bindery-based objects and NDS objects (such as Print Queues) that depend on object IDs should restore correctly because of the SSI information. In the event that Print Queues, for example, are not recovered correctly, you need to recreate them.

16. Reinstall, if necessary, any server-based add-on products.

17. Using the information recorded in the DSMISC.LOG file, use NDS Manager or Partition Manager to reestablish replicas.

Disk Space Problems

When restoring files to a volume that was nearly full during the backup, you may run into insufficient disk space issues. This is especially true when volume compression is used. Although SMS-compliant backup software can back up and restore a compressed file in its compressed format, that's not the default in most backup software; therefore, chances are good that you'll restore previously compressed files in their uncompressed format. And because compression is a background OS process, files are not compressed right away until the compression start time is reached. You can, however, flag files as immediate compress but that's an extra manual step you have to take. And afterwards, you have to remember to unflag them else they'll always be compressed again after access, causing unnecessary high server utilization.

Another volume-related issue that you can get caught with during a restore is suballocation. Again, because it is a background process, files are not suballocated as they are restored; therefore, if you're restoring many (small) files, you can also run out of disk space before the complete restore is done.

To work around these two problems, it is best you try to maintain at least 15 to 20 percent free disk space on each volume, or that the replacement drive capacity is larger.

NOTE

This procedure should work with NetWare 4.10 but we have not tested it in that environment. Also, there's a bug in TSA410 for NetWare 4.10 where replica information is not recorded in the DSMISC.LOG file. A workaround is to use MakeSSI (discussed in Chapter 8) on NetWare 4.10 servers as MakeSSI creates a PARTINFO.LST, which is equivalent to the DSMISC.LOG file. Also, you need to use the most recent TSA410 as older versions (before v4.14) doesn't support SSI.

As an added bonus, MakeSSI also makes a record of all the files in the server's DOS partition so you know what third-party drivers you may need when rebuilding the server.

Novell Technical Support has a Technical Information Document (TID #2908056) titled "Removing a Crashed Server from the NDS Tree" that covers how to recover from a server crash. This document tells you to delete the Server and Volume objects, which renders all your Directory Map, Print Queue, and other objects nonfunctional, and you'll have to manually recreate these objects after a restore. When you don't have SSI data to work with, the information in this TID may be used.

These steps work well when you have replicas on other servers to recover NDS data from; however, there is also the unlikely situation where you lose one partition within the tree and, for some reason, no replica of that partition exists. What can you do? First of all, take a deep breath and *don't panic!* Depending on the partition location within your tree structure, all may not be lost.

Consider the example NDS tree shown in Figure 11.4. Two of the servers in this tree contain the following replicas:

Server S1	Server S2
Master of [Root]	
Master of B	
Subordinate reference of C	Master of C
Read/Write of E	Read/Write of E

Because server S1 has a copy of B (the parent) but not C (the child), NDS automatically placed a subordinate reference of C on server S1.

NOTE

If server S2 is lost due to hardware failure and no other servers hold a replica of C, you lose the only full replica of the C partition (SubRefs are not full replicas, and they only contain enough information to locate other replicas and track synchronization.). When this happens, you now have a hole in your NDS tree between OU=B and OU=E. You can't use the procedure discussed earlier in this section to recover the C partition, because no other full replicas exist.

▶ . . . . ◀

F I G U R E   11.4

If the servers holding the replicas for the C partition are lost, you'll have a hole in your NDS tree between OU=B and OU=E.

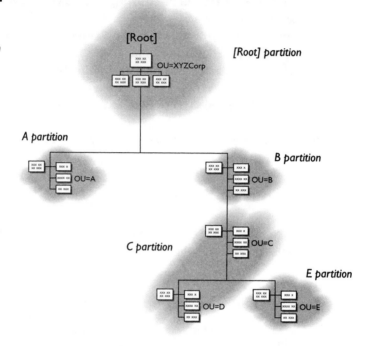

In this scenario where a subordinate reference of the lost partition exists, it is possible to rebuild the links to the lost portion of the NDS tree and then restore the objects from a recent backup. The following procedure explains how you may recover from the loss of a single partition in a multipartition tree and have no replicas of that partition:

WARNING

The following procedure may not work for all cases, and if this is the case, you should consider acquiring the assistance of Novell Technical Support's NDS Support group to rebuild the links to the missing partition in your tree. At the very least, you should test out the procedure in a lab environment first.

1. *Don't panic!* Don't attempt any NDS recovery or repair procedures.

2. Follow the steps outlined earlier in this section to clean up your replica rings for other partitions that have a replica on this crashed server, and make sure your other partitions are synchronizing without errors.

3. If there's more than one server that has a subordinate reference of the lost partition, pick one to work with. The best choice would be a server that has the least number of replicas on it.

4. On this server, load DSRepair with the -A command-line switch. Select the Advanced options menu ⇨ Replica and partition operations. Select the lost partition from the list and press Enter, and select "Designate this server" as the new master replica. This changes the subordinate reference into a real replica; however, because a subordinate reference replica doesn't contain any object information, the recovered replica will be empty.

Depending on your replica placement of this lost partition, SubRefs of this partition on other servers may be upgraded into a read/write.

5. Use DSTRACE to check that this partition is synchronizing correctly. If not, you should consider opening an incident with Novell's NDS Support group for assistance.

6. Once the replica ring is synchronizing, you can perform a selective restore of your NDS objects that were in the lost partition from your most recent backup. Take note of any objects in other parts of your tree that may have turned into Unknowns due to their lost mandatory attributes. You may need to do a selective restore on those objects or recreate them.

You'll need to recreate any bindery objects and NDS objects (such as Print Queues) that depend on object IDs. You may also need to reassign any NDS object trustee assignments.

7. Once the NDS is recovered, you can proceed with the installation of the new server and then restore the file system. Reinstall any add-on products as necessary. One example is Lightweight Directory Access Protocol (LDAP) Services. It may be necessary to remove the restored LDAP Server and LDAP Group objects in NDS and reinstall LDAP Services.

If you don't have a subordinate reference to work with, first make sure no one attempts any repair operations as they can make a bad situation worse. Then you should open a call with Novell's NDS Support group for assistance.

Dealing with Stealth Objects

In Chapter 8 we discussed how you can handle hidden objects. The following is another possible solution using existing tools (DSVIEW) that you can readily obtain for free without having to call Novell or use a third-party utility.

In a distributed management environment, a network administrator may lockout a branch of an NDS tree from administration by other network administrators. This is done by granting one or more users Supervisory objects rights to the container and revoking the inheritance of rights from higher in the tree using Inherited Rights Masks (IRMs). This branch of the NDS tree becomes invisible if none of the trustees of the container at a later stage are available or forget their password.

In such a situation where there are trustees to the parent container, you can make use of Bindery Services and change the password of one of the administrators. Here are the steps:

1. Find a user that has explicit rights to the container in question. In case you don't know what container(s) are invisible or hidden, the hidden object locator NLM (see Chapters 8 and 13) can assist you in locating them. If the user(s) having rights to the container(s) in question also are unknown, DSVIEW can be used:

a. Load the DSVIEW NLM on a server that has a replica of the partition containing the block container.

b. Use DSVIEW to tree walk to the blocked container object.

c. Browse through the values of the ACL attribute until you find a user object that has supervisory objects. The DSVIEW screen looks similar to this (the relevant fields are highlighted for emphasis):

```
Key<Action> 1<Next Attribute> 2<Next Value> 3<View Entry>

        4<Previous Attribute/Value> 5<Toggle Display Mode>

        6<Go To Entry> ESC<Return to Main Menu>



********—  Value Information  —********



Entry ID: 0100016E    "O=HideMe"

Attribute Name: "ACL"



Value Flags:  Present

TimeStamp: 98/10/27 00:39:01; rep# = 0003; event = 03E0



syntax: Object ACL

Trustee Name: CN=Peter2

Attribute Name: [Entry Rights]

Privileges:  Browse, Add, Delete, Rename, Supervisor



More Attributes: Yes     More Attribute Values: Yes
```

d. If the context of the user object is unknown, it can be found by going to the user object. Press g (or 6), and it will take you to the user object, which displays the object's full context in the Entry ID field.

2. Once you've located a user that has supervisory rights to the block container on a server holding a writable replica (master or read/write) of the partition, set the server's bindery context to the location of the user that has rights.

3. Log in to that particular server as Supervisor (in bindery mode).

4. Change the password of the administrator user with SETPASS.EXE (that is, SETPASS username).

5. You can now log in with the revived user and either grant other users rights or remove the IRMs from the container, so it can be administered again.

The same procedure can be applied to block objects.

NOTE
This procedure assumes there is at least one trustee with supervisory rights to the blocked object. If there are no trustees or if the amount of time to track down a trustee is long, you should consider the solutions outlined in Chapter 8.

Maximum Concurrent Logins Reached

One of the more common problems encountered since the initial release of NDS in 1993 is a problem involving maximum concurrent logins. The first you probably hear of an instance of this problem involves a user calling you or your help desk and saying that they are receiving a message indicating the maximum concurrent logins have been reached but that they are not logged in on any other computer on the network.

When a user logs into the network, the login process compares the current number of values in the Network Address attribute of the user object to the value of the Login Maximum Simultaneous attribute. If the number of network addresses is less than to the maximum logins allowed, the login is allowed to proceed; otherwise, the server returns the error code -217 (ERR_MAXIMUM_LOGINS_EXCEEDED) to the client, which then displays an appropriate error message to the user.

The issue here is that there are circumstances where old network addresses are never removed from the network address property for the user. This most commonly occurs when a workstation the user is logged onto ends its session with the server abnormally. In a NetWare 3.x environment, this was not a problem, because the user object had separate authentication credentials for each server. In a NetWare 4 or NetWare 5 environment, however, the credentials are valid for all servers the client is connected to, and the servers do not communicate a loss of communication with each other. During a normal shutdown, the client logout results in the address being properly cleaned up because the client disconnects from all servers. In an abnormal shutdown, however, none of the servers is told the disconnect occurred — they all use the watchdog to clear connections that are terminated abnormally.

Cleaning up this type of problem can be done in a few different ways:

▶ Increase the maximum concurrent logins allowed.

▶ Remove the concurrent login restriction.

▶ Use DSREPAIR to expire network addresses on the user objects that are no longer valid.

▶ Use DSDIAG to expire network addresses on the user objects that are no longer valid.

The first two of these options are easy to implement but may not be desirable for security reasons. If the first two options are not viable for your environment, you will have to use one of the other two options.

The first of these other options is available in NetWare 4 and in NetWare 5 — DSREPAIR automatically purges network address values older than 60 days during an unattended repair or during a repair of the local database from the Advanced Options menu.

You can control the time period to purge unused network address values using the -N switch for DSREPAIR. To do this, load DSREPAIR as follows:

```
LOAD DSREPAIR -N <number of days>
```

Once loaded, execute either an unattended repair or a repair on the local database. During the repair, the value after the -N is used instead of 60.

The biggest drawback to this solution is that it requires that a database repair be run. Running the repair locks the database on the server the repair is being run on. This may not be desirable to correct a problem that many consider to be nothing more than a nuisance.

The second repair option is to use DSDIAG to remove network addresses from user objects. This option does not have the major drawback that DSREPAIR does — it doesn't require that you lock the database on the servers. DSDIAG is capable of making this change on a tree-wide basis using a server that is not connected into the tree; however, the version of DSDiag that performs this option only runs on NetWare 5. At the NetWare 5 server console, type **DSDIAG** to start the program.

To start this operation, select the Preferences item from the main menu. Running this sort of distributed repair requires rights other than the default that DSDIAG starts with. From the Preferences menu, select the Manage Identities option and log in as an administrative user.

Once you have logged in as an administrative user, return to the main menu and select the Distributed Repair option. The only option available here is the option to Remove Monitored Network Addresses.

When selected, you are presented with the screen shown in Figure 11.5. This screen provides you with several options to control the search for unused network addresses. Table 11.1 shows the different options available in Figure 11.5 and the different selections for each option.

Options for Remove Monitored Network Addresses

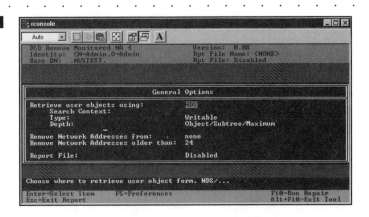

TABLE 11.1

DSDIAG Remove Monitored
Network Address options

OPTION	DESCRIPTION	VALUES
Retrieve user objects using	Tells DSDIAG where to look for user object names. Currently only NDS is an option.	NDS
Search Context	Starting context for the repair	Any valid context in the NDS tree
Type	Determines the type of replicas used for the operation	Master/writable/readable
Depth	How far from the starting search context do you want to search?	Object/Subtree/Maximum. Each of the second two items here can have other values. Subtree can also be self or subordinates, and maximum can also be partition boundary
Remove Network Addresses from	Which objects should have the address removed?	None, all users, or restricted users
Remove Network Addresses older than	How many hours old does an address have to be to be purged?	Any numeric value; 24 hours is the default.
Report file	Options to generate a text or tab-delimited report	Disabled or enabled. When enabled, several other options are enabled to specify the file name and output type.

If you set the Remove Network Addresses from value to NONE, DSDIAG only runs a report of unused network addresses. If you set it to ALL USERS, the program removes the addresses that are no longer used.

As with the DSREPAIR method of removing addresses, this is a manual process, although it can be automated with utilities such as STUFFKEY and CRON or with other task-scheduling software. Unlike the DSREPAIR method, this procedure does not require that you lock the NDS database on any of the servers involved.

If you are not yet ready to introduce a NetWare 5 server into your NDS tree, you can still use DSDIAG to repair this problem by specifying a different tree in the Preferences for DSDIAG. Under the entry for Base DN you will see a default value for the current tree (in our examples, the base DN is .NW5TEST.). By changing the value to another tree—such as .XYZCorp. —you can run the report on a second tree. If you do this, make sure you specify an identity in the target tree and not an identity in the tree the server DSDIAG is running on is in.

Group Membership Recovery

One situation that we have seen occur is when an administrator accidentally deleted group memberships from a large number of users. In this circumstance, the administrator was attempting to add a number of users to a group using the UIMPORT utility. Unfortunately for the site in question, the administrator used a control file that specified REPLACE VALUE=Y, resulting in the new group membership being added, but all of the other group memberships were deleted. Because these group memberships were used to assign rights in the file system and determine which applications are available to each user, this became a problem very quickly.

Fortunately, the change was made off hours, so the immediate impact was minimal. Of even more importance was the backup of the NDS tree that had been made several weeks earlier. While it is true that in many cases backups of NDS are not of much use, in this case, the backup did contain a large percentage of the users in the tree and the information necessary to rebuild the majority of the users' group memberships.

The tools used for this recovery were:

▶ The backup of NDS made several weeks earlier

▶ A server not connected to the production network

▶ NLIST

▶ UIMPORT

▶ Two awk scripts

The first step in this recovery was the restoration of the old NDS group information. The backup product used was only capable of restoring to a server named the same as the server the backup was taken from. In order to accommodate this limitation, we took a lab server from our isolated network and renamed it.

Once that was done, the NDS tree was restored to that server. To ensure the dependencies for group memberships were restored properly, we restored the data twice.

While the NDS tree was restored, two awk scripts were developed. The first script was designed to create a batch file to list the group memberships for each user listed in the original UIMPORT data file. Because the number of users affected was about 100 out of 5,000, it did not make sense to restore group membership information for all users. The awk script written took input in the format of

```
".UserID.Context",".GroupName.Context2"
```

and converted it to a batch file in the format of

```
del grpinfo.txt

cx .context1

nlist user = user1 show "group membership" > grpinfo.txt

nlist user = user2 show "group membership" > grpinfo.txt

cx .context2

nlist user = user3 show "group membership" > grpinfo.txt

nlist user = user4 show "group membership" > grpinfo.txt
```

The script that performs this conversion is as follows:

```
BEGIN { print "del grpinfo.txt" }


{

        count = split($0, object, ".")
```

```
        printf("cx ")

        for (x = 3; x<= count; x++)

                printf(".%s", object[x])

        printf("\n")

        print "nlist user = " object[2] " show \"group
membership\" > grpinfo.txt"

    }
```

Once this batch file was completed and the restore finished, this script could be run to generate a file called GRPINFO.TXT showing all group memberships for the user objects in question. This file was in the format:

```
Object Class: User

Current context: context1

User: user1

        Group Membership: Group1.Admin.Groups.Admin...

        Group Membership: Group2

One User object was found in this context


One User object was found.

Object Class: User

Current context: context1

User: user2

        Group Membership: Group3.Admin.Groups.Admin...

        Group Membership: Group4

One User object was found in this context


One User object was found.
```

```
Object Class: User

Current context: context2

User: user3

        Group Membership: Group1.Admin.Groups.Admin...

        Group Membership: Group2

One User object was found in this context


One User object was found.

Object Class: User

Current context: context2

User: user4

        Group Membership: Group3.Admin.Groups.Admin...

        Group Membership: Group4

One User object was found in this context


One User object was found.
```

This file was then parsed to create the data file used for the new run of UIMPORT. This file ended up being in the format

```
".user1.context1",".Group1.Admin.Groups.Admin"

".user1.context1",".Group2"

".user2.context1",".Group3.Admin.Groups.Admin"

".user2.context1",".Group4"

".user3.context2",".Group1.Admin.Groups.Admin"

".user3.context2",".Group2"

".user4.context2",".Group3.Admin.Groups.Admin"

".user4.context2",".Group4"
```

You should note a couple of things about the data file created. First, the user ID contains a leading dot. This is done so the script can be run from any context and the input is valid. The second thing you might notice is that there are multiple entries for a given user ID; UIMPORT handles this just fine and prevents us from having to determine the maximum number of groups for any of the users and replace those with empty strings for users with less than the maximum number of groups.

The challenge is in parsing the trailing dots on the group memberships and coming up with a script that works reliably to perform the conversion. The script that does this is shown below.

```
/Current context:/ { cx = $3 }


/User:/ {cn = $2}


/Group Membership:/ {
        printf("\".%s.%s\",", cn, cx)
        gsub(/\tGroup Membership: /, "")
        grptmp = $0
        num = split(cx, tmpcx, ".")
        counter = 1
        while (substr(grptmp, length(grptmp)) == ".")
        {
                counter++
                sub(/\.$/,"",grptmp)
        }


        printf("\".%s", grptmp)
```

```
for (y=counter;y<=num;y++)

{

        printf(".%s", tmpcx[y])

}

printf("\"\n")

}
```

In this script, we count the number of trailing dots and compare that to the number of parts in the current context. We then remove the leading portions of the current context until we have run out of dots at the end of the group name. Once that is done, concatenating the group name to the remaining portion of the context results in the correct context for the group.

Now that the new data file is created, we create a control file that uses two fields — one for the user login ID and one for the group membership being processed. Upon watching the run of UIMPORT, we were then able to determine which user IDs had been moved or deleted. Even though all of the users weren't covered in this move, there were sufficient users fixed to prevent a major outage the following day.

The remaining users were either located in the tree manually, and the UIMPORT script updated by hand, or another user object that was similar to that user was located, and those group memberships were used. In total, out of 100 users, only about 10 had to be modified.

NOTE

This example serves as a reminder that a disaster recovery solution need not be a 100 percent solution; if you can automate a large portion of the work in a reasonable amount of time, any remnants can be handled by hand or on a case-by-case basis.

Replica Ring Inconsistency

While not very common, replica ring inconsistencies can reflect serious problems in the NDS tree. A replica ring inconsistency is present when two or more servers holding a replica of a partition do not agree on what the replica rings look like.

The most common cause of this problem is a change in the replica ring while a server in the ring is down combined with a time stamp problem where the server that is down has a future time stamp on its replica information. When this occurs, the replica on the server that was down does not change its replica list to reflect the recent change.

This can result in a number of odd situations: two servers holding the master replica or inconsistent views for subordinate reference replicas and servers missing from the replica ring.

The easiest way to diagnose this type of problem is to use NDS Manager to view partition continuity. This option, as discussed in Chapter 7, provides a view of the NDS partition from each server's perspective. If the rows shown do not match on all servers, there is an inconsistency in the replica ring. Figure 11.6 shows what this might look like in a small tree.

There are two ways to approach resolving this type of issue. The first and most advisable is to contact Novell Technical Support to examine the replica list information on the servers, using their diagnostic tools, and repair the database manually. This is the most common resolution we recommend, because there are a number of different sets of circumstances that can lead to this sort of situation.

If you have worked with the situation for a while, you may be able to correct the problem without involving Novell. Let us look at a second way that does not involve using Novell's support services.

WARNING

It is important to realize that this is one of the types of problems where proceeding without Novell's direct assistance can result in the loss of part of your tree. Proceed with caution!

To start working with this problem, the first thing to do is use NDS Manager to determine which server has the inconsistent view. If you have more than two servers, the more consistent view is the one you want to work with. The server with the view that does not match the others is the one you want to correct in most circumstances.

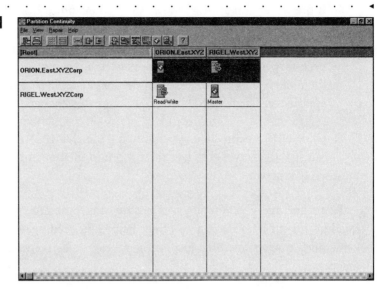

FIGURE 11.6

Replica ring inconsistency shown in NDS Manager

The most direct way to correct the problem is to uninstall NDS from the server in question and reinstall it. This ensures that the time stamps on the affected server are correct. The procedure is as follows:

1. Use NDS Manager to locate the server that has an incorrect view of the replica ring.

2. Remove NDS from that server using the INSTALL (NetWare 4.*x*) or NWCONFIG (NetWare 5.*x*) utility.

3. Wait a few minutes. How long depends on the WAN links involved and the number of replicas the change needs to replicate to.

4. Use NDS Manager to confirm that the replica lists on all servers in the ring show that the server is gone.

5. If NDS Manager still thinks the server is in the replica ring, there may be an additional problem with the server remote ID list. If this happens, use DSREPAIR on each server left to verify the remote IDs for each server.

6. If the server still appears in the ring, you can use DSREPAIR with the -A switch (that is, LOAD DSREPAIR -A) to manually remove the server from the replica ring on the server that holds the master replica. This is only necessary on the server with the master, as the rest of the servers receive the update from the server with the master replica, and the list should appear consistent in NDS Manager once this change has propagated.

7. Once NDS has finished synchronizing the changes to the replica ring, reinstall the server that was removed into the tree and replace the replicas on that server.

There are many different variations to this problem, so it is important to examine the entire situation carefully before proceeding with a plan of action. Remember: doing something just for the sake of doing something can make things much worse.

Synthetic Time

The last example we examine is a very common situation referred to as synthetic time. This problem is one we see more often than any other problem in the Novell Support Connection forums, and in many cases, the advice given by users does not include the first few steps necessary to determine if simply waiting is sufficient to enable the problem to resolve itself. As examples go, this one is the most common situation where waiting is the best alternative.

Synthetic time occurs when the modification time stamp on at least one object in the partition is set to a time that is in the future according to the real time clock on the server reporting the problem. Because it can be caused by a single object, it is important to find out how far ahead the modification time stamp is.

DSREPAIR can tell you this when you run either an unattended full repair or a local database repair. Objects with future modification time stamps are reported in the DSREPAIR.LOG file.

The way this problem is corrected depends on how far ahead the modification time stamp is. If it is measurable in days, you can simply wait for the time to catch up. What synthetic time does is ensure that the future modification time stamp and the current real time converge; this convergence typically takes half the time of the difference between the future time stamp and the current time. So, if the modification time stamp is reported to be an hour into the future, it should take about 30 minutes for the problem to resolve itself.

If, however, the time differential is measurable in months or years, we recommend that you repair the time stamps.

IMPORTANT

Repairing time stamps is a very traffic intensive operation, because all nonmaster replicas of the partition are destroyed and recreated. This can cause loss of services that require bindery contexts for the duration of the repair. Depending on the number of replicas, this operation can take hours to complete; make sure you schedule time off-hours to perform this operation if it is necessary.

In DSREPAIR, start by issuing a LOAD DSREPAIR -A. This enables the option to show up in the menu presented when you select a replica from the Replica and Partition Operations menu on the advanced menu. This option is shown in Figure 11.7.

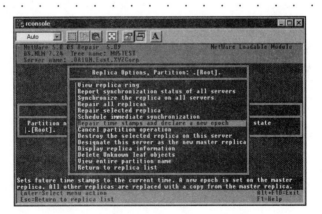

FIGURE 11.7

Repair time stamps option in DSREPAIR

Once this option is selected, you will be prompted for a user login and password; this login ID must have supervisory rights to the portion of the tree where the time stamp repair is taking place.

Once initiated, you must wait for this operation to complete before issuing a second time stamp repair. If the server has multiple replicas with future time stamps, wait for each repair to complete before starting the next one; otherwise, you may flood other servers on the network with too much traffic and introduce further problems. Because this operation destroys replicas on nonmaster servers, you want to make sure you minimize the number of changes taking place from one repair to the next. Run the first repair, and verify that it has completed (all replicas return to an on state in NDS Manager when the repair is complete) before initiating another — even if the other is in a different part of the tree.

Summary

In this chapter, you learned how the concepts and various tools that have been discussed in previous chapters can be applied to specific NDS issues.

In the following chapters, you'll find out how to proactively manage NDS to prevent these issues from developing.

## PART IV

Manage NDS to Prevent Problems

## CHAPTER 12

Upgrading to NetWare 5

NetWare 5 introduced a number of changes and enhancements, such as a new file system, integration of Domain Name System (DNS) and Dynamic Host Configuration Protocol (DHCP) services with NDS, and server-based Java support. NetWare 5 introduced some changes to NDS and the NDS schema that previous versions of NDS for NetWare 4.1x did not support; therefore, when upgrading your NetWare 4 network to NetWare 5, it is important to have a good understanding of the implications of mixing DS.NLM versions and to follow the proper upgrade procedures. This chapter covers the following topics:

▸ Differences in NDS between NetWare 5 and NetWare 4.1x

▸ NetWare 5 licensing scheme

▸ Upgrading a single NetWare 4 server to NetWare 5

▸ Upgrading multiple NetWare 4 servers to NetWare 5

▸ Moving bindery data into NDS

▸ Migration tools and methodologies.

NDS Differences between NetWare 4 and NetWare 5

NetWare 5 included many new features and changes in NDS that are not found in previous versions of NDS. Many of these changes are internal, such as improved performance, better error checking, and support for IP as transport protocol. NetWare 5 also introduced new schema extensions and containment rules into the NDS that previous versions of DS.NLM for NetWare 4.1x do not support. The three major changes that makes the DS.NLM in NetWare 5 incompatible with the older versions of DS.NLM for NetWare 4.10 and NetWare 4.11 are:

▸ Transitive synchronization

▸ ACL inheritance

▸ Handling of schema changes

▸ Handling of object references.

Transitive Synchronization

Transitive synchronization changes the process of how NDS replicas synchronize. As discussed in Chapter 6, previous versions of DS.NLM require all servers that hold a replica of an NDS partition to communicate with all of the other servers in the replica ring. This means there can be as many as $n \times (n-1)$ synchronization attempts between the servers (where n is the number of servers in the replica ring).

Previous versions of DS.NLM has a Synchronized Up To (SyncUpTo) attribute for each replica whose value is kept local on each server (that is, this value is not synchronized to other servers in the replica ring). This means at the beginning of each synchronization cycle, a server must query each target server's SyncUpTo value and decide if synchronization is necessary. In effect, this SyncUpTo attribute is functioning as a Received Up To attribute, because it contains the time stamp of when the server was last synchronized. Transitive synchronization changed this SyncUpTo attribute into a synchronizing attribute, meaning each server in the replica ring will have a list of SyncUpTo time stamps of all the other servers. This enables rapid determination of the need to start an NDS replica synchronization process.

Before a server synchronizes with another server in the replica list, it checks the replica up to (ReplicaUpTo) vectors on the target server (the first server it contacts for synchronization) for other servers in the replica list. Comparing the target server ReplicaUpTo vectors against the source servers determines whether the source server needs to synchronize with any other servers in the replica list. If the target server has more recently synchronized with other servers in the list than the source server, it is not necessary for the source server to synchronize with those servers. This cuts down on synchronization traffic a great deal, facilitates larger replica lists, and reduces the number of communications from $n \times (n-1)$ to $(n-1)$. In addition, changes made on a replica can be synchronized to other replicas via intermediaries. This eliminates the problem of DS servers being unable to connect with one another.

Also added to the schema definition for replicas are the Synchronization Tolerance and Purge Vector attributes. The Synchronization Tolerance attribute specifies the tolerance level of a replica ring for being considered in sync; this attribute's function is similar to the timesync synchronization radius setting. At the time of this writing, this attribute is defined in the schema and NDS Manger makes use of it, but its value is not currently adjustable. The Purge Vector attribute is used by NDS Manager, in conjunction with Synchronization Tolerance, to determine each replica's synchronization status. Figure 12.1 shows the Transitive Synchronization Information dialog box from NDS Manager with the purge vector and a transitive vector.

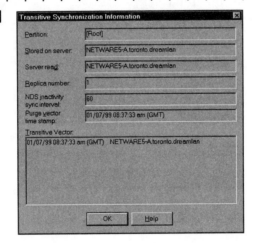

F I G U R E   12.1

Transitive Synchronization Information dialog box for the [Root] partition

>
>
> **NOTE**
>
> **To interoperate with NetWare 5, you need to be running DS.NLM v6.00 or higher on any NetWare 4.11 servers and DS.NLM v5.15 or higher on NetWare 4.10 servers that are in the same NDS tree. At the very least, any server in the same replica ring as a NetWare 5 server must have the updated DS.NLM.**

ACL Inheritance

One of the new features in NetWare 5 is the capability to make a specific attribute's Access Control List (ACL) inheritable. You will find a new NDS container attribute right called Inheritable. In the past, if you want to make someone an administrator for the Telephone Number attribute for all the users, for example, you must grant this person NDS rights to the Telephone Number attribute of *every* user. You're unable to simply grant the necessary property rights to a container (say, the container's Telephone Number attribute) and expect this user to have the necessary rights to the Telephone Number attribute of all objects subordinate to that container; however, you can accomplish this now with NetWare 5. This ACL inheritance feature only applies to container objects and is functional only with versions of NDS that ships with NetWare 5 or later.

NOTE

An immediate use of ACL inheritance is in setting up user password management. You can refer to Novell's TID #2942076 (Password Management in NetWare 5) on how to set this up from `http://support.novell.com/cgi-bin/search/tidfinder.cgi?2942076.`

You'll find an Inheritable option in NWAdmin to enable or not enable inheritance of rights to a container object, including both object and property rights (see Figure 12.2). When this option is checked, the trustee assignment is inherited to objects and containers below this object in the directory tree. This applies to object rights, rights to all properties, and rights to specific properties.

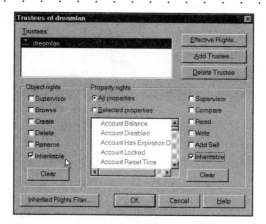

F I G U R E 12.2

Using 32-bit NWAdmin (NWADMN32) to see and manage ACL inheritance

To ensure that the synchronization of the inherited ACLs is consistent, any NetWare 4.11 server in the same replica ring as a NetWare 5 server must be upgraded to DS.NLM v5.99 (and NetWare 4.10 servers must be upgraded to DS.NLM v5.12 or higher). Otherwise, this inheritance behavior will be *masked out* (or filtered out) if the inheritance path includes a server running prior versions of DS.NLM. Although the newer versions of DS.NLM for NetWare 4.10 and NetWare

4.11 synchronize the inherited ACLs and enable them to properly flow through to a NetWare 5, they will not act upon these inheritable ACLs.

NOTE DS.NLM v5.99/5.12 supports ACL inheritance but not transitive synchronization; therefore, in an environment where you have NetWare 5 servers, it is best to use DS.NLM v6.00/5.15 and higher for full compatibility.

If you plan to use the inherited ACL feature, ensure all servers in the replica ring are NetWare 5. This ensures that no matter what server in the ring a user attaches to, the inherited rights will be available. (Remember that inherited ACL is a feature of NetWare 5 servers only.) Furthermore, you need to ensure DS v5.99 or higher is installed on any NetWare 4.11 servers (and DS v5.12 or higher on NetWare 4.10 servers) that are in the (logical) tree path between NetWare 5 servers. This ensures that ACL rights flow down to the NetWare 5 servers. To better understand this, consider the example NDS tree structure shown in Figure 12.3.

F I G U R E   12.3

Flow of inherited ACLs in a mixed NetWare 4 and NetWare 5 environment

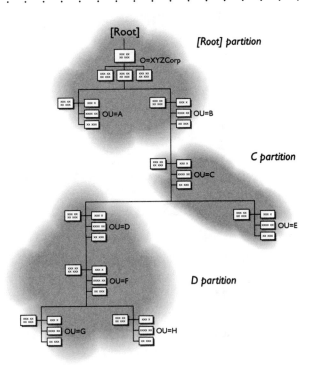

If you want to exercise the inherited ACL feature in partition [Root], all the servers holding replicas of [Root] must be NetWare 5 servers. If you then decide to use inherited ACLs in the subtree consisting of partition D and want those ACLs to flow down from [Root], in addition to upgrading all servers holding replicas of D to NetWare 5, you *must* upgrade all NetWare 4.1x servers holding a replica of C to DS.NLM v6.00/5.15 or higher. This ensures that the ACLs can flow down the tree.

Even with DS.NLM v6.00/5.15 and higher installed, NetWare 4.1x servers holding replicas of the C partition will not and cannot act upon the inherited ACLs from [Root]. They can, however, enable the ACLs to flow through to the NetWare 5 servers (holding replicas of the D partition) lower in the tree.

Schema Changes

NetWare 5.0 servers introduce new schema extensions and containment rules into the tree that previous versions of DS.NLM for NetWare 4.1x do not support. In addition to the inherited ACLs discussed previously, there are two other main issues arising from these changes:

▶ Deleting schema definitions

▶ Tree root dependency.

The first issue is the deletion of schema definitions (both classes and attributes). Because of issues with schema synchronization, most, if not all, schema deletes will not correctly synchronize to NetWare 4.1x servers without replicas. This is not particularly bad in most instances, because it means that some items that are defined in the schema are not being used; however, this does, technically, mean the schema definition in this tree is out of sync between servers. Fortunately, running DS.NLM v6.00/5.15 and higher, even on servers without a replica and using the new Reset Schema option in DSREPAIR v4.59 and higher, will fix these problems.

NOTE

Any servers which did not have a replica at one time and then later received a replica may have inconsistent schema from deletions which occurred before adding the replica. These servers should also have DS.NLM v6.00/5.15 and higher installed. Optionally, after upgrading to the new DS.NLM run the Reset Schema option of

DSRepair v4.59 or higher on these NetWare 4.1x servers. This cleans up any previously existing inconsistencies.

In NetWare 5 a new tree root dependency (with a new T=*treename* naming attribute) was added to the schema. This new schema is synchronized correctly from a NetWare 5 server to a NetWare 4.1x server, but the NetWare 4.1x server (if running DS.NLM prior to v6.00/5.15 or higher) does not pass the same new schema on to other NetWare 4.1x servers correctly.

Object References

As discussed in Chapters 8 and 11, it is important to maintain proper object references in a disaster recovery situation. You should be aware of this issue when you are restoring an object reference on a NetWare 5 server that requires the referenced object to also be restored. If the referenced object resides on a NetWare 4.1x server that is not running DS.NLM v6.00/5.15 or higher, the reference object will not be created properly.

Consider the following example:

You need to restore a group object (called Group1.East.XYZCorp) where there are many membership entries. Group1 has a member called User1.West.XYZCorp. User1 does not currently exist in the tree, and all replicas of West.XYZCorp exist only on NetWare 4.1x servers and none of which are running DS.NLM v6.00/5.15. When you restore this group object, the result could be one of the following:

1. The object Group1.East.XYZCorp cannot be created correctly.

2. The restore fails.

3. The restore does not fail, but the group membership User1.West.XYZCorp will not be created.

You should update the NetWare 4 servers to DS.NLM v6.00/5.15 or higher before attempting the restore.

NetWare 5 Licensing

NetWare 5 uses Novell Licensing Services (NLS) to manage its licenses and uses NDS to store the licensing information. Although NLS is available in NetWare 4.11 to track application license usage (such as BorderManager), NLS is not used to track NetWare 4.11 server licenses. While NetWare 5 licensing and NDS are not directly tied to each other, there are a number of things that you need to be aware of when managing NDS objects so that you don't cause unwanted licensing problems.

NetWare 4 stores each license as a separate file in the SYS:_NETWARE directory. Even though SYS:_NETWARE is the same directory in which all NDS database files are kept, the license files (which are named MLS.000, MLS.001, and so on) are not part of NDS.

 At the time of this writing, NetWare 5 licensing is still server-centric. For more details about licensing, see the "Assigning Licenses" section.
NOTE

When you install a NetWare 5 server into an NDS tree, the NLS extends the base schema (if not already extended) and creates the following NDS objects in the same context in which the NetWare server is installed into:

▸ **NLS License Server**. A leaf object named NLS_LSP_*servername* where *servername* is the name of the NetWare 5 server. (The object type is NLS:license Server.)

▸ **NLS Product Containers**. The base server license is associated with a container object named Novell+NetWare 5 Server+500 (where 500 refers to the version of NetWare, not the number of connections). A container named Novell+NetWare 5 Conn SLC+500 (again, the 500 refers to the version of NetWare, not the number of connections) is associated with connection licenses. (The object type is NLS:Product Container.)

▸ **NLS License Certificate**. A leaf object named the same as the serial number of the certificate (such as SN:*xxxxxxxxx* where *xxxxxxxxx* is the serial number). This object is created in one of the two NLS product containers. (The object type is NLS:license certificate.)

► · ◄

Naming Conventions

The naming convention for a NLS product container is

```
Publisher_name+Product_name+Version_number
```

If an application specified a decimal in the version number when creating the product container (such as Dreamlan+Demo+5.17), NDS puts a backslash in front of the decimal; in this case, the resulting object name is Dreamlan+Demo_5\.17.

NOTE

The NetWare 5 license file comes in one of two formats: certificate envelope (*.NLF) or user connection licenses (*.NLS or *.CLS). The envelope format contains both the base server license and connection license. If you install the full certificate envelope, an NLS:license certification object (with the name of the format SN:xxxxxxxx) is created in both NLS:product container objects. If you install only the base server license, the license certificate object is created only in the Novell+NetWare 5 Server+500 container. If you install only connection license, the license certificate object is created only in the Novell+NetWare 5 Conn SLC+500 container.

The schema is extended the first time you run SETUPNLS.NLM or NWCONFIG.NLM (NWConfig ⇨ License Options ⇨ Set up Licensing service). SetupNLS/NWConfig creates the NLS_LSP server object and this object has an attribute that tells it where the License Service Provider (LSP) objects are located in the tree. Each NetWare 5 server *must* has its own NLS_LSP_*servername* object.

NOTE

You need to have an LSP running on a server with a writeable replica. This replica can be a master or read/write. You can run LSPs on servers without replicas as long as they can communicate with the LSP that has a writeable replica. The server with a writeable replica can make changes to the NDS database in behalf of the other servers.

There is a license container object for the installed base server licenses and a separate license container for the installed connection licenses (see Figure 12.4). (Server and connection licenses are discussed in the "NetWare 5 Licensing Types" section in this chapter.) The license containers must be in the same container as the NetWare Server object or in a container above the one which contains the NetWare Server object. This requirement is due to the way the NLS Policy Manager searches for license objects — the Policy Manager only walks *up* the tree to find the license containers and not down the tree. What this means is that if the license containers are moved down the tree and the NetWare Server object is not moved to the same location, licensing ceases to function. On the other hand, you can move the license containers up the tree (toward the [Root]) to facilitate centralized license object management without having to move the NetWare Server objects.

► • • • • • • • • • • • • • • • • • • • ◄

You can only properly view and manage NetWare 5 licenses using NetWare 5's 32-bit NWAdmin utility.

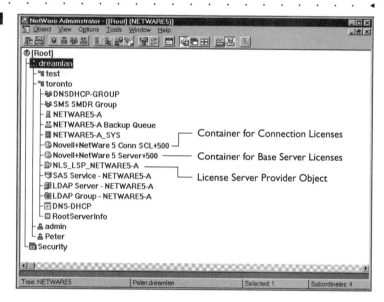

If the NetWare server object is moved to a container above the original container, the licenses must be deleted and reinstalled, because the Policy Manager will be unable to locate the associated licenses. The solution is as follows:

1. Using NWAdmin to open each license container and delete the certificate objects. The license containers can then be deleted.

2. Delete the NLS_LSP_*servername* object. (If you have not yet moved the NetWare server object, you can move it at this point.)

3. Reinstall the license(s) using NWAdmin or NWCONFIG.NLM. The license containers and certificates now appear in the same OU as the NetWare server object.

Moving Licenses

You can easily move license certificates from one context or location in the NDS tree to another. The easiest way is to drag and drop using NLSMan32. You can also follow these steps:

1. Select View ⇨ Tree View.

2. Select the license certificate you wish to move.

3. Select Edit ⇨ Move. You can also press Ctrl+M or right-click the certificate and select Move. (See Figure 12.5.)

Note that you can only move the certificates, not the license container. A new license container will be created after the move if one doesn't already exist.

NOTE

4. Select the new context for the license certificate using the tree icon next to the destination field. Browse by clicking the + or – symbols in the Select Context window. Double-click the location you prefer, or click the location and then click OK.

5. Click OK. Click Yes to confirm the new location, then click OK to acknowledge that the certificate object was successfully moved.

6. If the license container is empty, select Yes to delete it or No to leave it in the NDS tree.

License certificate objects can be moved to another location as long as the associated NLS_LSP_*servername* object is moved with it to the same destination. Other than NLSMan32, you can also use NWAdmn32 to move license certificates.

NOTE

To move license certificates using NWAdmn32, simply locate and highlight the license certificate object in the tree, then use the Tools ➪ Move License option to enter the name of the destination container (see Figure 12.6).

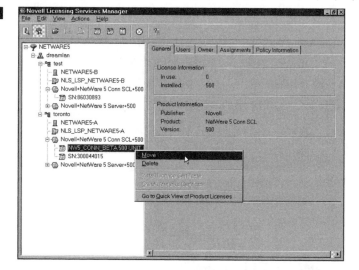

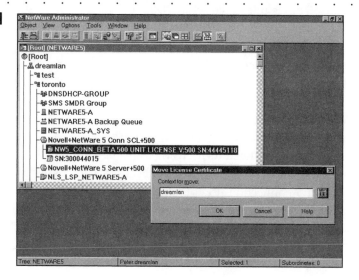

Site Licenses versus Unique Licenses

There are two types of NetWare 5 licenses that can be installed: *nonrestricted license* and *restricted license* (where you need a unique license per server). The nonrestricted license, commonly known as a Master License Agreement (MLA) license, doesn't check for duplicate serial numbers, and, therefore, the same license can be installed on multiple servers. The restricted license, on the other hand, cannot be installed on more than one server; each server is required to have its own unique server license, otherwise the servers complain "duplicate license detected" constantly. In addition, one or more unique server connection licenses may be installed per server.

WARNING

Unlike the MLA license, the restricted license does not allow you to change the name of the server in the AUTOEXEC.NCF file without any adverse effect. If the server name is changed in the AUTOEXEC.NCF, the file server assignment must be changed using NWAdmin (see the "Assigning Licenses" section).

NetWare 5 Licensing Types

NetWare 5 uses the Novell Licensing Services (NLS) to manage its licenses. And because NLS is integrated with NDS, you need to understand the different types of licenses available and the implications of installing certain types of licenses (such as the NetWare 5 evaluation license). Be aware that the version of NLS used by NetWare 5 is incompatible with previous versions of NLS available for NetWare 4; therefore, you need to apply the latest support pack for NetWare 4 to obtain the latest NLS for NetWare 4 servers.

Base Licenses and Connection Licenses

NetWare 5 separated its licensing into a base (server) license, which each server must have, and connection (or user) licenses. Each base server license comes with at least a 5-connection license, and you can add multiple connection licenses on top of this. For example, if your NetWare 5 server is to support 510 users, you can install a base server license that has 500 connections plus a 10-connection license. Without any license installed, NetWare 5 enables two login connections.

Evaluation Licenses

Novell has available evaluation/demo licenses for NetWare 5 which are full-blown, time-limited licenses. Before you install such a license, you must be aware of this one caveat: NetWare 5's evaluation licenses are intended to be used *once only* per server. Even if the evaluation license has reached the expiration date, once it has been installed on a server, it can't be reinstalled again on the same server. So, if the license has been completely removed from the server/tree, you can't reinstall the same license back on the same server that was previously installed with the same license. When you try to, you'll encounter messages similar to the following:

```
Cannot install this license because it has already been
installed into the Directory Service tree. (LICENSE_INSTALL-
5-9)

1 UNIT NetWare 5 Server LICENSE

This operation could not be completed. The License
Certificate selected is either damaged or already installed
somewhere in the Directory.
```

If you wish to reinstall the same license on the same server, you'll need to delete the SYS volume and reinstall the NetWare 5 OS; unless you have a utility that enables you access to the hidden SYS:_NETWARE directory where a file keeps track of the serial numbers installed. On the other hand, if after your evaluation is completed you wish to purchase the real NetWare 5 license, you need to remove the evaluation license and install the real license. You don't need to recreate the SYS volume.

The NetWare 5 evaluation license is typically a 1-server base server license with a 3-user connection license.

NOTE

Runtime Licenses

The NetWare 5 runtime license is not an evaluation license. The runtime license is a base server license without any connection licenses. By installing a runtime license, an SN:*serialnumber* object is added to the Novell+NetWare 5 Server+500 container. Because there is no connection license installed, the runtime server enables two connections to it.

Although a server without any licenses installed enables two logins just like a runtime server, the two are not equivalent. A server with a runtime license installed returns a success code to certain API function calls, while an unlicensed server returns a failure code to the same API calls, even under the same operating conditions.

NOTE

Assigning Licenses

Access to a license certificate is determined by the location of the license certificate and whether any assignments have been made to the license certificate. Each installed license certificate has an owner — the NDS user who installed the license certificate. The owner can assign the following objects access to the licenses: user, group, organization, organizational unit, and server.

Only the owner of a certificate can make and change access assignments.

NOTE

If you assign a container object to use a certificate, all users in and below this container are be able to use the certificate. If you do not want to restrict access to licenses in this way, do not make any assignments to the license certificates. Once you make assignments, only those objects that have been assigned to the license certificates can use the license.

At the time of this writing, NetWare 5 licenses are server-centric, much like previous versions of NetWare. If you examine the policy information (by selecting the license object in NLS Manager's tree view; see Figure 12.7) associated with the base server license or the connection license, you'll find that the certificate must be assigned to a file server. Because only one file server assignment can be made for each certificate, the license is server-based — you can't share a 50-connection license certificate among two or more servers (for example, 20 connections to one server and the remaining 30 connections to another). More than one certificate may be assigned to a given file server, however, and the connection count in each new license certificate is additive to the previous license certificate to give the total number of connections that can be granted for use. For example, you can assign two 50-connection license certificate to the same server, thus enabling 100 users to access resources on that server concurrently.

▶ · ◀

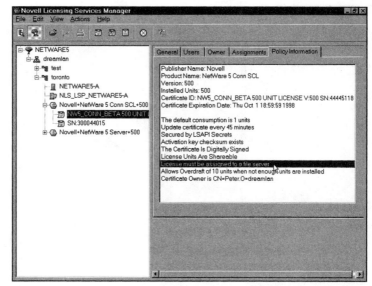

FIGURE 12.7

Viewing a certificate's policy information using NLSMan32

You assign and delete access to licenses through the assignments property page using the following steps. To add assignment (see Figure 12.8) using NLSMan32, do the following:

1. From NLS Manager's Browse window, select View ➪ Tree View.

2. Select the license certificate object you want to assign to a server.

3. Select the assignments tab and click the Add button.

4. Use the Select Object(s) To Assign window to locate the NetWare server object you want to assign as owner of this certificate object. Select the object and click OK.

Adding a file server assignment to a certificate using NLSMan32

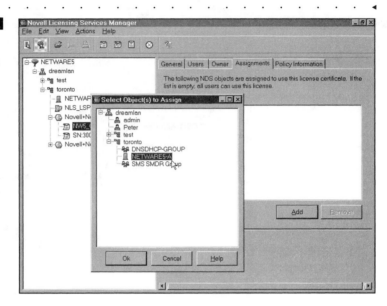

The following steps delete server assignment from a certificate:

1. From NLS Manager's Browse window, select View ⇨ Tree View..

2. Select the server object you want to delete.

3. Click Remove, click Yes, and click OK.

You can also make server assignments from NWAdmin by selecting the certificate you want to assign to a file server, right-clicking the object, and selecting Details ⇨ Assignments. Browse for the desired file server object using the Select Object window, select the object, and click OK.

Migration Tools and Methodologies

Depending on how you plan to upgrade your existing NetWare 4 network to NetWare 5, there are a number of methods and tools that can help to ensure a smooth and easy transition. This section covers the following NetWare 5 migration scenarios:

▸ A network with a single NetWare 4 server

▸ A network with multiple NetWare 4 servers

▸ Moving from NetWare for Small Business servers to NetWare 5

▸ Moving from NetWare 3 to NetWare 5

▸ Changing server hardware at the same time as upgrading the OS

NOTE

Because NetWare for Small Business uses the same code base as NetWare 4.1 (and higher), the same procedure for upgrading NetWare 4 to NetWare 5 is applicable.

Premigration Checklist

Prior to installing a NetWare 5 server into an existing 4.1*x* NDS tree, the following three things must first be verified:

1. All NetWare 4.10 servers are running DS.NLM v5.15 or higher.

2. All NetWare 4.11 servers are running DS.NLM v6.00 or higher.

3. All NetWare 4.1*x* servers should have DSREPAIR v 4.59 or higher installed.

You can always find the latest DS.NLM from the Novell support Web site at http://support.novell.com. **The NDS update files are either included in the latest Support Pack for the specific version of NetWare or in DS411x.EXE (or DS410x.EXE), if a newer DS.NLM is made available after the current Support Pack was released.**

If the NDS tree was originally installed using NetWare version 4.0*x*, you should execute the Repair local DS database option under the Advanced options menu with DSREPAIR v4.59 or greater on a NetWare 4.1*x* server holding the Master or a Read/Write replica of [Root]. This addresses schema definitions that may not have been properly time-stamped if your tree began life as a NetWare 4.0x NDS tree. With the introduction of newer versions of DS, this could cause possible corruption with the backlink attribute.

If your tree did not start out as a NetWare 4.0x tree, it is not necessary to run this DSREPAIR option; however, if you are unsure at what version the tree started out, you should run DSREPAIR
NOTE **(execute the Repair local DS database option under the Advanced options menu) on the server holding the Master or a Read/Write replica of [Root] to be on the safe side.**

NetWare Licenses with a Nine-Digit Serial Number

If the serial number printed on your NetWare 5 license diskette label has nine digits, it can't be installed while upgrading an existing server to NetWare 5. You must check the Install without licenses box on the License Installation screen during the server install and install this license later using NWAdmin or NWConfig.

If you didn't notice you have a nine-digit license and attempted to install it, selecting the Install without a license box after the failure may cause the remaining of the install process to fail. In some cases
WARNING **it is necessary to start the installation again and select the Install without a license box without first browsing for a license.**

Upgrade Options

There are two ways in which you can upgrade a server running one version of NetWare to another: in-place upgrade and across-the-wire upgrade. With the in-place upgrade method, the same server hardware is used and all existing data is preserved; therefore, the in-place upgrade is the fastest and least troublesome method, provided your server's hardware meets the requirement for the new version of the OS. The drawback of the in-place upgrade, however, is that if for any reason you need to back out of the process, you need to rebuild your server from backup. Therefore, when performing an in-place upgrade, it is vital that you have verified backups.

The industry-standard recommendation is that you should make at least two backups of your system prior to upgrading. In the (very) unlikely event that both backups are corrupted, chances are good that the corruption didn't happen on the same files or at the same location on the backup media.

TIP

The in-place upgrade is performed using the standard NetWare 5 install routine by choosing the Upgrade from 3.1x or 4.1x option.

The across-the-wire method is preferable if you are moving to new server hardware at the same time that you're upgrading the OS. This method requires you to have your NetWare 5 server installed; then the user information and files are copied from the source server to the NetWare 5 server. You can use either MIGRATE.EXE (a DOS application) shipped with NetWare 4 or the new Novell Upgrade Wizard (a 32-bit MS Windows program) included with NetWare 5. The across-the-wire method offers the safest migration method, because the source server is left untouched, but the drawback is speed. During the across-the-wire migration process, the workstation-based application performs the data transfer; thus the workstation itself becomes the bottleneck. The user-related data (such as user and group information) is first retrieved from source server to the workstation and is then written out to the target server (see Figure 12.9). Even during file transfer, the data does not flow directly between servers.

MIGRATE.EXE may be used to move information to NetWare 5 servers, but because it was not originally designed for NetWare 5, you should be using Upgrade Wizard; furthermore, the Upgrade Wizard is the Novell-supported replacement tool for MIGRATE.EXE. We simply mention MIGRATE.EXE here for the sake of completeness.

WARNING

There are many advantages the Upgrade Wizard has over MIGRATE.EXE. The two most notable advantages are speed and the password migration functionality. Because Upgrade Wizard is a 32-bit application, it is much more efficient than the 16-bit DOS MIGRATE.EXE program. Upgrade Wizard is able to migrate user passwords from the old server to the new, whereas MIGRATE.EXE cannot. MIGRATE.EXE is only able to assign no password or create a random password for each migrated user; therefore, if you wish to preserve user passwords during a

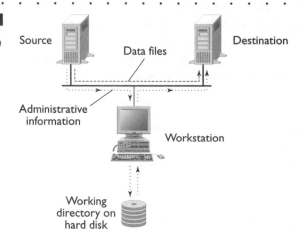

The data must flow through the workstation during an across-the-wire migration; thus the process is slower than an in-place upgrade.

migration, Upgrade Wizard is preferred over MIGRATE.EXE. You can, however, migrate user passwords without using the Upgrade Wizard, as discussed in the "Bindery-to-NDS Conversion" section.

You can't use MIGRATE.EXE or Upgrade Wizard to migrate from one NetWare 5 server to another NetWare 5 server (or from a NetWare 4 server to another NetWare 4 server), as would be the case if you need to upgrade or change the server hardware (such as replacing the disk which has the SYS volume) but not the version of the OS. To accomplish this, you need to use the DSMAINT.NLM shipped with NetWare. This process is very well documented in the Novell Technical Information Document (TID #2934033) "4.x or 5.x Migration / DSMaint Procedure."

To summarize:

▶ When upgrading a NetWare 3 or NetWare 4 server to NetWare 5 using the same hardware, use the in-place upgrade method.

▶ When upgrading a NetWare 3 or NetWare 4 server to NetWare 5 and switching hardware at the same time, use the across-the-wire upgrade method.

▶ If you plan to just upgrade the disks (and not the CPU, for example) as part of the migration, you should first do the in-place upgrade for the OS change over, *then* use DSMAINT for the hardware upgrade.

▸ When switching the disk(s) holding the SYS volume of a server with NDS on it (that is, a NetWare 4 or NetWare 5 server, regardless if it holds any replicas or not), use the DSMAINT procedure.

Postmigration Checklist

Any remaining NetWare 4.1x servers in the tree that receive the following or a similar NLS error on the server console must be upgraded to DS.NLM v6.00/5.15 or higher:

```
"Novell Licensing Services (NLS): An older NLS schema
extension has been detected. If you have not converted your
old licensing data, you may do so by running SETUPNLS.NLM."
```

If you receive the previous message, perform the following steps:

1. Run SETUPNLS.NLM on the server. If the message is still displayed, continue with step 2.

2. Upgrade the server to DS.NLM v6.00/5.15 or later.

3. Run the Reset Schema option in DSREPAIR v4.59 or later on the server where the error is being displayed. This updates the schema and removes the old attribute.

Renaming a NetWare 5 Server

When upgrading to NetWare 5, you should give some thought in advance and decide if you're changing the name of your servers or not. As noted in the "Site Licenses Versus Unique Licenses" section, changing the name of your NetWare 5 file server may affect licensing. The AUTOEXEC.NCF contains the following warning message:

```
If you change the name of this server, you must update

all the licenses that are assigned to this server. Using

NWAdmin, double-click on a license object and click on
```

the Assignments button. If the old name of
this server appears, you must delete it and add the
new server name. Do this for all license objects.

Therefore, switching the name of a NetWare 5 server is a little more involved than renaming a NetWare 3 or NetWare 4 server. And if there is any NDS corruption, you may have to also perform the following procedure:

I. Run NWAdmin.

2. Delete the license objects and license containers.

3. Delete NLS_LSP_*oldservername* object.

4. On the renamed server, set up licensing service using NWConfig.

5. Install the license using NWConfig or NWAdmin.

NOTE

Changing a file server's name may have other consequences, such as workstation configurations, and will affect other products that make use of the server name.

· ·

Upgrading in a Single-Server Environment

Upgrading a single server from NetWare 3 or NetWare 4 to NetWare 5 is rather straightforward. You can use either the in-place upgrade or across-the-wire migration method as appropriate. If the server is a NetWare 4 server, there is no need to upgrade the DS.NLM first. You don't even need to run the new DSREPAIR to fix time stamps on backlinks, because none are created in a single-server environment.

Backlinks are related to External References (ExRefs). When a server must hold information about entries in partitions that the server does not store (such as a file system trustee for a user object), the information is stored in ExRefs. ExRefs are not real entries, because they do not contain complete entry information; they are place holders containing information about entries that the server does not hold. ExRefs are very much like SubRefs for replicas.

In short, an ExRef is a reference to an entry that is not physically located on the local server, and it enables a reference to an entry without duplicating the entry on every server in the NDS tree. When NDS creates an ExRef for an entry not stored on the local server, a backlink is created on the real entry. The Backlink points to the server that holds the ExRef.

The main thing to keep in mind is the new licensing scheme: with single-server NetWare 5 tree, if for any reason you removed and reinstalled NDS, you may receive Policy Manager errors such as:

```
POLICY MANAGER - (5.00-24); The NLS licensing services are
not available on Server name. Please make sure the
NLSLSP.NLM is loaded. Error # C0001003.
```

You may also see similar errors with an error # of C0001002. The problem results from the fact that when DS is reinstalled, in the case of a single-server tree, the NLS and server license objects are lost. This problem would not occur in a multiserver tree because objects in NDS are replicated. If this happens, two things need to be done:

1. Reinstall NLS. This is done through NWConfig by selecting License Options ⇨ Set up licensing service.

2. Reinstall the server license(s). This can be done through NWConfig by selecting License Options ⇨ Install licenses. Alternatively, you can go through NWAdmn32 by selecting Tools ⇨ Install License ⇨ Install Envelope.

TIP
If you still don't see the license objects after using NWConfig, use NWAdmn32 to install your licenses, because it gives additional information and messages that may help you troubleshooting.

When you're done, you should have the following three NLS-related objects:

▸ NLS_LSP_*servername*

▸ Novell+NetWare 5 Conn SCL+500

▸ Novell+NetWare 5 Server+500.

► · ◄

Upgrading in a Multiserver Environment

Upgrading a multi-NetWare 4 network to NetWare 5 requires some advanced planning. Before installing a NetWare 5 server into an existing NetWare 4.1x tree, it is essential that the requirements listed in the "Premigration Checklist" (mentioned earlier in this chapter) are fulfilled. It would make your upgrade so much easier if you can have all your NetWare 4.1x servers running the latest DS.NLM prior to installing your first NetWare 5 server into this tree. If for technical or other reasons you cannot have all your NetWare 4.1x servers running the latest DS.NLM, observe the following implementation guidelines:

► Run the latest DSREPAIR on the NetWare 4.1x server holding the Master of [Root] to correct any improperly time-stamped schema definitions.

► Determine the version of DS.NLM that is running on each of your NetWare 4.1x servers. This can be accomplished using either NDS Manager or the DSDIAG NLM.

► Upgrade the DS.NLM on any NetWare 4.1x without a replica to deal with the schema deletion issue.

► If the new NetWare 5 server will hold a replica, identify the servers that are currently in that replica ring. This can be accomplished using either DSREPAIR or NLIST. Upgrade the DS.NLM on all servers in this replica ring to the latest versions. This ensures that the synchronization of the inherited ACLs is consistent and facilitates transitive synchronization.

► When adding your second and subsequent NetWare 5 servers, upgrade the DS.NLM on any NetWare 4.1x servers that lay in the (logical) path between the NetWare 5 servers. (Refer to the "ACL Inheritance" section earlier in this chapter.)

► Upgrade the DS.NLM on any NetWare 4.1x servers on which an object referenced by a NetWare 5 is stored. This is to address the possible loss of object reference during an object restore (refer to the "Object References" section earlier in this chapter).

As you can tell, the phased upgrade of DS.NLM is rather messy; therefore, it is best that you simply upgrade the DS.NLM on all your NetWare 4.1x servers prior to the start of your NetWare 5 implementation project.

Tree Merges

You may be running your current production network using NetWare 4.1x servers and have a separate NetWare 5 network for testing. At some point in time you may wish to merge the NetWare 4 tree and NetWare 5 tree together into a single NetWare 5 tree. You can easily accomplish this using the DSMERGE NLM utility.

DSMERGE enables you to join two NDS trees so that the new combined tree can be accessed by clients of both of the previous trees. A source tree and target tree are selected for the merge operation. The source tree is merged into the target tree at the root and becomes part of the target tree. The tree name of the combined tree is that of the target tree.

When the tree merge operation involves a NetWare 5 tree, you must use the DSMERGE.NLM (v2.00 or higher) that is shipped with NetWare 5. You need to load it on the server that holds the master of [Root] of the source tree. Shown in Table 12.1 is a DSMERGE placement matrix for merging NDS trees involving NetWare 5.

NOTE

If DSMERGE is loaded on a server that does not hold the master of [Root], it reports back the name of the correct server from which to run DSMerge.

T A B L E 12.1

*Different Merge Scenarios
and DSMERGE Placement*

SCENARIO	PLACEMENT
Merging two NetWare 5 trees	Load DSMERGE on the server that holds the master of [Root] of the source tree.
Merging a NetWare 5 tree into a NetWare 4.1x tree	Load DSMERGE on the server that holds the master of [Root] of the NetWare 5 tree.

Continued

T A B L E   12.1

*Different Merge Scenarios
and DSMERGE Placement
(continued)*

SCENARIO	PLACEMENT
Merging a NetWare 4.1x tree into a NetWare 5 tree	In order to merge a NetWare 4.1x tree into a NetWare 5 tree, the server holding the master of [Root] of the NetWare 4.1x tree must be a NetWare 5 server. If it's not, then you need to upgrade it to NetWare 5 first; however, only this one server in the NetWare 4.1x source tree needs to be NetWare 5, and the rest can remain as NetWare 4.1x until they are upgraded. Run DSMERGE on this NetWare 5 server.

When merging a pure NetWare 4.1x tree with a NetWare 5 tree, you can expect DSMERGE to report a schema mismatch between the two trees if you didn't first use DSREPAIR to synchronize the schemas between the trees. To synchronize the schemas, load DSREPAIR on the server that does *not* have the schema modification (the NetWare 4.1x tree in this case), go to Advanced options and choose Global Schema Options ⇨ Import remote schema. After entering the admin name and password, perform the option to import remote schema. If you have installed some products that extend the schema, such as NDS for NT, it is necessary to import the schema from source tree to target tree, then from target tree to source tree, and finally, once again, from source tree to target tree.

▶ · ◀

Bindery-to-NDS Conversion

We mentioned earlier in this chapter that you can use either MIGRATE.EXE or Novell Upgrade Wizard to move the bindery data, across-the-wire, from a NetWare 3.1x server into NDS; however, there is an alternative method that you can use — you can import the bindery information into NDS directly using NWConfig (or Install in NetWare 4), and the files and file system trustee assignments can be moved using the server-to-server copy feature available in many SMS-compliant tape backup software. The following simplified steps (assuming the NetWare 5 server is already installed) illustrate the process:

1. Place a replica on the NetWare 5 server so you can set the bindery context to the container into which the bindery data will be imported. Ensure only one bindery context is specified.

2. Clean up your bindery, such as removing obsolete users and groups. Delete all print queues and print servers; they'll need to be recreated in NDS anyway, and this gives you the opportunity to place the queue directories on a volume other than SYS.

3. Use Dupbind (a DOS utility from Novell Research) or visually scan the bindery (using SYSCON), and determine if you have any objects that are of different object classes but have the same name. For example, you may have a user called *test* and a group called *test*. If any conflicts are found, you need to rename one of the objects, because NDS does not permit two objects to have the same common name (CN) in the same container even if they are of different object classes.

Dupbind and a few other related utilities can be found at
`ftp://ftp.dreamlan.com/an304x.zip.`

4. Run Bindfix twice; the first time diagnoses and repairs any cross-links in the database, and the second creates a backup copy of the bindery.

5. Copy the three resulting NET$*.OLD files from the NetWare 3 server to the SYS:SYSTEM directory on the NetWare 5 server and rename them to NET$*.SYS.

6. Load NWConfig on the NetWare 5 server and select Directory options ➪ Upgrade NetWare 3.x bindery information to Directory.

NOTE

You may find some bindery objects showing up in your NDS tree after the import process. These are due to third-party applications which use the NetWare bindery to record their serial number and other information. You should verify if they are still needed and delete the obsolete objects.

7. If any of the imported users and groups already exist in the server's bindery context you'll have the option to merge or not import the bindery data for conflicting objects.

8. After all the users and groups data has been imported, you can use the server-to-server copy option in your tape backup software to move the files from the old server to the NetWare 5 server. Ensure the option to copy file system trustees is used.

9. Select a few user and group objects in NDS at random and check their properties to ensure they are imported correctly. For example, check login time restrictions and password expiration settings.

WARNING

You should not use NCOPY or similar DOS/Windows commands to copy files between the servers, because file system trustees will not be copied.

WARNING

When running the server-to-server copy using ARCserve, you must install and run ARCserve from the NetWare 3.1x server; otherwise the file system trustees will not be transferred correctly. The same may apply to other tape backup software.

If you don't need a replica on the NetWare 5 server, you can remove it after the files are transferred over from the bindery server. The replica and bindery context settings are only required for the bindery import process.

NOTE

The group name field in the bindery is not imported into the NDS, so you'll have to manually enter them.

At ftp://www.dreamlan.com/mig2nds.zip, **you can find some utilities useful in cleaning up the NDS. For example, the Grpname program can be used to repopulate the missing group name.**

Summary

This chapter discussed a number of enhancements and changes to NDS and to the NDS schema introduced by NetWare 5. Because these changes are not supported by previous versions of NDS for NetWare 4.1x, it is important that you have a good handle on the implications of mixing DS.NLM versions and follow the proper upgrade procedures.

In Chapter 13, you'll learn about various tools that can assist you in managing NDS more easily.

NDS Management Tools

A key component of avoiding NDS problems is understanding how to effectively manage the tree. Novell provides several good tools for accomplishing administrative tasks. In this chapter, we look at the tools supplied with the NetWare 5 product as well as tools available from Novell Consulting Services and third-party vendors.

▶ . . . . ◀

NetWare Administrator

Novell's NetWare Administrator utility has been around as long as NetWare 4 has been shipping, and it is the primary interface most administrators are familiar with for administering their NDS trees. Features of NetWare Administrator include

- Graphical view of the NDS tree

- Ability to view and modify NDS object attributes

- Ability to manage NDS and file system rights from a single interface

- Snap-in capabilities to manage extensions to NDS

- Manage multiple trees

- Ability to search the tree for objects based on a single criteria (for example, *Given Name* is equal to *Peter*)

Figure 13.1 shows the main NetWare Administrator browser window.

Over the years, Novell has shipped different versions of the NetWare Administrator tool for different platforms. The tool has evolved considerably. Table 13.1 outlines some of the differences between the different versions.

*NetWare Administrator for
NetWare 5*

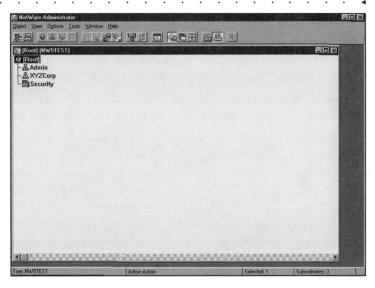

In this chapter, we examine NWADMN32, the version that Novell ships with
NetWare 5.

NOTE

**Snap-in DLLs written for older versions of NetWare Administrator
may not work with the newer version of the utility. If you are currently
using an older version of NetWare Administrator and find that the
newer version does not support the snap-ins you need, contact the
manufacturer of the product the snap-in is written for to get an
update.**

NetWare Administrator can be extended through the use of snap-ins. There are
two types of snap-ins that can be set up for the utility: snap-in object DLLs and
snap-in view DLLs.

Snap-in object DLLs enable you to administer additional object classes with
NetWare Administrator. The snap-in object DLL handles object creation and
modification and is used to define the property pages shown by NetWare
Administrator.

T A B L E 13.1

*Releases of NetWare
Administrator and Their
Features*

UTILITY EXE NAME	SHIPPED WITH	FEATURES/LIMITATIONS
NWADMIN	NetWare 4.0x	Extendable through snap-in development
NWADMN3X	NetWare 4.10 and NetWare 4.11	16-bit for Windows 3.x, extendable through snap-in development
NWADMN95	NetWare 4.11	32-bit version for Windows95/98; snap-in information stored in registry; extendable through snap-in development
NWADMNNT	NetWare 4.11	32-bit version for Windows NT; snap-in information stored in registry; extendable through snap-in development
NWADMN32	NetWare 5.0	Snap-in information not stored in registry — snap-ins loaded from the snap-ins directory on the server; 32-bit version for Windows95/98 and Windows NT; extendable through snap-in development

Snap-in view DLLs enable you to look at objects in NDS differently than through the tree view. These viewer DLLs add items to the tools menu. Several Novell products add snap-in view DLLs; GroupWise and Novell Replication Services are two of the more commonly used products that include this type of snap-in DLL.

Installation of snap-in DLLs with the version of NetWare Administrator that ships with NetWare 5 is very easy. In the SYS:PUBLIC\WIN32 directory on the server there is a subdirectory called "SNAPINS"; simply copy the DLLs into that directory. When NetWare Administrator starts, it uses the DLLs located in that directory.

Some snap-ins are compiled only for use on Windows 95/98 or Windows NT. Especially when moving DLLs from older versions of NetWare Administrator, there may be features only supported by one operating system or another. The new NetWare Administrator takes this into account by adding subdirectories underneath the snap-ins directory — one for Windows NT only snap-ins (NTONLY) and one for Windows 95/98 snap-ins (95ONLY). If you find that a snap-in doesn't work with one operating system or the other, you can copy it into the respective directory and prevent error messages from appearing on the unsupported operating system.

Snap-ins are created using Novell's Software Development Kit (SDK), available for free from Novell's developer Web site (http://developer.novell.com). Development of snap-ins is beyond the scope of this book; for more information on developing snap-ins, visit the Novell DeveloperNet website.

X-REF

If you are not a programmer but have a need for snap-ins, you may want to look into a product from Netoria called ScheMAX. We look at ScheMAX later in this chapter in the "Third Party Management Tools" section.

The primary function NetWare Administrator is typically used for is managing users. Figure 13.2 shows the different options available for modifying users using NetWare Administrator.

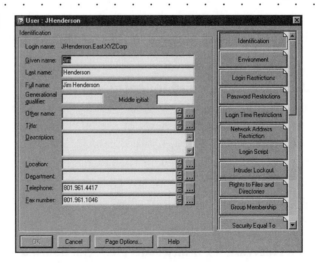

F I G U R E 13.2

User details pages in NetWare Administrator

The identification page shown by default includes information used to identify the user; none of this is used by either the workstation or the server. The other tabs include information about password limitations, login restrictions, the personal login script, and other information.

In most networks, user administration is the most time-consuming task for the administrator. Once the network is established, the users are the most dynamic part of the network and require the most attention.

Because user administration tends to be the most time-consuming task you will use NetWare Administrator for, it is also the part of NetWare Administrator you are probably the most familiar with. We will move on from user administration into administration of the other standard class objects in this chapter. Chapter 14 includes tips and tricks we have discovered that make administration simpler and will cover more information on user creation and administration.

NDS Manager

In Chapter 6, we examine a number of features of the NDS Manager from the perspective of the server. NDS Manager can be used for partitioning and replication operations, but it also has several other features to increase the manageability of NDS.

First, let us review using NDS Manager to manage partitions and replicas.

Partition and Replica Management

Managing partitions and replicas is the primary function of NDS Manager. NDS Manager provides two separate views of the NDS tree; the first view is the tree view, shown in Figure 13.3.

The tree view is the default view in NDS manager and starts more quickly than the list view. This is the view you want to use when creating new partitions, because it is the only view that shows all containers, whether they are a partition root or not.

NOTE

The NetWare 4.x utility PARTMGR can be used for the addition and deletion of replicas as well as the split/join partition operations. It is not included with NetWare 5, but if you have a NetWare 4 server available, you can use this utility instead of NDS Manager for some operations.

FIGURE 13.3

NDS Manager's tree view

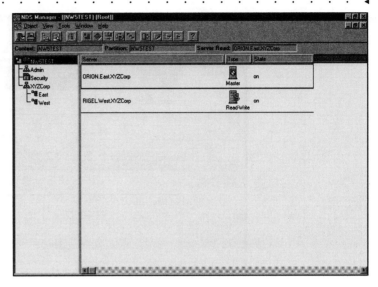

The list view, shown in Figure 13.4, scans the NDS tree and displays all servers in the lower half of the screen and all of the containers that are the root object of a partition in the upper half.

The list view takes more time to start because of the tree scan. In a large tree, this can take some time, particularly if there are slow WAN links involved.

The list view provides a feature that is not present in the tree view: the capability to check the synchronization status across multiple partitions. When a partition is selected in the list view and the synchronization status is checked, the option to check all partitions listed in the partition list is not grayed out, as shown in Figure 13.5.

TIP

The view item on the menu includes an option to set the context—this enables you to limit the scope of containers shown in the partition list window. Limiting the scope to something other than [Root] speeds up the tree scan and reduces the amount of time needed to perform the synchronization check.

FIGURE 13.4

NDS Manager's list view

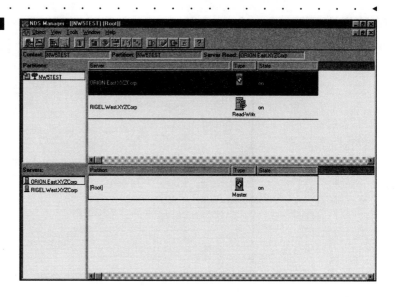

FIGURE 13.5

Checking partition sync across multiple partitions

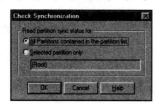

The partition synchronization check only checks the synchronization status from one server — if there is a problem with synchronization, it may not show up in the check synchronization status item. The way to look for more evasive problems is with the partition continuity option.

Partition Continuity

As with NetWare Administrator, we looked briefly at this part of NDS Manager in Chapter 6. We now look at this feature to see how it builds the information presented on the screen (see Figure 13.6).

▶ · ◀

F I G U R E   1 3 . 6

*Partition Continuity screen
in NDS Manager*

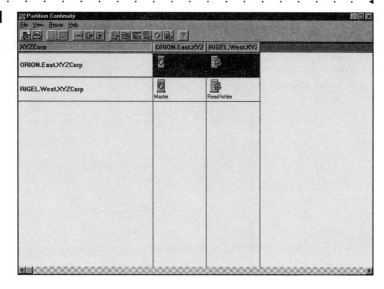

The first thing the partition continuity option does is request the list of servers holding any replica of the partition being examined — this includes master, read/write, read-only, and subordinate reference replica types.

Once the list is retrieved, NDS Manager checks connectivity to all servers in the list. If a server cannot be contacted, the row for that server reflects that there is a problem by showing a message indicating it was unable to connect. This is shown in Figure 13.7.

Once the connectivity check is completed, NDS Manager requests the replica list information for each server found from the server that was initially contacted. Each server's information is shown on a separate row and is presented to reflect the way the replica list looks from that server's perspective. From this, it is easy to spot an inconsistency in the replica lists between two servers — if the replica types are not consistent between two rows, there is a problem in the replica list consistency, and you need to troubleshoot the problem. If two servers are shown as having the master, there will be problems when you try to perform partitioning or replication options, and there may be problems with operations that require the workstation to talk only to the master (for example, a move object operation).

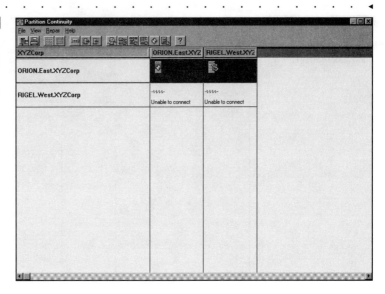

FIGURE 13.7

Partition continuity when a server can not be contacted. In this example, the server Rigel is down and cannot be checked.

While the replica list information is gathered, the synchronization status is also collected from each server. This status shows the state of communication from each server pair as viewed by all of the servers. If you see a yellow warning indicator in any of the boxes, there is a synchronization error being reported for that server pair. Right-click the indicated error, and select the information item from the context-sensitive menu. The replica information reports the error information from the replica pair, as shown in Figure 13.8. Pressing the ? button next to the sync error brings up help for the specific error being reported.

FIGURE 13.8

Replica information for a replica that is reporting an error condition

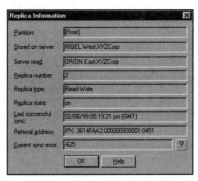

The partition synchronization screen also enables you to schedule immediate synchronization and perform other server-level operations. The toolbar has the common operations on it, but the repair menu lists all of the available options.

IMPORTANT

The *Repair* menu and the toolbar displayed in the partition continuity screen contain many options that remotely launch DSREPAIR tasks. Running a local database repair from within NDS Manager really launches DSREPAIR to perform the operation, and as such locks the DS database just as if you had gone to the server console and launched DSREPAIR manually. These options are presented in NDS Manager for convenience.

The server-level operations are executed by selecting the row in which the server appears in the leftmost column, and then initiating the operation from the menu or the toolbar.

The view menu contains an item that can be of use — if you want to update just a single server's information, the Update Synchronization Information option refreshes information from a single server. In a highly distributed network where it may take time to refresh the entire table, this option can save you time.

Other Features

NDS Manager is a well-rounded utility. We have already seen options it has for checking partition synchronization status as well as the features used for manipulating the layout of partitions and replicas.

There are two lesser-known management features of NDS manager — the Schema Manager and the NDS Version/Update option. These features add even more functionality to NDS Manager. Both of these features are available from the object menu on the main NDS Manager window.

Schema Manager

The Schema Manager, shown in Figure 13.9, is a utility that provides both information about your NDS tree's schema and enables you to make changes to the schema.

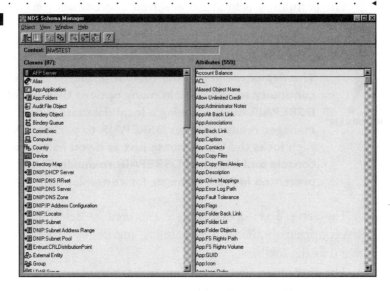

F I G U R E   13.9

NDS Manager's Schema Manager

When Schema Manager is started, it displays two panes in the window: the left-hand pane contains all of the classes defined in the schema; the right-hand pane shows all of the attributes defined.

Double-clicking on a class in the left-hand pane shows information about the selected class. Figure 13.10 shows an example using the App:Application class, an extension used by the ZENworks product.

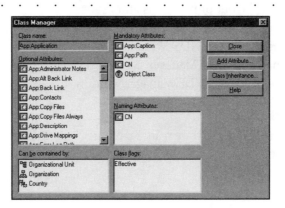

F I G U R E   13.10

App:Application class definition shown in Schema Manager

Similarly, double-clicking on an attribute name in the right-hand pane displays information about the selected attribute. This is shown in Figure 13.11.

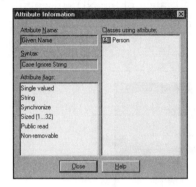

Given Name attribute definition

The Schema Manager component also offers features to extend the schema and add your own customizations. To extend the schema, you select either Create New Class or Create New Attribute from the Object menu.

WARNING

Extending the schema is usually a nonreversible operation. When testing schema extensions, it is advised that you work on a nonproduction tree until the extensions work the way you want them to. Extensions to base classes (for example, addition of attributes to a class such as the user class) are not currently removable. Removal of extended classes is possible but only after all objects of the extended class type are deleted from the tree.

Starting either of these options launches a wizard that walks you through the creation of your new class or attribute.

DS Version Check/Update

The final option in NDS manager we will examine is the DS Version Check/Update option. This feature is invoked by selecting the Object ⇨ NDS Version item on the object menu. Selecting this item produces a submenu with two options, only one of which will be active. The active choice is determined by the selection of either a container (not necessarily a container that is a partition root) or a server. If a container is selected, the View option is available; if a server is selected, the Update option is available.

The View option searches a branch of the NDS tree and reports all versions of NDS found on servers located in that branch of the tree. Figure 13.12 shows this with one server.

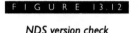

F I G U R E 13.12

NDS version check

The Update option enables you to select a server that contains the source files for the DS.NLM update and any number of target servers to update with the version of DS.NLM loaded on the source server.

IMPORTANT

It is strongly recommended that the update be performed with the latest version of NDS Manager available. Updates to the way DS.NLM is designed have resulted in additional files being needed during the distribution of DS.NLM updates. Older versions of NDS Manager are not programmed to distribute all of the necessary files and result in DS.NLM being unable to load on the target servers. The dialog box displayed is shown in Figure 13.13.

NDS version update

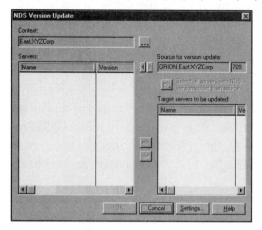

WARNING

Make sure the version of DS you are updating to is supported on the version of NetWare each server has. Updating a NetWare 4.11 system with a NetWare 5.0 version of DS.NLM results in problems—the best case is that the DS.NLM update will not load and the server becomes inaccessible.

Once the files are updated on a target server, the old version of DS.NLM is unloaded and the new one is loaded.

Server Management

In addition to partition and replica management in NDS manager, there are a few server management features to be aware of.

Under certain circumstances, you need to delete a server from within NDS manager. This is typically needed when:

▸ The server in question has had an unrecoverable SYS volume crash.

▸ Some other event occurs that shuts the server down unexpectedly, and the server cannot be brought back onto the network.

WARNING

If at all possible, remove the server from the tree by removing all replicas from the server and using INSTALL.NLM to remove directory services from the server. Using NDS Manager to remove the server from the tree should only be used as a last resort in a disaster recovery situation.

If a server needs to be deleted from the tree in this manner, you may also need to clean up the replica ring information using DSREPAIRDSREPAIR on other servers that are still up. Please see the example on repairing replica ring inconsistencies in Chapter 11 for information on how to do this.

UIMPORT

The UIMPORT utility is one of the most powerful — and underused — utilities included with NetWare 5. The history of this utility dates back to NetWare 4, but its roots can be traced back to the MAKEUSER utility introduced before NetWare 2.15 started shipping.

The idea behind UIMPORT is very simple: Provide a batch-driven process to enable mass user creation and modification. In pre-NetWare 4 environments, the MAKEUSER utility provided this functionality, but because the bindery definition for a user was fixed, it was a very simple utility to use. UIMPORT is capable of handling extensions to the NDS schema, and because of this, it is a somewhat more complex utility.

UIMPORT uses two data files: a control file and a data file. The file format for these files is easy to understand — they both can be created in any text editor. The following is a review of the format and use of these files.

The control file contains two sections — an import control section and a fields section. Each of these sections is prefaced by the section name. Table 13.2 provides examples for the import control section of the file.

T A B L E 13.2

*UIMPORT Import Control
Field Definitions*

FIELD	DEFINITION	SAMPLE
Create Home Directory	Boolean Value (Y/N) that tells UIMPORT whether or not to create a home directory in the file system for the user being created	CREATE HOME DIRECTORY=N
Delete Mailbox Dirs	Boolean Value used to determine whether or not the mail directory (used for bindery services) for the user should be deleted	DELETE MAILBOX DIRS=Y
Delete Property	Used to specify a special value for UIMPORT to search for in the data file that means the field should be deleted	DELETE PROPERTY= #DEL
Home Directory Path	Path for the parent directory where the home directory is to be created.	HOME DIRECTORY PATH=USERS
Home Directory Volume	DN of the volume object the home directory will be created on	HOME DIRECTORY= USERS.East.XYZCorp
Import Mode	C (Create) U (Update) B (Both Create and Update) R (Remove)	IMPORT MODE=U
Maximum Directory Retries	Number of attempts to assign the user as a trustee to the home directory. This is necessary because of synchronization delays if the user is created on a server that the home directory is not on.	MAXIMUM DIRECTORY RETRIES=5
Name Context	Default context to use for the UIMPORT operation	NAME CONTEXT= .East.XYZCorp
Quote	Character that represents a quote. This can be changed in order to enable quotation characters to be embedded in property values.	QUOTE="
Replace Value	With multivalued fields, this option enables you to overwrite the existing value (when set to Y) or add a new value to the attribute (when set to N).	REPLACE VALUE=Y

Continued

TABLE 13.2
UIMPORT Import Control
Field Definitions (continued)

FIELD	DEFINITION	SAMPLE
Separator	Character that is used to delimit fields within a record.	Separator=,
User Template	Boolean value used to designate whether UIMPORT uses the USER_TEMPLATE user in the context being used for creation as a template for new user objects	USER TEMPLATE=Y

There are some important notes about some of the fields that you need to keep in mind when working with UIMPORT:

▸ The delete property control field is used to specify a special value to be included in the data file. If you set this value to #DEL and you want to delete the given name property for a group of users, you would put #DEL in the field in the data file that represents the Given Name attribute.

▸ The delete property control field also has a few fields it does not affect — these fields are the volume restrictions field, the password field, and the home directory field. Deleting the volume restrictions field is accomplished by specifying a volume restrictions field and putting a space restriction of –1 in the field. To delete the password field, specify the field in the fields section and put a blank value in the data file. For the home directory property, you must manually delete the property using NetWare Administrator.

▸ The replace value control field can be very dangerous if not used properly. For example, if you are adding groups to a large number of users and you specify REPLACE VALUE=Y in the control file, you need to delete all previous group memberships and explicitly add the memberships specified in the data file.

▸ The USER_TEMPLATE object is just another user object not a template object that can be created in NetWare Administrator. If you use this type of template, the following list of fields is copied from the USER_TEMPLATE object: account balance, account has expiration date, allow unlimited credit, allow user to change password, city, days between forced changes, default server, department, description, fax number, foreign email address, foreign email alias, full name, generational qualifier, given name, grace logins allowed, group membership, home directory, language, location, login allowed time, login script, low balance limit, mailbox location, mailing label information, maximum connections, minimum password length, network address restriction, postal (ZIP) code, postal office box, profile, remaining grace logins, require a password, require unique passwords, security equal to, see also, state or province, street address, telephone, and title.

After the import control section is complete, a fields section is needed.

The absolute minimum number of fields needed depends on the operation being performed. Table 13.3 shows which fields are needed for which operation. The name field refers to the common name (CN) of the object; name is what UIMPORT uses to designate this attribute.

TABLE 13.3	IMPORT MODE	MINIMUM FIELDS REQUIRED
Minimum Fields Required for the Various Import Modes	C	name, surname
	U	name, another field to modify
	B	name, surname
	R	name

The update mode only requires the name field, however specifying only the name field would not be useful — you also need to specify another field to update. The both mode (create and update) requires both the name and surname, because users are created if they do not exist, and the surname is a mandatory attribute for the user class.

Once the control section is completed, you need to define the fields section. This section starts with the line fields and then lists the NDS attributes the data file contains, one per line.

TIP

If you cannot determine the name of a particular NDS attribute you want to use, use the DSVIEW.NLM module at the server to get the attribute name. Other than the name field, the other fields use the NDS attribute name.

Determining the syntax of some of the fields can be tricky. For example, if you look at the definition for the Volume Space Restrictions attribute, you will find there are multiple parts to the attribute. To specify the different parts of the value, separate them with colons. For example, if you wanted to specify that the user is limited to 100MB (102,400K) of disk space on Rigel's data volume, you would specify .RIGEL_DATA.EAST.XYZCorp:102400 in the field used in your data file to represent the desired space restriction.

A sample control file might look like this:

```
IMPORT CONTROL

IMPORT MODE=U

USER TEMPLATE=N

NAME CONTEXT=.East.XYZCorp

DELETE PROPERTY=#DEL


FIELDS

NAME

GIVEN NAME

SURNAME

FULL NAME

TELEPHONE NUMBER
```

This control file, named UPDATE.CTL, specifies the following options:

▶ Update existing users, do not create new ones

▶ Do not apply the USER_TEMPLATE object's values to these users

▶ The context the users exist in is East.XYZCorp

▶ Fields filled in with #DEL should be deleted

▶ The data file contains the fields name, given name, surname, full name, telephone number.

The data file must now be constructed. To do this, you can use a database program that outputs comma delimited files (sometimes referred to as Comma Separated Variable, or CSV, text files), or you can create the file using your favorite text editor.

The fields specified need to appear in the order specified and need to all be present. The file can contain as many records as you need to update, though with larger files it may be desirable to break the operation into smaller pieces.

For the discussion here, our data file is named UPDATE.DAT and contains the following records:

```
"JHenderson","Jim","Henderson","Jim Henderson","801-555-1234"

"PKuo","Peter","Kuo","Peter Kuo","907-555-5678"

"JimH","Jim","Henderson","Jim Henderson -Administrative
Acct","801-555-1234"

"PeterK","Peter","Kuo","Peter Kuo -Administrative
Acct","907-555-5678"
```

Once done, invoke UImport with the following command:

```
UIMPORT UPDATE.CTL UPDATE.DAT /C
```

The /C parameter tells UImport not to pause on every screen of information.

UIMPORT can be used to manipulate users in multiple contexts. The easiest way to do this is specify the full DN of the user with a leading period in the name field.

TIP

In Chapter 14, we examine some advanced techniques for building the data file using output from the second most underutilized tool included with NetWare 5 — NLIST.

► · ◄

NLIST

The NLIST utility provided with NetWare 4 and NetWare 5 is an extremely powerful tool for examining the information in your NDS tree. Its power, however, is masked by a fairly complex command-line interface. As with UIMPORT, the NLIST utility is not used by many administrators because it takes time to learn it and the output can take a significant amount of time to interpret.

The NLIST command line consists of three parts:

1. The class to list with an optional value to look for

2. An optional where component, used to filter requests

3. An optional show component, used to select fields to display.

In addition to these components, there are several switches used to modify the output of the NLIST command.

The first of these components is the class component. Whenever you use NLIST, you must specify a single class to find information on. The class name used is the name found in the class definitions list, viewable with DSVIEW from the server console or with the Schema Manager component of NDS Manager.

The class component can also be limited by specifying that the name be equal to a single value. The value can also include wildcards, so you can look for only users starting with *J*, for example. The format of this command would be:

```
NLIST USER = J*
```

This would provide a list of all users whose login name starts with the letter *J*.

TIP

If you don't know the name of the class, you can list all classes by specifying the * character in place of a class name. This shows you all objects regardless of class. Using the NLIST command in this way can be limited by specifying an object name by using the format *NLIST * = ObjectName*. This produces a listing showing the object and its class.

The second piece of the NLIST command, the optional where component, lets you limit the scope based on an attribute value defined for the object. If the attribute does not fit the values searched for by the where component, the object will not be displayed.

> **NOTE**
> **Some values, particularly date and time values, are difficult to perform numeric comparisons against. If you want to limit the scope based on a date, you may need to experiment a bit with the value. In cases such as this, it might make more sense to use techniques we describe in Chapter 14 to build a data file and then use an external program, such as Microsoft Excel, to filter the data more effectively.**

If you wanted to list all users whose login name starts with the letter *J* but only if the last name starts with an *H*, the command you would use would be:

```
NLIST USER = J* WHERE SURNAME = H*
```

As with the class scope, wildcards are supported in the where component of the command.

> **TIP**
> **If the class or attribute name includes a space, you need to enclose the name in quotes. For example, if you are looking for a print queue, you would type NLIST "PRINT QUEUE", not NLIST PRINT QUEUE.**

There are a number of comparison operators that can be used in the where component of the query. Table 13.4 lists them.

T A B L E 13.4	COMPARISON	DEFINITION
Comparison Operators for the Where Component of an NLIST Command	EQ	Equality; can use = instead
	NE	Not equal
	LT	Less than
	LE	Less than or equal
	GT	Greater than
	GE	Greater than or equal
	EXISTS	Exists
	NEXISTS	Does not exist

The only comparison operator that can use a numeric equivalent is testing for equality. The greater than (>) and less than (<) operators are used by the operating system to pipe information either from a file or to a file.

NOTE

When testing numeric values, the use of comparisons is very straightforward; however, when comparing other values, such as dates or string values, the comparison becomes a bit more difficult to determine. For example, if you execute the command:

```
NLIST USER SHOW "Last Login Time"
```

The information presented includes a date and time in the format *hh:mm:ss [ap]m mm-dd-yy*. However, using this format in a where clause results in an error message indicating that dates prior to 1980 are invalid.

After a bit of experimentation, we find that performing a comparison on this attribute requires just a date value — a time value will not be accepted. Thus the command

```
NLIST USER WHERE "Last Login Time" GE "8:00:00 am 2-5-99"
```

results in an error message, but the command

```
NLIST USER WHERE "Last Login Time" GE "2-5-99"
```

results in a listing of users.

String comparisons, conversely, cannot use the LT, LE, GE, or GE comparison operators; strings can only be checked for existence or nonexistence and for equality or inequality.

Thus the command

```
NLIST USER WHERE SURNAME GE HE
```

is invalid, but the command

```
NLIST USER WHERE SURNAME EQ H*
```

returns a list of all users where the surname attribute starts with the letter *H*.

The last of the primary sections of the NLIST command is the show section. This section determines which attributes should be displayed in the output. This section is optional, and if omitted the listing will include the object name and other general fields dependant on the class of object being listed.

If a show directive appears in the NLIST command, the list of attributes following the parameter is displayed in the output. The list can be comma delimited or not, but all attributes that include a space must be enclosed in quotes.

NOTE

The help displayed with the command NLIST /? D shows that commas are required; however, if you have a long list of attributes you wish to display, including the quotes can create problems with the length of the command. Omitting commas may free up enough space to include additional information you want to include.

Once the three main sections are entered, there are a few command line switches that are of use. The first is the /S switch, which is used to search the entire subtree. This is useful if you want to include information on all users from a particular context down.

The /C parameter tells NLIST not to pause output at the screen boundaries and wait for user intervention. This is useful if you want to just scan the information visually and pause the output or if you want to use your own paging program — such as MORE. When redirecting the output to a file, this parameter is not needed.

The /CO parameter enables you to specify a start context; when used in conjunction with the /S parameter, this enables you to search any subtree. The /R switch is similar to the /CO switch, except that it starts at the [Root] of the tree.

TIP

By default, NLIST uses the current workstation context. Rather than use the /CO switch, set the context with the CX command instead. This saves you space on the command line and has the same effect as specifying the /CO switch in NLIST.

The /A switch is used to show active connection or server information. If you want to view just information about users who are currently logged into the tree, for example, you can specify this switch to limit the scope of your query to the users who are logged in.

The /B switch is used to display bindery information. The typical use for this is to display users currently logged into a particular server. The command **NLIST USER /A /B** results in the same output as the NetWare 3.x utility USERLIST. Similarly, the command **NLIST SERVER /A /B** results in the same type of output as the NetWare 3.x SLIST parameter.

The /TREE parameter enables you to list the trees available and optionally select a tree to run the command against. The command **NLIST /TREE** shows all trees available to the workstation.

TIP

Similar to the /CO switch, the /TREE switch can be bypassed by setting the workstation's current tree from Network Neighborhood (in Windows 95/98 and Windows NT) before starting the command interpreter. This is recommended rather than using the /TREE switch to set the current tree, because it saves space on the command line for the scope and display parameters.

Specifying /D on the command line displays detailed information about the object; it lists all of the attributes defined for the object. This can be a useful way of obtaining attribute values for a number of attributes when the command line might otherwise be too long.

Using /N on the command line instructs NLIST to display just the object name. This is a more minimalist option than specifying no show fields and can speed up output if all you want is a list of the object names.

NLIST is an extremely powerful utility for reporting on NDS information. As we demonstrate in Chapter 14, the output from this program is designed to be human-readable but can be easily manipulated into a machine-readable format. Once converted, it can then be reported using database and spreadsheet programs, as well as being converted into a format to be used by UIMPORT.

ConsoleOne

With the introduction of NetWare 5, Novell is starting to change direction in how administration of NetWare and NDS services is performed. The ConsoleOne utility is a Java application designed to ultimately replace the 32-bit NetWare Administrator utility. It may be some time before that happens, because the shift in administration to Java-based utilities requires a change in thinking on the part of administrators.

As of this writing, the ConsoleOne utility is a shipped product but includes very limited functionality. It is intended to be a proof-of-concept utility that will grow as acceptance of Java for NDS administration grows.

As Java support with the Abstract Windowing Toolkit (AWT) is available on the NetWare 5 server console, the ConsoleOne utility can be run either on a NetWare 5 server console or on any workstation with connectivity to the NDS tree. This includes Windows 95/98, Windows NT, Macintosh, or Sun Solaris.

Figure 13.14 shows the main ConsoleOne screen as shown on a Windows 95 workstation. To expand a branch of the tree, click the circle to the left of the container in the left pane of the window.

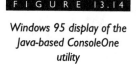

F I G U R E 13.14

Windows 95 display of the Java-based ConsoleOne utility

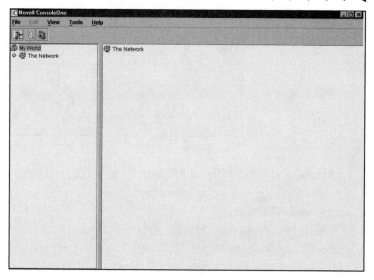

The console-based utility provides a little additional functionality. You can display information about configuration files on the server, look at the file system on the local server, and perform administration of some objects in the NDS tree.

Administration of the NDS tree from the server console requires a login; ConsoleOne handles the authentication upon startup. Workstation-based administration uses the credentials established when you logged in to the NDS tree.

Object administration in ConsoleOne is currently limited to the User and NCP Server classes. Figure 13.15 shows the user administration component of ConsoleOne.

► · ◄

FIGURE 13.15

User administration with ConsoleOne

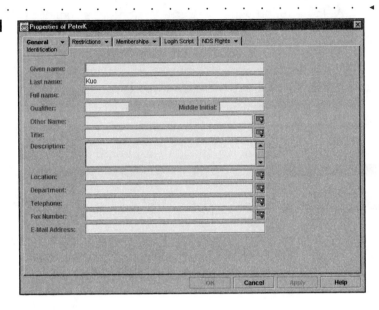

Across the top of the administration window, there are five categories of information that can be administered: general, restrictions, memberships, login script, and NDS rights.

Clicking the category brings up a list of panels available for the information category. As shown in Figure 13.16, clicking the general category brings up several options: identification, environment, postal address, see also, and others.

Information for a number of other object classes is available on a limited basis. In most cases, you will be able to look at trustee information and other generic information. The only four classes that can be administered are Organization, Organizational Unit, User, and Group.

Right clicking a NetWare server object brings up an option to launch a remote console to the server. This option is functional for NetWare 5 servers only, because it uses the new IP-based remote console utility, RConj. Figure 13.17 shows how this utility looks.

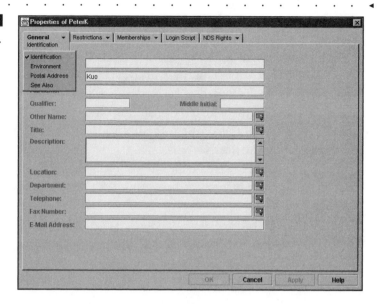

F I G U R E   13.16

Information available under the general information category

F I G U R E   13.17

The Java-based RConj utility

In order to use RConj, you need to have support for NCP over TCP/IP installed. This is done by installing Client32 3.x on the workstation and enabling IP support. Note that RConj does not show the Java GUI console on the server—it only displays the text-based screens on the console.

NOTE

OIMPORT/OEXPORT

The last tool available from Novell for performing NDS object management is the OIMPORT/OEXPORT utility pair available from Novell Consulting Services. This utility is not included with NetWare 5 but is a separate pay-for product available through the Novell Consulting Web site at `http://consulting.novell.com`. As of this writing, the licensing for the product is either a single-user license or a site license.

These two utilities use data files in a similar fashion to the way UIMPORT uses data files. The main differences between UIMPORT and the OIMPORT/OEXPORT tools are

- ▶ UIMPORT is an import-only tool

- ▶ UIMPORT only supports the User object class

- ▶ OEXPORT enables you to specify class filters as well as attribute filters using a file rather than needing to specify everything on the command line.

- ▶ OEXPORT's output file can be used directly as an import file for OIMPORT.

- ▶ OIMPORT/OEXPORT supports the use of rule files to control their processes.

- ▶ Full logging capabilities are present in OIMPORT/OEXPORT that are not present in UImport.

Because of interdependencies between objects, the OIMPORT utility pair supports the use of sequencing. Sequencing sets a priority for a particular class of object. For example, in order to create user objects with the home directory property filled in, you have to have the volume object in the tree that the home directory exists on. This means that you have to have a precedence for the creation of objects that puts the volume objects at a higher priority than the user objects.

Similarly, when creating users, the container the users are to be created in needs to exist prior to the creation of the user. Setting a sequence enables you to specify that containers have to be created before other objects.

The OIMPORT/OEXPORT utility is extremely flexible—if you have a large network to administer, it is well worth looking into this utility pair.

▶ · ◀

Third-Party Tools

There are many excellent third-party tools available to enhance management of NDS. In this section, we discuss three of the tools we have looked at and used in production networks: Netoria's ScheMAX tool, DS Expert from NetPro, and BindView EMS from BindView Development.

ScheMAX

Netoria's ScheMAX product is a fairly new product. It is, as many of Netoria's products are, a niche product designed to make administration easier. The product is available for download for a 60-day evaluation from Netoria's Web site at `http://www.netoria.com`.

ScheMAX consists of three components: the Schema Administrator, Snapin Builder, and the ScheMAX Viewer.

Schema Administrator

The Schema Administrator component of ScheMAX is accessible through the tools menu of NetWare Administrator. When activated, it displays a graphical browser that shows the schema class inheritance tree (see Figure 13.18).

As with the Schema Manager in NDS Manager, you can add classes and attributes into the DS schema; the real power in ScheMAX's schema administrator is the presentation. The graphical overview of the schema tree enables you to determine where your new object class appears in the schema tree and gives you greater precision in locating the proper place to put your schema extension.

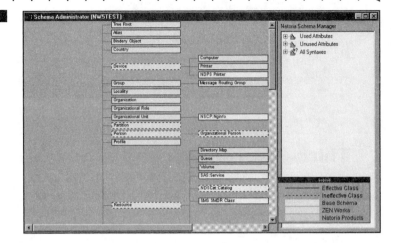

FIGURE 13.18

*ScheMAX Schema
Administrator*

Snapin Builder

ScheMAX doesn't stop where NDS Manager's schema manager does; through an ingenious twist, rather than create snap-in DLLs with a development tool, ScheMAX includes facilities to build pages for NetWare Administrator and associate them with NDS objects. The end result is that you can create schema extensions and build pages right into NetWare Administrator to administer your schema extension with. The pages built with ScheMAX are stored directly in NDS, so installation of the snap-in is as easy as associating a container, group, or user object with the snap-in.

Figure 13.19 shows a sample snap-in page in development. This page includes several standard attributes that are spread through normal administration pages.

The end result of the new attribute page is shown in Figure 13.20. As you can see, the page is accessible directly through the standard NetWare Administrator interface — it appears just the way it would if you spent hours or days developing a snap-in DLL but only takes a few minutes.

FIGURE 13.19

ScheMAX graphical snap-in designer

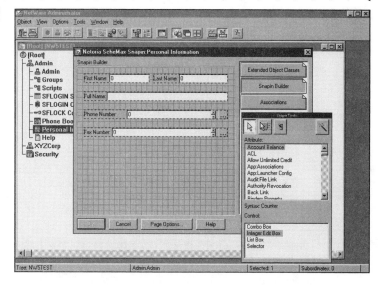

FIGURE 13.20

ScheMAX-built snap-in added to the user class

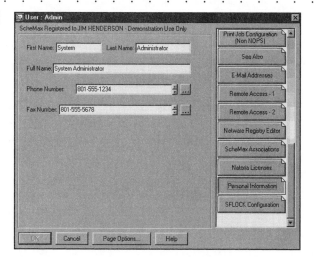

ScheMAX Viewer

The final component of ScheMAX is the viewer. In many cases, it would be much easier if users could populate the data in the NDS database themselves. The viewer can be used to do this. The initial view, shown in Figure 13.21, lets the user pick a view to be displayed.

▶ • ◀

*ScheMAX Viewer view
selection screen*

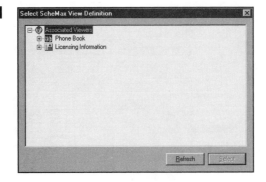

Once the view is selected, the user can display information for a particular subtree or for objects in a specific context. Administration of information is just a double-click away—selecting a record from the view brings up associated snap-ins created for the view. The same snap-ins created for NetWare Administrator are available in the viewer.

The view is also stored in NDS and is created with NetWare Administrator. Figure 13.22 shows how the view is created.

▶ • ◀

*Creating a view for use with
the ScheMAX Viewer*

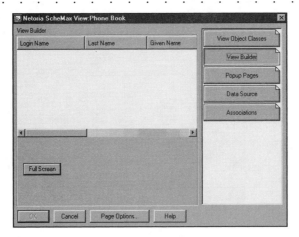

Adding the capability to edit fields just requires associating a ScheMAX snap-in object with the view, shown in Figure 13.23.

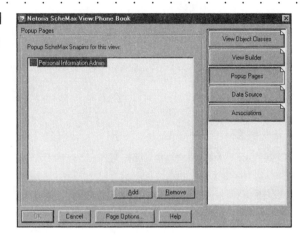

FIGURE 13.23

Associating a snap-in with a view to enable editing of NDS attributes from the viewer

A number of other options are available with the viewer: for example, you can force the viewer to run for the specific user object logged in and require the viewer fields to be updated before the program can be exited. This is one way you might update a telephone list with current employee information.

Another option is the capability to pass a specific view directly into the executable — this prevents the selection screen shown in Figure 13.20 from appearing, but launches the desired view directly.

DS Expert

NetPro is a leading developer of NDS management tools. Their DS Expert product is for viewing the overall health of your NDS tree. There are two components to the DS Expert product: a server agent and a workstation-based tool to gather and view the information from the agents loaded on your servers.

DS Expert has the capability to send SNMP alerts to any standard SNMP management console and react based on user-defined thresholds.

A unique feature of DS Expert is its capability to provide a multiserver DSTRACE functionality. This functionality is provided through the workstation-based management console and enables you to discover more about how NDS functions as well as view real-time information about problems in your NDS tree.

An evaluation of DS Expert is available through NetPro's Web site at `http://www.netpro.com`.

BindView EMS

The final product we touch on is BindView EMS. Bindview has been around for a very long time; it was first available for bindery-based servers (in fact, the company derives their name from the idea of viewing the bindery). More information about the product is available from BindView's Web site at `http://www.bindview.com`.

BindView EMS evolves the idea of the original BindView product beyond reporting on information into a full management product. Through a feature called ActiveAdmin, you can make changes to objects in your tree on a large scale. While not all attributes can be edited with ActiveAdmin in version 5.2 (the shipping version as of this writing), the product's flexibility is tremendous.

This product is well suited for management tasks as well as disaster recovery tasks. Proactively, it can be used to document aspects of your tree that you might not otherwise be able to document easily. Reactively, it can be used to repopulate information in NDS using standard values.

The strongest part of BindView, however, is its capability to produce security-based reports. As we will discuss in Chapter 15, implementing effective NDS security in your tree may turn out to be the most critical part of preventing problems with NDS. By using BindView EMS, you can check security throughout your tree and save the reports to rerun them later to see how effective your security implementation is.

Summary

In this chapter, we examined a number of different tools used to manage NDS and looked at how to use these tools to better prevent problems. Through a better understanding of the use of Novell-supplied tools such as NetWare Administrator, NDS Manager, and ConsoleOne, as well as third-party administration tools, it is easy to prevent many problems from occurring.

In Chapter 14, we look at ways to use these tools more effectively to manage your tree.

NDS Management Techniques

Knowing how to use the NDS management tools is the first step towards understanding strategies to manage to prevent problems. Understanding effective techniques for using the tools is as important — if not more important — than understanding how the tools work themselves.

In this chapter, we look at effective techniques for managing single objects and multiple objects using the tools described in Chapter 13 and a few additional tools available from DreamLAN Network Consulting Ltd. After looking at basic techniques for single-and multiple-object modification, we delve into advanced techniques of combining tools. These techniques overlap with some of the techniques presented for recovery in Chapter 10; good techniques are effective in both reactive maintenance and preventative maintenance.

Strategies

The specific strategies used for managing NDS may vary from environment to environment; however, any strategy for good management is based in three principles:

- ▸ Planning ahead

- ▸ Saving time

- ▸ Knowing your tools

Planning Ahead

This is a very difficult task for many administrators — partly because most work reactively rather than proactively. When reacting to situations on a continual basis, you have a constant drain on your time. This drain results in not spending the time to figure out a better way of doing things. Reacting to situations on a constant basis also frequently results in having to spend time figuring out how to do the same task each time you do it, because you cannot remember how you did it the last time.

A good way to start planning ahead is to spend a little extra time documenting solutions to problems as you go along. This is not always an easy task when moving from crisis to crisis. Remind yourself—and your management—that documenting your solutions ultimately saves you time and the company money.

Start small when documenting solutions: take some notes along the way and refer back to them. When dealing with problems, one of the more critical phases of evaluating the solution is reviewing the problem and what happened between the time the problem was discovered and the time the problem was resolved.

Documenting changes also is a way to save time during the troubleshooting process—with a record of recent changes made, you frequently stand a better chance of solving the problem.

By documenting changes, you also can start to lay down a framework for standard ways of doing things. Standards—even if you have several—are a good way to meet the second strategy: saving time.

Saving Time

By spending a little extra time looking at how certain repetitive tasks are done, you may find ways to reduce the amount of time spent doing them. By shaving a little bit of time off of each time you do something, you can make yourself more productive—and in many environments, being productive is a key to promotion or to working on other projects.

Let's take a simple example: starting NetWare Administrator. On a 300MHz Celeron-based machine running Windows 95, NetWare Administrator takes about 30 seconds to start, depending on the number of snap-ins to be loaded and the other applications running on the system. If you need to add a user to a group, that operation can take a minute or two—significantly more time than the startup of the utility.

However, if you shut down NetWare Administrator and have to restart it to perform another administrative task, there is a repeat on the startup. While 30 seconds may not seem like much, it adds up quickly—if you start NetWare Administrator an average of ten times a day, that's 25 minutes worth of time just waiting for the utility to start up over the course of a week.

That may not seem like much at first, but if you can find a number of places where you can make small changes, the time adds up. Reducing the time you spend performing repetitive—and frequently boring—tasks gives you time to work on projects you want to be working on.

Coming up with standard ways of doing tasks also makes it possible to train others to do repetitive tasks. If you are a programmer, knowing when you can save time by writing a program—as opposed to using standard tools to complete the task at hand—is important. If you know your programming skills can make shorter work of a repetitive task, spend a little extra time writing the program. Using automated tools—even homegrown tools—can help ensure consistency in how tasks are performed and make your network easier to administer.

Knowing Your Tools

There is nothing worse for a new administrator than the overwhelming task of learning how to effectively use all of the tools available. Knowing when to use UIMPORT instead of NetWare Administrator depends on knowing the features of both utilities and being able to ascertain when one utility is better than another is.

Spend time with the different utilities: learn what the strengths and weaknesses of each utility are. What works for you may not work for someone else, but knowledge works to your advantage, particularly when trying to save time.

Look at older tools if they are available—Novell does not provide the DOS-based NETADMIN utility with NetWare 5, but a NetWare 4.11 server on your network would have a copy of it. NETADMIN has its own features that can prove useful when making lots of changes when UIMPORT cannot be applied, for example, when updating console operators on multiple servers or making a quick change to a login script. One limitation of NETADMIN is that it cannot support extended schema classes and attributes.

This applies to third-party tools as well. If your company spends money on a management tool, the best return they can get on investment is only realized if the tool is used effectively.

If possible, reuse parts of tools. For example, in Chapter 13, we talk about the product BindView EMS from BindView Development. BindView is an extremely powerful tool, but using it fully involves reusing reports that you have created or that are part of the standard reports included with the product. Not having to recreate reports that already exist—or modifying existing reports that almost contain the information you are in need of—saves you time. The only way you can do this, though, is by knowing what comes with the product and organizing your reports so you can find reports for reuse later.

Similarly, if you create a data file for a mass user modification with UIMPORT, save the control and data files as well as the tools used to create the data files. You never know when they may come in handy—particularly in a disaster recovery situation.

Knowing your tools also involves knowing shortcuts for certain functions. Why would you use the mouse to open the Object menu and select the Move item, when you could select the object and press F7 to accomplish the same task more quickly? Train yourself to use shortcut keystrokes instead of using the mouse.

A Secret Fourth Idea: Multitasking

No, we are not talking about the capabilities in your operating system of choice to run more than one program, though we are talking conceptually of a similar way of doing things.

Desktop operating systems typically do not do true multitasking—they do what is called *task switching*. Task switching between multiple computers is what you need to do as an administrator.

This is particularly effective if you use a tool like BindView which can tie up a machine for a significant amount of time (hours to days sometimes). Having a separate machine to perform tasks like this one can save you time and enable you to work on multiple tasks.

Many administrators benefit from having more than one computer at their disposal. It does take some time to get used to the idea of working on more than one project at a time, and it takes a bit of practice to keep from getting lost. If you can master the skill of task switching, though, you'll find your job a whole lot easier.

Single-Object Modification

At first, it may seem obvious to use a tool like NetWare Administrator for administering single objects: the interface is intuitive and easy to use for making single object changes. There are several techniques, however, than can be applied to single object administration. In addition, there are instances where using NetWare Administrator is possible, but a repetitive change made to users one by one (for example, during an office move) may make more sense to automate.

Through simple automation of single object changes, it is possible to reduce the time spent performing administrative tasks. For everything that NetWare Administrator does well, it does not excel at automated tasks. This is a key place where UIMPORT (for user objects) or the OIMPORT/OEXPORT utility from Novell Consulting Services can make more sense and save you a lot of time. Mass object modification is something that can save some time: it's the single object modifications that can take a lot of your time. A single change doesn't seem to be much, but compounded over time, these tasks can take more time than any other task you work on.

Let us first look at techniques in NetWare Administrator.

NetWare Administrator

The first of our single object tricks is the creation of users using NetWare Administrator. As an administrator, you undoubtedly often get a request from a manager to create a new user that looks exactly like another user: "We have a new accounts payable clerk named Carl who will be working alongside Jane and needs to access the same information Jane does." Normally, the administrator creates a new user ID for Carl and then spends time examining the group memberships and security equivalences and looking through the file system to make sure that Carl has the same rights as Jane.

With the new 32-bit version of NetWare Administrator and its support for templates, there is a much quicker way to accomplish this task through the use of a template. To use this shortcut, we start by creating a template object using the Object ⇨ Create menu item, as shown in Figure 14.1.

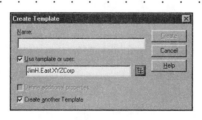

Creation of a template object

As you can see in Figure 14.1, we can create the template with the use template or user option checked. This enables us to create the template based on the values in another template object or in a user object. We simply create the template based on Jane's user ID.

Once the template is created, we then create Carl's ID using the new template, and we have granted Carl the rights that Jane has.

NOTE

This technique does not create a security equivalence to Jane — rather, it creates a user with the same security equivalences and group memberships that Jane has. This particular method does not duplicate rights in the file system. As part of your management strategy, it is recommended that you keep explicit trustee assignments to a minimum and always grant rights through a group or container membership if possible.

NETADMIN and Other DOS-Based Tools

Earlier in this chapter, we discussed the use of the NetWare 4.*x* NETADMIN utility, which is not included with NetWare 5. The NETADMIN utility, along with the other DOS-based utilities included with NetWare 4 and NetWare 5, are some of the most valuable tools for managing your NDS tree. The reasons these tools are so valuable is because of the time saved in launching the tool as well as the quick access to various standard attributes used in the base class objects in your tree.

In Chapter 10, we discussed the use of NLIST and UIMPORT for disaster recovery and building UIMPORT data files using information extracted from NDS with NLIST to rapidly recover from large-scale mistakes. Administration on a large scale is just as effective as disaster recovery. UIMPORT can actually serve as the fastest tool for single object modification as well.

Many people know how to write a quick program in C or BASIC to create and manipulate text files. Rather than learn the NetWare API so you can create or modify users, you can cut a lot of time just by writing a script or program to create the data file and use UIMPORT to make the changes for you. Even a single user creation can be done very rapidly using UIMPORT if you have a tool to create a standardized data file for the object creation.

TIP

Using scripted object creation/modification provides you another means of disaster recovery. Save the data files once you have finished with them; you never know when they might come in handy.

Suppose you have a need to make a quick change to your own personal login script. You could start NetWare Administrator, locate your object, and maneuver through the different tabs to find the login script. If you followed the advice found earlier in this chapter, you probably already have NetWare Administrator running, so you've saved some time. You might even have the context your user is in open or use the search feature in NetWare Administrator.

For many people, using the keyboard is more natural and faster than using the mouse. Zipping out to a DOS prompt, using the CX utility to change to the context your user object is contained in, and starting NETADMIN to make that script change will still be faster, particularly if you type quickly.

TIP

Some people have reported that some of the menu-driven DOS-based NetWare utilities do not work with NetWare 5 — specifically, the problems seem to be related to using the utilities in a pure IP environment. When they do not work, you receive error messages that you would not expect. Try the utilities and see what works and what does not. The better you know the limitations of each utility, the better able you will be to decide which tool is the best for the job.

For most administrators, management of single objects takes more time than any other task they perform. This is the best place to start with trying to find ways to save time by standardizing how you do things. Once you standardize single object management, you can apply the same techniques to multiple object management.

▶ . . . . ◀

Multiple Object Modification

Many of the techniques discussed in the previous section apply to multiple object manipulation as well as to single object manipulation.

As with single object manipulation, use of standardized programs to create scripts for utilities like UIMPORT and the OIMPORT/OEXPORT utility pair from Novell Consulting Services can be a tremendous timesaver. In the extreme case of a university environment — where you may be creating thousands of users each term — there really is no other approach to mass management than using batch tools.

In this type of environment, being able to manipulate data is the key. Suppose you receive a list of students from the university administration or the enrollment department, you need to be able to extract the information from the data provided in order to create user objects with standardized names and information. With a project of this scale, standardization is the key to being successful.

The logical starting place for standardization is with the user account names themselves. This is particularly important if you have multiple systems where you want to use the same login identifier for the users. There are several factors to take into consideration when coming up with a standardized naming convention:

▸ Maximum login name length on all systems

▸ Resolving naming clashes

▸ Potentially identifying multiple accounts for the same user

▸ Removing duplication

Let us talk about each of these in a little more detail.

Maximum Login Name Length

Unlike other systems, NetWare has a fairly long name length: the NetWare login ID in NDS has a maximum DN length of 256 characters. This means the user name and all contexts back to the [Root] context must be less than 256 characters. This should be more than adequate for any environment; if it is not adequate for your environment, you need to rethink your naming conventions.

With this in mind, though, there may be other systems that you or another department uses login names for that have different limitations. The AS/400 platform, for example, has a maximum login name length of nine characters. Many Unix platforms limit you to eight characters. In situations where you want to use the same login ID across platforms — even if the user information is not shared — you want to keep the maximum login name lengths in mind for all platforms concerned.

NOTE **When considering what sort of maximum length should be used, remember that in NDS, the user name the user typically needs to know is their object's CN; thus, if you create a user ID called HendersJ in a Unix environment, the DN for that user name may end up being something like HendersJ.East.XYZCorp—the CN portion of the full DN is the part that should match between platforms.**

Resolving Naming Clashes

The next challenge is to determine a way to handle name clashes. A naming clash occurs when

▸ Your standard dictates a way to generate login IDs

▸ Two or more users end up with the same generated login ID

For example, suppose you opt for an eight-character naming convention that uses up to the first seven characters of the last name and the first initial. This would result in the name Jim Henderson generating the login name HendersJ. The name John Henderson, however, would also result in the login name HendersJ.

Resolving this type of name clash ahead of time in your naming convention—particularly if using an automated system—can prove to be difficult. Some sites using this convention switch to using the first six characters of the last name and the first and middle initials—if no middle initial is present, replace the initial with an uncommon letter—say the letter x. So, Jim Henderson would now become HenderJS, while John Henderson might become HenderJX. If your organization is small enough, this sort of change in the convention might be sufficient.

For larger environments—such as the university environment described earlier in the chapter—that might not be sufficient. You may want to use some other unique identifier in conjunction with part of the user's name, for example, their initials and the last four digits of their student number; thus, John Henderson's login ID could end up being JXH1234. In an environment where thousands of users are being created at a time, you do not want to tie the user's name to an arbitrary value. Such a value could be referred to as an instance number: the first user being JXH01, the second being JXH02, and so on. Automating the creation of accounts in this manner becomes more and more difficult. The idea is to use the data provided to create a unique key to be used as the user login name.

In smaller environments, such measures might not be necessary; it may be sufficient to use first name and last initial or the user's first name or nickname.

Choosing a way to resolve name clashes is very dependent on your environment. However you choose to handle it, always keep in mind that you may run into a clash and decide ahead of time how you want to handle it.

Identifying Multiple Accounts for the Same User

Earlier in this book, we discussed the need to keep administrative accounts separate from nonadministrative accounts. Administrative accounts, by their very nature, have the capability to make changes to your network during normal operation that you may not want.

For example, an administrative user might be able to make changes to default templates used by the Microsoft Office product suite or, worse, could accidentally delete part of a critical application.

The best solution to this is to create a separate nonadministrative account for each user who has administrative authority. That way, they can perform normal operational tasks such as preparing status reports and project plans without risk to the software installations. Their administrative ID should be used only for administrative tasks such as creating users.

This also gives you the ability to restrict that user's rights if they should leave your information systems department (or at least leave the role where they perform administrative tasks). Simply disable the administrative account and modify their nonadministrative account to fit their new job role.

This idea works very well if the administrative staff has more than one computer to work on.

Administrative accounts should be easy to identify at a glance — possibly as obvious as using their regular user ID with a special modifier to show the administrative account. Such an identifier could be something obvious, such as a suffix of _Admin_ (making John Henderson's administrative account JXH1234_Admin), but something a little more subtle might be called for if your environment is likely to have people attempting to hack into the system. Making the administrative accounts easy for anyone to identify removes a barrier to someone attempting to break into your system.

Maybe instead of using a suffix on the account, use a different middle initial — say Q — for the user. Searching for administrative accounts that are logged in then becomes a simple matter of searching for all accounts with a middle initial of Q.

NetWare Administrator

NetWare Administrator has the capability to perform modifications on multiple user objects. To use this feature, select multiple user objects while holding down the Ctrl key. Select either Object ⇨ Details on Multiple Users, or click the details on multiple users button on the toolbar. This brings up the dialog box shown in Figure 14.2.

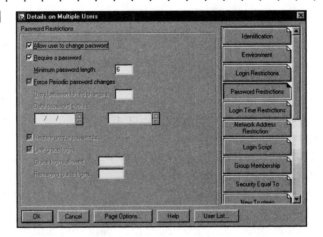

F I G U R E   1 4 . 2

Viewing Password Restriction details on multiple users

As you can see, the dialog box looks nearly identical to the dialog box for a single object modification. The primary difference is that you have the ability to set the values for multiple users or to leave values alone. The checkboxes on each page allow three states — clear, set, and unchanged — represented by a cleared box, a checked box, and a grayed checked box.

This particular method of changing multiple users can be easy to use, but it can also create problems if not used properly. For example, changing user group memberships on a large-scale results in the user group membership lists being the same, rather than just adding the desired group memberships. A better approach in this case is to add multiple users to the group from the group perspective or to use UIMPORT to make this type of mass change.

Tips and Tricks

There are a number of tips and tricks that can be applied to administering your system. We cover two different classes of tips and tricks here: standards and NDS replication and partitioning.

Standards

When creating data files for a mass import, regardless of whether you are using the files for a single object or multiple objects, you should have a standardized way of mapping fields from one file to another. For example, if the data file you receive with the new user information contains the fields Name (consisting of the first and last name of the user), Middle Initial, Employee Number, and Telephone Extension, ensure that the data is always presented in a consistent way — the fields should always appear in the same order in the data file.

Also ensure that your data conversion program performs the conversions in a consistent manner. Regardless of the programming language you use or if you use something like Excel to generate the data from another spreadsheet, ensure that the conversion process handles exceptions such as commas in the data fields and the use of special characters.

When using UIMPORT to do object creation, you have the option of setting the initial password for the user. The initial password should be fairly easy to remember but should also have a requirement to be changed when the user first logs in. Creating long initial passwords can be difficult to manage; you have to remember that not all platforms support long passwords the way NetWare does. While NetWare's password algorithm enables a maximum password length of 128 characters, Windows platforms typically only enable 15 characters.

TIP

Earlier in this book, we talked about locking away your Admin account's password for use as an emergency backdoor account. By making the password on this account longer than the maximum allowed by your management platform, you can add an additional level of security to the account. You must be sure, however, to have a platform available where the longer password can be entered — such as an MS-DOS platform.

Another standard to consider is the default rights given to the user for their home directory. You will find that depending on which utility is used for creating the accounts you will have different rights granted to the home directory.

If you use a batch procedure to create the accounts, use the RIGHTS command to set the default rights to what you want them to be. Many administrators prefer that users not be able to grant rights to other users for their home directory; however, creation with some of the utilities grants the user either Supervisory or Access Control rights for the user to their home directory.

Additionally, disk space management is also important: if your environment permits, set space restrictions on the home directories and shared data directories. This will save you problems down the road when space starts to get a little thin.

NDS Replication and Partitioning

Create home directories on a volume other than the SYS volume. NDS uses the SYS volume exclusively, and if that volume should fill up, you will run into synchronization problems that will be compounded by not being able to attach to the server to delete unnecessary files from the volume.

When partitioning an NDS tree, use common sense: try to keep partitions from crossing multiple WAN links. Part of the reason for partitioning your tree is to cut down on traffic over the WAN; however, if you only have two sites partitioning does not make a lot of sense, because you still want to maintain three to five copies of each partition in an ideal setup. If you only have two servers, you should leave just a single partition and keep two copies of the NDS tree.

When removing replicas from a server, you may find that you receive the following error message:

```
TTS Disabled because of an error growing the TTS memory
tables.
```

The way to fix this problem is to decrease the maximum number of transactions using the SET MAXIMUM TRANSACTIONS set parameter. The default for this parameter is 1000, but for systems with smaller amounts of memory, this can cause a problem. Decreasing the maximum number of transactions causes the TTS backout file to grow more because the transactions are queued, but the server will not run out of memory while trying to process the transactions.

When starting a replica deletion from a server, always ensure that you have plenty of disk space on the SYS volume.

IMPORTANT

With regard to your SYS volume's free space, there are frequently several things on the SYS volume that can be deleted to free up space. These include

▶ Client software in SYS:PUBLIC\CLIENT

▶ OS/2 Utilities in SYS:LOGIN\OS2 and SYS:PUBLIC\OS2

▶ Extra language support for utilities. These files include unicode files and multiple language support at the server. If you only use one language at the server, there is no need to keep the other languages on the server.

▶ Utilities that you do not use or that you intend to use on a more restricted basis (such as AUDITCON)

▶ Extra LAN and DSK/HAM drivers in the SYS:SYSTEM directory

By deleting these utilities, you can get by with a smaller SYS volume or at least free up space for larger NDS operations where the extra disk space would be of use.

► · ◄

Summary

In this chapter, we looked at a number of different techniques for administration of single objects as well as multiple objects. By understanding the four strategies for management, you can more efficiently provide consistency between objects in the tree.

In Chapter 15, we examine how to implement security in a way that provides flexibility and prevents self-inflicted problems.

Effectively Setting Up NDS Security

Management tools and techniques are very important to effectively prevent NDS problems, but they do not address a serious issue facing modern network administrative staff: securing resources from unauthorized access.

Experience has shown that the danger of an unauthorized access comes more from internal sources than from outside your organization. And the modern-day war is an information war—having information as opposed to not having it, and figuring out ways to obtain information about an organization.

Another reason to provide security on your network is to prevent accidental destruction of data. Security is an effective means to limit the scope of potential damage done by people who do not fully understand how to administer the system or how to properly use the administrative tools. Security can save you from nonadministrative users inadvertently causing a problem because they deleted something they should have been unable to or moved a directory that should not have been moved.

Effectively securing your system—whether from an attack or from unintentional error—needs to start with the basic premise that your system is not secure. A good security policy puts enough barriers in the way that the cost to a would-be information thief is higher than the value of the information. These barriers, however, have to be balanced against usability of the system.

In this chapter, we take an in-depth look at the features of NDS security and how to effectively implement security policies so the system is secure and usable.

Physical Security

Before addressing NDS security, we need to touch on the need for physical security of the servers holding NDS replicas. If at all possible, you should

- Lock the server room

- Limit access to that room

- If possible, use an access method that includes a mechanism to trace access to the room.

If these steps are not possible, find a way to physically secure the system. If someone breaks in and steals the server, they have all the access they need and more than enough time to break into the system.

Console Security

Console security is the next important piece of securing the server. If someone can obtain access to your file server's console, they can copy the NDS database files to a publicly accessible directory and take those files offsite for an offline attack. While the NDS database files only yield the password hash, user ID, and length of the password, that is enough to perform a brute-force attack to determine what the password is.

Using RCONSOLE, XCONSOLE, ACONSOLE, or RCONAG6 opens you up to attacks on the console remotely. They provide enough access to obtain the NDS database files for such an offline attack.

Evaluations of remote console security have turned up a couple of problems with using RCONSOLE, even when using encrypted passwords (using REMOTE ENCRYPT and storing the password in LDREMOTE.NCF).

Several services that can be installed on the server grant access to the SYS:ETC directory, where the network configuration information is stored if you configure your system with INETCFG. If you configure remote access to your system and use Unix Print Services, NFS, or FTP services, the possibility exists that access to your SYS:ETC directory is open.

If you set up remote access with RCONSOLE through INETCFG and if unauthorized users can read the SYS:ETC\NETINFO.CFG file, your console is not secure, because the RCONSOLE password is stored in that file in plain text.

Unfortunately, the best policy for remote access is the one that is least feasible — do not use it. Many system administrators are dependent on having remote console access to the server for various administrative tasks.

A potentially better solution is to not load remote console access unless you need it. It is possible to remotely load and unload NLMs on the server console using a tool like Novell's Onsite Administrator. Setting up RCONSOLE in this way provides more control over who has access to the console and when.

NOTE
Using remote LOAD/UNLOAD commands requires console operator privileges on the server you want to execute the command on.

Good security for the console is not an easy thing to achieve, but it can be done. An Australian company called Protocom Development Systems Ltd. has developed a product that addresses many needs for console security. The product is called SecureConsole and provides a high degree of console security. Information about how to contact Protocom is listed in Appendix D. Among other things, SecureConsole

- ► Requires a valid NetWare user login ID and password

- ► Requires the login ID be granted explicit access to the server's console — having supervisory rights to the server is not sufficient (much like having supervisory rights is not sufficient to perform print queue operator functions)

- ► Is capable of creating an audit trail of all console commands

- ► Has the capability to restrict console commands and access to special console functions, such as the NetWare kernel debugger and the fast restart key sequence introduced in NetWare 4.11

- ► Has a configurable login screen

- ► Can have multiple emergency users (non-NDS users) in case the NDS database is locked or corrupted

- ► Supports the use of passwords that are available for a specified amount of time for emergency user accounts

Figure 15.1 shows a screenshot of the login screen for SecureConsole.

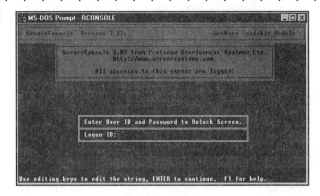

F I G U R E 15.1

SecureConsole login screen

Additionally, SecureConsole can be configured through NetWare Administrator or through a server-based administration utility, SCADMIN.

IMPORTANT

All conversations between a server and a workstation using RCONSOLE are conducted over an SPX connection: someone with a packet analyzer may be able to capture the conversation and learn the password of an administrative account. If this type of threat is a possibility in your environment, consider finding another method of communicating remotely with the server — possibly using an encrypting protocol stack.

Many people ask about the security of MONITOR's console lock (in NetWare 4.11 and earlier) and the screen saver NLM SCRSAVER in NetWare 5.

The MONITOR console lock is based on either an entered password or on the bindery SUPERVISOR password for the server — even if a bindery context is not present. MONITOR does not, however, prevent someone from unlocking the console through the debugger. A password entered at the MONITOR console lock prompt is stored in memory in plain text. If you know where to look, you can read the password directly from memory, continue the server's execution with the G debugger command, and then work from the server console by entering the password discovered in memory.

However, if you hit Enter at the MONITOR lock, the only password that unlocks the console is the SUPERVISOR password, and this password is stored like any other NetWare password — after being passed through a one-way hash.

However, there is a problem with this as well — it is possible through the NetWare kernel debugger to completely bypass the security checks in MONITOR and cause MONITOR to think you entered the correct password when you did not. For someone who knows what they are doing, they can do this quickly enough so that services hosted by the server are not interrupted. This demonstrates how dangerous it can be to have access to the kernel debugger.

Breaking into the kernel debugger is a simple task — press both shift keys, an Alt key, and Esc: the so-called four-finger salute.

WARNING

Do *not* attempt this on a production system. Breaking into the debugger causes the system to stop responding to client requests. It can be restarted with the G debugger command, but it is not recommended that you experiment with production systems.

NetWare 5 removes the screen saver and console lock components from the MONITOR utility and puts them in a separate NLM called SCRSAVER. SCRSAVER, however, requires that the person accessing the console have supervisory rights to the server object in the NDS tree. This may not be practical in all cases, and the screen saver NLM also does not restrict access to the kernel debugger.

Security Policies

A well-written data security policy is like a good disaster recovery policy: everybody says it is important, but only a few people actually implement it. Part of the reason people may be reluctant to write an official security policy is that they hope they never need it — just like a disaster recovery policy. Most people realize they need it only after a problem has been discovered.

Such a policy does not need to be very complicated. It should establish the following:

► Procedures for users requesting access to resources

▸ Procedures for granting users access to resources once the request is approved

▸ Consequences for accessing unauthorized resources.

Additionally, if your IT organization has multiple levels of administrative authority, the security policy documentation should outline which groups have responsibility for which aspects of the network. In many organizations that implement such a written policy, the policy can be added to the human resources manuals or documentation.

It is also recommended that competency testing be implemented as well. This enables you to verify that people who have a certain level of administrative access know how to properly use their access to perform their job functions. Granting administrative authority of any kind to resource on the network should be something done only if you (or management) have confidence in the people that have been assigned duties that involve administrative tasks.

Now that we have covered the physical aspects of security, we can talk about logical security — this security is the security inherent in NDS.

▸ · ◂

Principles of Good Security

There are many principles for good security — many of the easiest ones to implement are overlooked because they are not completely obvious. Because many attacks on a network's security system come from inside the organization and can come from people who have help-desk-level authority (that is, authority to change passwords), it is important to protect against that sort of attack.

Figure 15.2 shows a basic structure for granting administrative rights that will be used throughout the rest of the chapter. The idea behind this particular architecture is to remove the security administration from the main part of the tree and lock it away where only a few people can make changes — that way, you increase your accountability without compromising flexibility.

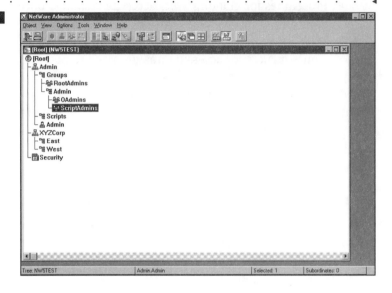

FIGURE 15.2

Administrative container
structure

There are many other ways to structure security, but experience has shown that this model provides a high degree of flexibility and security, because the groups used to assign rights are contained in a separate container that only a few people have access to.

As shown in Figure 15.2, the Admin ID is also located in this container. By default, it is recommended that this branch not be browseable by [Public], limiting not-logged-in stations from being able to login easily as Admin.

Do not use the Admin ID for daily administrative tasks — use it for emergency situations only. By not using it for daily administrative tasks, you increase accountability for various changes made to the tree.

TIP

Another good idea is to generate a long password for the Admin account and store it in a safe place. In one production environment we have worked with, the Admin account is protected with a 40-character randomly generated password.

Only two people in the organization — an organization of over 100,000 people — know where that password is stored. Note that if this organization did not implement proper physical security access controls, it could be only a matter of time before that password is compromised.

When granting rights in the tree that are supervisor-equivalent, it is generally considered good practice to assign explicit rights to the [Root] object in the tree, rather than to grant a security equivalence to Admin. If something should happen to the Admin account that results in the object being corrupted or deleted, any accounts that are security equivalent to the account will lose their rights to the tree.

Protecting Administrative Accounts

The first level of providing good security is to protect your administrative accounts. This may seem fairly obvious as a need, but the how-to aspect is something that many administrators do not give thought to.

Protecting administrative accounts is quite easy to do. First, try to limit the number of partitions that contain administrative accounts and make sure the replicas that hold those objects are on servers that have an extra degree of physical and console security. As discussed earlier in this chapter, if someone can gain access to a server console, they can grab the NDS database files and attack them offline.

Second, containers where there are administrative accounts should have intruder detection turned on. This can be done in NetWare Administrator by selecting the details of the container and selecting the intruder detection tab. By default, this feature is turned off, and when turned off, someone trying to break into your system can try as many passwords as they want in an online brute-force attack. Figure 15.3 shows how to set this feature up.

Third, you want to limit the number of stations administrative accounts can login at simultaneously. You may elect to enable administrators to only login from certain workstations; this can also be done using a network address restriction. As shown in Figure 15.4, you can enable network address restrictions for a number of different address types — IPX, TCP/IP, Ethernet/Token-Ring, and so on.

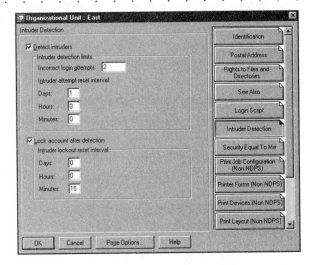

FIGURE 15.3

Enabling Intruder Detection

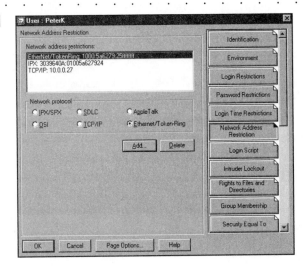

FIGURE 15.4

Enabling network address restrictions

NOTE Enabling some of these options may require you to limit administrators' access to modify their own accounts. If you choose to restrict the number of simultaneous workstations the administrator can use, you may want to prevent them from changing that value on their own.

In NDS, it is possible to block supervisory rights to an object or branch of the tree. The only caveat is that at least one user object must have supervisory rights explicitly assigned to the object that is being protected with an inherited rights filter (IRF).

NOTE The checks performed to validate that some user has supervisory access to a container that has the IRF are performed in the more recent versions of the NetWare Administrator utility and not performed by NDS itself.

Figure 15.5 shows the IRF dialog box in its default state. To change whether a particular right is blocked, uncheck it. The arrow next to the check box reflects the state of the filter; when blocked, the arrow is also blocked. For protecting an administrative account, we recommend blocking all object rights except Browse rights and all property rights except Read and Compare. This prevents someone from deleting the account and recreating it without the IRF, as well as preventing other changes to the account.

FIGURE 15.5

The Inherited Rights Filter dialog box in NetWare Administrator

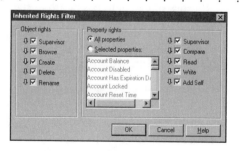

With the property rights portion of the box, you can block rights to specific attributes, such as Password Management, or to all attributes. The default is to set up the IRF for all properties. By selecting a specific property, though, you can be very granular in what you revoke rights to, just as you can when granting rights.

When protecting an administrative account, we recommend that in addition to the user having explicit supervisory rights to their own object, another user or group of users have rights as well. From the structure in Figure 15.2, we have a group called RootAdmins located in the Groups.Admin container — this group would be ideal for that type of role. The idea behind doing this is if an administrative user locks themselves out of their account, somebody else should be able to unlock the account or change the password. Remember that by applying an IRF to an object, you remove some degree of administrative access to that object.

You may wonder why a special group called RootAdmins exists in this example — after all, Admin has explicit rights to root, and the discussion thus far has suggested granting explicit rights to [Root] for objects that need Admin equivalence.

In a large environment, it may make sense to use a group to house administrative accounts other than Admin and possibly one other account — that way, at least one person can get back in if something should happen to both the Admin user and RootAdmins groups. Using a group membership is somewhat easier to manage if you have a few people with that level of access.

It is also strongly recommended that administrative users change their passwords on a regular basis; it is very easy for an administrator to make an exception for themselves with their own administrative account and remove otherwise standard password restrictions and length limitations. If anything, administrative accounts should have their passwords changed more frequently, have a longer minimum password length than standard user accounts, and should ideally only be used for performing administrative tasks. Any other work the administrator does should be performed through a separate account set up as a typical user account.

Also in the structure suggested is a special group called OAdmins. As the name might imply, this group is used for granting rights to all Organization objects and all objects under those Organizational objects. The only exception to this is the Admin container itself; rights to the Admin resources are granted based on membership in groups within the container.

You may be wondering what the difference is between the RootAdmins group and the OAdmins group — after all, you could achieve the same thing by putting an IRF on the Admin container, could you not?

Protecting the Schema

Having supervisory rights at the [Root] of the tree grants you another special right: the capability to make changes in the schema partition on all servers. Extending the schema is one of the things that makes NDS so versatile. At the same time, changes to the schema need to be controlled, or else you might run into problems due to schema definition clashes — this is a real danger if you have programmers who write programs using the Novell Developer Kit for NDS. In most cases, extensions added to the schema can be very difficult to remove, and in a few cases, they cannot be removed.

The newer versions of NDS Manager include a schema manager that has the capability of adding extensions to the schema. Administrators who are learning may have a tendency to play with this feature and create new object classes and attribute definitions. If you or another part of the administrative staff want to experiment with this functionality, it is best to test it on a nonproduction NDS tree. For this reason, we recommend using a group for rights at [Root] and a second group that has rights to all objects under [Root].

Limiting the access to [Root] also limits the possibility of someone trying to break into your system from causing damage. If the administrative accounts are few and relatively difficult to locate, and if the accounts that are found do not have administrative access to [Root], the capability for a would-be hacker to extend the schema and create a special class object to be a back door into the system is limited.

Protecting Login Scripts

Another aspect of NDS that should be closely controlled is the capability to modify login scripts. Referring back to Figure 15.2, you see another special group called ScriptAdmins. The idea behind the ScriptAdmins group is that only members of the ScriptAdmins group can change the majority of login scripts.

One large company has implemented this on a rather large scale — all of the organizational units in the tree contain a subcontainer called scripts. The scripts container contains profile objects that make up the login scripts for that container. The container script itself only contains one line, as shown in Figure 15.6.

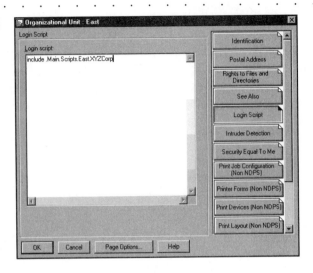

The main script indicated in the INCLUDE statement contains all of the standard script components—validation of network address for dial-up accounts (to abort the script and not run programs in the script over a dial-up connection), and execution of an operating-system specific login script.

The operating-system specific script is called with the following line:

```
INCLUDE .%OS.Scripts.East.XYZCorp
```

The client performing the login request fills in the %OS portion of the command with the name of the operating system. The scripts container then contains the following scripts to be included:

- MSDOS

- PCDOS

- DRDOS

- WIN95

▸ WIN98

▸ WINNT

These are all created as profile objects and contain commands specific to the operating system in question. The reason this is done is because as Client32 has evolved, its login script interpreter includes capabilities that are not supported in the older LOGIN.EXE program.

One of those commands is the @ command. On 32-bit Windows platforms, this command executes an external program and immediately continues the script. It is very similar to the # command (which these interpreters also support), except that it does not wait for the program that was run to return.

Unfortunately, the LOGIN.EXE script interpreter does not understand this command, and even if you attempt to check for the operating system in the login script as shown here, the script interpreter still interprets the line and returns an error:

```
IF "%OS" = "WIN95" BEGIN

    @NALEXPLD

END
```

You may notice that the list of different script names includes three DOS names and both WIN95 and WIN98. This is because the OS variable actually returns these values; however, in cases such as MSDOS, PCDOS, and DRDOS, the scripts are really the same. Rather than copy the script and have to maintain three copies, you can simply work with one (MSDOS is what we use) and then include that script in the others using the login script INCLUDE command. The same holds true for Windows 98, which is frequently considered by software to be an upgraded Windows 95 — the client is the same, the environment is the same, so the script probably should be the same as well.

Protecting login scripts really serves two purposes:

▸ Prevents accidental errors in login scripts from causing widespread problems

▸ Prevents a hacker from inserting commands in the login script to capture passwords or other information.

When a change is made to a script that causes problems, it can be difficult to determine what change was made and who made the change. By limiting editing access to the login scripts, you reduce the number of people who might have caused the problem. A good side effect of this is that you can more easily create an environment where script changes are thought out and discussed before implementation.

To limit access to edit the scripts, you need to secure the container. First grant Admin and the ScriptAdmins group explicit supervisory rights to the Scripts container, as shown in Figure 15.7.

F I G U R E   15.7

Granting supervisory rights to the Scripts container

Once that is done, block all rights to the container except for browse object rights and read and compare rights to all properties.

IMPORTANT

In addition to the container rights, the profile scripts need to have read rights assigned to the Login Script property; otherwise your users will not be able to read the scripts in order to run them when they log in.

Protecting Logical Portions of the Tree

In some environments where administration is decentralized, it may be necessary to set up regional administration — possibly even to the level of site-level administration. If you have administrative groups in Salt Lake City and Toronto, you may not want the administrative group in Toronto to be able to make changes to the users in the Salt Lake City container.

Setting up administrative authority to do this is easy to do. Using the base model created in Figure 15.4, add two groups to the Groups.Admin container — one called *TorontoAdmins* and another called *SaltLakeAdmins*. For the high-level container in the tree for Salt Lake City, grant the SaltLakeAdmins group supervisory object rights. Similarly, for the Toronto high-level container, grant the *TorontoAdmins* group supervisory object rights.

If you have multiple sites within a location that have their own administration, you can take this a step further. In Salt Lake City, you may have a regional office but also several branch offices with their own IT staff in Murray, Provo, and Logan. Assuming these containers are listed under Salt Lake City's container, you would create a container in Groups.Admin called *Salt Lake City* and under that container create the groups *MurrayAdmins, ProvoAdmins,* and *LoganAdmins.*

The reason for this setup is that you may want to design a hierarchy for adding people to these groups. Putting the branch office administrators in a container named after the region means that you can now grant the regional Admins groups Supervisory (S) rights to the container, and they can add people to those groups without having the capability to add people to the regional group.

This type of design is very scalable and easy to manage — while at the same time providing a foundation for smaller organizations that will not have to change as the organization grows.

Evaluating Security Equivalences

Security equivalence checks are something that you should do from time to time — it never hurts to make sure the security is set up the way you think it is.

The first thing you need to understand is how security equivalence works. Figure 15.8 shows three users, AmyP, JimH, and PeterK, and how security equivalence works.

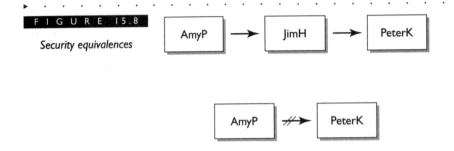

FIGURE 15.8

Security equivalences

In this figure, JimH is assigned a security equivalence to PeterK, and AmyP is assigned a security equivalence to JimH. In some environments, the result might be that AmyP receives security equivalence to PeterK, but in an NetWare environment — either NDS or Bindery — that is not the case. Security equivalences are not transitive — they only are evaluated to a single level. This makes the evaluation of security equivalence much simpler.

NetWare 5 introduces a new feature called an inheritable access control list value. As you will see in the section "Setting Up NDS Security Access for a Help Desk" in this chapter, the capability to set this up simplifies administration greatly, but it introduces an additional complexity to evaluating security equivalence — also commonly referred to as the *effective rights* of an object.

Fortunately, NetWare Administrator has the capability to perform the evaluation for you, even with the changes made in NetWare 5. Figure 15.9 shows the effective rights window in NetWare Administrator

FIGURE 15.9

Using NetWare Administrator to evaluate effective rights

The evaluation of effective rights to a particular object or attri[ ] several things:

▸ The trustees of the object being examined (the target object)

▸ Objects that are equivalent to objects with direct rights to the target object

▸ Rights granted to parent containers for the target object

▸ Security equivalences of the source object

▸ Rights flagged as inheritable for the parent container objects to the target object

You may notice that group membership is not one of the things tested. Group membership does not grant rights to another object. The action of adding a user to a group with NetWare Administrator makes a total of four major changes in NDS:

▸ The group receives a new value in its Member attribute

▸ The group receives a new value in its Equivalent To Me attribute

▸ The user receives a new value in its Groups I'm In attribute

▸ The user receives a new value in its Security Equivalences attribute

NOTE

The current implementations of DS.NLM do not automatically make these changes all happen simultaneously. If you are a developer writing a program to accomplish this task, you must make all four of these changes in your program's code.

Accountability and Auditing

Starting with the release of NetWare 4, Novell included a feature for providing an audit trail. The original auditing in NetWare 4.0, and even as late as NetWare 4.10, it was not very easy to use. The utility used for manipulating auditing, AUDITCON, was fairly cryptic, and the reports contained too much information for determining who was doing what. In short, it was difficult to find specific information you might look for, because the reports were so difficult to read.

In NetWare 4.11, the AUDITCON utility became more robust. Gone were the auditing passwords—in their place was an object placed in the tree to control access to various features of auditing.

Auditing in NetWare 5 is still handled through AUDITCON, shown in Figure 15.10. The utility still maintains its somewhat cryptic interface, but the tool has improved. Because this is a largely unfamiliar utility for administrators, we examine it in detail.

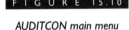

FIGURE 15.10

AUDITCON main menu

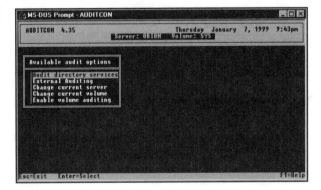

NetWare Auditing in NetWare 5 is capable of auditing a large number of events, listed here:

Directory Services Events

Abort join partitions	Close bindery
Abort partition	Close stream
Add attribute to schema	Compare attribute value
Add class to schema	Create backlink
Add entry	Create bindery property
Add member to group property	Disable user account
Add partition	Enable user account
Add replica	End replica update
Add subordinate reference to partition	End schema update

Backup entry
Change ACL
Change bindery object security
Change bindery property security
Change password
Change replica type
Change security also equals
Change security equivalence
Change station restriction
Clear NDS statistics
Modify class definition
Modify entry
Move entry
Move tree
Mutate entry
New schema epoch
Open bindery
Open stream
Read entry
Read references
Receive replica update
Reload NDS software
Remove attribute from schema
Remove backlink
Remove bindery property
Remove class from schema
Remove entry
Remove entry directory
Remove member from group
  property
Remove partition

Inspect entry
Intruder lockout change
Join partitions
List containable classes
List partitions
List subordinates
Log in user
Log out user
Merge entries
Merge trees
Remove replica
Rename object
Rename tree
Repair time stamps
Resend entry
Restore entry
Send replica update
Send/receive NDS fragmented
  request/reply
Split partition
Start partition join
Start replica update
Start schema update
Synchronize partitions
Synchronize schema
Update replica
Update schema
User locked
User unlocked
Verify console operator
Verify password

Accounting Events

Get account status
Submit account charge

Submit account hold
Submit account note

Extended Attribute Events

Duplicate extended attribute

Enumerate extended attribute

Read extended attribute

Write extended attribute

File System Events

Allocate directory handle

Convert handle to directory entry

Create directory - global

Create directory - user and directory

Create directory - user or directory

Delete directory - global

Delete directory - user and directory

Delete directory - user or directory

File close - global

File close - user and file

File close - user or file

File create - global

File create - user and file

File create - user or file

File delete - global

File delete - user and file
file

File delete - user or file

File open - global

File open - user and file

File open - user or file

File purge

File read - user and file

File read - user or file

File rename/move - global

File rename/move - user and file

File rename/move - user or file

File salvage

File search

File write - user and file

File write - user or file

Generate directory base and
  volume number

Get entry access rights

Get reference count for directory
  entry

Get specific information for entry

Get user's effective rights

Lock file

Modify directory entry - global

Modify directory entry - user and

Modify directory entry - user or file

Obtain entry information

Scan deleted files

Scan trustee list

Scan volume's user disk restriction

Search specified directory

Set compressed file size

Set directory handle

Message Events

Broadcast to console

Disable broadcasts

Enable broadcasts

Get broadcast message

Send broadcast message

Queue Management Services Events

Get queue job from form list

Get queue job list

Get queue job size

Get queue server status

Move queue job

Queue attach server

Queue create

Queue create job

Queue destroy

Queue detach server

Queue edit job

Queue job finish

Queue job service

Queue job service abort

Queue job swap rights

Queue remove job

Queue set job priority

Queue set status

Queue start job

Read queue job entry

Read queue status

Restore queue server rights

Set print job environment

Set queue server status

Server Events

Change Date/Time

Convert path to directory entry

Disable login

Disable transaction tracking

Down server

Enable login

Enable transaction tracking

Get connection's open files

Get connection's semaphores

Get connection's task information

Get connections using a file

Get logical record information

Get logical records by connection

Get objects remaining disk space

Get physical record locks by
   connection and file

Get physical record locks by file

Get semaphore information
   disk utilization

Graded authentication get
   volume access label

Graded authentication set
   volume access label

Map directory number to path

NLM add audit record

NLM add user ID record

Relinquish connection

Remote add name space

Remote dismount volume

Remote execute configura-
   tion file

Remote load NLM

Remote mount volume

Remote set console parameters

Remote unload NLM

Send console broadcast

Server console commandGet user

Verify server serial number

Graded authentication failed access control service

Graded authentication get connection range

Volume dismount

Volume mount

User Events

Clear connection

Disable account

Grant trustee

Log in user

Log out user

Remove trustee

User space restrictions

Auditing in NetWare 5 is a good way to keep track of what changes are made on your network and who makes them. Auditing is a very powerful tool, but if overused it can become burdensome to maintain and evaluate. Auditing all events is generally not a good idea because of the space needed on all servers and because of the amount of information returned. As you can see, there are many events that can be audited, and many of those events happen very frequently.

Instead, auditing is a good tool to use when you want to figure out why something is happening. For example, you may want to audit the container objects, but you only see changes in the ACL—this would indicate that someone is granting rights or removing rights in a way that you do not want them to.

You may also want to audit changes to passwords or resets of intruder lockouts. In conjunction with a help-desk setup, this is a way to provide checks to verify that only the people you want to be able to make the changes are actually the ones making the changes.

Another use for auditing is to record changes in the NDS partitioning and replication scheme. In the directory services auditing events, there are items to audit partition split/join operations as well as replica additions, deletions, and changes of replica types.

Because auditing is controlled by an object in the NDS tree, you can block access to even see the object, thus making the auditing operation transparent to the users and other administrators on the system.

Once you have AUDITCON running, select Audit Directory Services and select a container to audit by pressing F10. If the container does not have auditing enabled, you will see a menu like the one in Figure 15.11.

► . . . . ◄

F I G U R E   15.11

Enabling auditing with AUDITCON

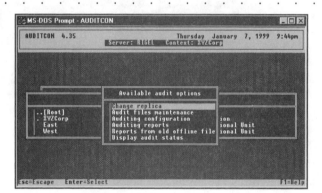

Once auditing is enabled, the menu in Figure 15.12 will be displayed.

► . . . . ◄

F I G U R E   15.12

Menu shown when container auditing is enabled

The first option on the menu, change replica, enables you to select the directory services replica you wish to view. Directory Services auditing is stored along with the directory itself, and is a part of the partition. As such, its information is replicated along with the rest of the partition.

IMPORTANT

Because Directory Services auditing is replicated with the rest of the information in NDS, you need to ensure that you have sufficient space on the SYS volumes for the servers that hold replicas of audited containers. If there is insufficient space, you will encounter problems with server utilization and potentially have issues with directory services corruption due to insufficient space.

When setting up auditing, the menu item you want next is Auditing configuration. This menu, shown in Figure 15.13, is where you select what you want to audit and which objects in the tree you want auditing enabled for.

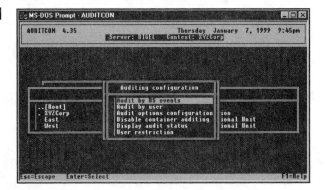

FIGURE 15.13

The Auditing configuration menu

The first item on this menu, Audit by DS events, enables you to toggle specific events by highlighting the event and pressing F10.

Once you have auditing enabled and have selected the events and users you want to audit, you want to extract the auditing information from the audit logs. The reporting option from the menu shown in Figure 15.12 brings up the menu shown in Figure 15.14.

There are several options on the reporting menu — the report options create a readable file that can be browsed offline. If you have few events enabled, this can be a fast way to see what has been happening on the system.

F I G U R E   15.14

The Auditing reports menu

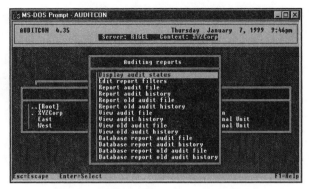

The second type of report is one viewed on the screen—this is similar to the report options, except the information is displayed on the screen.

The most useful of the different reporting methods is a database report. This creates a comma-delimited file that can be imported into a database or spreadsheet for more detailed analysis. This file format does not lend itself to easy visual examination, but if you are attempting to keep a history of old audit files to establish trends in certain events, this is the best format to work in.

There is an option on this menu to edit report filters as well—these can be edited either from the menu or after selecting a reporting method. Figure 15.15 shows the options available for creating reporting filters.

In addition to directory services auditing, there are a number of other services that can be audited. By returning to the main AUDITCON menu and enabling volume auditing, you can select the other types of events that can be audited. When volume auditing is enabled, the screen looks like Figure 15.16.

These other types of events include:

► Accounting

► Extended attributes

Audit report filter options

*AUDITCON main menu
when volume auditing
is enabled*

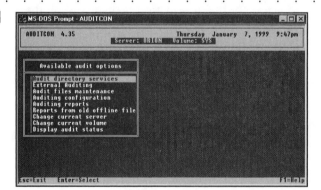

- ► File system

- ► Message events

- ► Queue management services

- ► Server events

- ► User events

The specifics of each of these types are shown earlier in this section. The information recorded for these auditing events is stored on the volume being audited in the _NETWARE directory on that volume.

All of the different types of auditing include the capability to control the configuration of auditing. We mentioned earlier that auditing can cause disk space problems if you are not careful with how you use it. The auditing configuration menu — shown in Figure 15.17 — enables you to limit the use of disk space and define what should happen when the audit log is full.

F I G U R E   15.17

Auditing configuration options

These options are set on a per-volume or per-container basis. Another configuration option is the capability to audit not-logged-in users or to enable auditing of specified users as opposed to all users. These options are shown in Figure 15.18.

The second option on this menu, User restriction, enables you to specify whether all users are audited (value set to No) or to just the specified users

F I G U R E 1 5 . 1 8

Special User restriction configuration options

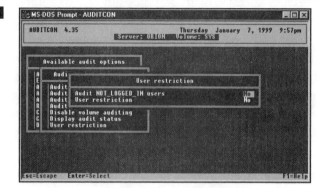

selected from the audit configuration menu (value set to Yes). This is useful if you have containers with a large number of users in them and do not want to have to enable auditing for every user manually or figure out when users are created so you can enable auditing for the user.

Because auditing takes a fair amount of time and energy to use, it should not be turned on frivolously — rather, it should be used as a preventative tool. There are two differing philosophies when using auditing:

▸ Let people know you are using an auditing tool.

▸ Do not let people know you are using an auditing tool.

There are advantages to either option. With the first option, people know you are watching what is happening on the network and know that they will be held accountable for the changes they make. This tends to make people think more before they make a change, because they know you will find out if something goes wrong.

On the other hand, by not telling people you are using auditing, they do not feel that big brother is watching everything they do. Used in this way, auditing can be a tool for helping you learn what shortcomings other administrators have in their education, and you can teach them how to properly do things.

With the second option, if you are not careful, people will find out that you are watching every move they make. It is important when dealing with people that they be at ease and not fearful that you are going to make life difficult for them when they make a mistake. A big part of successfully implementing auditing without letting people know you are auditing them is making sure they cannot see the Audit:File objects in the NDS tree. If those objects are not blocked, they will likely know that something is up, particularly if they are familiar with how auditing works.

While no method is completely effective for keeping people from knowing auditing is going on, it is possible to make it more difficult to detect. Using an IRF to block rights to the object is a starting place.

Keeping Hackers Out

The majority of the discussion so far has been about internal threats to your NDS tree and servers. External threats can present themselves, though, and because of this it is necessary to take steps to limit the possibility of someone outside your organization from breaking in.

The easiest way to accomplish this is to not enable external access to your production network. Not being connected to outside networks, however, is becoming more and more difficult when you have a need for external e-mail and Internet connectivity.

Because NetWare 5's default protocol is TCP/IP, this can become more of a threat if you do not protect your network adequately using a firewall (if connected directly to the Internet). Using the IPX protocol on your LAN puts a distinct barrier into your system—it becomes impossible to connect to IPX resources without some sort of IPX to IP translation gateway.

There are several things you can do to address this issue:

► Use a firewall at your point of presence on the Internet.

► Use a TCP/IP Network Address Translation (NAT) gateway.

▸ Use a product like Novell's BorderManager to provide a demilitarized zone between the Internet and your intranet.

▸ Perform your own tests and try to break in to your network from outside your network.

A problem as serious as the threat of someone breaking into your network is the threat of a denial-of-service attack. This is an attack on a service hosted on one of your systems that denies users access to the service. Several denial of service attacks have surfaced recently, but the concept of a denial of service attack has been around for a long time — though it has not always been known by that name.

For more specific information on how to accomplish the last two items, you may want to refer to "Novell's BorderManager Administrator's Handbook," by Laura Y. Pan, from Novell Press.

No matter what vendor's product you use at your connection to the outside world, you should be certain you are current with any patches the vendor makes available — especially patches that address denial of service attacks. Denial of service can take many forms, from flooding a network interface on a router or server with garbage traffic to actually crashing a system that hosts critical services intentionally.

Another recommendation is that you keep up on security issues — there are several newsgroups on USENET as well as mailing lists that discuss security issues. Additionally, you may want to search on the Internet for sites that specialize in hacking networks. The hackers out there use the information on those sites to learn how to break into other people's systems — you should search those sites and be familiar with the tools of the trade. By being familiar with these tools, you are better equipped to defend against them.

WARNING

If you do decide to experiment with hacking or cracking tools, we *strongly* **suggest that you test on an isolated nonproduction system. Many of the hacker-programmers out there do not always take precautions that professional programmers would take — it is not worth taking a risk with your production network. If you choose to work with these types of tools, it may be wise to let others in your organization know what you are doing and why; otherwise, when they find out what you are doing, they may not understand your motivations.**

Hidden Objects

Earlier in this chapter, we discussed the use of IRFs to block access to certain objects in your tree. Using IRFs in your tree can be beneficial if done properly, but it can be disastrous if the only user object with S rights to a container or object is deleted.

Additionally, you may find that an ex-administrator created a back door account in the system and hid the object. Locating hidden objects with excessive authority is not very difficult — the ones that are difficult to find are the ones that are hidden and have no special rights. This type of object is referred to as a *zero-footprint* hidden object.

Tracking down hidden objects with excessive rights is a simple task; however, it can be very repetitive and time consuming in a large tree. If you have a large network, you may want to look at some of the NDS reporting tools or spend more time learning how to combine NLIST with awk scripts, as we discussed in Chapter 10.

Locating objects with authority involves looking at the following:

- ► Objects with administrative rights at [Root]

- ► Objects with administrative rights at all container levels

- ► Objects that are listed in the Equivalent To Me attribute for administrative objects

Once you have looked in these places, you will have a list of objects that potentially have supervisory access to your tree. You can then search your tree for each of the objects you have found to have administrative rights.

Objects that do not have administrative rights but exist in the tree can be a nuisance — if you are attempting to reorganize your tree and need to delete a container, a hidden object or container makes this impossible.

Novell Consulting Services created a utility in 1996 that is capable of locating hidden objects in the tree. The Hidden Object Locator utility is located on Novell Consulting Services' Web site at `http://consulting.novell.com/` in the tool kit section of the site.

This tool can be extremely useful when trying to determine the cause of problems when attempting to delete a container object — if NetWare Administrator indicates the object could not be deleted because there are still subordinate objects, there are two possibilities:

▸ There are obituaries for objects that used to be in the container that have not purged yet.

▸ There are one or more hidden objects in the container.

It is easy to use the Hidden Object Locator utility to rule out the second option as the cause of the problems. If the Hidden Object Locator finds an object, there are at least two options:

▸ Call Novell and ask them to correct the problem.

▸ Visit the DreamLAN Consulting Web site and obtain the NDS Toolkit.

Setting Up NDS Security Access for a Help Desk

The final topic we want to cover in this chapter is setting up help desks to perform password administration and reset intruder lockouts on accounts.

When NetWare 4.0 was first released, a number of people using the product told Novell it would be nice to be able to set up password administration in NDS without having to grant rights that enabled modification of other parts of the user object or tree.

There have been many solutions created to solve this need — Novell's own developer group developed a sample utility that involved setting up an NLM on the server and building a custom snap-in for NetWare Administrator that communicated the password change to the server.

Many companies resorted to granting a group write access to the ACL of every single user object in the tree — a very long and tedious process. The idea behind using this method was that the password administrators could only damage users if they knew that they could grant themselves additional rights to the user object. This sort of security through obscurity works, but is dangerous because it leaves the door wide open for those who know what they are doing.

However, in order to achieve the desired goal without purchasing an additional product, this method of granting rights was the only way to solve the problem — until NetWare 5 shipped. With the release of NetWare 5, Novell has introduced two features to make setting up help desks a very simple task. The first feature is pseudo-attributes that can be used to grant rights to change passwords and reset intruder lockouts. The second feature is one we have already discussed — the capability to set rights on a container and make those rights inheritable through the tree. By using these two new features, it is now possible to set up password administration for the entire tree with just a few mouse clicks in NetWare Administrator.

To set this up in our tree, we created a group in the Admin.Groups.Admin container called PasswordAdmins. This group is going to be granted rights to set passwords and reset intruder lockouts on accounts through the tree. In Figure 15.19, we start by adding this group to the trustee list.

▶ . . . . ◀

Granting the password administrators group rights to change passwords in the tree

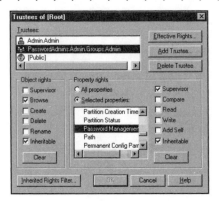

Select the Selected Properties item and scroll down to the Password Management option. Grant supervisor rights, and check the Inheritable box.

Next, find the Reset Intruder Lockout item. Check the Supervisor and Inheritable checkboxes, just as you did with the Password Management item.

Once this is set up, all you need to do is add your Help Desk staff to the PasswordAdmins group, and they will be able to change passwords and reset intruder detection.

NOTE

Password Administration is a new feature in NetWare 5. In order for it to function correctly, all servers in the tree must be running NetWare 5. NetWare 4.11 servers running DS.NLM 5.99a or later and NetWare 4.10 servers running DS.NLM 5.12 or later pass the inheritable attributes on but do not evaluate the security properly for rights flagged as inheritable. In order for this feature to work, the password administrator's workstation must be communicating with a NetWare 5 server.

Earlier in this chapter, we talked about protecting administrative accounts. Part of that process was not enabling users with less administrative authority than an account to change administrative account passwords. With this setup, how do we accomplish this?

Figure 15.20 shows the rights the PasswordAdmins group has to the Admin user.

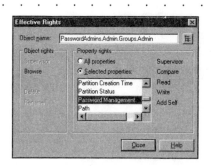

FIGURE 15.20

Effective rights that PasswordAdmins has to the Admin account

Clearly this is a problem — members of PasswordAdmins should not be able to change the Admin account's password.

There are a couple of approaches to resolving this issue — one would be to grant the PasswordAdmins group rights at the Organizational level and not at the [Root]. This works well if the administrative accounts are all located in other organizations in the tree. If they are mixed in with the typical user accounts, though, this is not going to work.

Instead, let us look at what happens if we set up an IRF on the Admin account that specifically blocks rights to the Password Management attribute.

▶ • ◀

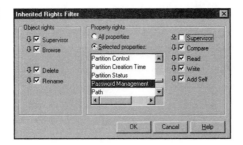

FIGURE 15.21

Changing the IRF on the Admin user to block access to the Password Management attribute

The default rights users will have are Browse, and we only granted the PasswordAdmins group supervisory rights to the attribute, so all we need to do is block the supervisory right to the attribute on the Admin user.

A quick check of the PasswordAdmins group's effective rights to the Admin user reveals the results in Figure 15.22.

▶ • ◀

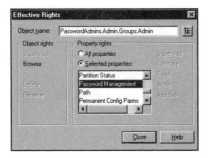

FIGURE 15.22

Results of checking PasswordAdmins' effective rights to Admin's Password Management attribute after setting up the IRF

As you can see in this figure, the IRF is working — PasswordAdmins can no longer modify the Admin account's password.

When users call a help desk for assistance with logging in, there might be a second item that they need the help desk to fix: the number of grace logins. Intruder detection can lock an account out, but so can using up all of your grace logins. Help desk staff should also be able to make this change.

In Figure 15.23, all that needs to be set is write rights to the Remaining Grace Logins attribute. By also checking the Inheritable option, this item only needs to be set at the [Root] level, and the rights will be inherited for all objects not explicitly blocked with an IRF.

▶ . . . . ◀

FIGURE 15.23

Granting rights to enable help desks to increase the remaining grace logins

▶ . . . . ◀

Summary

In this chapter, we looked at a number of techniques that can be used to secure NDS in order to proactively prevent administrator-created problems through either accidental or intentional misuse of the management tools. We also discussed different ways of protecting your network from external hackers and described how to set up security access for Help Desk personnel in order to perform common tasks such as changing passwords and resetting grace logins.

NDS Error Codes

This appendix provides an exhaustive listing and explanation of all the published NDS error codes you can use as a starting point to further determine the actual cause of the problem and then formulate a corrective action plan. For each NDS error, the following information is shown, in a tabular format:

▶ Error code in decimal

▶ Error code in hexadecimal

▶ Name of constant as used in the Novell Developer Kit (NDK) that corresponds to the error code

▶ An explanation of the error

The error code listings are separated according to their source: the server, client, or DSA.

Shown in Table A.1 are NetWare OS error codes returned through Directory Services. Many of the errors are generated by bindery-based API calls.

 Notice that some of these error codes (such as -254 and -255) have multiple meanings. Since -001 to -255 are really NetWare OS error codes reported as DS errors, you need to be aware of the context under which the error code is returned in order to correctly interpret the cause of the error.

NOTE

Shown in Table A.2 are the Directory Services client API library error codes.

Shown in Table A.3 are Directory Services client API library error codes specific to NLMs only.

Shown in Table A.4 are the error codes returned by DSA.

T A B L E   A . 1

OS-Released DS Error Codes

DECIMAL	HEXADECIMAL	CONSTANT	DESCRIPTION
-001	0xFFFFFFFF	DSERR_INSUFFICIENT_SPACE	Insufficient space to process an auditing request.
-002 through -118	0xFFFFFFFE through 0xFFFFFF8A		Unused.
-119	0xFFFFFF89	DSERR_BUFFER_TOO_SMALL	The buffer allocated is too small for the amount of data to be passed back. This error can also suggest that the server has insufficient IPX sockets available. If this is the case, you can increase the maximum number of IPX sockets using SPXCONFG.NLM.
-120	0xFFFFFF88	DSERR_VOLUME_FLAG_NOT_SET	The service requested is not available on the selected volume.
-121	0xFFFFFF87	DSERR_NO_ITEMS_FOUND	Requested to identify any accounting changes pending on the specified object and none were found.
-122	0xFFFFFF86	DSERR_CONN_ALREADY_TEMPORARY	Trying to convert a temporary connection to a temporary connection.
-123	0xFFFFFF85	DSERR_CONN_ALREADY_LOGGED_IN	The connection is already authenticated.
-124	0xFFFFFF84	DSERR_CONN_NOT_AUTHENTICATED	Trying to perform an operation (which requires an authenticated connection) using a connection that is not yet authenticated.
-125	0xFFFFFF83	DSERR_CONN_NOT_LOGGED_IN	Trying to log out of a connection that you're not logged into.

Continued

TABLE A.I

OS-Released DS Error Codes (continued)

DECIMAL	HEXADECIMAL	CONSTANT	DESCRIPTION
-126	0xFFFFFF82	DSERR_NCP_BOUNDARY_CHECK_FAILED	Size of NCP data received doesn't match NCP subfunction size. This can be due to faulty LAN drivers or networking hardware. This error can also arise from an improperly formatted auditing request.
-127	0xFFFFFF81	DSERR_LOCK_WAITING	Timed out while trying to put a lock on a file.
-128	0xFFFFFF80	DSERR_LOCK_FAIL	Attempt to open or create a file that's already opened.
-129	0xFFFFFF7F	DSERR_OUT_OF_HANDLES	The server's out of file handles.
-130	0xFFFFFF7E	DSERR_NO_OPEN_PRIVILEGE	Attempt to open a file without the Open privilege.
-131	0xFFFFFF7D	DSERR_HARD_IO_ERROR	Hard disk I/O error on a NetWare volume; possible bad sector found on disk and could be fatal.
-132	0xFFFFFF7C	DSERR_NO_CREATE_PRIVILEGE	Attempt to create a file without the Create privilege.
-133	0xFFFFFF7B	DSERR_NO_CREATE_DELETE_PRIV	Trying to create an already existing file without the Create/Delete privilege.
-134	0xFFFFFF7A	DSERR_R_O_CREATE_FILE	Cannot create an already existing file with read-only status.
-135	0xFFFFFF79	DSERR_CREATE_FILE_INVALID_NAME	Attempt to create a file using an ambiguous filename (for example, contains wildcard characters).

DECIMAL	HEXADECIMAL	CONSTANT	DESCRIPTION
-136	0xFFFFFF78	DSERR_INVALID_FILE_HANDLE	Attempt to perform I/O operation on a file with an invalid file handle (for example, trying to write to a file that has been closed).
-137	0xFFFFFF77	DSERR_NO_SEARCH_PRIVILEGE	Trying to search a directory without Search privilege (File Scan) in that directory.
-138	0xFFFFFF76	DSERR_NO_DELETE_PRIVILEGE	Unable to delete a file without File Deletion privilege in that file's directory.
-139	0xFFFFFF75	DSERR_NO_RENAME_PRIVILEGE	Unable to rename a file without Rename privilege in that file's directory.
-140	0xFFFFFF74	DSERR_NO_SET_PRIVILEGE	Cannot set a file's attribute without Modify privilege in that file's directory.
-141	0xFFFFFF73	DSERR_SOME_FILES_IN_USE	Attempt to delete, rename, or modify file attributes using a wildcard filename while some of the files matching the filename are in use by another process.
-142	0xFFFFFF72	DSERR_ALL_FILES_IN_USE	Attempt to delete, rename, or modify file attributes using a wildcard filename while all of the files matching the filename are in use by another process.
-143	0xFFFFFF71	DSERR_SOME_READ_ONLY	Trying to delete, rename, or set file attributes using a filename when some of the files specified have read-only status.
-144	0xFFFFFF70	DSERR_ALL_READ_ONLY	Cannot delete, rename, or modify file attributes using a wildcard filename while all of the files matching the filename are read-only.

Continued

TABLE A.1

OS-Released DS Error Codes *(continued)*

DECIMAL	HEXADECIMAL	CONSTANT	DESCRIPTION
-145	0xFFFFFF6F	DSERR_SOME_NAMES_EXIST	Failed to rename files using a wildcard filename when one or more files matching the new filename specification already exist.
-146	0xFFFFFF6E	DSERR_ALL_NAMES_EXIST	Failed to rename files using a wildcard filename when all of the files matching the new filename specification already exist.
-147	0xFFFFFF6D	DSERR_NO_READ_PRIVILEGE	Cannot read from a file without Read privilege to that file.
-148	0xFFFFFF6C	DSERR_NO_WRITE_PRIVILEGE	Cannot write to a file without Write privilege to that file, or the specified file is opened as read-only.
-149	0xFFFFFF6B	DSERR_FILE_DETACHED	This is caused by an internal auditing error. You need to contact Novell about this error.
-150	0xFFFFFF6A	ERR_INSUFFICIENT_MEMORY	The server does not have sufficient dynamic memory to process the current auditing request. This is the same as OS error ERR_NO_ALLOC_SPACE (0x96).
-150	0xFFFFFF6A	DSERR_NO_ALLOC_ SPACE	The server failed to allocate memory for the current NDS request, process, or operation.
-150	0xFFFFFF6A	DSERR_TARGET_NOT_A_SUBDIR	The target is not a subdirectory.
-151	0xFFFFFF69	DSERR_NO_SPOOL_ SPACE	There is insufficient disk space left on the NetWare volume for spool files.

DECIMAL	HEXADECIMAL	CONSTANT	DESCRIPTION
-152	0xFFFFFF68	DSERR_INVALID_VOLUME	A bindery API call was made to retrieve a bindery-emulated object's file system rights but the specified volume name cannot be found. Perhaps the volume is not mounted.
-153	0xFFFFFF67	DSERR_DIRECTORY_FULL	Cannot write to volume due to out of directory space.
-154	0xFFFFFF66	DSERR_RENAME_ACROSS_VOLUME	Cannot rename a file and move the renamed file from one volume to another volume; the rename command may only move the file between directories on the same volume.
-155	0xFFFFFF65	DSERR_BAD_DIR_HANDLE	Trying to use an invalid directory (not file) handle. This could happen if the server was brought down and brought back up without rebooting the client.
-156	0xFFFFFF64	DSERR_INVALID_PATH	A bindery API call was made to create a bindery-emulated queue object. However, the specified (directory/filename) path is invalid or not accessible. This error can also be caused by faulty LAN driver or networking hardware.
-156	0xFFFFFF64	DSERR_NO_SUCH_EXTENSION	No more trustees are listed in the directory entry table.
-157	0xFFFFFF63	DSERR_NO_DIR_HANDLES	The server's directory handle table is full. (Each client is allowed up to 255 directory handles.)
-158	0xFFFFFF62	DSERR_BAD_FILE_NAME	Cannot create a file whose name contains illegal character(s).
-159	0xFFFFFF61	DSERR_DIRECTORY_ACTIVE	Unable to delete a directory that is currently in use by another process.

Continued

T A B L E   A . I

OS-Released DS Error Codes (continued)

DECIMAL	HEXADECIMAL	CONSTANT	DESCRIPTION
-160	0xFFFFFF60	DSERR_DIRECTORY_NOT_EMPTY	Cannot delete a directory that contains other directories or files.
-161	0xFFFFFF5F	DSERR_DIRECTORY_IO_ERROR	A non-recoverable I/O error when trying to access the Directory Entry Table (DET). Both copies of the DET are not accessible and the error is fatal.
-162	0xFFFFFF5E	DSERR_IO_LOCKED	Attempt to read a file where data is physically locked.
-163	0xFFFFFF5D	DSERR_TRANSACTION_RESTARTED	An aborted TTS transaction has been restarted.
-164	0xFFFFFF5C	DSERR_RENAME_DIR_INVALID	The rename operation specified a directory name that contains one or more invalid characters.
-165	0xFFFFFF5B	DSERR_INVALID_OPENCREATE_MODE	An invalid combination of Open/Create mode option was specified.
-166	0xFFFFFF5A	DSERR_ALREADY_IN_USE	The auditor is trying to access an object that is currently being accessed by another auditor.
-167	0xFFFFFF59	DSERR_INVALID_RESOURCE_TAG	An application is trying to register an NDS event using an invalid resource tag. This is due to faulty applications.
-168	0xFFFFFF58	DSERR_ACCESS_DENIED	Access to resource has been denied.

DECIMAL	HEXADECIMAL	CONSTANT	DESCRIPTION
-169 through -187	0xFFFFFF57 through 0xFFFFFF45		Unused.
-188	0xFFFFFF44	DSERR_LOGIN_ SIGNING_REQUIRED	Packet signing is required for the login process.
-189	0xFFFFFF43	DSERR_LOGIN_ ENCRYPT_REQUIRED	Data encryption is required for the login process.
-190	0xFFFFFF42	DSERR_INVALID_DATA_STREAM	The specified data stream is invalid. An internal auditing error.
-191	0xFFFFFF41	DSERR_INVALID_NAME_SPACE	The specified name space is not supported.
-192	0xFFFFFF40	DSERR_NO_ACCOUNTING_ PRIVILEGES	Trying to perform accounting function without the proper privileges.
-193	0xFFFFFF3F	DSERR_NO_ACCOUNT_BALANCE	A bindery login was attempted but the object has no accounting balance, and the server's accounting is enabled.
-194	0xFFFFFF3E	DSERR_CREDIT_LIMIT_ EXCEEDED	Attempt to log in with no credit available or attempt to perform an operation that will exceed its accounting credit limit.
-195	0xFFFFFF3D	DSERR_TOO_MANY_ HOLDS	Too many accounting transactions on hold.
-196	0xFFFFFF3C	DSERR_ACCOUNTING_ DISABLED	Trying to perform accounting function when the server's accounting is disabled.
-197	0xFFFFFF3B	DSERR_LOGIN_LOCKOUT	Attempt to log in after the system had locked the account due to intruder detection.

Continued

T A B L E   A . I

OS-Released DS Error Codes (continued)

DECIMAL	HEXADECIMAL	CONSTANT	DESCRIPTION
-198	0xFFFFFF3A	DSERR_NO_ CONSOLE_RIGHTS	Attempt to perform console functions (such as changing the server's time) without operator privileges.
-199 through -207	0xFFFFFF39 through 0xFFFFFF31		Unused.
-208	0xFFFFFF30	DSERR_Q_IO_FAILURE	I/O error when trying to access queue.
-209	0xFFFFFF2F	DSERR_NO_QUEUE	Queue directory not found.
-210	0xFFFFFF2E	DSERR_NO_Q_SERVER	No queue server associated with the queue.
-211	0xFFFFFF2D	DSERR_NO_Q_RIGHTS	Insufficient rights to service queue.
-212	0xFFFFFF2C	DSERR_Q_FULL	Queue is full. A QMS-based queue can hold up to 250 jobs.
-213	0xFFFFFF2B	DSERR_NO_Q_JOB	There is no serviceable job in the queue.
-214	0xFFFFFF2A	DSERR_NO_Q_JOB_ RIGHTS	Cannot assume the rights of a queue job's submitter in order to service that queue job. (This is controlled by the Allow Change To Client Rights SET command.)
-214	0xFFFFFF2A	DSERR_ UNENCRYPTED_NOT_ ALLOWED	A bindery API call was made using an unencrypted password when the server does not permit it. (This is controlled by the Allow Unencrypted Passwords SET command.)
-215	0xFFFFFF29	DSERR_Q_IN_SERVICE	The specified queue is already being serviced by the queue server.

DECIMAL	HEXADECIMAL	CONSTANT	DESCRIPTION
-215	0xFFFFFF29	DSERR_DUPLICATE_PASSWORD	Attempt to change the (NDS or bindery) password to a previously used password when the unique password requirement is specified for the account.
-216	0xFFFFFF28	DSERR_Q_NOT_ACTIVE	Trying to service a queue that does not allow queue servers to service jobs in the queue.
-216	0xFFFFFF28	DSERR_PASSWORD_TOO_SHORT	The new (NDS or bindery) password has fewer characters than the required minimum specified for the account.
-217	0xFFFFFF27	DSERR_Q_STN_NOT_SERVER	The station making the queue service request is not logged in as a queue server.
-217	0xFFFFFF27	DSERR_MAXIMUM_LOGINS_EXCEEDED	Attempt to log in using an (NDS or bindery) account which has limits on the number of concurrent connections when that number has already been reached.
-218	0xFFFFFF26	DSERR_Q_HALTED	Trying to place a job into a queue that does not allow new jobs to be added.
-218	0xFFFFFF26	DSERR_BAD_LOGIN_TIME	Attempt to log in during an unauthorized time of day as specified in the Login Time Restriction for the (NDS or bindery) user account.
-219	0xFFFFFF25	DSERR_Q_MAX_SERVERS	The queue already has its maximum number of queue servers attached. Each QMS-based queue can be serviced by up to 16 queue servers.
-219	0xFFFFFF25	DSERR_NODE_ADDRESS_VIOLATION	Attempt to log in from an unauthorized station using an (NDS or bindery) account with limits to a specific network and/or node.

Continued

TABLE A.1

OS-Released DS Error Codes (continued)

DECIMAL	HEXADECIMAL	CONSTANT	DESCRIPTION
-220	0xFFFFFF24	DSERR_LOG_ACCOUNT_EXPIRED	Trying to log in using an (NDS or bindery) account that has expired or has been disabled.
-222	0xFFFFFF22	DSERR_BAD_PASSWORD	Attempt to log in using an (NDS or bindery) account whose password has expired and all grace logins have been used up.
-223	0xFFFFFF21	DSERR_PASSWORD_EXPIRED	Trying to log in using an expired (NDS or bindery) password and the login was allowed because the account had a grace login.
-224	0xFFFFFF20	DSERR_NO_LOGIN_CONN_AVAILABLE	The server is out of connections and rejected the login request.
-225 through -231	0xFFFFFF1F through 0xFFFFFF19		Unused.
-232	0xFFFFFF18	DSERR_WRITE_TO_GROUP_PROPERTY	Attempt to write a data segment to a group property using the call to write a property value. Wrong bindery API call used. This error can also be caused by an attempt to use an item not associated with this group or an item which has been deleted from this group.
-233	0xFFFFFF17	DSERR_MEMBER_ALREADY_EXISTS	Trying to redundantly add an object to a group.
-234	0xFFFFFF16	DSERR_NO_SUCH_MEMBER	Trying to access an object that is not a member of the specified group.
-235	0xFFFFFF15	DSERR_PROPERTY_NOT_GROUP	Attempt to access data that is not a property of the specified group.

DECIMAL	HEXADECIMAL	CONSTANT	DESCRIPTION
-236	0xFFFFFF14	DSERR_NO_SUCH_VALUE_SET	Attempt to access a nonexistent data set.
-237	0xFFFFFF13	DSERR_PROPERTY_ALREADY_EXISTS	Trying to redundantly add a (single-valued) property to an object; you need to first delete the existing property value before adding the new information.
-238	0xFFFFFF12	DSERR_OBJECT_ALREADY_EXISTS	Trying to create an object that already exists.
-239	0xFFFFFF11	DSERR_ILLEGAL_NAME	Request made with an object or property name containing illegal characters, such as a control character, comma, colon, semicolon, slash, backslash, question mark, asterisk, or tilde. This error may also be due to the fact that DS.NLM can't map the supplied name to its unicode representation. (This is the same as -638, ERR_NO_CHARACTER_MAPPING.)
-240	0xFFFFFF10	DSERR_ILLEGAL_WILDCARD	Attempt to use a wildcard character or wild object type in an API call where wildcards are not allowed.
-241	0xFFFFFF0F	DSERR_BINDERY_SECURITY	Trying to assign a security level of a bindery object or property to be higher than the requester's security level. This would make the object or property inaccessible to the requester.
-242	0xFFFFFF0E	DSERR_NO_OBJECT_READ_RIGHTS	Attempt to access an object's information or scan the object's properties by a station without the necessary security to access this information.

Continued

T A B L E   A . I

OS-Released DS Error Codes (continued)

DECIMAL	HEXADECIMAL	CONSTANT	DESCRIPTION
-243	0xFFFFFF0D	DSERR_NO_OBJECT_ RENAME_RIGHTS	Attempt to rename an object without the necessary security. Requires Supervisor or Rename object rights to rename objects.
-244	0xFFFFFF0C	DSERR_NO_OBJECT_ DELETE_RIGHTS	Cannot delete an object without the necessary security. Requires Supervisor or Delete object rights to delete objects.
-245	0xFFFFFF0B	DSERR_NO_OBJECT_ CREATE_RIGHTS	Cannot create or modify an object without the necessary security. Requires Supervisor or Create object rights to create objects.
-246	0xFFFFFF0A	DSERR_NO_ PROPERTY_DELETE_ RIGHTS	Attempt to delete a property by a client that doesn't have the necessary security privilege to delete a property from the give object. Requires Supervisor or Delete property rights to delete a property.
-247	0xFFFFFF09	DSERR_NO_ PROPERTY_CREATE_ RIGHTS	Unable to add a new property value by a client that doesn't have the necessary security privilege to add a property to the give object. Requires Supervisor or Write property rights to add a property or property value.
-248	0xFFFFFF08	DSERR_NO_ PROPERTY_WRITE_ RIGHTS	Unable to write to a property by a client that doesn't have the necessary security privilege. Requires Supervisor or Write property rights to write change the property data.

DECIMAL	HEXADECIMAL	CONSTANT	DESCRIPTION
-249	0xFFFFFF07	DSERR_NO_PROPERTY_READ_RIGHTS	Attempt to read a property by a client that doesn't have the necessary read security to access the property data. Requires Supervisor or Read property rights to retrieve a property value.
-250	0xFFFFFF06	DSERR_TEMP_REMAP	Attempt to use an unknown or invalid directory path.
-251	0xFFFFFF05	ERR_REQUEST_UNKNOWN	Request with an invalid parameter (drive number, path, or flag value) during a set drive path API call.
-251	0xFFFFFF05	DSERR_UNKNOWN_REQUEST	An unknown request was received. This is the same as OS error ERR_UNKNOWN_REQUEST (0xFB).
-251	0xFFFFFF05	DSERR_NO_SUCH_PROPERTY	Trying to access a property which doesn't exist for the specified object.
-252	0xFFFFFF04	DSERR_MESSAGE_QUEUE_FULL	The message queue (as used by the console BROADCAST command or the NetWare SEND.EXE utility) is full. No new messages can be queued.
-252	0xFFFFFF04	DSERR_TARGET_ALREADY_HAS_MSG	There is already waiting message in the message queue. No new messages can be added.

Continued

TABLE A.1
OS-Released DS Error Codes (continued)

DECIMAL	HEXADECIMAL	CONSTANT	DESCRIPTION
-252	0xFFFFFF04	DSERR_NO_SUCH_OBJECT	Attempt to use an object which doesn't exist, or the calling station doesn't have the proper security to access the object. Note that the object name and type must both match for the object to be found. This is the bindery equivalent of -601 error.
-253	0xFFFFFF03	DSERR_BAD_STATION_NUMBER	Attempt to use a bad (undefined, unavailable, and so on) station number. For example, the connection was cleared just prior to trying to access that connection.
-254	0xFFFFFF02	DSERR_BINDERY_LOCKED	Trying to access a locked bindery. On NDS servers, this can be due to DSRepair being run and the local DS database being temporarily locked.
-254	0xFFFFFF02	DSERR_DIR_LOCKED	Attempt to access a directory whose data area on the volume is physically locked.
-254	0xFFFFFF02	DSERR_SPOOL_DELETE	Trying to access a spool file that doesn't exist.
-254	0xFFFFFF02	DSERR_TRUSTEE_NOT_FOUND	The specified trustee is not found.
-254	0xFFFFFF02	DSERR_TIMEOUT	Request timed out.

DECIMAL	HEXADECIMAL	CONSTANT	DESCRIPTION
-255	0xFFFFFF01	DSERR_HARD_FAILURE	A bindery-emulation error has occurred. This can be a result from an attempt to verify a bindery object's password while Bindery Services was not enabled on the server, or an unsupported bindery API call was used. You can gather additional information by using DSTrace on the source server with the Bindery Emulation flag (EMU) turned on.
-255	0xFFFFFF01	DSERR_FILE_NAME	An illegal file name was specified.
-255	0xFFFFFF01	DSERR_FILE_EXISTS	The specified file already exists. An internal auditing error.
-255	0xFFFFFF01	DSERR_CLOSE_FCB	Error closing File Control Block (FCB).
-255	0xFFFFFF01	DSERR_IO_BOUND	Attempt to write beyond the end of file or disk. An internal auditing error.
-255	0xFFFFFF01	DSERR_NO_SPOOL_ FILE	The specified spool file does not exist.
-255	0xFFFFFF01	DSERR_BAD_SPOOL_ PRINTER	Attempt to use a bad (undefined, unavailable, and so on) printer.
-255 parameter.	0xFFFFFF01	DSERR_BAD_ PARAMETER	The API called tried to pass an illegal
-255	0xFFFFFF01	DSERR_NO_FILES_ FOUND	No files matching the search parameter were found.

Continued

T A B L E   A.1

OS-Released DS Error Codes (continued)

DECIMAL	HEXADECIMAL	CONSTANT	DESCRIPTION
-255 rights.	0xFFFFFF01	DSERR_NO_TRUSTEE_ CHANGE_PRIV	Unable to change trustee due to insufficient
-255	0xFFFFFF01	DSERR_TARGET_NOT_ LOGGED_IN	Trying to send a message to a user that is not logged in.
-255	0xFFFFFF01	DSERR_TARGET_NOT_ ACCEPTING_MSGS	Trying to send a message to a user that has disabled broadcast message reception. (The user has issued a "castoff" command using SEND /A=N.)
-255	0xFFFFFF01	DSERR_MUST_FORCE_ DOWN	The server cannot be downed gracefully (perhaps due to opened files) when a down-server API (such as NWDownFileServer) was issued.
-255	0xFFFFFF01	ERR_OF_SOME_SORT	An unknown error was encountered. This is the same as OS error ERR_OF_SOME_SORT (0xFF).
-255	0xFFFFFF01	ERR_NOT_ENOUGH_MEMORY	The server does not have sufficient memory to process the request.

TABLE A.2

Client API Library Error Codes

DECIMAL	HEXADECIMAL	CONSTANT	DESCRIPTION
-301	0xFFFFFED3	ERR_NOT_ENOUGH_MEMORY	Unable to allocate memory. The client (workstation) may be low on memory or the application has been repeatedly allocating buffers and failed to release them.
-302	0xFFFFFED2	ERR_BAD_KEY	An unknown key value was passed when making a context API call (NWDSSetContext or NWDSGetContext).
-303	0xFFFFFED1	ERR_BAD_CONTEXT	Trying to pass an invalid context value to a DS API call. Most likely cause of this error is that NWDSCreateContext or NWDSCreateContextHandle was not first called to obtain a context value.
-304	0xFFFFFED0	ERR_BUFFER_FULL	The buffer is full when trying to add data to an input buffer. The default buffer size is 4Kbytes and the maximum is 63Kbytes.
-305	0xFFFFFECF	ERR_LIST_EMPTY	An empty list (a NULL pointer) was passed to the NWDSPutAttrVal call when using the SYN_CI_LIST or SYN_OCTET_LIST syntax type.
-306	0xFFFFFECE	ERR_BAD_SYNTAX	An invalid syntax ID was being passed. Could be due to an internal auditing error.
-307	0xFFFFFECD	ERR_BUFFER_EMPTY	Attempt to retrieve data from an empty buffer.

Continued

T A B L E   A.2

Client API Library Error Codes (continued)

DECIMAL	HEXADECIMAL	CONSTANT	DESCRIPTION
-308	0xFFFFFECC	ERR_BAD_VERB	Trying to initialize a buffer using a verb that is not associated with the API call. For example, a call to NWDSInitBuf was made with the DSV_RESOLVE_NAME verb, which is not a valid verb for this API call.
-309	0xFFFFFECB	ERR_EXPECTED_IDENTIFIER	The NDS object name being parsed is not typed.
-310	0xFFFFFECA	ERR_EXPECTED_EQUALS	The expected equal sign in the object name is not found.
-311	0xFFFFFEC9	ERR_ATTR_TYPE_EXPECTED	The name being parsed must be typed.
-312	0xFFFFFEC8	ERR_ATTR_TYPE_NOT_EXPECTED	The name being parsed must *not* be typed.
-313	0xFFFFFEC7	ERR_FILTER_TREE_EMPTY	Trying to delete an empty filter.
-314	0xFFFFFEC6	ERR_INVALID_OBJECT_NAME	The specified object name is invalid. Perhaps the name contained both a leading *and* a trailing period, or a NULL string was passed.
-315	0xFFFFFEC5	ERR_EXPECTED_RDN_DELIMITER	The specified relative distinguished name (RDN) doesn't have the expected delimiter (a period, ".").
-316	0xFFFFFEC4	ERR_TOO_MANY_TOKENS	Too many trailing delimiter dots in the specified name; a maximum of three context levels and four trailing dots are allowed.

DECIMAL	HEXADECIMAL	CONSTANT	DESCRIPTION
-317	0xFFFFFEC3	ERR_INCONSISTENT_ MULTIAVA	An error occurs when checking the name field for the specified multivalued attribute. (An AVA, Attribute Value Association, is one of the values in a multivalued attribute, and multiAVA refers to a link in a values linked list.)
-318	0xFFFFFEC2	ERR_COUNTRY_ NAME_TOO_LONG	Too many characters in the specified country name. A country name can only be two characters long.
-319	0xFFFFFEC1	ERR_SYSTEM_ERROR	An internal system error.
-320	0xFFFFFEC0	ERR_CANT_ADD_ ROOT	Unable to add or restore object at [Root].
-321	0xFFFFFEBF	ERR_UNABLE_TO_ATTACH	Unable to attach to the specified server.
-322	0xFFFFFEBE	ERR_INVALID_HANDLE	Invalid iteration handle. Functions such as NWDSList, NWDSRead, and NWDSSearch can retrieve data from the server iteratively. To do this, a valid iteration handle is needed on each API call.
-323	0xFFFFFEBD	ERR_BUFFER_ZERO_ LENGTH	An API call to NWDSAllocBuf was made with a zero-length buffer size.
-324	0xFFFFFEBC	ERR_INVALID_ REPLICA_TYPE	The specified replica type is not one of RT_MASTER (Master), RT_SECONDART (ReadWrite), or RT_READONLY (ReadOnly).
-325	0xFFFFFEBB	ERR_INVALID_ATTR_ SYNTAX	The specified attribute syntax ID is invalid.
-326	0xFFFFFEBA	ERR_INVALID_FILTER_ SYNTAX	The specified filter syntax is invalid.
-327	0xFFFFFFB9		Unused.

Continued

· · · · ·

T A B L E   A . 2

Client API Library Error Codes (continued)

DECIMAL	HEXADECIMAL	CONSTANT	DESCRIPTION
-328	0xFFFFFEB8	ERR_CONTEXT_ CREATION	Unable to create a context handle. This may be caused by not having call the NWInitUnicodeTables API first.
-329	0xFFFFFEB7	ERR_INVALID_ UNION_TAG	The server-returned data does not agree with the data type (attribute name, attribute value, or effective privileges) you specified.
-330	0xFFFFFEB6	ERR_INVALID_SERVER_ RESPONSE	The NWDSGetSyntaxID API call is unable to retrieve the syntax ID of the specified attribute.
-331	0xFFFFFEB5	ERR_NULL_POINTER	A NULL pointer was found when a real pointer was expected.
-332	0xFFFFFEB4	ERR_NO_SERVER_ FOUND	Attempted connect failed to find any servers responding.
-333	0xFFFFFEB3	ERR_NO_ CONNECTION	Attempted to get connection information from a server that's not currently attached to.
-334	0xFFFFFEB2	ERR_RDN_TOO_LONG	The specified relative distinguished name (RDN) is longer than 128 bytes.
-335	0xFFFFFEB1	ERR_DUPLICATE_TYPE	Multiple AVAs specified and they can't contain the same data. (An AVA is one of the values in a multivalued attribute.)
-336	0xFFFFFEB0	ERR_DATA_STORE_ FAILURE	Internal error.
-337	0xFFFFFEAF	ERR_NOT_LOGGED_IN	Internal error. The client is not logged into any servers.
-338	0xFFFFFEAE	ERR_INVALID_PASSWORD_CHARS	One or more characters specified in the password is invalid.

DECIMAL	HEXADECIMAL	CONSTANT	DESCRIPTION
-339	0xFFFFFEAD	ERR_FAILED_SERVER_AUTHENT	Unable to authenticate to server using the cached credentials.
-340	0xFFFFFEAC	ERR_TRANSPORT	Communication fault detected.
-341	0xFFFFFEAB	ERR_NO_SUCH_SYNTAX	The specified syntax is not found.
-342	0xFFFFFEAA	ERR_INVALID_DS_NAME	A NULL or empty string is specified for an object name.
-343	0xFFFFFEA9	ERR_ATTR_NAME_TOO_LONG	The specified attribute name is longer than 32 bytes.
-344	0xFFFFFEA8	ERR_INVALID_TDS	Internal (Tagged Data Store) error. Usual cause of this error is that NWDSLogin wasn't first called.
-345	0xFFFFFEA7	ERR_INVALID_DS_VERSION	The version of DS.NLM is incompatible with the version of the operating system.
-346	0xFFFFFEA6	ERR_UNICODE_TRANSLATION	A unicode translation error from NWDSListPartitions, NWDSSyncPartition, or NWDSSyncSchema API call.
-347	0xFFFFFEA5	ERR_SCHEMA_NAME_TOO_LONG	Specified schema name is longer than 32 bytes.
-348	0xFFFFFEA4	ERR_UNICODE_FILE_NOT_FOUND	The required unicode file or files could not be found.
-349	0xFFFFFEA3	ERR_UNICODE_ALREADY_LOADED	The NWInitUnicodeTables call was made more than once.
-350	0xFFFFFEA2	ERR_NOT_CONTEXT_OWNER	The specified context handle doesn't belong to the current NDS tree or NLM thread.
-351	0xFFFFFEA1	ERR_ATTEMPT_TO_AUTHENTICATE_0	Internal error.

Continued

TABLE A.2
Client API Library Error Codes (continued)

DECIMAL	HEXADECIMAL	CONSTANT	DESCRIPTION
-352	0xFFFFFEA0	ERR_NO_WRITABLE_ REPLICAS	Cannot locate a writeable replica of a partition.
-353	0xFFFFFE9F	ERR_DN_TOO_LONG	The specified distinguished name is longer than 256 bytes. (Because NDS stores all characters using unicode representation, the maximum internal object name length is 512 bytes.)
-354	0xFFFFFE9E	ERR_RENAME_NOT_ALLOWED	Not permitted to rename specified object.
-355	0xFFFFFE9D	ERR_NOT_NDS_ FOR_NT	The server is not running NDS for NT.
-356	0xFFFFFE9C	ERR_NDS_FOR_NT_ NO_DOMAIN	No NDS for NT domain found.
-357	0xFFFFFE9B	ERR_NDS_FOR_NT_ SYNC_DISABLED	Synchronization between NDS for NT and NT PDC is disabled.
-358 through -399	0xFFFFFF9A through 0xFFFFFE71		Unused.

T A B L E   A.3

NLM-Specific Client API Library Error Codes

DECIMAL	HEX.ADECIMAL	CONSTANT	DESCRIPTION
-400	0xFFFFFE70	ERR_BAD_SERVICE_CONNECTION	An invalid server connection handle was specified.
-401	0xFFFFFE6F	ERR_BAD_NETWORK	The specified network address is unreachable.
-402	0xFFFFFE6E	ERR_BAD_ADDRESS	The specified MAC address is unknown.
-403	0xFFFFFE6D	ERR_SLOT_ALLOCATION	Unable to allocate a server connection slot.
-404	0xFFFFFE6C	ERR_BAD_BROADCAST	An invalid broadcast address was specified.
-405	0xFFFFFE6B	ERR_BAD_SERVER_NAME	There are one or more invalid characters in the specified server name.
-406	0xFFFFFE6A	ERR_BAD_USER_NAME	There are one or more invalid characters in the specified user name.
-407	0xFFFFFE69		Unused.
-408	0xFFFFFE68	ERR_NO_MEMORY	Unable to allocate memory.
-409	0xFFFFFE67		Unused.
-410	0xFFFFFE66	ERR_BAD_SOCKET	Request attempted with an invalid socket number.
-411	0xFFFFFE65	ERR_TAG_ALLOCATION	Unable to allocate resource tag.
-412	0xFFFFFE64	ERR_CONNECTION_ABORTED	The connection attempt to a server was aborted.
-413	0xFFFFFE63	ERR_TIMEOUT	The request has timed out.
-414	0xFFFFFE62	ERR_CHECKSUM	CRC checksum error detected.

Continued

T A B L E   A.3

NLM-Specific Client API Library Error Codes (continued)

DECIMAL	HEX.ADECIMAL	CONSTANT	DESCRIPTION
-415	0xFFFFFE61	ERR_NO_FRAGMENT_ LIST	No request fragment list was found when one was expected. (An NCP request/reply may be split into multiple packets, called fragments, if the information doesn't fit in a single packet.)
-416 through -496	0xFFFFFE60 through 0xFFFFFE10		Unused.
-497	0xFFFFFE0F	UNI_HANDLE_BAD	The unicode table in use is invalid. This error is from UNICODE.NLM. This error can prevent the NDS database from being initialized and opened because NDS data is stored in unicode representation. If the UNICODE.NLM is unable to translate the data for NDS, the data can't be used. During server boot up, UNICODE.NLM looks for its unicode files in the SYS:LOGIN\NLS directory. If any of the required files are missing from this directory, the NDS database may not open.
-498	0xFFFFFE0E		Unused.
-499	0xFFFFFE0D	UNI_NO_DEFAULT	The data contained one or more characters that can't be mapped to the corresponding unicode representation.

T A B L E   A . 4

DSA Error Codes

DECIMAL	HEXADECIMAL	CONSTANT	DESCRIPTION
-601	0xFFFFFDA7	ERR_NO_SUCH_ENTRY	The specified object is not found on the server replying to the request. The context could be a factor. Or, the client doesn't have sufficient rights to the object.
-602	0xFFFFFDA6	ERR_NO_SUCH_VALUE	The requested attribute value is not found on the server replying to the request. The client may not have sufficient rights to the attribute.
-603	0xFFFFFDA5	ERR_NO_SUCH_ATTRIBUTE	The requested attribute is not found on the server replying to the request. The client may not have sufficient rights to the attribute.
-604	0xFFFFFDA4	ERR_NO_SUCH_CLASS	The specified schema class is not found on the server replying to the request.
-605	0xFFFFFDA3	ERR_NO_SUCH_ PARTITION	The specified partition doesn't exist on the server replying to the request. There may be a communication problems between servers in the NDS tree.
-606	0xFFFFFDA2	ERR_ENTRY_ALREADY_ EXISTS	Trying to create, rename, or restore an object when an object with the same name already exists at the same context level of the tree.
-607	0xFFFFFDA1	ERR_NOT_EFFECTIVE_ CLASS	Attempt to create an object using a schema class definition that is not an effective class.
-608	0xFFFFFDA0	ERR_ILLEGAL_ATTRIBUTE	Attempt to add an attribute that's not listed as an optional or mandatory in the object's class.

Continued

T A B L E A . 4

DSA Error Codes (continued)

DECIMAL	HEXADECIMAL	CONSTANT	DESCRIPTION
-609	0xFFFFFD9F	ERR_MISSING_ MANDATORY	Trying to create an object that's missing one or more mandatory attributes. For example, a User object must have its Surname attribute defined when being created. (You can use Schema Manager to determine which attributes are mandatory for a given schema class; see Chapter 7).
-610	0xFFFFFD9E	ERR_ILLEGAL_DS_ NAME	The specified object name is incorrectly formatted or is longer than 256 bytes. (Because NDS stores all characters using unicode representation, the maximum internal object name length is 512 bytes.)
-611	0xFFFFFD9D	ERR_ILLEGAL_ CONTAINMENT	Attempt was made to add an object that violates the schema's containment rules.
-612	0xFFFFFD9C	ERR_CANT_HAVE_MULTIPLE_VALUES	An attempt was made to add more than one attribute value to a single-value attribute. If you wish to replace the value, you need to either delete the old value first or overwrite it with the new value.
-613	0xFFFFFD9B	ERR_SYNTAX_VIOLATION	Trying to modify an attribute using data that doesn't conform to the syntax specified for the attribute. For example, your API call specified SYN_INTEGER instead of SYN_STRING.

DECIMAL	HEXADECIMAL	CONSTANT	DESCRIPTION
-614	0xFFFFFD9A	ERR_DUPLICATE_VALUE	Attempt to add the same value-attribute combination to an object. For example, an User object already has a telephone number of 555-1212 and you're trying to add another telephone number whose value is also 555-1212.
-615	0xFFFFFD99	ERR_ATTRIBUTE_ALREADY_EXISTS	Attempt to create a schema attribute that already exists.
-616	0xFFFFFD98	ERR_MAXIMUM_ENTRIES_EXIST	Unable to add a new object to the NDS database as the maximum number of entries (16,777,215) in the Object database has been reached.
-617	0xFFFFFD97	ERR_DATABASE_FORMAT	The record structure of the NDS database doesn't match the structure expected by the version of DS.NLM being used. The database cannot be used. If you ever encounter this error, it will be while DS.NLM is trying to open the database or when you're attempting to abort an NDS operation, such as partitioning.
-618	0xFFFFFD96	ERR_INCONSISTENT_ DATABASE	The DS.NLM is unable to open the NDS database. This can be due to unexpected data returned from the local database to DS.NLM or due to a problem with the database. This error may be rectified using DSRepair by running a local database repair.
-619	0xFFFFFD95	ERR_INVALID_ COMPARISON	Attempt to compare two attributes whose syntaxes are not comparable, or you may have used an invalid compare syntax.

Continued

T A B L E   A . 4

DSA Error Codes (continued)

DECIMAL	HEXADECIMAL	CONSTANT	DESCRIPTION
-620	0xFFFFFD94	ERR_COMPARISON_FAILED	The two attribute values specified for comparison are not the same.
-621	0xFFFFFD93	ERR_TRANSACTIONS_DISABLED	No NDS request can be processed because the server's TTS has been disabled.
-622	0xFFFFFD92	ERR_INVALID_TRANSPORT	The specified type of transport is not supported by the server.
-623	0xFFFFFD91	ERR_SYNTAX_INVALID_IN_NAME	The naming attribute specified for the new schema class definition is not of the character string type.
-624	0xFFFFFD90	ERR_REPLICA_ALREADY_EXISTS	Trying to place a replica on a server that is already holding a (non-subref) replica of the same partition.
-625	0xFFFFFD8F	ERR_TRANSPORT_FAILURE	Unable to communicate with the target server. Generally a result of target server being down, a LAN/WAN outage, or some sort of routing problem.
-626	0xFFFFFD8E	ERR_ALL_REFERRALS_FAILED	The local server has no objects that match the request, and all attempts to tree-walk to other servers to find the objects have failed. This error is not the same as -634 (0xFFFFFD8E), ERR_NO_REFERRALS. This error could be an indirect result of SAP/RIP filtering on the network.

DECIMAL	HEXADECIMAL	CONSTANT	DESCRIPTION
-627	0xFFFFFD8D	ERR_CANT_REMOVE_NAMING_VALUE	Cannot remove the attribute value that's flagged as a naming attribute of an object. You can use Schema Manager to determine the naming attributes of a particular object class.
-628	0xFFFFFD8C	ERR_OBJECT_CLASS_VIOLATION	Trying to create an object without specifying its base class.
-629	0xFFFFFD8B	ERR_ENTRY_IS_NOT_LEAF	Attempt to delete an object containing subordinates, such as an Organizational Unit, that still has objects in it.
-630	0xFFFFFD8A	ERR_DIFFERENT_TREE	The request was sent to a server that is not located in the current NDS tree.
-631	0xFFFFFD89	ERR_ILLEGAL_REPLICA_TYPE	The server responding to the request doesn't have a replica with the required replica type to service the request. For example, the server has a ReadOnly replica and not a Read/Write. This error is generally due to an application bug.
-632	0xFFFFFD88	ERR_SYSTEM_FAILURE	An unknown and unexpected error. This can be a result of memory corruption in the server or inconsistent NDS database. Restarting the server or DSRepair may resolve the problem.
-633	0xFFFFFD87	ERR_INVALID_ENTRY_FOR_ROOT	Trying to restore an object as [Root] but the object's base class is not "Top". Or attempting to assign an object as a partition root object but the object's base class is not of a "container class".

Continued

T A B L E A.4

DSA Error Codes (continued)

DECIMAL	HEXADECIMAL	CONSTANT	DESCRIPTION
-634	0xFFFFFD86	ERR_NO_REFERRALS	The local server has no objects that match the request and has no referrals on which to search for the object. This error is not the same as -626 (0xFFFFFD8E), ERR_ALL_REFERRALS_FAILED. This error could be an indirect result of SAP/RIP filtering on the network.
-635	0xFFFFFD85	ERR_REMOTE_FAILURE	Unable to connect to another server. Unlike -625, this is not an error due to the network. Rather, it is due to the requester using an invalid server handle or unsupported NCP call, or the remote server returned an invalid reply. Therefore, this is mostly an application-related error.
-636	0xFFFFFD84	ERR_UNREACHABLE_ SERVER	A partition operation can't be performed because one or more of the servers in the replica ring is unreachable due to -625 error.
-637	0xFFFFFD83	ERR_PREVIOUS_MOVE_ IN_PROGRESS	Cannot process the current request because a previous Object Move operation is still in progress.
-638	0xFFFFFD82	ERR_NO_CHARACTER_ MAPPING	Request made with an object or property name containing illegal characters, such as a control character, comma, colon, semicolon, slash, backslash, question mark, asterisk, or tilde. This error may also be due to the fact that DS.NLM can't map the supplied name to its unicode representation. (This is the same as -239, DSERR_ILLEGAL_NAME.)

DECIMAL	HEXADECIMAL	CONSTANT	DESCRIPTION
-639	0xFFFFFD81	ERR_INCOMPLETE_AUTHENTICATION	An error happened during the final phase of the NDS authentication process. This is generally due to LAN/WAN's hardware or software as it is suggestive of packet corruption.
-640	0xFFFFFD80	ERR_INVALID_ CERTIFICATE	An invalid security certificate was specified. This error is NetWare 5-specific.
-641	0xFFFFFD7F	ERR_INVALID_REQUEST	The request was invalid or unsupported by the running version of DS.NLM.
-642	0xFFFFFD7E	ERR_INVALID_ ITERATION	The iteration handle in a message fragment of an NDS request is invalid. This could be a result of packet corruption.
-643	0xFFFFFD7D	ERR_SCHEMA_IS_ NONREMOVABLE	Attempt to delete a base schema class flagged as non-removable.
-644	0xFFFFFD7C	ERR_SCHEMA_IS_IN_USE	Attempt to delete a schema class definition that still contains an object using that definition.
-645	0xFFFFFD7B	ERR_CLASS_ALREADY_ EXISTS	Trying to add a schema class definition that already exists in the schema.
-646	0xFFFFFD7A	ERR_BAD_NAMING_ATTRIBUTES	Trying to add a schema class definition whose naming attribute is not a valid attribute for the class.
-647	0xFFFFFD79	ERR_NOT_ROOT_ PARTITION	Attempt to perform a partitioning operation on a non-partition root object.

Continued

T A B L E   A.4

DSA Error Codes (continued)

DECIMAL	HEXADECIMAL	CONSTANT	DESCRIPTION
-648	0xFFFFFD78	ERR_INSUFFICIENT_ STACK	Internal error. The server ran out of stack.
-649	0xFFFFFD77	ERR_INSUFFICIENT_ BUFFER	The server ran out of memory, or the calling application didn't provide sufficient buffer space for the request.
-650	0xFFFFFD76	ERR_AMBIGUOUS_ CONTAINMENT	Attempt to create a schema class definition that contained an ambiguous containment rule.
-651	0xFFFFFD75	ERR_AMBIGUOUS_ NAMING	Attempt to create a schema class definition that contained an ambiguous containment name.
-652	0xFFFFFD74	ERR_DUPLICATE_ MANDATORY	Attempt to create a schema class definition that contained a duplicate mandatory attribute name.
-653	0xFFFFFD73	ERR_DUPLICATE_ OPTIONAL	Attempt to create a schema class definition that contained a duplicate optional attribute name.
-654	0xFFFFFD72	ERR_PARTITION_BUSY	Cannot process the request because the specified partition is currently involved in a partition operation, or the replica's state is not On.
-655	0xFFFFFD71	ERR_MULTIPLE_ REPLICAS	Attempt to add a new replica attribute value to the partition root object that already has a replica attribute with the same value.
-656	0xFFFFFD70	ERR_CRUCIAL_REPLICA	An illegal partition operation was requested (such as trying to add a ReadWrite replica to a server holding the Master replica of the same partition).

DECIMAL	HEXADECIMAL	CONSTANT	DESCRIPTION
-657	0xFFFFFD6F	ERR_SCHEMA_SYNC_ IN_PROGRESS	The request can't be processed because the schema sync process is in progress.
-658	0xFFFFFD6E	ERR_SKULK_IN_ PROGRESS	The request can't be processed because the skulk process is in progress.
-659	0xFFFFFD6D	ERR_TIME_NOT_ SYNCHRONIZED	The time between the source and target server is not synchronized. Consequently, partition operation can't be performed.
-660	0xFFFFFD6C	ERR_RECORD_IN_USE	NDS tried to purge an NDS database record that's still in use. DSRepair may be used to resolve this error.
-661	0xFFFFFD6B	ERR_DS_VOLUME_ NOT_MOUNTED	Internal error. You should "never" encounter this error as it is used by the OS to indicate that DS.NLM shouldn't be loaded at this time because the SYS volume is not yet mounted.
-662	0xFFFFFD6A	ERR_DS_VOLUME_IO_ FAILURE	Internal error. I/O operation attempted on the SYS volume failed. Possibly because the volume is not yet mounted.
-663	0xFFFFFD69	ERR_DS_LOCKED	Can't process request because The NDS database is locked (or closed); analogous to bindery being locked. The database may be locked by DSRepair while it is doing a repair, or it was closed because the server's TTS was shutdown. In some cases, this error is due to -497 (UNI_HANDLE_BAD) from UNICODE.NLM.

Continued

T A B L E   A . 4
DSA Error Codes (continued)

DECIMAL	HEXADECIMAL	CONSTANT	DESCRIPTION
-664	0xFFFFFD68	ERR_OLD_EPOCH	Trying to modify objects on a server that is using an older epoch of the data. This can happen either during a replica sync process or a schema sync process. This is a transitory error and will disappear once the sync process updates the epoch on the servers. (An epoch is an arbitrary time and date that marks the beginning of an event. In the context of NDS schema, a schema epoch defines the time at which the schema was last updated or changed.)
-665	0xFFFFFD67	ERR_NEW_EPOCH	Trying to modify objects on a server that is using a newer epoch of the data. This can happen either during a replica sync process or a schema sync process. This is a transitory error and will disappear once the sync process updates the epoch on the servers.
-666	0xFFFFFD66	ERR_INCOMPATIBLE_ DS_VERSION	Unable to synchronize with target server due to either incompatible DS.NLM versions between the source and target servers, or the version of the DS.NLM on the source server is on the target server's restricted version list. You can check a server's restricted DS version list using the "NDS do not synchronize with" console SET command.

DECIMAL	HEXADECIMAL	CONSTANT	DESCRIPTION
-667	0xFFFFFD65	ERR_PARTITION_ROOT	Attempt to perform an NDS operation on a partition root object when it is not allowed. For example, you tried to delete a container root object without first merging it with its parent partition.
-668	0xFFFFFD64	ERR_ENTRY_NOT_CONTAINER	Attempt to perform a partition operation on a leaf object.
-669	0xFFFFFD63	ERR_FAILED_AUTHENTICATION	An invalid password was used to authenticate into NDS.
-670	0xFFFFFD62	ERR_INVALID_CONTEXT	Internal error. A request was made using an invalid context handle. The server's task and connection management table may be corrupt. Reloading DS.NLM may help to resolve the problem.
-671	0xFFFFFD61	ERR_NO_SUCH_PARENT	Attempt to modify an object whose parent object cannot be found.
-672	0xFFFFFD60	ERR_NO_ACCESS	The requester doesn't have sufficient rights to the requested information. For example, you're trying to perform a partitioning operation, but you don't have the necessary rights to the specified partition root objects.
-673	0xFFFFFD5F	ERR_REPLICA_NOT_ON	Cannot process the request because the specified partition's replica state is not On. You can check the current state of the replica using DSRepair.
-674	0xFFFFFD5E	ERR_INVALID_NAME_SERVICE	The specified name service is not available or is not supported.

Continued

T A B L E   A . 4

DSA Error Codes (continued)

DECIMAL	HEXADECIMAL	CONSTANT	DESCRIPTION
-675	0xFFFFFD5D	ERR_INVALID_TASK	Internal server error. A request was made using a Task ID of 0 of an NCP connection. The server's task and connection management table may be corrupt. Reloading DS.NLM may help to resolve the problem.
-676	0xFFFFFD5C	ERR_INVALID_CONN_ HANDLE	Internal server error. A request was made using an invalid NCP connection handle or an invalid Task ID of an NCP connection. The server's task and connection management table may be corrupt. Reloading DS.NLM may help to resolve the problem.
-677	0xFFFFFD5B	ERR_INVALID_ IDENTITY	Internal NDS error. A request was made using an invalid NDS identity. The server's identity tables may be corrupt. Reloading DS.NLM may help to resolve the problem.
-678	0xFFFFFD5A	ERR_DUPLICATE_ACL	Attempt to add an ACL attribute value to an object that already has same ACL attribute value and trustee.
-679	0xFFFFFD59	ERR_PARTITION_ALREADY_EXISTS	Trying to create a partition on a server that already has the specified object as a partition root object.

DECIMAL	HEXADECIMAL	CONSTANT	DESCRIPTION
-680	0xFFFFFD58	ERR_TRANSPORT_MODIFIED	A communication inconsistency occurred when attempting to connect to a remote server. The initial attempt resulted in a -625 error. However, a subsequent retry succeeded by re-negotiating the IPX checksum, IPX Packet Signatures, or maximum packet size. This error is generally caused by faults in the LAN/WAN hardware or software components.
-681	0xFFFFFD57	ERR_ALIAS_OF_AN_ALIAS	Trying to create an Alias of an Alias object.
-682	0xFFFFFD56	ERR_AUDITING_FAILED	Internal error due to NDS auditing operations. This error may be a result of an attempt to audit an object that has not been flagged for auditing or a failure to reset the auditing files.
-683	0xFFFFFD55	ERR_INVALID_API_VERSION	An API call specified a version number that is not supported by the currently running DS.NLM. The application may have been created using an outdated library.
-684	0xFFFFFD54	ERR_SECURE_NCP_VIOLATION	The source server or client attempted to authenticate with a remote server using IPX Packet Signatures, but the remote server doesn't support packet signing.
-685	0xFFFFFD53	ERR_MOVE_IN_PROGRESS	The specified object is currently involved in an NDS Object Move operation; the object has either a Move Obituary or an Inhibit Move Obituary. (For more information about obits, see Chapter 6.)

Continued

TABLE A.4

DSA Error Codes *(continued)*

DECIMAL	HEXADECIMAL	CONSTANT	DESCRIPTION
-686	0xFFFFFD52	ERR_NOT_LEAF_ PARTITION	Attempt to perform a Move Subtree partition operation but the specified object is not a "leaf" partition. You must first merge any subordinate partition root object with its parent partition first.
-687	0xFFFFFD51	ERR_CANNOT_ABORT	The current partition operation can't be aborted as it has progressed past a specific "turnaround" state. Typically when a Change Replica Type, Split Partition, or Merge Partition operation has gone beyond its initial phase (e.g., state RS_CRT_0, or replica state 4 during a Change Replica Type operation), the operation cannot be aborted. The same is true during a Move Subtree operation: when any of the Move Tree-related obits are changed to Notified, OK To Purge, or Purgeable, the operation can't be aborted.
-688	0xFFFFFD50	ERR_CACHE_ OVERFLOW	An internal error from the cache used by the NDS Replica Synchronization process.
-689	0xFFFFFD4F	ERR_INVALID_SUBORDINATE_COUNT	The subordinate object count in the object's database record doesn't match the number of presently found child objects. A repair local database operation using DSRepair may resolve the error.

DECIMAL	HEXADECIMAL	CONSTANT	DESCRIPTION
-690	0xFFFFFD4E	ERR_INVALID_RDN	The relative distinguished name specified in the object's database record doesn't match the name found in the object's naming attribute. Or the specified object's parent object, as identified by the database record, is invalid. A repair local database operation using DSRepair may resolve the error.
-691	0xFFFFFD4D	ERR_MOD_TIME_NOT_CURRENT	The modification timestamp of an object attribute is newer than the modification timestamp found in the object's database record. A repair local database operation using DSRepair may resolve the error.
-692	0xFFFFFD4C	ERR_INCORRECT_BASE_CLASS	The base class of an object doesn't match the base class specification found in the object's database record. A repair local database operation using DSRepair may resolve the error.
-693	0xFFFFFD4B	ERR_MISSING_REFERENCE	The specified object has an attribute value that references another object in the local database, but the referenced object doesn't have a reference attribute indicating the specified object that references it. A repair local database operation using DSRepair may resolve the error.
-694	0xFFFFFD4A	ERR_LOST_ENTRY	When the NDS Replica Synchronization process tried to update an object on the target server, the object had not yet been received by the target server. This is a transitory error, as the NDS Replica Synchronization process will resend the lost object before trying to update it.

Continued

T A B L E   A . 4

DSA Error Codes (continued)

DECIMAL	HEXADECIMAL	CONSTANT	DESCRIPTION
-695	0xFFFFFD49	ERR_AGENT_ALREADY_ REGISTERED	Trying to load DS.NLM when another NLM has already registered with the OS as an NDS agent.
-696	0xFFFFFD48	ERR_DS_LOADER_BUSY	The DS Loader was busy when a request was made to unload and reload DS.NLM. You should try the operation again at a later time.
-697	0xFFFFFD47	ERR_DS_CANNOT RELOAD_	Trying to unload and reload DS.NLM when one or more DS.NLM-dependent NLMs (such as DSRepair) was still loaded.
-698	0xFFFFFD46	ERR_REPLICA_IN_ SKULK	Attempt to start the NDS Replica Synchronization process with a target server, but the target server is busy synchronizing with another server. This is a transitory error, and the NDS Replica Synchronization process will reschedule.
-699	0xFFFFFD45	ERR_FATAL	An internal error. If this happens during normal NDS operations, it is generally transitory. However, if the error persists, you can try reloading DS.NLM or restarting the server. If the standard repair methods (such as performing a local database repair using DSRepair) do not resolve the error, you need to open a call with Novell.
-700	0xFFFFFD44	ERR_OBSOLETE_API	An API request that's no longer supported by the running version of DS.NLM. This is the opposite to error -714, ERR_NOT_IMPLEMENTED.

DECIMAL	HEXADECIMAL	CONSTANT	DESCRIPTION
-701	0xFFFFFD43	ERR_SYNCHRONIZATION_DISABLED	The NDS Replica Synchronization process is unable to sync with the target server as its Inbound Replica Synchronization is disabled using the SET DSTRACE=!D or SET DSTRACE=!DI command. You can re-enable the inbound sync using the SET DSTRACE=!E or SET DSTRACE=!EI command.
-702	0xFFFFFD42	ERR_INVALID_PARAMETER	Attempt to register for an unsupported DS event or to unregister an unregistered event. This error is due to logic faults in (NLM) applications.
-703	0xFFFFFD41	ERR_DUPLICATE_TEMPLATE	This is an internal error and is expected during schema initialization.
-704	0xFFFFFD40	ERR_NO_MASTER_REPLICA	Unable to locate the Master replica of the partition. The server holding the Master may be unavailable.
-705	0xFFFFFD3F	ERR_DUPLICATE_CONTAINMENT	This is an internal error and is expected during schema initialization.
-706	0xFFFFFD3E	ERR_NOT_SIBLING	The objects specified in a Merge Entries operation are not siblings to each one another. A repair local database operation using DSRepair may resolve the error.
-707	0xFFFFFD3D	ERR_INVALID_SIGNATURE	The packet signature is invalid. This may be due to packet corruption.
-708	0xFFFFFD3C	ERR_INVALID_RESPONSE	The data received by DS.NLM is invalid or contains unexpected information. This may be due to packet corruption.

Continued

T A B L E   A . 4

DSA Error Codes (continued)

DECIMAL	HEXADECIMAL	CONSTANT	DESCRIPTION
-709	0xFFFFFD3B	ERR_INSUFFICIENT_SOCKETS	All available NCP sockets are currently in use. This is a transitory error. However, if the error persists, you can increase the number of sockets using SPXCONFG.NLM.
-710	0xFFFFFD3A	ERR_DATABASE_READ_FAIL	Unable to read the NDS database.
-711	0xFFFFFD39	ERR_INVALID_CODE_PAGE	The code page used by the OS is not supported by the currently running DS.NLM.
-712	0xFFFFFD38	ERR_INVALID_ESCAPE_CHAR	The specified escape character is not supported by the currently running DS.NLM. An escape character tells NDS to treat the following character as a regular text character, as opposed to whatever meaning that character might normally have for NDS.
-713	0xFFFFFD37	ERR_INVALID_DELIMITERS	The specified delimiters are not supported by the currently running DS.NLM. (NDS uses dots, ".", as delimiters in object names.)
-714	0xFFFFFD36	ERR_NOT_IMPLEMENTED	The requested operation or function is not supported by the currently running DS.NLM. You'll need to upgrade to a newer version of DS.NLM. This is the opposite to error -700, ERR_OBSOLETE_API.

DECIMAL	HEXADECIMAL	CONSTANT	DESCRIPTION
-715	0xFFFFFD35	ERR_CHECKSUM_ FAILURE	The NDS checksum in the request packet is invalid. This error is generally caused by faults in the LAN/WAN hardware or software components. NDS checksumming is generally not recommended as the current versions of DS.NLM use a transport-independent CRC checking for all traffic between servers. You can enable NDS checksumming using the SET DSTRACE=CHECKSUM command or disable it with the SET DSTRACE=NOCHECKSUM command. Note that NDS checksumming is not supported on all frame types, such as Novell's Ethernet_802.3.
-716	0xFFFFFD34	ERR_CHECKSUMMING_NOT_SUPPORTED	Attempt to negotiate an NCP connection with a server that doesn't support NDS checksumming, while the source server has NDS checksumming enabled.
-717	0xFFFFFD33	ERR_CRC_FAILURE	The NDS CRC (different from NDS checksum) in the request packet is invalid. This error is generally caused by faults in the LAN/WAN hardware or software components.
-718	0xFFFFFD32	ERR_INVALID_ENTRY_ HANDLE	The file handle for the Object Entry database file is invalid.
-719	0xFFFFFD31	ERR_INVALID_VALUE_ HANDLE	The file handle for the Attribute Value database file is invalid.
-720	0xFFFFFD30	ERR_CONNECTION_ DENIED	NDS outbound traffic or NCP connection to a remote server is not permitted because of WanMan (WAN Traffic Manager) restriction policies.

Continued

TABLE A.4

DSA Error Codes (continued)

DECIMAL	HEXADECIMAL	CONSTANT	DESCRIPTION
-721	0xFFFFFD2F	ERR_NO_SUCH_FEDERATION_LINK	Reserved error code for Federated Partition implementation.
-722	0xFFFFFD2E	ERR_OP_SCHEMA_MISMATCH	A mismatch in operational schema was detected.
-723	0xFFFFFD2D	ERR_STREAM_NOT_FOUND	The specified stream file doesn't exist. This could be a result of no database files found in the SYS:_NETWARE directory.
-724	0xFFFFFD2C	ERR_DCLIENT_UNAVAILABLE	The DSA is not running.
-725	0xFFFFFD2B	ERR_MASV_NO_ACCESS	Cannot access Mandatory Access Control Service. (NetWare 5-specific.)
-726	0xFFFFFD2A	ERR_MASV_INVALID_REQUEST	The Mandatory Access Control Service received an invalid request. (NetWare 5-specific.)
-727	0xFFFFFD29	ERR_MASV_FAILURE	A failure condition was detected in the Mandatory Access Control Service. (NetWare 5-specific.)
-728	0xFFFFFD28	ERR_MASV_ALREADY_EXISTS	The Mandatory Access Control Service is already running. (NetWare 5-specific.)
-729	0xFFFFFD27	ERR_MASV_NOT_FOUND	The Mandatory Access Control Service is not running. (NetWare 5-specific.)
-730	0xFFFFFD26	ERR_MASV_BAD_RANGE	The Mandatory Access Control Service data is out of range. (NetWare 5-specific.)
-731	0xFFFFFD25	ERR_VALUE_DATA	The value received is invalid.
-732	0xFFFFFD24	ERR_DATABASE_LOCKED	The database files are locked.

DECIMAL	HEXADECIMAL	CONSTANT	DESCRIPTION
-733 through -734	0xFFFFFD23 through 0xFFFFFD22		Unused.
-735	0xFFFFFD21	ERR_NOTHING_TO_ABORT	Cannot abort the specified NDS operation as it has already completed or has been aborted.
-736	0xFFFFFD20	ERR_END_OF_STREAM	End-of-file encountered while accessing the stream file.
-737	0xFFFFFD1F	ERR_NO_SUCH_TEMPLATE	The specified User Template doesn't exist.
-738	0xFFFFFD1E	ERR_SAS_LOCKED	The Secure Authentication Services database is locked. (NetWare 5-specific.)
-739	0xFFFFFD1D	ERR_INVALID_SAS_VERSION	The version information in the SAS request is not supported by the currently running SAS.NLM. (NetWare 5-specific.)
-740	0xFFFFFD1C	ERR_SAS_ALREADY_ REGISTERED	The SAS.NLM is already running. (NetWare 5-specific.)
-741	0xFFFFFD1B	ERR_NAME_TYPE_ NOT_SUPPORTED	The specified object type is not supported.
-742	0xFFFFFD1A	ERR_WRONG_DS_ VERSION	The specified DS version is not supported.
-743	0xFFFFFD19	ERR_INVALID_ CONTROL_FUNCTION	The specified control function is not supported.
-744	0xFFFFFD18	ERR_INVALID_ CONTROL_STATE	The specified control function state is not supported.
-745	0xFFFFFD17	ERR_CACHE_IN_USE	Trying to use the data cache while it is in use by another process.
-746	0xFFFFFD16	ERR_ZERO_ CREATION_TIME	The specified object has a zero creation timestamp. A repair local database operation using DSRepair may resolve the error.

Continued

T A B L E   A . 4

DSA Error Codes (continued)

DECIMAL	HEXADECIMAL	CONSTANT	DESCRIPTION
-747	0xFFFFFD15	ERR_WOULD_BLOCK	The specified API call will block (control is not returned to the calling client until the execution of the API function is completed).
-748	0xFFFFFD14	ERR_CONN_TIMEOUT	The connection has timed out.
-749	0xFFFFFD13	ERR_TOO_MANY_ REFERRALS	The tree-walking process has reached the maximum number of servers for which the local server can contact to retrieve an object's information.
-750	0xFFFFFD12	ERR_OPERATION_ CANCELLED	The specified NDS operation has been (successfully) cancelled.
-751	0xFFFFFD11	ERR_UNKNOWN_ TARGET	The specified server is unknown.
-752	0xFFFFFD10	ERR_GUID_FAILURE	The SGUID.NLM (Global Unique Identifier Services) can't process the request, or can't find the required GUID. (NetWare 5-specific.)
-753	0xFFFFFD0F	ERR_INCOMPATIBLE_OS	The NLM can't be loaded on this version of the OS.
-754	0xFFFFFD0E	ERR_CALLBACK_ CANCEL	The execution of the callback routine has been cancelled.
-755	0xFFFFFD0D	ERR_INVALID_SYNCHRONIZATION_DATA	Invalid data was found in the data sent by the NDS Replica Synchronization process.
-756	0xFFFFFD0C	ERR_STREAM_EXISTS	The specified stream file already exists.
-757 through -799	0xFFFFFD0B through 0xFFFFFCE1		Unused.

DS Verbs

Directory Services Verbs are issued by the Directory Services Agent on a server or by a client requesting the server perform some action on DS. Many of the verbs can be observed in the DSTRACE screen by using the command:

```
SET DSTRACE=+DSA
```

This command enables tracing of the Directory Services Agent (DSA) on the server and shows all inbound and outbound DSA requests.

The DSTRACE screen will show the information in the format:

```
DSA: DSACommonRequest(r) conn:c for client <ObjectName>
```

The request value is shown in decimal format for value *r*. The connection number making the request is value *c*, and the object name (if known) is *ObjectName*.

For example, if **Jim.East.XYZCorp** on connection 42 on the server attempts to read the last name attribute of his user object, the DSTRACE screen would show:

```
DSA: DSACommonRequest(3) conn:42 for client
<Jim.East.XYZCorp>
```

If you turn the **BUFFERS** flag on as well, you would also see the request/reply buffers that go along with this request and would see the last name attribute referenced in the request buffer and the value of the last name returned in the reply buffer.

Table B.1 is a list of all the current Directory Services Agent Common Request values and their definitions.

TABLE B.1

Common Request Values

DEFINE VALUE	DECIMAL	HEXADECIMAL	DESCRIPTION
DSV_UNUSED_0	0	0x00	Not Used
DSV_RESOLVE_NAME	1	0x01	NDS Name Lookup
DSV_READ_ENTRY_INFO	2	0x02	Read Basic Information about an Entry
DSV_READ	3	0x03	Read Attribute Values in an Object
DSV_COMPARE	4	0x04	Perform Comparison with an Attribute Value
DSV_LIST	5	0x05	List Subordinate Objects
DSV_SEARCH	6	0x06	Search the Tree for an Object Based on an Attribute Value
DSV_ADD_ENTRY	7	0x07	Create an Object
DSV_REMOVE_ENTRY	8	0x08	Delete an Object
DSV_MODIFY_ENTRY	9	0x09	Commit Changes to an Entry's Attributes
DSV_MODIFY_RDN	10	0x0A	Move Object
DSV_DEFINE_ATTR	11	0x0B	Create a New Attribute in the Schema
DSV_READ_ATTR_DEF	12	0x0C	Read Schema Definition for an Attribute
DSV_REMOVE_ATTR_DEF	13	0x0D	Delete Attribute Definition from the Schema
DSV_DEFINE_CLASS	14	0x0E	Create a New Class in the Schema
DSV_READ_CLASS_DEF	15	0x0F	Read Schema Definition for a Class
DSV_MODIFY_CLASS_DEF	16	0x10	Change Schema Definition for a Class (typically used when adding attributes to a class)
DSV_REMOVE_CLASS_DEF	17	0x11	Delete Class Definition from the Schema

Continued

TABLE B.1

Common Request Values (continued)

DEFINE VALUE	DECIMAL	HEXADECIMAL	DESCRIPTION
DSV_LIST_CONTAINABLE_CLASSES	18	0x12	List All Classes That Are Flagged as Being Container Classes
DSV_GET_EFFECTIVE_RIGHTS	19	0x13	Determine Currently Logged-In Object's Effective Rights to Another Object
DSV_ADD_PARTITION	20	0x14	Add Partition to a Replica List
DSV_REMOVE_PARTITION	21	0x15	Remove Partition from a Replica List
DSV_LIST_PARTITIONS	22	0x16	List Partitions in a Replica List
DSV_SPLIT_PARTITION	23	0x17	Create Partition Operation
DSV_JOIN_PARTITIONS	24	0x18	Merge Partition Operation
DSV_ADD_REPLICA	25	0x19	Create Replica Operation
DSV_REMOVE_REPLICA	26	0x1A	Delete Replica Operation
DSV_OPEN_STREAM	27	0x1B	Open a Stream File (e.g., Login Script)
DSV_SEARCH_FILTER search	28	0x1C	Used for building an NDS server-based
DSV_CHANGE_REPLICA_TYPE	31	0x1F	Change Replica Type Operation
DSV_UPDATE_REPLICA	37	0x25	Synchronize Replica
DSV_SYNC_PARTITION	38	0x26	Partition Synchronization
DSV_SYNC_SCHEMA	39	0x27	Schema Synchronization
DSV_READ_SYNTAXES	40	0x28	List All Defined Syntaxes
DSV_GET_REPLICA_ROOT_ID	41	0x29	Get Object ID for the Replica Root Object
DSV_BEGIN_MOVE_ENTRY	42	0x2A	Issued during an Object or Partition Move

DEFINE VALUE	DECIMAL	HEXADECIMAL	DESCRIPTION
DSV_FINISH_MOVE_ENTRY	43	0x2B	Issued during an Object or Partition Move
DSV_RELEASE_MOVED_ENTRY	44	0x2C	Issued during an Object or Partition Move
DSV_BACKUP_ENTRY	45	0x2D	Object Backup
DSV_RESTORE_ENTRY	46	0x2E	Object Restore
DSV_CLOSE_ITERATION	50	0x32	End Iteration for Large Operations
DSV_GET_SERVER_ADDRESS	53	0x35	Get Referenced Server's Network Address
DSV_SET_KEYS	54	0x36	Generate Public Key/Private Key Pair
DSV_CHANGE_PASSWORD	55	0x37	Change Object Password
DSV_VERIFY_PASSWORD	56	0x38	Verify Object Password
DSV_BEGIN_LOGIN	57	0x39	Start Login
DSV_FINISH_LOGIN	58	0x3A	End Login
DSV_BEGIN_AUTHENTICATION	59	0x3B	Start Background Authentication
DSV_FINISH_AUTHENTICATION	60	0x3C	End Background Authentication
DSV_LOGOUT	61	0x3D	Logout
DSV_REPAIR_RING	62	0x3E	Repair Replica Ring
DSV_REPAIR_TIMESTAMPS	63	0x3F	Issue Repair Timestamps
DSV_DESIGNATE_NEW_MASTER	69	0x45	Server Forced to Become New Master
DSV_CHECK_LOGIN_RESTRICTIONS	72	0x48	Validate Login Can Occur
DSV_ABORT_PARTITION_OPERATION	76	0x4C	Abort Partition Operation
DSV_READ_REFERENCES	79	0x4F	Read Object Reference Information
DSV_INSPECT_ENTRY	80	0x50	Inspect Entry in ENTRY.NDS

NDS Classes, Objects, and Attributes

The schema defines what attributes an NDS object (such as users, printers, and groups) will have. For example, a User object will have login restriction properties associated with it. The schema also defines which information (attribute) is required or optional at the time that NDS object is created. Every NDS object has a schema class that has been defined for that type of object.

The schema that originally shipped with NetWare is called the base schema. Once the base schema has been modified in any way—such as by adding a new class or a new attribute—then it is considered the extended schema. NetWare 5 is shipped with 66 base class and 409 base attribute definitions.

Class Definitions

The following are 75 class definitions for a NetWare 5 tree; there are nine DHCP/DNS-related classes (DNIP:*) included here for your reference. Out of the 66 base classes, there are only 29 effective classes that you can use in NWAdmin to create NDS objects. These 29 NDS objects are shown below:

AFP Server	Alias
Certificate Authority	Computer
Country	Directory Map
Group	Key Material
LAN Area	LDAP Group
Locality	NDPS Broker
NDPS Manager	NDPS Printer
NDSCat:Master Catalog	NDSCat:Slave Catalog
NetWare Server	Organization
Organizational Role	Organizational Unit
Print Queue	Print Server (Non NDPS)
Printer (Non NDPS)	Profile
SLP Directory Agent	SLP Scope Unit
Template	User
Volume	

AFP Server

▶ **Super Class:** Server

▶ **Containment:** Organization,Organizational Unit

▶ **Naming Attribute:** CN

▶ **Mandatory Attributes:** CN Object Class

▶ **Optional Attributes:** CN, Object Class, Account Balance, ACL, Allow Unlimited Credit, Audit:File Link, Authority Revocation, Back Link, Bindery Property, CA Private Key, CA Public Key, Certificate Revocation, Certificate Validity Interval, Cross Certificate Pair, Description, Equivalent To Me, Full Name, GUID, Host Device, L, Last Referenced Time, MASV:Authorized Range, MASV:Default Range, MASV:Proposed Label, Minimum Account Balance, Network Address, O, Obituary, Other GUID, OU, Private Key, Public Key, Reference, Resource, Revision, Security Equals, Security Flags, See Also, Serial Number, Status, Supported Connections, SvcInfo, SvcType, SvcTypeID, Timezone, Used By, User, Version

Alias

▶ **Super Class:** Top

▶ **Containment:** n/a

▶ **Naming Attribute:** n/a

▶ **Mandatory Attributes:** Aliased Object Name, Object Class

▶ **Optional Attribute:** ACL, Audit:File Link, Authority Revocation, Back Link, Bindery Property, CA Private Key, CA Public Key, Certificate Revocation, Certificate Validity Interval, Cross Certificate Pair, Equivalent To Me, GUID, Last Referenced Time, MASV:Authorized Range, MASV:Default Range, MASV:Proposed Label, Obituary, Other GUID, Reference, Revision, Used By

Audit:File Object

▸ **Super Class:** Top

▸ **Containment:** Country, Locality, Organization, Organizational Unit, Top, Tree Root

▸ **Naming Attribute:** CN

▸ **Mandatory Attributes:** Audit:Contents, Audit:Policy, CN, Object Class

▸ **Optional Attributes:** ACL, Audit:A Encryption Key, Audit:B Encryption Key, Audit:Current Encryption Key, Audit:File Link, Audit:Link List, Audit:Path, Audit:Type, Authority Revocation, Back Link, Bindery Property, CA Private Key, CA Public Key, Certificate Revocation, Certificate Validity Interval, Cross Certificate Pair, Description, Equivalent To Me, GUID, Last Referenced Time, MASV:Authorized Range, MASV:Default Range, MASV:Proposed Label, Obituary, Other GUID, Reference, Revision, Used By

Bindery Object

▸ **Super Class:** Top

▸ **Containment:** Organization, Organizational Unit

▸ **Naming Attribute:** Bindery Type, CN

▸ **Mandatory Attributes:** Bindery Object Restriction, Bindery Type, CN, Object Class

▸ **Optional Attributes:** ACL, Audit:File Link, Authority Revocation, Back Link, Bindery Property, CA Private Key, CA Public Key, Certificate Revocation, Certificate Validity Interval, Cross Certificate Pair, Equivalent To Me, GUID, Last Referenced Time, MASV:Authorized Range, MASV:Default Range, MASV:Proposed Label, Obituary, Other GUID, Reference, Revision, Used By

Bindery Queue

▸ **Super Class:** Queue

▸ **Containment:** Organization, Organizational Unit

▸ **Naming Attribute:** Bindery Type, CN

▸ **Mandatory Attributes:** Bindery Type, CN, Object Class, Queue Directory

▸ **Optional Attributes:** ACL, Audit:File Link, Authority Revocation, Back Link, Bindery Property, CA Private Key, CA Public Key, Certificate Revocation, Certificate Validity Interval, Cross Certificate Pair, Description, Device, Equivalent To Me, GUID, Host Resource Name, Host Server, L, Last Referenced Time, MASV:Authorized Range, MASV:Default Range, MASV:Proposed Label, Network Address, O, Obituary, Operator, Other GUID, OU, Reference, Revision, See Also, Server, Used By, User, Uses, Volume

CommExec

▸ **Super Class:** Server

▸ **Containment:** Organization, Organizational Unit

▸ **Naming Attribute:** CN

▸ **Mandatory Attributes:** CN, Object Class

▸ **Optional Attributes:** Account Balance, ACL, Allow Unlimited Credit, Audit:File Link, Authority Revocation, Back Link, Bindery Property, CA Private Key, CA Public Key, Certificate Revocation, Certificate Validity Interval, Cross Certificate Pair, Description, Equivalent To Me, Full Name, GUID, Host Device, L, Last Referenced Time, MASV:Authorized Range, MASV:Default Range, MASV:Proposed Label, Minimum Account Balance, Network Address, Network Address Restriction, O, Obituary, Other GUID, OU, Private Key, Public Key, Reference, Resource, Revision, Security Equals,

Security Flags, See Also, Status, SvcInfo, SvcType, SvcTypeID, Timezone, Used By, User, Version

Computer

▸ **Super Class:** Device

▸ **Containment:** Organization, Organizational Unit

▸ **Naming Attribute:** CN

▸ **Mandatory Attributes:** CN, Object Class

▸ **Optional Attributes:** ACL, Audit:File Link, Authority Revocation, Back Link, Bindery Property, CA Private Key, CA Public Key, Certificate Revocation, Certificate Validity Interval, Cross Certificate Pair, Description, Equivalent To Me, GUID, L, Last Referenced Time, MASV:Authorized Range, MASV:Default Range, MASV:Proposed Label, Network Address, O, Obituary, Operator, Other GUID, OU, Owner, Reference, Revision, See Also, Serial Number, Server, Status, SvcInfo, SvcType, SvcTypeID, Used By

Country

▸ **Super Class:** Top

▸ **Containment:** Top Tree Root [Nothing]

▸ **Naming Attribute:** C

▸ **Mandatory Attributes:** C, Object Class

▸ **Optional Attributes:** ACL, Audit:File Link, Authority Revocation, Back Link, Bindery Property, CA Private Key, CA Public Key, Certificate Revocation, Certificate Validity Interval, Cross Certificate Pair, Description, Equivalent To Me, GUID, Last Referenced Time, MASV:Authorized Range,

MASV:Default Range, MASV:Proposed Label, Obituary, Other GUID, Reference, Revision, Used By

Device

▸ **Super Class:** Top

▸ **Containment:** Organization, Organizational Unit

▸ **Naming Attribute:** CN

▸ **Mandatory Attributes:** CN, Object Class

▸ **Optional Attributes:** ACL, Audit:File Link, Authority Revocation, Back Link, Bindery Property, CA Private Key, CA Public Key, Certificate Revocation, Certificate Validity Interval, Cross Certificate Pair, Description, Equivalent To Me, GUID, L, Last Referenced Time, MASV:Authorized Range, MASV:Default Range, MASV:Proposed Label, Network Address, O, Obituary, Other GUID, OU, Owner, Reference, Revision, See Also, Serial Number, SvcInfo, SvcType, SvcTypeID, Used By

Directory Map

▸ **Super Class:** Resource

▸ **Containment:** Organization, Organizational Unit

▸ **Naming Attribute:** CN

▸ **Mandatory Attributes:** CN, Host Server, Object Class

▸ **Optional Attributes:** ACL, Audit:File Link, Authority Revocation, Back Link, Bindery Property, CA Private Key, CA Public Key, Certificate Revocation, Certificate Validity Interval, Cross Certificate Pair, Description, Equivalent To Me, GUID, Host Resource Name, L, Last Referenced Time, MASV:Authorized Range, MASV:Default Range,

MASV:Proposed Label, O, Obituary, Other GUID, OU, Path, Reference, Revision, See Also, Used By, Uses

DNIP:DHCP Server

▸ **Super Class:** Top

▸ **Containment:** Country, Locality, Organization, Organizational Unit

▸ **Naming Attribute:** CN

▸ **Mandatory Attributes:** CN, DNIP:DHCP Version, Object Class

▸ **Optional Attributes:** ACL, Audit:File Link, Authority Revocation, Back Link, Bindery Property, CA Private Key, CA Public Key, Certificate Revocation, Certificate Validity Interval, Cross Certificate Pair, DNIP:AuditLevel, DNIP:Comment, DNIP:FT Automatic, DNIP:FT Sync Delay, DNIP:FT Update Interval, DNIP:IP Assignment Policy, DNIP:Message ID, DNIP:New Attrib, DNIP:Ping Enable, DNIP:Primary Server Reference, DNIP:Public Key, DNIP:Secondary Server Reference, DNIP:Secondary ServerIPAddress, DNIP:ServerIPAddress, DNIP:SNMP Trap Flag, DNIP:Subnet Address Range Attr, Equivalent To Me, GUID, Last Referenced Time, MASV:Authorized Range, MASV:Default Range, MASV:Proposed Label, Obituary, Other GUID, Reference, Revision, Used By

DNIP:DNS RRset

▸ **Super Class:** Top

▸ **Containment:** DNIP:DNS Zone

▸ **Naming Attribute:** CN

▸ **Mandatory Attributes:** CN, DNIP:DNS Domain Name, Object Class

▸ **Optional Attributes:** ACL, Audit:File Link, Authority Revocation, Back Link, Bindery Property, CA Private Key, CA Public Key, Certificate Revocation, Certificate Validity Interval, Cross Certificate Pair, Description, DNIP:Aliased Object Name, DNIP:MAC Address, DNIP:RR, DNIP:RR Status, DNIP:RRSet Options, Equivalent To Me, GUID, Last Referenced Time, MASV:Authorized Range, MASV:Default Range, MASV:Proposed Label, Obituary, Other GUID, Reference, Revision, Used By

DNIP:DNS Server

▸ **Super Class:** Top

▸ **Containment:** Country, Locality, Organization, Organizational Unit, Top, Tree Root

▸ **Naming Attribute:** CN

▸ **Mandatory Attributes:** CN, Object Class

▸ **Optional Attributes:** ACL, Audit:File Link, Authority Revocation, Back Link, Bindery Property, CA Private Key, CA Public Key, Certificate Revocation, Certificate Validity Interval, Cross Certificate Pair, Description, DNIP:AuditLevel, DNIP:DNS Server Options, DNIP:Fwd List, DNIP:Message ID, DNIP:NoFwd List, DNIP:Public Key, DNIP:Server DN, DNIP:Server DNS Names, DNIP:ServerIPAddress, DNIP:SNMP Trap Flag, DNIP:Zone List, Equivalent To Me, GUID, Last Referenced Time, MASV:Authorized Range, MASV:Default Range, MASV:Proposed Label, Obituary, Other GUID, Reference, Revision, Used By

DNIP:DNS Zone

▸ **Super Class:** Top

▸ **Containment:** Country, Locality, Organization, Organizational Unit, Top, Tree Root

▶ **Naming Attribute:** CN

▶ **Mandatory Attributes:** CN, DNIP:Secondary Zone, DNIP:SOA Admin Mailbox, DNIP:SOA Expire, DNIP:SOA Minimum, DNIP:SOA Refresh, DNIP:SOA Retry, DNIP:SOA Serial, DNIP:SOA Zone Master, DNIP:Zone Domain Name, Object Class

▶ **Optional Attributes:** ACL, Audit:File Link, Authority Revocation, Back Link, Bindery Property, CA Private Key, CA Public Key, Certificate Revocation, Certificate Validity Interval, Cross Certificate Pair, Description, DNIP:Designated Server, DNIP:Master Server IP Addr, DNIP:RR Count, DNIP:Zone Options, DNIP:Zone Out Filter, DNIP:Zone Servers, DNIP:Zone Type, Equivalent To Me, GUID, Last Referenced Time, MASV:Authorized Range, MASV:Default Range, MASV:Proposed Label, Obituary, Other GUID, Reference, Revision, Used By

DNIP:IP Address Configuration

▶ **Super Class:** Top

▶ **Containment:** DNIP:Subnet

▶ **Naming Attribute:** CN

▶ **Mandatory Attributes:** CN, DNIP:Address Number, DNIP:Assignment Type, Object Class

▶ **Optional Attributes:** ACL, Audit:File Link, Authority Revocation, Back Link, Bindery Property, CA Private Key, CA Public Key, Certificate Revocation, Certificate Validity Interval, Cross Certificate Pair, DNIP:Boot Parameter, DNIP:Client Identifier, DNIP:Comment, DNIP:Config Options, DNIP:FQ Domain Name, DNIP:Host Name, DNIP:Last Used, DNIP:Lease Expiration, DNIP:Lease Time, DNIP:MAC Address, DNIP:Object Reference, Equivalent To Me, GUID, Last Referenced Time, MASV:Authorized Range, MASV:Default Range, MASV:Proposed Label, Obituary, Other GUID, Reference, Revision, Used By

DNIP:Locator

▸ **Super Class:** Top

▸ **Containment:** Country, Locality, Organization, Organizational Unit

▸ **Naming Attribute:** CN

▸ **Mandatory Attributes:** CN, Object Class

▸ **Optional Attributes:** ACL, Audit:File Link, Authority Revocation, Back Link, Bindery Property, CA Private Key, CA Public Key, Certificate Revocation, Certificate Validity Interval, Cross Certificate Pair, DNIP:CfgPreferences, DNIP:Config Options, DNIP:DHCPServers, DNIP:DNSServers, DNIP:DNSZones, DNIP:Excluded MAC, DNIP:Group Reference, DNIP:Subnet Attr, DNIP:Subnet Pool List, DNIP:UI Signature, Equivalent To Me, GUID, Last Referenced Time, MASV:Authorized Range, MASV:Default Range, MASV:Proposed Label, Obituary, Other GUID, Reference, Revision, Used By

DNIP:Subnet

▸ **Super Class:** Top

▸ **Containment:** Country, Locality, Organization, Organizational Unit

▸ **Naming Attributes:** CN

▸ **Mandatory Attributes:** CN, DNIP:Subnet Address, DNIP:Subnet Mask, Object Class

▸ **Optional Attributes:** ACL, Audit:File Link, Authority Revocation, Back Link, Bindery Property, CA Private Key, CA Public Key, Certificate Revocation, Certificate Validity Interval, Cross Certificate Pair, DNIP:Boot Parameter, DNIP:Comment, DNIP:Config Options, DNIP:Domain Name, DNIP:Lease Time, DNIP:New Attrib, DNIP:Subnet Pool Reference, DNIP:Subnet Type, DNIP:Zone Reference, Equivalent To Me, GUID,

Last Referenced Time, MASV:Authorized Range, MASV:Default Range, MASV:Proposed Label, Obituary, Other GUID, Reference, Revision, Used By

DNIP:Subnet Address Range

▸ **Super Class:** Top

▸ **Containment:** DNIP:Subnet

▸ **Naming Attribute:** CN

▸ **Mandatory Attributes:** CN, DNIP:End Address Number, DNIP:Start Address Number, Object Class

▸ **Optional Attributes:** ACL, Audit:File Link, Authority Revocation, Back Link, Bindery Property, CA Private Key, CA Public Key, Certificate Revocation, Certificate Validity Interval, Cross Certificate Pair, DNIP:Auto Host Name Start, DNIP:Comment, DNIP:DHCP Server Reference, DNIP:DNS Update Option, DNIP:Range Type, Equivalent To Me, GUID, Last Referenced Time, MASV:Authorized Range, MASV:Default Range, MASV:Proposed Label, Obituary, Other GUID, Reference, Revision, Used By

DNIP:Subnet Pool

▸ **Super Class:** Top

▸ **Containment:** Country, Locality, Organization, Organizational Unit

▸ **Naming Attribute:** CN

▸ **Mandatory Attributes:** CN, DNIP:Subnet Type, Object Class

▸ **Optional Attributes:** ACL, Audit:File Link, Authority Revocation, Back Link, Bindery Property, CA Private Key, CA Public Key, Certificate

Revocation, Certificate Validity Interval, Cross Certificate Pair, DNIP:Comment, DNIP:Subnet Attr, Equivalent To Me, GUID, Last Referenced Time, MASV:Authorized Range, MASV:Default Range, MASV:Proposed Label, Obituary, Other GUID, Reference, Revision, Used By

Entrust:CRLDistributionPoint

▸ **Super Class:** Top

▸ **Containment:** Organizational Unit

▸ **Naming Attribute:** CN

▸ **Mandatory Attributes:** CN, Object Class

▸ **Optional Attributes:** ACL, Audit:File Link, Authority Revocation, Back Link, Bindery Property, CA Private Key, CA Public Key, Certificate Revocation, Certificate Validity Interval, Cross Certificate Pair, Equivalent To Me, GUID, Last Referenced Time, LDAP:ARL, LDAP:caCertificate, LDAP:CRL, LDAP:crossCertificatePair, MASV:Authorized Range, MASV:Default Range, MASV:Proposed Label, Obituary, Other GUID, Reference, Revision, Used By

External Entity

▸ **Super Class:** Top

▸ **Containment:** Organization, Organizational Unit

▸ **Naming Attribute:** CN, OU

▸ **Mandatory Attributes:** CN, Object Class

▸ **Optional Attributes:** ACL, Audit:File Link, Authority Revocation, Back Link, Bindery Property, CA Private Key, CA Public Key, Certificate

Revocation, Certificate Validity Interval, Cross Certificate Pair, Description, EMail Address, Equivalent To Me, External Name, Facsimile Telephone Number, GUID, L, Last Referenced Time, Mailbox ID, Mailbox Location, MASV:Authorized Range, MASV:Default Range, MASV:Proposed Label, Obituary, Other GUID, OU, Physical Delivery Office Name, Postal Address, Postal Code, Postal Office Box, Reference, Revision, S, SA, See Also, Title, Used By

Group

▸ **Super Class:** Top

▸ **Containment:** Organization, Organizational Unit

▸ **Naming Attribute:** CN

▸ **Mandatotry Attributes:** CN, Object Class

▸ **Optional Attributes:** ACL, Audit:File Link, Authority Revocation, Back Link, Bindery Property, CA Private Key, CA Public Key, Certificate Revocation, Certificate Validity Interval, Cross Certificate Pair, Description, EMail Address, Equivalent To Me, Full Name, GID, GUID, L, Last Referenced Time, Login Script, Mailbox ID, Mailbox Location, MASV:Authorized Range, MASV:Default Range, MASV:Proposed Label, Member, O, Obituary, Other GUID, OU, Owner, Profile, Profile Membership, Reference, Revision, See Also, Used By

LDAP Group

▸ **Super Class:** Top

▸ **Containment:** Country, Locality, Organization, Organizational Unit

▸ **Naming Attribute:** CN

▸ **Mandatory Attributes:** CN, Object Class

▸ **Optional Attributes:** ACL, Audit:File Link, Authority Revocation, Back Link, Bindery Property, CA Private Key, CA Public Key, Certificate Revocation, Certificate Validity Interval, Cross Certificate Pair, Equivalent To Me, GUID, Last Referenced Time, LDAP ACL v11, LDAP Allow Clear Text Password, LDAP Anonymous Identity, LDAP Attribute Map v11, LDAP Class Map v11, LDAP Referral, LDAP Server List, LDAP Suffix, MASV:Authorized Range, MASV:Default Range, MASV:Proposed Label, Obituary, Other GUID, Reference, Revision, Used By, Version

LDAP Server

▸ **Super Class:** Top

▸ **Containment:** Country, Locality, Organization, Organizational Unit

▸ **Naming Attribute:** CN

▸ **Mandatory Attributes:** CN, Object Class

▸ **Optional Attributes:** ACL, Audit:File Link, Authority Revocation, Back Link, Bindery Property, CA Private Key, CA Public Key, Certificate Revocation, Certificate Validity Interval, Cross Certificate Pair, Equivalent To Me, GUID, Last Referenced Time, LDAP Backup Log Filename, LDAP Enable SSL, LDAP Enable TCP, LDAP Enable UDP, LDAP Group, LDAP Host Server, LDAP Log Filename, LDAP Log Level, LDAP Log Size Limit, LDAP Screen Level, LDAP Search Size Limit, LDAP Search Time Limit, LDAP Server Bind Limit, LDAP Server Idle Timeout, LDAP SSL Port, LDAP TCP Port, LDAP UDP Port, LDAP:bindCatalog, LDAP:bindCatalogUsage, LDAP:keyMaterialName, LDAP:searchCatalog, LDAP:searchCatalogUsage, MASV:Authorized Range, MASV:Default Range, MASV:Proposed Label, Obituary, Other GUID, Reference, Revision, Used By, Version

List

- ▸ **Super Class:** Top

- ▸ **Containment:** Organization, Organizational Unit

- ▸ **Naming Attribute:** CN

- ▸ **Mandatory Attributes:** CN, Object Class

- ▸ **Optional Attributes:** ACL, Audit:File Link, Authority Revocation, Back Link, Bindery Property, CA Private Key, CA Public Key, Certificate Revocation, Certificate Validity Interval, Cross Certificate Pair, Description, EMail Address, Equivalent To Me, Full Name, GUID, L, Last Referenced Time, Mailbox ID, Mailbox Location, MASV:Authorized Range, MASV:Default Range, MASV:Proposed Label, Member, O, Obituary, Other GUID, OU, Owner, Reference, Revision, See Also, Used By

Locality

- ▸ **Super Class:** Top

- ▸ **Containment:** Country, Locality, Organization, Organizational Unit

- ▸ **Naming Attribute:** L, S

- ▸ **Mandatory Attributes:** Object Class

- ▸ **Optional Attributes:** ACL, Audit:File Link, Authority Revocation, Back Link, Bindery Property, CA Private Key, CA Public Key, Certificate Revocation, Certificate Validity Interval, Cross Certificate Pair, Description, Equivalent To Me, GUID, L, Last Referenced Time, MASV:Authorized Range, MASV:Default Range, MASV:Proposed Label, Obituary, Other GUID, Reference, Revision, S, SA, See Also, Used By

MASV:Security Policy

▸ **Super Class:** Top

▸ **Containment:** SAS:Security

▸ **Naming Attribute:** CN

▸ **Mandatory Attributes:** CN, Object Class

▸ **Optional Attributes:** ACL, Audit:File Link, Authority Revocation, Back Link, Bindery Property, CA Private Key, CA Public Key, Certificate Revocation, Certificate Validity Interval, Cross Certificate Pair, Description, Equivalent To Me, GUID, Last Referenced Time, MASV:Authorized Range, MASV:Default Range, MASV:Domain Policy, MASV:Proposed Label, Obituary, Other GUID, Reference, Revision, Used By

Message Routing Group

▸ **Super Class:** Group

▸ **Containment:** Organization, Organizational Unit

▸ **Naming Attribute:** CN

▸ **Mandatory Attributes:** CN, Object Class

▸ **Optional Attributes:** ACL, Audit:File Link, Authority Revocation, Back Link, Bindery Property, CA Private Key, CA Public Key, Certificate Revocation, Certificate Validity Interval, Cross Certificate Pair, Description, EMail Address, Equivalent To Me, Full Name, GID, GUID, L, Last Referenced Time, Login Script, Mailbox ID, Mailbox Location, MASV:Authorized Range, MASV:Default Range, MASV:Proposed Label, Member, O, Obituary, Other GUID, OU, Owner, Profile, Profile Membership, Reference, Revision, See Also, Used By

Messaging Server

▸ **Super Class:** Server

▸ **Containment:** Organization, Organizational Unit

▸ **Naming Attribute:** CN

▸ **Mandatory Attributes:** CN, Object Class

▸ **Optional Attributes:** Account Balance, ACL, Allow Unlimited Credit, Audit:File Link, Authority Revocation, Back Link, Bindery Property, CA Private Key, CA Public Key, Certificate Revocation, Certificate Validity Interval, Cross Certificate Pair, Description, Equivalent To Me, Full Name, GUID, Host Device, L, Last Referenced Time, MASV:Authorized Range, MASV:Default Range, MASV:Proposed Label, Message Routing Group, Messaging Database Location, Messaging Server Type, Minimum Account Balance, Network Address, O, Obituary, Other GUID, OU, Postmaster, Private Key, Public Key, Reference, Resource, Revision, Security Equals, Security Flags, See Also, Status, Supported Gateway, Supported Services, SvcInfo, SvcType, SvcTypeID, Timezone, Used By, User, Version

NCP Server

▸ **Super Class:** Server

▸ **Containment:** Organization, Organizational Unit

▸ **Naming Attribute:** CN

▸ **Mandatory Attributes:** CN, Object Class

▸ **Optional Attributes:** Account Balance, ACL, Allow Unlimited Credit, Audit:File Link, Authority Revocation, Back Link, Bindery Property, CA Private Key, CA Public Key, Certificate Revocation, Certificate Validity Interval, Cross Certificate Pair, Description, DNIP:DHCP Server Reference, DNIP:DNS Server Reference, DNIP:LocatorPtr, DS Revision, Equivalent To

Me, Full Name, GUID, Host Device, L, Last Referenced Time, LDAP Server, MASV:Authorized Range, MASV:Default Range, MASV:Proposed Label, Messaging Server, Minimum Account Balance, NDSCat:Catalog List, NDSCat:Max Threads, NDSCat:Synch Interval, Network Address, NLS:License Service Provider, O, Obituary, Operator, Other GUID, OU, Permanent Config Parms, Private Key, Public Key, Reference, Resource, Revision, SAS:Service DN, Security Equals, Security Flags, See Also, SLP Directory Agent DN, Status, Supported Services, SvcInfo, SvcType, SvcTypeID, Timezone, Used By, User, Version, WANMAN:Cost, WANMAN:Default Cost, WANMAN:LAN Area Membership, WANMAN:WAN Policy

NDPS Broker

▸ **Super Class:** Server

▸ **Containment:** Organization, Organizational Unit

▸ **Naming Attribute:** CN

▸ **Mandatory Attributes:** CN, Object Class

▸ **Optional Attributes:** Account Balance, ACL, Allow Unlimited Credit, Audit:File Link, Authority Revocation, Back Link, Bindery Property, CA Private Key, CA Public Key, Certificate Revocation, Certificate Validity Interval, Cross Certificate Pair, Delivery Methods Installed, Description, Equivalent To Me, Full Name, GUID, GW API Gateway Directory Path, GW API Gateway Directory Volume, Host Device, L, Last Referenced Time, MASV:Authorized Range, MASV:Default Range, MASV:Proposed Label, MHS Send Directory Path, MHS Send Directory Volume, Minimum Account Balance, NDPS SMTP Server, Network Address, Notification Service Enabled, Notification Srvc Net Addr, Notification Srvc Net Address, O, Obituary, Other GUID, OU, Private Key, Public Key, Reference, Registry Advertising Name, Registry Service Enabled, Registry Srvc Net Addr, Registry Srvc Net Address, Resource, Resource Mgmt Service Enabled, Resource Mgmt Srvc Net Addr, Resource Mgmt Srvc Net Address,

Resource Mgr Database Path, Resource Mgr Database Volume, Revision, Security Equals, Security Flags, See Also, Status, SvcInfo, SvcType, SvcTypeID, Timezone, Used By, User, Version

NDPS Manager

▶ **Super Class:** Server

▶ **Containment:** Organization, Organizational Unit

▶ **Naming Attribute:** CN

▶ **Mandatory Attributes:** CN, Database Dir Path, Database Volume Name, NDPS Manager Status, Object Class,

▶ **Optional Attributes:** Account Balance, ACL, Allow Unlimited Credit, Audit:File Link, Authority Revocation, Back Link, Bindery Property, CA Private Key, CA Public Key, Certificate Revocation, Certificate Validity Interval, Cross Certificate Pair, Datapool Locations, Description, Equivalent To Me, Full Name, GUID, Host Device, L, Last Referenced Time, MASV:Authorized Range, MASV:Default Range, MASV:Proposed Label, Minimum Account Balance, NDPS Database Saved Data Image, NDPS Database Saved Index Image, NDPS Database Saved Timestamp, Network Address, O, Obituary, Other GUID, OU, Printer to PA ID Mappings, Private Key, Public Key, Reference, Resource, Revision, Security Equals, Security Flags, See Also, Status, SvcInfo, SvcType, SvcTypeID, Timezone, Used By, User, Version

NDPS Printer

▶ **Super Class:** Device

▶ **Containment:** Organization, Organizational Unit

▶ **Naming Attribute:** CN

- ▶ **Mandatory Attributes:** CN, NDPS Operator Role, NDPS User Role, Object Class, Printer Status

- ▶ **Optional Attributes:** ACL, Audit:File Link, Authority Revocation, Back Link, Bindery Property, CA Private Key, CA Public Key, Certificate Revocation, Certificate Validity Interval, Client Install Candidate, Color Supported, Cross Certificate Pair, Datapool Location, Description, Equivalent To Me, GUID, Host Device, IPP URI, IPP URI Security Scheme, L, Last Referenced Time, MASV:Authorized Range, MASV:Default Range, MASV:Proposed Label, Maximum Speed, Maximum Speed Units, NDPS Accountant Role, NDPS Job Configurations, NDPS Printer Queue List, NDPS Printer Siblings, Network Address, Notification Consumers, Notification Profile, O, Obituary, Other GUID, OU, Owner, Page Description Languages, Primary Notification Service, Primary Resource Service, Printer Agent Name, Printer Manufacturer, Printer Mechanism Types, Printer Model, Printer to PA ID Mappings, Private Key, PSM Name, Public Key, Reference, Resolution, Revision, See Also, Serial Number, Sides Supported, SvcInfo, SvcType, SvcTypeID, Used By

NDSCat:Catalog

- ▶ **Super Class:** Resource, Top

- ▶ **Containment:** Organization, Organizational Unit

- ▶ **Naming Attribute:** CN

- ▶ **Mandatory Attributes:** CN, Object Class

- ▶ **Optional Attributes:** ACL, Audit:File Link, Authority Revocation, Back Link, Bindery Property, CA Private Key, CA Public Key, Certificate Revocation, Certificate Validity Interval, Cross Certificate Pair, Description, Equivalent To Me, GUID, Host Resource Name, L, Last Referenced Time, MASV:Authorized Range, MASV:Default Range, MASV:Proposed Label, NDSCat:Actual All Attributes, NDSCat:Actual Attribute Count, NDSCat:Actual Attributes, NDSCat:Actual Base Object,

NDSCat:Actual Catalog Size, NDSCat:Actual End Time, NDSCat:Actual Filter, NDSCat:Actual Object Count, NDSCat:Actual Return Code, NDSCat:Actual Scope, NDSCat:Actual Search Aliases, NDSCat:Actual Start Time, NDSCat:Actual Value Count, NDSCat:AttrDefTbl, NDSCat:CatalogDB, NDSCat:IndexDefTbl, NDSCat:Label, NDSCat:Log, O, Obituary, Other GUID, OU, Reference, Revision, See Also, Used By, Uses

NDSCat:Master Catalog

▶ **Super Class:** NDSCat:Catalog

▶ **Containment:** Organization, Organizational Unit

▶ **Naming Attribute:** CN

▶ **Mandatory Attributes:** CN, Object Class

▶ **Optional Attributes:** ACL, Audit:File Link, Authority Revocation, Back Link, Bindery Property, CA Private Key, CA Public Key, Certificate Revocation, Certificate Validity Interval, Cross Certificate Pair, Description, Equivalent To Me, GUID, Host Resource Name, Host Server, L, Last Referenced Time, MASV:Authorized Range, MASV:Default Range, MASV:Proposed Label, NDSCat:Actual All Attributes, NDSCat:Actual Attribute Count, NDSCat:Actual Attributes, NDSCat:Actual Base Object, NDSCat:Actual Catalog Size, NDSCat:Actual End Time, NDSCat:Actual Filter, NDSCat:Actual Object Count, NDSCat:Actual Return Code, NDSCat:Actual Scope, NDSCat:Actual Search Aliases, NDSCat:Actual Start Time, NDSCat:Actual Value Count, NDSCat:All Attributes, NDSCat:AttrDefTbl, NDSCat:Attributes, NDSCat:Auto Dredge, NDSCat:Base Object, NDSCat:CatalogDB, NDSCat:Dredge Interval, NDSCat:Filter, NDSCat:IndexDefTbl, NDSCat:Indexes, NDSCat:Label, NDSCat:Log, NDSCat:Max Log Size, NDSCat:Max Retries, NDSCat:Retry Interval, NDSCat:Scope, NDSCat:Search Aliases, NDSCat:Slave Catalog List, NDSCat:Start Time, O, Obituary, Other GUID, OU, Private Key, Public Key, Reference, Revision, Security Equals, See Also, Used By, Uses

NDSCat:Slave Catalog

▸ **Super Class:** NDSCat:Catalog

▸ **Containment:** Organization, Organizational Unit

▸ **Naming Attribute:** CN

▸ **Mandatory Attributes:** CN, Object Class

▸ **Optional Attributes:** ACL, Audit:File Link, Authority Revocation, Back Link, Bindery Property, CA Private Key, CA Public Key, Certificate Revocation, Certificate Validity Interval, Cross Certificate Pair, Description, Equivalent To Me, GUID, Host Resource Name, L, Last Referenced Time, MASV:Authorized Range, MASV:Default Range, MASV:Proposed Label, NDSCat:Actual All Attributes, NDSCat:Actual Attribute Count, NDSCat:Actual Attributes, NDSCat:Actual Base Object, NDSCat:Actual Catalog Size, NDSCat:Actual End Time, NDSCat:Actual Filter, NDSCat:Actual Object Count, NDSCat:Actual Return Code, NDSCat:Actual Scope, NDSCat:Actual Search Aliases, NDSCat:Actual Start Time, NDSCat:Actual Value Count, NDSCat:AttrDefTbl, NDSCat:CatalogDB, NDSCat:IndexDefTbl, NDSCat:Label, NDSCat:Log, NDSCat:Master Catalog, O, Obituary, Other GUID, OU, Reference, Revision, See Also, Used By, Uses

NDSPKI:Certificate Authority

▸ **Super Class:** Top

▸ **Containment:** SAS:Security

▸ **Naming Attribute:** CN

▸ **Manditory Attributes:** CN, Object Class

▸ **Optional Attributes:** ACL, Audit:File Link, Authority Revocation, Back Link, Bindery Property, CA Private Key, CA Public Key, Certificate

Revocation, Certificate Validity Interval, Cross Certificate Pair, Equivalent To Me, GUID, Host Server, Last Referenced Time, MASV:Authorized Range, MASV:Default Range, MASV:Proposed Label, NDSPKI:Certificate Chain, NDSPKI:Parent CA, NDSPKI:Parent CA DN, NDSPKI:Private Key, NDSPKI:Public Key, NDSPKI:Public Key Certificate, NDSPKI:Subject Name, Obituary, Other GUID, Reference, Revision, Used By

NDSPKI:Key Material

- ▶ **Super Class:** Top

- ▶ **Containment:** Organization, Organizational Unit, SAS:Security

- ▶ **Naming Attribute:** CN

- ▶ **Mandatory Attributes:** CN, Object Class

- ▶ **Optional Attributes:** ACL, Audit:File Link, Authority Revocation, Back Link, Bindery Property, CA Private Key, CA Public Key, Certificate Revocation, Certificate Validity Interval, Cross Certificate Pair, Equivalent To Me, GUID, Host Server, Last Referenced Time, MASV:Authorized Range, MASV:Default Range, MASV:Proposed Label, NDSPKI:Certificate Chain, NDSPKI:Given Name, NDSPKI:Key File, NDSPKI:Private Key, NDSPKI:Public Key, NDSPKI:Public Key Certificate, NDSPKI:Subject Name, Obituary, Other GUID, Reference, Revision, Used By

NetSvc

- ▶ **Super Class:** Server

- ▶ **Containment:** Organization, Organizational Unit

- ▶ **Naming Attribute:** CN

- ▶ **Mandatory Attributes:** CN, Object Class, SvcTypeID

▶ **Optional Attributes:** Account Balance, ACL, Allow Unlimited Credit, Audit:File Link, Authority Revocation, Back Link, Bindery Property, CA Private Key, CA Public Key, Certificate Revocation, Certificate Validity Interval, Cross Certificate Pair, Description, Equivalent To Me, Full Name, GUID, Host Device, L, Last Referenced Time, MASV:Authorized Range, MASV:Default Range, MASV:Proposed Label, Minimum Account Balance, Network Address, O, Obituary, Other GUID, OU, Private Key, Public Key, Reference, Resource, Revision, Security Equals, Security Flags, See Also, Status, SvcInfo, SvcType, SvcTypeID, Timezone, Used By, User, Version

NLS:License Certificate

▶ **Super Class:** Top

▶ **Containment:** NLS:Product Container

▶ **Naming Attribute:** NLS:License ID

▶ **Mandatory Attributes:** NLS:Common Certificate, NLS:License ID, NLS:Revision, Object Class

▶ **Optional Attributes:** ACL, Audit:File Link, Authority Revocation, Back Link, Bindery Property, CA Private Key, CA Public Key, Certificate Revocation, Certificate Validity Interval, Cross Certificate Pair, Equivalent To Me, GUID, Last Referenced Time, MASV:Authorized Range, MASV:Default Range, MASV:Proposed Label, NLS:Owner, Obituary, Other GUID, Reference, Revision, Used By

NLS:License Server

▶ **Super Class:** Server

▶ **Containment:** Organization, Organizational Unit

▶ **Naming Attribute:** CN

▸ **Mandatory Attributes:** CN, Host Server, NLS:License Database, NLS:LSP Revision, NLS:Transaction Database, Object Class

▸ **Optional Attributes:** Account Balance, ACL, Allow Unlimited Credit, Audit:File Link, Authority Revocation, Back Link, Bindery Property, CA Private Key, CA Public Key, Certificate Revocation, Certificate Validity Interval, Cross Certificate Pair, Description, Equivalent To Me, Full Name, GUID, Host Device, L, Last Referenced Time, MASV:Authorized Range, MASV:Default Range, MASV:Proposed Label, Minimum Account Balance, Network Address, NLS:Search Type, NLS:Transaction Log Name, NLS:Transaction Log Size, O, Obituary, Other GUID, OU, Private Key, Public Key, Reference, Resource, Revision, Security Equals, Security Flags, See Also, Status, SvcInfo, SvcType, SvcTypeID, Timezone, Used By, User, Version

NLS:Product Container

▸ **Super Class:** Top

▸ **Containment:** Organization, Organizational Unit

▸ **Naming Attribute:** NLS:Product, NLS:Publisher, NLS:Version

▸ **Mandatory Attributes:** NLS:Product, NLS:Publisher, NLS:Revision, NLS:Version, Object Class

▸ **Optional Attributes:** ACL, Audit:File Link, Authority Revocation, Back Link, Bindery Property, CA Private Key, CA Public Key, Certificate Revocation, Certificate Validity Interval, Cross Certificate Pair, Equivalent To Me, GUID, Last Referenced Time, MASV:Authorized Range, MASV:Default Range, MASV:Proposed Label, NLS:Current Installed, NLS:Current Peak Installed, NLS:Current Peak Used, NLS:Current Used, NLS:Hourly Data Size, NLS:Peak Installed Data, NLS:Peak Used Data, NLS:Summary Update Time, NLS:Summary Version, Obituary, Other GUID, Reference, Revision, Used By

NSCP:groupOfUniqueNames5

▸ **Super Class:** NSCP:mailGroup5

▸ **Containment:** Country, Locality, Organization, Organizational Unit,

▸ **Naming Attribute:** CN,

▸ **Mandatory Attributes:** CN, Object Class

▸ **Optional Attributes:** ACL, Audit:File Link, Authority Revocation, Back Link, Bindery Property, CA Private Key, CA Public Key, Certificate Revocation, Certificate Validity Interval, Cross Certificate Pair, Description, EMail Address, Equivalent To Me, Full Name, GUID, Internet EMail Address, L, Last Referenced Time, Mailbox ID, Mailbox Location, MASV:Authorized Range, MASV:Default Range, MASV:Proposed Label, Member, NSCP:mailAlternateAddress, NSCP:mailForwardingAddress, NSCP:mailHost, NSCP:mgrpRFC822mailmember, O, Obituary, Other GUID, OU, Owner, Reference, Revision, See Also, Used By

NSCP:mailGroup5

▸ **Super Class:** List

▸ **Containment:** Country, Locality, Organization, Organizational Unit

▸ **Naming Attribute:** CN

▸ **Mandatory Attributes:** CN, Object Class

▸ **Optional Attributes:** ACL, Audit:File Link, Authority Revocation, Back Link, Bindery Property, CA Private Key, CA Public Key, Certificate Revocation, Certificate Validity Interval, Cross Certificate Pair, Description, EMail Address, Equivalent To Me, Full Name, GUID, Internet EMail Address, L, Last Referenced Time, Mailbox ID, Mailbox Location, MASV:Authorized Range, MASV:Default Range, MASV:Proposed Label, Member, NSCP:mailAlternateAddress, NSCP:mailForwardingAddress,

NSCP:mailHost, NSCP:mgrpRFC822mailmember, O, Obituary, Other GUID, OU, Owner, Reference, Revision, See Also, Used By

NSCP:NetscapeMailServer5

▸ **Super Class:** NSCP:NetscapeServer5

▸ **Containment:** Country, Locality, NSCP:NetscapeServer5, Organization, Organizational Unit

▸ **Naming Attribute:** CN

▸ **Mandatory Attributes:** CN, Object Class

▸ **Optional Attributes:** Account Balance, ACL, Allow Unlimited Credit, Audit:File Link, Authority Revocation, Back Link, Bindery Property, CA Private Key, CA Public Key, Certificate Revocation, Certificate Validity Interval, Cross Certificate Pair, Description, Equivalent To Me, Full Name, GUID, Host Device, L, Last Referenced Time, MASV:Authorized Range, MASV:Default Range, MASV:Proposed Label, Minimum Account Balance, Network Address, NSCP:administratorContactInfo, NSCP:adminURL, NSCP:installationTimeStamp, NSCP:serverHostName, NSCP:serverProductName, NSCP:serverRoot, NSCP:serverVersionNumber, O, Obituary, Other GUID, OU, Private Key, Public Key, Reference, Resource, Revision, Security Equals, Security Flags, See Also, Status, SvcInfo, SvcType, SvcTypeID, Timezone, Used By, User, Version

NSCP:NetscapeServer5

▸ **Super Class:** Server

▸ **Containment:** Country, Locality, Organization, Organizational Unit

▸ **Naming Attribute:** CN

▶ **Mandatory Attributes:** CN, Object Class

▶ **Optional Attributes:** Account Balance, ACL, Allow Unlimited Credit, Audit:File Link, Authority Revocation, Back Link, Bindery Property, CA Private Key, CA Public Key, Certificate Revocation, Certificate Validity Interval, Cross Certificate Pair, Description, Equivalent To Me, Full Name, GUID, Host Device, L, Last Referenced Time, MASV:Authorized Range, MASV:Default Range, MASV:Proposed Label, Minimum Account Balance, Network Address, NSCP:administratorContactInfo, NSCP:adminURL, NSCP:installationTimeStamp, NSCP:serverHostName, NSCP:serverProductName, NSCP:serverRoot, NSCP:serverVersionNumber, O, Obituary, Other GUID, OU, Private Key, Public Key, Reference, Resource, Revision, Security Equals, Security Flags, See Also, Status, SvcInfo, SvcType, SvcTypeID, Timezone, Used By, User, Version

NSCP:Nginfo

▶ **Super Class:** Organizational Unit

▶ **Containment:** Country, Locality, Organization, Organizational Unit

▶ **Naming Attribute:** CN, OU

▶ **Mandatory Attributes:** CN, Object Class, OU

▶ **Optional Attributes:** ACL, Audit:File Link, Authority Revocation, Back Link, Bindery Property, CA Private Key, CA Public Key, Certificate Revocation, Certificate Validity Interval, Cross Certificate Pair, Description, Detect Intruder, EMail Address, Entrust:AttributeCertificate, Equivalent To Me, Facsimile Telephone Number, GUID, Intruder Attempt Reset Interval, Intruder Lockout Reset Interval, L, Last Login Time, Last Referenced Time, Lockout After Detection, Login Intruder Limit, Login Script, Login Time, Mailbox ID, Mailbox Location, MASV:Authorized Range, MASV:Default Range, MASV:Proposed Label, NDPS Control Flags, NDPS Default Printer, NDPS Default Public Printer, NDPS Printer Install List, NDPS Printer Install Timestamp, NDPS Public Printer Install List, NDPS Replace All Client Printers,

Network Address, NNS Domain, NSCP:nsaclrole, NSCP:nscreator, NSCP:nsflags, NSCP:nsnewsACL, NSCP:nsprettyname, NSCP:subtreeACI, Obituary, Other GUID, Physical Delivery Office Name, Postal Address, Postal Code, Postal Office Box, Print Job Configuration, Printer Control, Private Key, Public Key, Reference, Revision, S, SA, See Also, Telephone Number, Used By

NSCP:Nginfo2

▸ **Super Class:** Top

▸ **Containment:** Country, Locality, Organization, Organizational Unit

▸ **Naming Attributes:** CN

▸ **Mandatory Attributes:** CN, Object Class

▸ **Optional Attributes:** ACL, Audit:File Link, Authority Revocation, Back Link, Bindery Property, CA Private Key, CA Public Key, Certificate Revocation, Certificate Validity Interval, Cross Certificate Pair, Equivalent To Me, GUID, Last Referenced Time, MASV:Authorized Range, MASV:Default Range, MASV:Proposed Label, NSCP:nsaclrole, NSCP:nscreator, NSCP:nsflags, NSCP:nsnewsACL, NSCP:nsprettyname, NSCP:subtreeACI, Obituary, Other GUID, Reference, Revision, Used By

Organization

▸ **Super Class:** Top

▸ **Containment:** Country, Locality, Top, Tree Root, [Nothing]

▸ **Naming Attribute:** O

▸ **Mandatory Attributes:** O, Object Class

▸ **Optional Attributes:** ACL, Audit:File Link, Authority Revocation, Back Link, Bindery Property, CA Private Key, CA Public Key, Certificate

Revocation, Certificate Validity Interval, Cross Certificate Pair, Description, Detect Intruder, EMail Address, Equivalent To Me, Facsimile Telephone Number, GUID, Intruder Attempt Reset Interval, Intruder Lockout Reset Interval, L, Last Referenced Time, LDAP:ARL, LDAP:caCertificate, LDAP:CRL, LDAP:crossCertificatePair, LDAPUserCertificate, Lockout After Detection, Login Intruder Limit, Login Script, Mailbox ID, Mailbox Location, MASV:Authorized Range, MASV:Default Range, MASV:Proposed Label, NDPS Control Flags, NDPS Default Printer, NDPS Default Public Printer, NDPS Printer Install List, NDPS Printer Install Timestamp, NDPS Public Printer Install List, NDPS Replace All Client Printers, NNS Domain, Obituary, Other GUID, Physical Delivery Office Name, Postal Address, Postal Code, Postal Office Box, Print Job Configuration, Printer Control, Reference, Revision, S, SA, See Also, Telephone Number, Used By

Organizational Person

▸ **Super Class:** Person

▸ **Containment:** Organization, Organizational Unit

▸ **Naming Attribute:** CN, OU

▸ **Mandatory Attributes:** CN, Object Class, Surname

▸ **Optional Attributes:** ACL, Audit:File Link, Authority Revocation, Back Link, Bindery Property, CA Private Key, CA Public Key, Certificate Revocation, Certificate Validity Interval, Cross Certificate Pair, Description, EMail Address, Equivalent To Me, Facsimile Telephone Number, Full Name, Generational Qualifier, Given Name, GUID, Initials, L, Last Referenced Time, Mailbox ID, Mailbox Location, MASV:Authorized Range, MASV:Default Range, MASV:Proposed Label, Obituary, Other GUID, OU, Physical Delivery Office Name, Postal Address, Postal Code, Postal Office Box, Reference, Revision, S, SA, See Also, Telephone Number, Title, Used By

Organizational Role

▶ **Super Class:** Top

▶ **Containment:** Organization, Organizational Unit

▶ **Naming Attribute:** CN

▶ **Mandatory Attributes:** CN, Object Class

▶ **Optional Attributes:** ACL, Audit:File Link, Authority Revocation, Back Link, Bindery Property, CA Private Key, CA Public Key, Certificate Revocation, Certificate Validity Interval, Cross Certificate Pair, Description, EMail Address, Equivalent To Me, Facsimile Telephone Number, GUID, L, Last Referenced Time, Mailbox ID, Mailbox Location, MASV:Authorized Range, MASV:Default Range, MASV:Proposed Label, Obituary, Other GUID, OU, Physical Delivery Office Name, Postal Address, Postal Code, Postal Office Box, Reference, Revision, Role Occupant, S, SA, See Also, Telephone Number, Used By

Organizational Unit

▶ **Super Class:** Top

▶ **Containment:** Locality, Organization, Organizational Unit

▶ **Naming Attribute:** OU

▶ **Mandatory Attributes:** Object Class, OU

▶ **Optional Attributes:** ACL, Audit:File Link, Authority Revocation, Back Link, Bindery Property, CA Private Key, CA Public Key, Certificate Revocation, Certificate Validity Interval, Cross Certificate Pair, Description, Detect Intruder, EMail Address, Entrust:AttributeCertificate, Equivalent To Me, Facsimile Telephone Number, GUID, Intruder Attempt Reset Interval, Intruder Lockout Reset Interval, L, Last Login Time, Last Referenced Time, Lockout After Detection, Login Intruder Limit, Login Script, Login Time,

Mailbox ID, Mailbox Location, MASV:Authorized Range, MASV:Default Range, MASV:Proposed Label, NDPS Control Flags, NDPS Default Printer, NDPS Default Public Printer, NDPS Printer Install List, NDPS Printer Install Timestamp, NDPS Public Printer Install List, NDPS Replace All Client Printers, Network Address, NNS Domain, Obituary, Other GUID, Physical Delivery Office Name, Postal Address, Postal Code, Postal Office Box, Print Job Configuration, Printer Control, Private Key, Public Key, Reference, Revision, S, SA, See Also, Telephone Number, Used By

Partition

▶ **Super Class:** Top

▶ **Containment:** n/a

▶ **Naming Attribute:** n/a

▶ **Mandatory Attributes:** Object Class

▶ **Optional Attributes:** ACL, Audit:File Link, Authority Revocation, Back Link, Bindery Property, CA Private Key, CA Public Key, Certificate Revocation, Certificate Validity Interval, Convergence, Cross Certificate Pair, Equivalent To Me, GUID, High Convergence Sync Interval, Inherited ACL, Last Referenced Time, Low Convergence Reset Time, Low Convergence Sync Interval, MASV:Authorized Range, MASV:Default Range, MASV:Label, MASV:Proposed Label, Obituary, Obituary Notify, Other GUID, Partition Control, Partition Creation Time, Partition Status, Purge Vector, Received Up To, Reference, Replica, Replica Up To, Revision, Synchronization Tolerance, Synchronized Up To, Transitive Vector, Used By

Person

▶ **Super Class:** Top

▶ **Containment:** n/a

▶ **Naming Attribute:** n/a

▶ **Mandatory Attributes:** CN, Object Class, Surname

▶ **Optional Attributes:** ACL, Audit:File Link, Authority Revocation, Back Link, Bindery Property, CA Private Key, CA Public Key, Certificate Revocation, Certificate Validity Interval, Cross Certificate Pair, Description, Equivalent To Me, Full Name, Generational Qualifier, Given Name, GUID, Initials, Last Referenced Time, MASV:Authorized Range, MASV:Default Range, MASV:Proposed Label, Obituary, Other GUID, Reference, Revision, See Also, Telephone Number, Used By

Print Server

▶ Super Class: Server

▶ Containment: Organization, Organizational Unit

▶ Naming Attribute: CN

▶ Mandatory Attributes: CN, Object Class

▶ Optional Attributes: Account Balance, ACL, Allow Unlimited Credit, Audit:File Link, Authority Revocation, Back Link, Bindery Property, CA Private Key, Certificate Revocation, Certificate Validity Interval, Cross Certificate Pair, Description, Equivalent To Me, Full Name, GUID, Host Device, L, Last Referenced Time, MASV:Authorized Range, MASV:Default Range, MASV:Proposed Label, Minimum Account Balance, Network Address, O, Obituary, Operator, Other GUID, OU, Printer, Private Key, Public Key, Reference, Resource, Revision, SAP Name, Security Equals, Security Flags, See Also, Status, SvcInfo, SvcType, ScvTypeID, Timezone, Used By, User, Version

Printer

- ▸ **Super Class:** Device

- ▸ **Containment:** Organization, Organizational Unit

- ▸ **Naming Attribute:** CN

- ▸ **Mandatory Attributes:** CN, Object Class

- ▸ **Optional Attributes:** ACL, Audit:File Link, Authority Revocation, Back Link, Bindery Property, CA Private Key, CA Public Key, Cartridge, Certificate Revocation, Certificate Validity Interval, Cross Certificate Pair, Default Queue, Description, Equivalent To Me, GUID, Host Device, L, Last Referenced Time, MASV:Authorized Range, MASV:Default Range, MASV:Proposed Label, Memory, Network Address, Network Address Restriction, Notify, O, Obituary, Operator, Other GUID, OU, Owner, Page Description Language, Print Server, Printer Configuration, Queue, Reference, Revision, See Also, Serial Number, Status, Supported Typefaces, SvcInfo, SvcType, SvcTypeID, Used By

Profile

- ▸ **Super Class:** Top

- ▸ **Containment:** Organization, Organizational Unit

- ▸ **Naming Attribute:** CN

- ▸ **Mandatory Attributes:** CN, Login Script, Object Class

- ▸ **Optional Attributes:** ACL, Audit:File Link, Authority Revocation, Back Link, Bindery Property, CA Private Key, CA Public Key, Certificate Revocation, Certificate Validity Interval, Cross Certificate Pair, Description, Equivalent To Me, Full Name, GUID, L, Last Referenced Time, MASV:Authorized Range, MASV:Default Range, MASV:Proposed Label, O, Obituary, Other GUID, OU, Reference, Revision, See Also, Used By

Queue

▶ **Super Class:** Resource

▶ **Containment:** Organization, Organizational Unit

▶ **Naming Attribute:** CN

▶ **Mandatory Attributes:** CN, Object Class, Queue Directory

▶ **Optional Attributes:** ACL, Audit:File Link, Authority Revocation, Back Link, Bindery Property, CA Private Key, CA Public Key, Certificate Revocation, Certificate Validity Interval, Cross Certificate Pair, Description, Device, Equivalent To Me, GUID, Host Resource Name, Host Server, L, Last Referenced Time, MASV:Authorized Range, MASV:Default Range, MASV:Proposed Label, Network Address, O, Obituary, Operator, Other GUID, OU, Reference, Revision, See Also, Server, Used By, User, Uses, Volume

Resource

▶ **Super Class:** Top

▶ **Containment:** Organization, Organizational Unit

▶ **Naming Attribute:** CN

▶ **Mandatory Attributes:** CN, Object Class

▶ **Optional Attributes:** ACL, Audit:File Link, Authority Revocation, Back Link, Bindery Property, CA Private Key, CA Public Key, Certificate Revocation, Certificate Validity Interval, Cross Certificate Pair, Description, Equivalent To Me, GUID, Host Resource Name, L, Last Referenced Time, MASV:Authorized Range, MASV:Default Range, MASV:Proposed Label, O, Obituary, Other GUID, OU, Reference, Revision, See Also, Used By, Uses

SAS:Security

▶ **Super Class:** Top

▶ **Containment:** Country, Organization, Top, Tree Root

▶ **Naming Attribute:** CN

▶ **Mandatory Attributes:** CN, Object Class

▶ **Optional Attributes:** ACL, Audit:File Link, Authority Revocation, Back Link, Bindery Property, CA Private Key, CA Public Key, Certificate Revocation, Certificate Validity Interval, Cross Certificate Pair, Equivalent To Me, GUID, Last Referenced Time, MASV:Authorized Range, MASV:Default Range, MASV:Proposed Label, NDSPKI:Tree CA DN, Obituary, Other GUID, Reference, Revision, Used By

SAS:Service

▶ **Super Class:** Resource

▶ **Containment:** Organization, Organizational Unit

▶ **Naming Attribute:** CN

▶ **Mandatory Attributes:** CN, Object Class

▶ **Optional Attributes:** ACL, Audit:File Link, Authority Revocation, Back Link, Bindery Property, CA Private Key, CA Public Key, Certificate Revocation, Certificate Validity Interval, Cross Certificate Pair, Description, Equivalent To Me, GUID, Host Resource Name, Host Server, L, Last Referenced Time, MASV:Authorized Range, MASV:Default Range, MASV:Proposed Label, NDSPKI:Key Material DN, O, Obituary, Other GUID, OU, Private Key, Public Key, Reference, Revision, See Also, Used By, Uses

Server

▶ **Super Class:** Top

▶ **Containment:** Organization, Organizational Unit

▶ **Naming Attribute:** CN

▶ **Mandatory Attributes:** CN, Object Class

▶ **Optional Attributes:** Account Balance, ACL, Allow Unlimited Credit, Audit:File Link, Authority Revocation, Back Link, Bindery Property, CA Private Key, CA Public Key, Certificate Revocation, Certificate Validity Interval, Cross Certificate Pair, Description, Equivalent To Me, Full Name, GUID, Host Device, L, Last Referenced Time, MASV:Authorized Range, MASV:Default Range, MASV:Proposed Label, Minimum Account Balance, Network Address, O, Obituary, Other GUID, OU, Private Key, Public Key, Reference, Resource, Revision, Security Equals, Security Flags, See Also, Status, SvcInfo, SvcType, SvcTypeID, Timezone, Used By, User, Version

SLP Directory Agent

▶ **Super Class:** Top

▶ **Containment:** Country, Locality, Organization, Organizational Unit

▶ **Naming Attribute:** CN

▶ **Mandatory Attributes:** Object Class

▶ **Optional Attributes:** ACL, Audit:File Link, Authority Revocation, Back Link, Bindery Property, CA Private Key, CA Public Key, Certificate Revocation, Certificate Validity Interval, CN, Cross Certificate Pair, Equivalent To Me, GUID, Last Referenced Time, MASV:Authorized Range, MASV:Default Range, MASV:Proposed Label, Obituary, Other GUID, Private Key, Public Key, Reference, Revision, SLP Cache Limit, SLP DA Back Link, SLP Scope Unit DN, SLP Start Purge Hour, SLP Status, Used By

SLP Scope Unit

▸ **Super Class:** Top

▸ **Containment:** Country, Locality, Organization, Organizational Unit

▸ **Naming Attribute:** SU

▸ **Mandatory Attributes:** Object Class

▸ **Optional Attributes:** ACL, Audit:File Link, Authority Revocation, Back Link, Bindery Property, CA Private Key, CA Public Key, Certificate Revocation, Certificate Validity Interval, Cross Certificate Pair, Equivalent To Me, GUID, Last Referenced Time, MASV:Authorized Range, MASV:Default Range, MASV:Proposed Label, Obituary, Other GUID, Reference, Revision, SLP Scope Name, SLP SU Back Link, SLP SU Type, SU, Used By

SLP Service

▸ **Super Class:** Top

▸ **Containment:** SLP Scope Unit

▸ **Naming Attribute:** CN

▸ **Mandatory Attributes:** Object Class, SLP Language, SLP Lifetime, SLP Type, SLP URL

▸ **Optional Attributes:** ACL, Audit:File Link, Authority Revocation, Back Link, Bindery Property, CA Private Key, CA Public Key, Certificate Revocation, Certificate Validity Interval, CN, Cross Certificate Pair, Equivalent To Me, GUID, Last Referenced Time, MASV:Authorized Range, MASV:Default Range, MASV:Proposed Label, Obituary, Other GUID, Reference, Revision, SLP Attribute, Used By

SMS SMDR Class

- ▶ **Super Class:** Resource

- ▶ **Containment:** Organization, Organizational Unit

- ▶ **Naming Attribute:** CN

- ▶ **Mandatory Attributes:** CN, Object Class

- ▶ **Optional Attributes:** ACL, Audit:File Link, Authority Revocation, Back Link, Bindery Property, CA Private Key, CA Public Key, Certificate Revocation, Certificate Validity Interval, Cross Certificate Pair, Description, Equivalent To Me, GUID, Host Resource Name, L, Last Referenced Time, MASV:Authorized Range, MASV:Default Range, MASV:Proposed Label, O, Obituary, Other GUID, OU, Reference, Revision, SAP Name, See Also, SMS Protocol Address, SMS Registered Service, Status, Used By, Uses, Version

Template

- ▶ **Super Class:** Top

- ▶ **Containment:** Organization, Organizational Unit

- ▶ **Naming Attribute:** CN

- ▶ **Mandatory Attributes:** CN, Object Class

- ▶ **Optional Attributes:** Account Balance, ACL, Allow Unlimited Credit, Audit:File Link, Authority Revocation, Back Link, Bindery Property, CA Private Key, CA Public Key, Certificate Revocation, Certificate Validity Interval, Cross Certificate Pair, Description, EMail Address, Equivalent To Me, Facsimile Telephone Number, Group Membership, GUID, Higher Privileges, Home Directory, Home Directory Rights, L, Language, Last Referenced Time, Login Allowed Time Map, Login Disabled, Login Expiration Time, Login Grace Limit, Login Maximum Simultaneous, Login Script, Mailbox ID, Mailbox Location, MASV:Authorized Range,

MASV:Default Range, MASV:Proposed Label, Member, Members Of Template, Message Server, Minimum Account Balance, Network Address Restriction, New Object's DS Rights, New Object's FS Rights, New Object's Self Rights, Obituary, Other GUID, OU, Password Allow Change, Password Expiration Interval, Password Expiration Time, Password Minimum Length, Password Required, Password Unique Required, Physical Delivery Office Name, Postal Address, Postal Code, Postal Office Box, Profile, Reference, Revision, Run Setup Script, S, SA, Security Equals, Security Flags, See Also, Set Password After Create, Setup Script, Telephone Number, Title, Trustees Of New Object, Used By, Volume Space Restrictions

Top

▶ **Super Class:** n/a

▶ **Containment:** n/a

▶ **Naming Attribute:** n/a

▶ **Mandatory Attributes:** Object Class

▶ **Optional Attributes:** ACL, Audit:File Link, Authority Revocation, Back Link, Bindery Property, CA Private Key, CA Public Key, Certificate Revocation, Certificate Validity Interval, Cross Certificate Pair, Equivalent To Me, GUID, Last Referenced Time, MASV:Authorized Range, MASV:Default Range, MASV:Proposed Label, Obituary, Other GUID, Reference, Revision, Used By

Tree Root

▶ **Super Class:** Top

▶ **Containment:** [Nothing]

> ▸ **Naming Attribute:** T

> ▸ **Mandatory Attributes:** Object Class, T

> ▸ **Optional Attributes:** ACL, Audit:File Link, Authority Revocation, Back Link, Bindery Property, CA Private Key, CA Public Key, Certificate Revocation, Certificate Validity Interval, Cross Certificate Pair, Equivalent To Me, GUID, Last Referenced Time, MASV:Authorized Range, MASV:Default Range, MASV:Proposed Label, Obituary, Other GUID, Reference, Revision, SAS:Security DN, Used By

Unknown

> ▸ **Super Class:** Top

> ▸ **Containment:** n/a

> ▸ **Naming Attribute:** n/a

> ▸ **Mandatory Attributes:** Object Class

> ▸ **Optional Attributes:** ACL, Audit:File Link, Authority Revocation, Back Link, Bindery Property, CA Private Key, CA Public Key, Certificate Revocation, Certificate Validity Interval, Cross Certificate Pair, Equivalent To Me, GUID, Last Referenced Time, MASV:Authorized Range, MASV:Default Range, MASV:Proposed Label, Obituary, Other GUID, Reference, Revision, Used By

User

> ▸ **Super Class:** Organizational Person

> ▸ **Containment:** Organization, Organizational Unit

> ▸ **Naming Attributes:** CN, OU

▶ **Mandatory Attributes:** CN, Object Class, Surname

▶ **Optional Attributes:** Account Balance, ACL, Allow Unlimited Credit, Audit:File Link, Authority Revocation, Back Link, Bindery Property, CA Private Key, CA Public Key, Certificate Revocation, Certificate Validity Interval, Cross Certificate Pair, Description, EMail Address, Employee ID, Entrust:User, Equivalent To Me, Facsimile Telephone Number, Full Name, Generational Qualifier, Given Name, Group Membership, GUID, Higher Privileges, Home Directory, Initials, Internet EMail Address, L, Language, Last Login Time, Last Referenced Time, LDAP:ARL, LDAP:caCertificate, LDAP:CRL, LDAP:crossCertificatePair, LDAPUserCertificate, Locked By Intruder, Login Allowed Time Map, Login Disabled, Login Expiration Time, Login Grace Limit, Login Grace Remaining, Login Intruder Address, Login Intruder Attempts, Login Intruder Reset Time, Login Maximum Simultaneous, Login Script, Login Time, Mailbox ID, Mailbox Location, MASV:Authorized Range, MASV:Default Range, MASV:Proposed Label, Message Server, Minimum Account Balance, Network Address, Network Address Restriction, NRD:Registry Data, NRD:Registry Index, NSCP:mailAccessDomain, NSCP:mailAlternateAddress, NSCP:mailAutoReplyMode, NSCP:mailAutoReplyText, NSCP:mailDeliveryOption, NSCP:mailForwardingAddress, NSCP:mailHost, NSCP:mailMessageStore, NSCP:mailProgramDeliveryInfo, NSCP:mailQuota, NSCP:nsLicensedFor, NSCP:nsLicenseEndTime, NSCP:nsLicenseStartTime, Obituary, Other GUID, OU, Password Allow Change, Password Expiration Interval, Password Expiration Time, Password Minimum Length, Password Required, Password Unique Required, Passwords Used, Physical Delivery Office Name, Postal Address, Postal Code, Postal Office Box, Print Job Configuration, Printer Control, Private Key, Profile, Profile Membership, Public Key, Reference, Revision, S, SA, Security Equals, Security Flags, See Also, Server Holds, Telephone Number, Timezone, Title, Type Creator Map, UID, Used By

Volume

▸ **Super Class:** Resource

▸ **Containment:** Organization, Organizational Unit

▸ **Naming Attribute:** CN

▸ **Mandatory Attributes:** CN, Host Server, Object Class

▸ **Optional Attributes:** ACL, Audit:File Link, Authority Revocation, Back Link, Bindery Property, CA Private Key, CA Public Key, Certificate Revocation, Certificate Validity Interval, Cross Certificate Pair, Description, Equivalent To Me, GUID, Host Resource Name, L, Last Referenced Time, MASV:Authorized Range, MASV:Default Range, MASV:Proposed Label, O, Obituary, Other GUID, OU, Reference, Revision, See Also, Status, Used By, Uses

WANMAN:LAN Area

▸ **Super Class:** Top

▸ **Containment:** Country, Locality, Organization, Organizational Unit

▸ **Naming Attribute:** CN

▸ **Mandatory Attributes:** CN, Object Class

▸ **Optional Attributes:** ACL, Audit:File Link, Authority Revocation, Back Link, Bindery Property, CA Private Key, CA Public Key, Certificate Revocation, Certificate Validity Interval, Cross Certificate Pair, Description, Equivalent To Me, GUID, L, Last Referenced Time, MASV:Authorized Range, MASV:Default Range, MASV:Proposed Label, Member, O, Obituary, Other GUID, OU, Owner, Reference, Revision, See Also, Used By, WANMAN:Cost, WANMAN:Default Cost, WANMAN:WAN Policy

[Anything]

- ▸ **Super Class:** Top

- ▸ **Containment:** n/a

- ▸ **Naming Attribute:** n/a

- ▸ **Mandatory Attributes:** Object Class

- ▸ **Optional Attributes:** ACL, Audit:File Link, Authority Revocation, Back Link, Bindery Property, CA Private Key, CA Public Key, Certificate Revocation, Certificate Validity Interval, Cross Certificate Pair, Equivalent To Me, GUID, Last Referenced Time, MASV:Authorized Range, MASV:Default Range, MASV:Proposed Label, Obituary, Other GUID, Reference, Revision, Used By

[Nothing]

- ▸ **Super Class:** Top

- ▸ **Containment:** n/a

- ▸ **Naming Attribute:** n/a

- ▸ **Mandatory Attributes:** Object Class

- ▸ **Optional Attributes:** ACL, Audit:File Link, Authority Revocation, Back Link, Bindery Property, CA Private Key, CA Public Key, Certificate Revocation, Certificate Validity Interval, Cross Certificate Pair, Equivalent To Me, GUID, Last Referenced Time, MASV:Authorized Range, MASV:Default Range, MASV:Proposed Label, Obituary, Other GUID, Reference, Revision, Used By

Base Attributes

Table C.1 lists the 409 base attributes plus 79 DHCP/DNS-related (DNIP:*) attributes for a NetWare 5 tree. For each attribute, its value's range is listed and any special definition flags used when the attribute is defined (such as if the attribute is single-valued or is non-removable) are also shown. The following definition flags are used:

- ▸ Single Valued—Attribute is single valued. By default, an attribute may contain multiple values.

- ▸ Sized Attribute—Attribute has length or range limits. For example, the Postal Code is limited to 0x28 or 40 bytes in size.

- ▸ Non-Removable—Attribute cannot be deleted. By default, an attribute definition may be removed from the schema.

- ▸ Read-Only Attribute—Clients cannot write to this attribute but can read its value.

- ▸ Hidden Attribute—Clients can neither read from nor write to the attribute.

- ▸ String Attribute—Attribute syntax is string.

- ▸ Sync Immediate—Attribute value is scheduled for immediate synchronization. This is required on some attributes, such as the Password Required attribute of a User object, to either maintain proper data integrity or security.

- ▸ Public Read—Attached workstations can read this attribute's values.

- ▸ Server Read—Server class objects can read attribute without inherited or explicit read right.

TABLE C.1

Base Attributes

ATTRIBUTE NAME	DEFINITION FLAGS	SYNTAX	LOWER LIMIT	UPPER LIMIT
Account Balance	Single Valued Non-Removable Sync Immediate	SYN_COUNTER	0x0000	0xFFFF
Allow Unlimited Credit	Single Valued Non-Removable Sync Immediate	SYN_BOOLEAN	0x0000	0xFFFF
ACL	Non-Removable Sync Immediate	SYN_OBJECT_ACL	0x0000	0xFFFF
Aliased Object Name	Single Valued Non-Removable Sync Immediate	SYN_DIST_NAME	0x0000	0xFFFF
Audit:A Encryption Key	Single Valued Sync Immediate	SYN_OCTET_STRING	0x0000	0xFFFF
Audit:B Encryption Key	Single Valued Sync Immediate	SYN_OCTET_STRING	0x0000	0xFFFF
Audit:Contents	Single Valued Sync Immediate	SYN_INTEGER	0x0000	0xFFFF
Audit:Current Encryption Key	Single Valued Sync Immediate	SYN_OCTET_STRING	0x0000	0xFFFF
Audit:File Link	Single Valued Sync Immediate	SYN_DIST_NAME	0x0000	0xFFFF
Audit:Link List	Sync Immediate	SYN_DIST_NAME	0x0000	0xFFFF
Audit:Path	Single Valued Sync Immediate	SYN_PATH	0x0000	0xFFFF

Continued

T A B L E   C . I

Base Attributes (continued)

ATTRIBUTE NAME	DEFINITION FLAGS	SYNTAX	LOWER LIMIT	UPPER LIMIT
Audit:Policy	Single Valued Sync Immediate	SYN_OCTET_STRING	0x0000	0xFFFF
Audit:Type	Single Valued Sync Immediate	SYN_INTEGER	0x0000	0xFFFF
Authority Revocation	Single Valued Non-Removable Read-Only Attribute Sync Immediate	SYN_OCTET_STRING	0x0000	0xFFFF
Back Link	Non-Removable Read-Only Attribute Server Read	SYN_BACK_LINK	0x0000	0xFFFF
Bindery Property	Non-Removable Read-Only Attribute	SYN_OCTET_STRING	0x0000	0xFFFF
Bindery Object Restriction	Single Valued Non-Removable Read-Only Attribute	SYN_INTEGER	0x0000	0xFFFF
Bindery Restriction Level	Single Valued Non-Removable Sync Immediate	SYN_INTEGER	0x0000	0xFFFF
Bindery Type	Single Valued Non-Removable Read-Only Attribute String Attribute	SYN_NU_STRING	0x0000	0xFFFF

ATTRIBUTE NAME	DEFINITION FLAGS	SYNTAX	LOWER LIMIT	UPPER LIMIT
C	Single Valued Sized Attribute Non-Removable Sync Immediate	SYN_CI_STRING	0x0002	0x0002
CA Private Key	Single Valued Non-Removable Read-Only Attribute Hidden Attribute Sync Immediate	SYN_OCTET_STRING	0x0000	0xFFFF
CA Public Key	Single Valued Non-Removable Read-Only Attribute Sync Immediate Public Read	SYN_OCTET_STRING	0x0000	0xFFFF
Cartridge	Non-Removable String Attribute Sync Immediate	SYN_CI_STRING	0x0000	0xFFFF
Certificate Validity Interval	Single Valued Sized Attribute Non-Removable Sync Immediate	SYN_INTERVAL	0x003C	0xFFFF
Certificate Revocation	Single Valued Non-Removable Read-Only Attribute Sync Immediate	SYN_OCTET_STRING	0x0000	0xFFFF
Client Install Candidate	Single Valued Public Read	SYN_BOOLEAN	0x0000	0xFFFF

Continued

NDS CLASSES, OBJECTS, AND ATTRIBUTES

T A B L E   C . I

Base Attributes (continued)

ATTRIBUTE NAME	DEFINITION FLAGS	SYNTAX	LOWER LIMIT	UPPER LIMIT
CN	Sized Attribute Non-Removable String Attribute Sync Immediate	SYN_CI_STRING	0x0001	0x0040
Color Supported	Single Valued Public Read	SYN_BOOLEAN	0x0000	0xFFFF
Convergence	Single Valued Sized Attribute Non-Removable Sync Immediate	SYN_INTEGER	0x0000	0x0001
Cross Certificate Pair	Non-Removable Sync Immediate	SYN_OCTET_STRING	0x0000	0xFFFF
Database Dir Path	Single Valued Sized Attribute String Attribute	SYN_CI_STRING	0x0001	0x0080
Database Volume Name	Single Valued	SYN_DIST_NAME	0x0000	0xFFFF
Datapool Location	Single Valued	SYN_TYPED_NAME	0x0000	0xFFFF
Datapool Locations	n/a	SYN_TYPED_NAME	0x0000	0xFFFF
Delivery Methods Installed	Sized Attribute String Attribute Public Read	SYN_CI_STRING	0x0001	0x0080
Default Queue	Single Valued Non-Removable Sync Immediate Server Read	SYN_DIST_NAME	0x0000	0xFFFF

ATTRIBUTE NAME	DEFINITION FLAGS	SYNTAX	LOWER LIMIT	UPPER LIMIT
Description	Sized Attribute, Non-Removable, String Attribute, Sync Immediate	SYN_CI_STRING	0x0001	0x04009
Detect Intruder	Single Valued, Non-Removable, Sync Immediate	SYN_BOOLEAN	0x0000	0xFFFF
Device	Non-Removable, Sync Immediate	SYN_DIST_NAME	0x0000	0xFFFF
dn	Single Valued, Sync Immediate	SYN_DIST_NAME	0x0000	0xFFFF
DNIP:Address Number	Single Valued	SYN_INTEGER	0x0000	0xFFFF
DNIP:Aliased Object Name	Single Valued, Sync Immediate	SYN_DIST_NAME	0x0000	0xFFFF
DNIP:Assignment Type	Single Valued	SYN_INTEGER	0x0000	0xFFFF
DNIP:AuditLevel	Single Valued, Sync Immediate	SYN_INTEGER	0x0000	0xFFFF
DNIP:Auto Host Name Start	Single Valued, String Attribute	SYN_CE_STRING	0x0000	0xFFFF
DNIP:Boot Parameter	Single Valued	SYN_OCTET_STRING	0x0000	0xFFFF
DNIP:CfgPreferences	n/a	SYN_OCTET_STRING	0x0000	0xFFFF
DNIP:Client Identifier	Single Valued	SYN_OCTET_STRING	0x0000	0xFFFF
DNIP:Comment	Single Valued, String Attribute	SYN_CE_STRING	0x0000	0xFFFF
DNIP:Config Options	Single Valued	SYN_OCTET_STRING	0x0000	0xFFFF

Continued

NDS CLASSES, OBJECTS, AND ATTRIBUTES

T A B L E C . I

Base Attributes (continued)

ATTRIBUTE NAME	DEFINITION FLAGS	SYNTAX	LOWER LIMIT	UPPER LIMIT
DNIP:Designated Server	Single Valued Sync Immediate	SYN_DIST_NAME	0x0000	0xFFFF
DNIP:DHCP Server Reference	Single Valued	SYN_DIST_NAME	0x0000	0xFFFF
DNIP:DHCP Version	Single Valued	SYN_INTEGER	0x0000	0xFFFF
DNIP:DHCPServers	Sync Immediate	SYN_DIST_NAME	0x0000	0xFFFF
DNIP:DNS Domain Name	Single Valued Sized Attribute String Attribute Sync Immediate	SYN_CI_STRING	0x0001	0x0100
DNIP:DNS Server Options	Single Valued Sync Immediate	SYN_INTEGER	0x0000	0xFFFF
DNIP:DNS Server Reference	Single Valued	SYN_DIST_NAME	0x0000	0xFFFF
DNIP:DNS Update Option	Single Valued	SYN_INTEGER	0x0000	0xFFFF
DNIP:DNSServers	Sync Immediate	SYN_DIST_NAME	0x0000	0xFFFF
DNIP:DNSZones	Sync Immediate	SYN_DIST_NAME	0x0000	0xFFFF
DNIP:Domain Name	Single Valued String Attribute	SYN_CE_STRING	0x0000	0xFFFF
DNIP:End Address Number	Single Valued	SYN_INTEGER	0x0000	0xFFFF
DNIP:Excluded MAC	n/a	SYN_OCTET_STRING	0x0000	0xFFFF
DNIP:Fwd List	Single Valued Sync Immediate	SYN_OCTET_STRING	0x0000	0xFFFF
DNIP:FQ Domain Name	Single Valued String Attribute	SYN_CE_STRING	0x0000	0xFFFF

ATTRIBUTE NAME	DEFINITION FLAGS	SYNTAX	LOWER LIMIT	UPPER LIMIT
DNIP:FT Automatic	Single Valued	SYN_BOOLEAN	0x0000	0xFFFF
DNIP:FT Sync Delay	Single Valued	SYN_INTEGER	0x0000	0xFFFF
DNIP:FT Update Interval	Single Valued	SYN_INTEGER	0x0000	0xFFFF
DNIP:Group Reference	Single Valued	SYN_DIST_NAME	0x0000	0xFFFF
DNIP:Last Used	Single Valued	SYN_TIME	0x0000	0xFFFF
DNIP:Lease Expiration	Single Valued	SYN_TIME	0x0000	0xFFFF
DNIP:Lease Time	Single Valued	SYN_INTEGER	0x0000	0xFFFF
DNIP:New Attrib	Single Valued	SYN_STREAM	0x0000	0xFFFF
DNIP:NoFwd List	Sized Attribute String Attribute Sync Immediate	SYN_CI_STRING	0x0001	0x0100
DNIP:Host Name	Single Valued String Attribute	SYN_CE_STRING	0x0000	0xFFFF
DNIP:IP Assignment Policy	Single Valued	SYN_INTEGER	0x0000	0xFFFF
DNIP:LocatorPtr	Single Valued	SYN_DIST_NAME	0x0000	0xFFFF
DNIP:MAC Address	Single Valued Sync Immediate	SYN_OCTET_STRING	0x0000	0xFFFF
DNIP:Master Server IP Addr	Single Valued Sync Immediate	SYN_OCTET_STRING	0x0000	0xFFFF
DNIP:Message ID	Single Valued Sync Immediate	SYN_INTEGER	0x0000	0xFFFF
DNIP:Object Reference	Single Valued	SYN_DIST_NAME	0x0000	0xFFFF
DNIP:Ping Enable	Single Valued	SYN_INTEGER	0x0000	0xFFFF

Continued

T A B L E C . I

Base Attributes (continued)

ATTRIBUTE NAME	DEFINITION FLAGS	SYNTAX	LOWER LIMIT	UPPER LIMIT
DNIP:Primary Server Reference	Single Valued	SYN_DIST_NAME	0x0000	0xFFFF
DNIP:Public Key	Single Valued Sync Immediate	SYN_OCTET_STRING	0x0000	0xFFFF
DNIP:Range Type	Single Valued	SYN_INTEGER	0x0000	0xFFFF
DNIP:RR	Sync Immediate	SYN_OCTET_STRING	0x0000	0xFFFF
DNIP:RR Count	Single Valued Sync Immediate	SYN_INTEGER	0x0000	0xFFFF
DNIP:RR Status	Single Valued Sync Immediate	SYN_INTEGER	0x0000	0xFFFF
DNIP:RRSet Options	Single Valued Sync Immediate	SYN_INTEGER	0x0000	0xFFFF
DNIP:Secondary Server Reference	Single Valued	SYN_DIST_NAME	0x0000	0xFFFF
DNIP:Secondary Zone	Single Valued Sync Immediate	SYN_BOOLEAN	0x0000	0xFFFF
DNIP:Secondary ServerIPAddress	Sync Immediate	SYN_OCTET_STRING	0x0000	0xFFFF
DNIP:Server DN	Single Valued Sync Immediate	SYN_DIST_NAME	0x0000	0xFFFF
DNIP:Server DNS Names	Sized Attribute String Attribute Sync Immediate	SYN_CI_STRING	0x0001	0x0100
DNIP:ServerIPAddress	Sync Immediate	SYN_OCTET_STRING	0x0000	0xFFFF

ATTRIBUTE NAME	DEFINITION FLAGS	SYNTAX	LOWER LIMIT	UPPER LIMIT
DNIP:SNMP Trap Flag	Single Valued Sync Immediate	SYN_INTEGER	0x0000	0xFFFF
DNIP:SOA Admin Mailbox	Single Valued Sized Attribute String Attribute Sync Immediate	SYN_CI_STRING	0x0001	0x0100
DNIP:SOA Expire	Single Valued Sync Immediate	SYN_INTEGER	0x0000	0xFFFF
DNIP:SOA Minimum	Single Valued Sync Immediate	SYN_INTEGER	0x0000	0xFFFF
DNIP:SOA Refresh	Single Valued Sync Immediate	SYN_INTEGER	0x0000	0xFFFF
DNIP:SOA Retry	Single Valued Sync Immediate	SYN_INTEGER	0x0000	0xFFFF
DNIP:SOA Serial	Single Valued Sync Immediate	SYN_INTEGER	0x0000	0xFFFF
DNIP:SOA Zone Master	Single Valued Sized Attribute String Attribute Sync Immediate	SYN_CI_STRING	0x0001	0x0100
DNIP:Start Address Number	Single Valued	SYN_INTEGER	0x0000	0xFFFF
DNIP:Subnet Address	Single Valued	SYN_INTEGER	0x0000	0xFFFF
DNIP:Subnet Address	n/a	SYN_DIST_NAME	0x0000	0xFFFF
DNIP:Subnet Attr	Sync Immediate	SYN_DIST_NAME	0x0000	0xFFFF
DNIP:Subnet Mask	Single Valued	SYN_INTEGER	0x0000	0xFFFF

Continued

T A B L E   C . I

Base Attributes (continued)

ATTRIBUTE NAME	DEFINITION FLAGS	SYNTAX	LOWER LIMIT	UPPER LIMIT
DNIP:Subnet Pool List	Sync Immediate	SYN_DIST_NAME	0x0000	0xFFFF
DNIP:Subnet Pool Reference	Single Valued	SYN_DIST_NAME	0x0000	0xFFFF
DNIP:Subnet Type	Single Valued	SYN_INTEGER	0x0000	0xFFFF
DNIP:UI Signature	n/a	SYN_OCTET_STRING	0x0000	0xFFFF
DNIP:Zone Domain Name	Single Valued Sized Attribute String Attribute Sync Immediate	SYN_CI_STRING	0x0001	0x0100
DNIP:Zone List	Sync Immediate	SYN_DIST_NAME	0x0000	0xFFFF
DNIP:Zone Options	Single Valued Sync Immediate	SYN_INTEGER	0x0000	0xFFFF
DNIP:Zone Out Filter	Sized Attribute String Attribute Sync Immediate	SYN_CI_STRING	0x0001	0x0100
DNIP:Zone Reference	n/a	SYN_DIST_NAME	0x0000	0xFFFF
DNIP:Zone Servers	Sync Immediate	SYN_DIST_NAME	0x0000	0xFFFF
DNIP:Zone Type	Single Valued Sync Immediate	SYN_INTEGER	0x0000	0xFFFF
DS Revision	Single Valued Non-Removable Sync Immediate Public Read	SYN_INTEGER	0x0000	0xFFFF

ATTRIBUTE NAME	DEFINITION FLAGS	SYNTAX	LOWER LIMIT	UPPER LIMIT
EMail Address	Non-Removable Sync Immediate Public Read	SYN_EMAIL_ADDRESS	0x0000	0xFFFF
Employee ID	Single Valued String Attribute Sync Immediate	SYN_CI_STRING	0x0000	0xFFFF
Entrust:AttributeCertificate	n/a	SYN_OCTET_STRING	0x0000	0xFFFF
Entrust:User	String Attribute	SYN_CE_STRING	0x0000	0xFFFF
Equivalent To Me	Non-Removable Sync Immediate Server Read	SYN_DIST_NAME	0x0000	0xFFFF
External Name	Single Valued Non-Removable Sync Immediate	SYN_OCTET_STRING	0x0000	0xFFFF
External Synchronizer	Non-Removable Sync Immediate	SYN_OCTET_STRING	0x0000	0xFFFF
Facsimile Telephone Number	Non-Removable Sync Immediate	SYN_FAX_NUMBER	0x0000	0xFFFF
Full Name	Sized Attribute Non-Removable String Attribute Sync Immediate	SYN_CI_STRING	0x0000	0x007F
Generational Qualifier	Single Valued Sized Attribute Non-Removable String Attribute Sync Immediate Public Read	SYN_CI_STRING	0x0001	0x0008

Continued

T A B L E C . I

Base Attributes (continued)

ATTRIBUTE NAME	DEFINITION FLAGS	SYNTAX	LOWER LIMIT	UPPER LIMIT
GID	Single Valued Non-Removable Sync Immediate	SYN_INTEGER	0x0000	0xFFFF
Given Name	Single Valued Sized Attribute Non-Removable String Attribute Sync Immediate Public Read	SYN_CI_STRING	0x0001	0x0020
Group Membership	Non-Removable Sync Immediate	SYN_DIST_NAME	0x0000	0xFFFF
GUID	Single Valued Sized Attribute Non-Removable Read-Only Attribute Sync Immediate Public Read	SYN_OCTET_STRING	0x0010	0x0010
GW API Gateway Directory Path	Single Valued Sized Attribute String Attribute	SYN_CI_STRING	0x0001	0x0080
GW API Gateway Directory Volume	Single Valued	SYN_DIST_NAME	0x0000	0xFFFF
High Convergence Sync Interval	Single Valued Non-Removable Sync Immediate	SYN_INTERVAL	0x0000	0xFFFF

ATTRIBUTE NAME	DEFINITION FLAGS	SYNTAX	LOWER LIMIT	UPPER LIMIT
Higher Privileges	Non-Removable Sync Immediate Server Read	SYN_DIST_NAME	0x0000	0xFFFF
Home Directory	Single Valued Sized Attribute Non-Removable Sync Immediate	SYN_PATH	0x0001	0x00FF
Home Directory Rights	n/a	SYN_INTEGER	0x0000	0xFFFF
Host Device	Single Valued Non-Removable Sync Immediate	SYN_DIST_NAME	0x0000	0xFFFF
Host Resource Name	Single Valued Non-Removable String Attribute Sync Immediate	SYN_CI_STRING	0x0000	0xFFFF
Host Server	Single Valued Non-Removable Sync Immediate	SYN_DIST_NAME	0x0000	0xFFFF
Inherited ACL	Non-Removable Read-Only Attribute Sync Immediate	SYN_OBJECT_ACL	0x0000	0xFFFF
Initials	Single Valued Sized Attribute Non-Removable String Attribute Sync Immediate Public Read	SYN_CI_STRING	0x0001	0x0008

Continued

T A B L E C . 1

Base Attributes (continued)

ATTRIBUTE NAME	DEFINITION FLAGS	SYNTAX	LOWER LIMIT	UPPER LIMIT
Internet EMail Address	String Attribute Sync Immediate Public Read	SYN_CI_STRING	0x0000	0xFFFF
Intruder Lockout Reset Interval	Single Valued Non-Removable Sync Immediate	SYN_INTERVAL	0x0000	0xFFFF
IPP URI	Single Valued Public Read	SYN_CI_LIST	0x0000	0xFFFF
IPP URI Security Scheme	Single Valued Public Read	SYN_CI_LIST	0x0000	0xFFFF
L	Sized Attribute Non-Removable String Attribute Sync Immediate	SYN_CI_STRING	0x0001	0x0080
Language	Single Valued Non-Removable Sync Immediate	SYN_CI_LIST	0x0000	0xFFFF
Last Login Time	Single Valued Non-Removable Read-Only Attribute	SYN_TIME	0x0000	0xFFFF
Last Referenced Time	Single Valued Non-Removable	SYN_TIMESTAMP	0x0000	0xFFFF
Locked By Intruder	Single Valued Non-Removable Sync Immediate	SYN_BOOLEAN	0x0000	0xFFFF
LDAP:ARL	Sync Immediate	SYN_OCTET_STRING	0x0000	0xFFFF

ATTRIBUTE NAME	DEFINITION FLAGS	SYNTAX	LOWER LIMIT	UPPER LIMIT
LDAP:bindCatalog	Sync Immediate	SYN_DIST_NAME	0x0000	0xFFFF
LDAP:bindCatalogUsage	Single Valued Sync Immediate	SYN_INTEGER	0x0000	0xFFFF
LDAP:caCertificate	Sync Immediate	SYN_OCTET_STRING	0x0000	0xFFFF
LDAP:CRL	Sync Immediate	SYN_OCTET_STRING	0x0000	0xFFFF
LDAP:crossCertificatePair	Sync Immediate	SYN_OCTET_STRING	0x0000	0xFFFF
LDAP:keyMaterialName	Single Valued String Attribute Sync Immediate	SYN_CI_STRING	0x0000	0xFFFF
LDAP:searchCatalog	Sync Immediate	SYN_DIST_NAME	0x0000	0xFFFF
LDAP:searchCatalogUsage	Single Valued Sync Immediate	SYN_INTEGER	0x0000	0xFFFF
LDAP ACL v11	Single Valued Sync Immediate	SYN_OCTET_STRING	0x0000	0xFFFF
LDAP Allow Clear Text Password	Single Valued Sync Immediate	SYN_BOOLEAN	0x0000	0xFFFF
LDAP Anonymous Identity	Single Valued Sync Immediate	SYN_DIST_NAME	0x0000	0xFFFF
LDAP Attribute Map v11	Single Valued Sync Immediate	SYN_OCTET_STRING	0x0000	0xFFFF
LDAP Backup Log Filename	Single Valued String Attribute Sync Immediate	SYN_CI_STRING	0x0000	0xFFFF
LDAP Class Map	Single Valued Sync Immediate	SYN_STREAM	0x0000	0xFFFF

Continued

ATTRIBUTE NAME	DEFINITION FLAGS	SYNTAX	LOWER LIMIT	UPPER LIMIT
LDAP Class Map v11	Single Valued Sync Immediate	SYN_OCTET_STRING	0x0000	0xFFFF
LDAP Enable SSL	Single Valued Sync Immediate	SYN_BOOLEAN	0x0000	0xFFFF
LDAP Enable TCP	Single Valued Sync Immediate	SYN_BOOLEAN	0x0000	0xFFFF
LDAP Enable UDP	Single Valued Sync Immediate	SYN_BOOLEAN	0x0000	0xFFFF
LDAP Group	Single Valued Sync Immediate	SYN_DIST_NAME	0x0000	0xFFFF
LDAP Host Server	Single Valued Sync Immediate	SYN_DIST_NAME	0x0000	0xFFFF
LDAP Log Filename	Single Valued String Attribute Sync Immediate	SYN_CI_STRING	0x0000	0xFFFF
LDAP Log Level	Single Valued Sized Attribute Sync Immediate	SYN_INTEGER	0x0000	0x8000
LDAP Log Size Limit	Single Valued Sized Attribute Sync Immediate	SYN_INTEGER	0x0800	0xFFFF
LDAP Referral	Single Valued String Attribute Sync Immediate	SYN_CI_STRING	0x0000	0xFFFF

ATTRIBUTE NAME	DEFINITION FLAGS	SYNTAX	LOWER LIMIT	UPPER LIMIT
LDAP Screen Level	Single Valued Sized Attribute Sync Immediate	SYN_INTEGER	0x0000	0x8000
LDAP Search Size Limit	Single Valued Sized Attribute Sync Immediate	SYN_INTEGER	0x0001	0xFFFF
LDAP Search Time Limit	Single Valued Sized Attribute Sync Immediate	SYN_INTEGER	0x0001	0xFFFF
LDAP Server	Sync Immediate	SYN_DIST_NAME	0x0000	0xFFFF
LDAP Server Bind Limit	Single Valued Sized Attribute Sync Immediate	SYN_INTEGER	0x0000	0xFFFF
LDAP Server Idle Timeout	Single Valued Sized Attribute Sync Immediate	SYN_INTEGER	0x0000	0xFFFF
LDAP Server List	Sync Immediate	SYN_DIST_NAME	0x0000	0xFFFF
LDAP SSL Port	Single Valued Sized Attribute Sync Immediate	SYN_INTEGER	0x0000	0xFFFF
LDAP Suffix	Sync Immediate	SYN_DIST_NAME	0x0000	0xFFFF
LDAP TCP Port	Single Valued Sized Attribute Sync Immediate	SYN_INTEGER	0x0000	0xFFFF
LDAP UDP Port	Single Valued Sized Attribute Sync Immediate	SYN_INTEGER	0x0000	0xFFFF

Continued

T A B L E   C . I

Base Attributes (continued)

ATTRIBUTE NAME	DEFINITION FLAGS	SYNTAX	LOWER LIMIT	UPPER LIMIT
LDAPUserCertificate	n/a	SYN_OCTET_STRING	0x0000	0xFFFF
Lockout After Detection	Single Valued Non-Removable Sync Immediate	SYN_BOOLEAN	0x0000	0xFFFF
Login Allowed Time Map	Single Valued Sized Attribute Non-Removable Sync Immediate	SYN_OCTET_STRING	0x002A	0x002A
Login Disabled	Single Valued Non-Removable Sync Immediate	SYN_BOOLEAN	0x0000	0xFFFF
Login Expiration Time	Single Valued Non-Removable Sync Immediate	SYN_TIME	0x0000	0xFFFF
Login Grace Limit	Single Valued Non-Removable Sync Immediate	SYN_INTEGER	0x0000	0xFFFF
Login Grace Remaining	Single Valued Non-Removable Sync Immediate	SYN_COUNTER	0x0000	0xFFFF
Login Intruder Address	Single Valued Non-Removable Sync Immediate	SYN_NET_ADDRESS	0x0000	0xFFFF
Login Intruder Attempts	Single Valued Non-Removable Sync Immediate	SYN_COUNTER	0x0000	0xFFFF

ATTRIBUTE NAME	DEFINITION FLAGS	SYNTAX	LOWER LIMIT	UPPER LIMIT
Login Intruder Limit	Single Valued Non-Removable Sync Immediate	SYN_INTEGER	0x0000	0xFFFF
Intruder Attempt Reset Interval	Single Valued Non-Removable Sync Immediate	SYN_INTERVAL	0x0000	0xFFFF
Login Intruder Reset Time	Single Valued Non-Removable Sync Immediate	SYN_TIME	0x0000	0xFFFF
Login Maximum Simultaneous	Single Valued Non-Removable Sync Immediate	SYN_INTEGER	0x0000	0xFFFF
Login Script	Single Valued Non-Removable Sync Immediate	SYN_STREAM	0x0000	0xFFFF
Login Time	Single Valued Non-Removable	SYN_TIME	0x0000	0xFFFF
Low Convergence Reset Time	Single Valued Non-Removable Sync Immediate	SYN_TIME	0x0000	0xFFFF
Low Convergence Sync Interval	Single Valued Non-Removable Sync Immediate	SYN_INTERVAL	0x0000	0xFFFF

Continued

TABLE C.1

Base Attributes (continued)

ATTRIBUTE NAME	DEFINITION FLAGS	SYNTAX	LOWER LIMIT	UPPER LIMIT
Mailbox ID	Single Valued Sized Attribute Non-Removable String Attribute Sync Immediate Public Read	SYN_CI_STRING	0x0001	0x0008
Mailbox Location	Single Valued Non-Removable Sync Immediate Public Read	SYN_DIST_NAME	0x0000	0xFFFF
MASV:Authorized Range	Read-Only Attribute Sync Immediate Public Read	SYN_OCTET_STRING	0x0000	0xFFFF
MASV:Default Range	Single Valued Read-Only Attribute Sync Immediate Public Read	SYN_OCTET_STRING	0x0000	0xFFFF
MASV:Domain Policy	Single Valued Read-Only Attribute Sync Immediate Public Read	SYN_OCTET_STRING	0x0000	0xFFFF
MASV:Label	Single Valued Read-Only Attribute Sync Immediate	SYN_OCTET_STRING	0x0000	0xFFFF
MASV:Proposed Label	Single Valued Read-Only Attribute Sync Immediate	SYN_OCTET_STRING	0x0000	0xFFFF

ATTRIBUTE NAME	DEFINITION FLAGS	SYNTAX	LOWER LIMIT	UPPER LIMIT
Maximum Speed	Single Valued Sized Attribute Public Read	SYN_INTEGER	0x0001	0x2710
Maximum Speed Units	Single Valued Sized Attribute Public Read	SYN_INTEGER	0x0001	0x4240
Member	Non-Removable Sync Immediate	SYN_DIST_NAME	0x0000	0xFFFF
Members Of Template	n/a	SYN_DIST_NAME	0x0000	0xFFFF
Memory	Single Valued Non-Removable Sync Immediate	SYN_INTEGER	0x0000	0xFFFF
Message Routing Group	Non-Removable Sync Immediate	SYN_DIST_NAME	0x0000	0xFFFF
Message Server	Single Valued Non-Removable Sync Immediate	SYN_DIST_NAME	0x0000	0xFFFF
Messaging Database Location	Single Valued Non-Removable Sync Immediate	SYN_PATH	0x0000	0xFFFF
Messaging Server	Non-Removable Sync Immediate	SYN_DIST_NAME	0x0000	0xFFFF
Messaging Server Type	Single Valued Sized Attribute Non-Removable String Attribute Sync Immediate	SYN_CI_STRING	0x0001	0x0020

Continued

NDS CLASSES, OBJECTS, AND ATTRIBUTES

TABLE C.1

Base Attributes (continued)

ATTRIBUTE NAME	DEFINITION FLAGS	SYNTAX	LOWER LIMIT	UPPER LIMIT
MHS Send Directory Path	Single Valued, Sized Attribute, String Attribute	SYN_CI_STRING	0x0001	0x0080
MHS Send Directory Volume	Single Valued	SYN_DIST_NAME	0x0000	0xFFFF
Minimum Account Balance	Single Valued, Non-Removable, Sync Immediate	SYN_INTEGER	0x0000	0xFFFF
NDPS Accountant Role	Sized Attribute, String Attribute	SYN_CI_STRING	0x0001	0x0080
NDPS Control Flags	Single Valued, Public Read	SYN_INTEGER	0x0000	0xFFFF
NDPS Database Saved Data Image	Single Valued	SYN_STREAM	0x0000	0xFFFF
NDPS Database Saved Index Image	Single Valued	SYN_STREAM	0x0000	0xFFFF
NDPS Database Saved Timestamp	Single Valued	SYN_INTEGER	0x0000	0xFFFF
NDPS Default Printer	Single Valued, Public Read	SYN_DIST_NAME	0x0000	0xFFFF
NDPS Default Public Printer	Single Valued, Sized Attribute, String Attribute, Public Read	SYN_CI_STRING	0x0001	0x0080
NDPS Job Configurations	Single Valued, Public Read	SYN_STREAM	0x0000	0xFFFF

ATTRIBUTE NAME	DEFINITION FLAGS	SYNTAX	LOWER LIMIT	UPPER LIMIT
NDPS Manager Status	Single Valued Public Read	SYN_OCTET_STRING	0x0000	0xFFFF
NDPS Operator Role	Sized Attribute String Attribute	SYN_CI_STRING	0x0001	0x0080
NDPS Printer Install List	Public Read	SYN_TYPED_NAME	0x0000	0xFFFF
NDPS Printer Install Timestamp	Single Valued Public Read	SYN_INTEGER	0x0000	0xFFFF
NDPS Printer Queue List	Public Read	SYN_TYPED_NAME	0x0000	0xFFFF
NDPS Printer Siblings	Public Read	SYN_DIST_NAME	0x0000	0xFFFF
NDPS Public Printer Install List	Public Read	SYN_OCTET_STRING	0x0000	0xFFFF
NDPS Replace All Client Printers	Single Valued Public Read	SYN_BOOLEAN	0x0000	0xFFFF
NDPS SMTP Server	Sized Attribute String Attribute	SYN_CE_STRING	0x0001	0x07D0
NDPS User Role	Sized Attribute String Attribute	SYN_CI_STRING	0x0001	0x0080
NDSCat:Actual All Attributes	Single Valued	SYN_BOOLEAN	0x0000	0xFFFF
NDSCat:Actual Attributes	String Attribute	SYN_CE_STRING	0x0000	0xFFFF
NDSCat:Actual Attribute Count	Single Valued	SYN_INTEGER	0x0000	0xFFFF
NDSCat:Actual Base Object	n/a	SYN_DIST_NAME	0x0000	0xFFFF
NDSCat:Actual Catalog Size	Single Valued	SYN_INTEGER	0x0000	0xFFFF
NDSCat:Actual End Time	Single Valued	SYN_TIME	0x0000	0xFFFF

Continued

T A B L E C.1

Base Attributes (continued)

ATTRIBUTE NAME	DEFINITION FLAGS	SYNTAX	LOWER LIMIT	UPPER LIMIT
NDSCat:Actual Filter	Single Valued String Attribute	SYN_CE_STRING	0x0000	0xFFFF
NDSCat:Actual Object Count	Single Valued	SYN_INTEGER	0x0000	0xFFFF
NDSCat:Actual Return Code	Single Valued	SYN_INTEGER	0x0000	0xFFFF
NDSCat:Actual Scope	Single Valued	SYN_INTEGER	0x0000	0xFFFF
NDSCat:Actual Search Aliases	Single Valued	SYN_BOOLEAN	0x0000	0xFFFF
NDSCat:Actual Start Time	Single Valued	SYN_TIME	0x0000	0xFFFF
NDSCat:Actual Value Count	Single Valued	SYN_INTEGER	0x0000	0xFFFF
NDSCat:All Attributes	Single Valued	SYN_BOOLEAN	0x0000	0xFFFF
NDSCat:AttrDefTbl	n/a	SYN_OCTET_LIST	0x0000	0xFFFF
NDSCat:Attributes	String Attribute	SYN_CE_STRING	0x0000	0xFFFF
NDSCat:Auto Dredge	Single Valued	SYN_BOOLEAN	0x0000	0xFFFF
NDSCat:Base Object	n/a	SYN_DIST_NAME	0x0000	0xFFFF
NDSCat:Catalog List	n/a	SYN_DIST_NAME	0x0000	0xFFFF
NDSCat:CatalogDB	Single Valued	SYN_STREAM	0x0000	0xFFFF
NDSCat:Dredge Interval	Single Valued	SYN_INTERVAL	0x0000	0xFFFF
NDSCat:Filter	Single Valued String Attribute	SYN_CE_STRING	0x0000	0xFFFF
NDSCat:IndexDefTbl	n/a	SYN_OCTET_LIST	0x0000	0xFFFF
NDSCat:Indexes	String Attribute	SYN_CI_STRING	0x0000	0xFFFF
NDSCat:Label	n/a	SYN_CI_LIST	0x0000	0xFFFF

ATTRIBUTE NAME	DEFINITION FLAGS	SYNTAX	LOWER LIMIT	UPPER LIMIT
NDSCat:Log	Single Valued	SYN_STREAM	0x0000	0xFFFF
NDSCat:Master Catalog	Single Valued	SYN_DIST_NAME	0x0000	0xFFFF
NDSCat:Max Log Size	Single Valued	SYN_INTEGER	0x0000	0xFFFF
NDSCat:Max Retries	Single Valued	SYN_INTEGER	0x0000	0xFFFF
NDSCat:Max Threads	Single Valued Sized Attribute	SYN_INTEGER	0x0001	0x0014
NDSCat:Retry Interval	Single Valued	SYN_INTERVAL	0x0000	0xFFFF
NDSCat:Scope	Single Valued	SYN_INTEGER	0x0000	0xFFFF
NDSCat:Search Aliases	Single Valued	SYN_BOOLEAN	0x0000	0xFFFF
NDSCat:Slave Catalog List	n/a	SYN_DIST_NAME	0x0000	0xFFFF
NDSCat:Start Time	Single Valued	SYN_TIME	0x0000	0xFFFF
NDSCat:Synch Interval	Single Valued	SYN_INTERVAL	0x0000	0xFFFF
NDSPKI:Certificate Chain	Sync Immediate Public Read	SYN_OCTET_STRING	0x0000	0xFFFF
NDSPKI:Given Name	Single Valued String Attribute Sync Immediate	SYN_CI_STRING	0x0000	0xFFFF
NDSPKI:Key File	Single Valued Sync Immediate	SYN_OCTET_STRING	0x0000	0xFFFF
NDSPKI:Key Material DN	Sync Immediate	SYN_DIST_NAME	0x0000	0xFFFF
NDSPKI:Parent CA	Single Valued String Attribute Sync Immediate	SYN_CI_STRING	0x0000	0xFFFF

Continued

T A B L E C.1

Base Attributes (continued)

ATTRIBUTE NAME	DEFINITION FLAGS	SYNTAX	LOWER LIMIT	UPPER LIMIT
NDSPKI:Parent CA DN	Single Valued Sync Immediate	SYN_DIST_NAME	0x0000	0xFFFF
NDSPKI:Private Key	Single Valued Sync Immediate	SYN_OCTET_STRING	0x0000	0xFFFF
NDSPKI:Public Key	Single Valued Sync Immediate Public Read	SYN_OCTET_STRING	0x0000	0xFFFF
NDSPKI:Public Key Certificate	Single Valued Sync Immediate Public Read	SYN_OCTET_STRING	0x0000	0xFFFF
NDSPKI:Subject Name	Single Valued String Attribute Sync Immediate	SYN_CI_STRING	0x0000	0xFFFF
NDSPKI:Tree CA DN	Sync Immediate	SYN_DIST_NAME	0x0000	0xFFFF
Network Address	Non-Removable Sync Immediate	SYN_NET_ADDRESS	0x0000	0xFFFF
Network Address Restriction	Non-Removable Sync Immediate	SYN_NET_ADDRESS	0x0000	0xFFFF
New Object's DS Rights	n/a	SYN_OBJECT_ACL	0x0000	0xFFFF
New Object's FS Rights	n/a	SYN_PATH	0x0000	0xFFFF
New Object's Self Rights	n/a	SYN_OBJECT_ACL	0x0000	0xFFFF
NLS:Common Certificate	Public Read	SYN_OCTET_STRING	0x0000	0xFFFF
NLS:Current Installed	Single Valued Public Read	SYN_INTEGER	0x0000	0xFFFF

ATTRIBUTE NAME	DEFINITION FLAGS	SYNTAX	LOWER LIMIT	UPPER LIMIT
NLS:Current Peak Installed	Single Valued Public Read	SYN_INTEGER	0x0000	0xFFFF
NLS:Current Peak Used	Single Valued Public Read	SYN_INTEGER	0x0000	0xFFFF
NLS:Current Used	Single Valued Public Read	SYN_INTEGER	0x0000	0xFFFF
NLS:Hourly Data Size	Single Valued Public Read	SYN_INTEGER	0x0000	0xFFFF
NLS:LSP Revision	Single Valued Public Read	SYN_INTEGER	0x0000	0xFFFF
NLS:License Database	Single Valued Public Read	SYN_BOOLEAN	0x0000	0xFFFF
NLS:License ID	Single Valued String Attribute Public Read	SYN_CE_STRING	0x0000	0xFFFF
NLS:License Service Provider	Single Valued Public Read	SYN_DIST_NAME	0x0000	0xFFFF
NLS:Owner	Single Valued Public Read	SYN_DIST_NAME	0x0000	0xFFFF
NLS:Peak Installed Data	Single Valued Public Read	SYN_OCTET_STRING	0x0000	0xFFFF
NLS:Peak Used Data	Single Valued Public Read	SYN_OCTET_STRING	0x0000	0xFFFF
NLS:Product	Single Valued String Attribute Public Read	SYN_CE_STRING	0x0000	0xFFFF

Continued

T A B L E   C . 1

Base Attributes (continued)

ATTRIBUTE NAME	DEFINITION FLAGS	SYNTAX	LOWER LIMIT	UPPER LIMIT
NLS:Publisher	Single Valued String Attribute Public Read	SYN_CE_STRING	0x0000	0xFFFF
NLS:Revision	Single Valued Public Read	SYN_INTEGER	0x0000	0xFFFF
NLS:Search Type	Single Valued Public Read	SYN_INTEGER	0x0000	0xFFFF
NLS:Summary Version	Single Valued Public Read	SYN_INTEGER	0x0000	0xFFFF
NLS:Summary Update Time	Single Valued Public Read	SYN_TIME	0x0000	0xFFFF
NLS:Transaction Database	Single Valued Public Read	SYN_BOOLEAN	0x0000	0xFFFF
NLS:Transaction Log Size	Single Valued Public Read	SYN_INTEGER	0x0000	0xFFFF
NLS:Version	Single Valued String Attribute Public Read	SYN_CI_STRING	0x0000	0xFFFF
NRD:Registry Data	Single Valued	SYN_STREAM	0x0000	0xFFFF
NRD:Registry Index	Single Valued	SYN_STREAM	0x0000	0xFFFF
NLS:Transaction Log Name	Single Valued String Attribute Public Read	SYN_CI_STRING	0x0000	0xFFFF

ATTRIBUTE NAME	DEFINITION FLAGS	SYNTAX	LOWER LIMIT	UPPER LIMIT
NNS Domain	Sized Attribute Non-Removable String Attribute Sync Immediate	SYN_CI_STRING	0x0001	0x0080
Notification Consumers	n/a	SYN_TYPED_NAME	0x0000	0xFFFF
Notification Profile	Single Valued	SYN_STREAM	0x0000	0xFFFF
Notification Service Enabled	Single Valued	SYN_BOOLEAN	0x0000	0xFFFF
Notification Srvc Net Addr	Public Read	SYN_NET_ADDRESS	0x0000	0xFFFF
Notification Srvc Net Address	Single Valued Public Read	SYN_NET_ADDRESS	0x0000	0xFFFF
Notify	Non-Removable Sync Immediate	SYN_TYPED_NAME	0x0000	0xFFFF
NSCP:adminURL	String Attribute	SYN_CI_STRING	0x0000	0xFFFF
NSCP:administratorContactInfo	String Attribute	SYN_CI_STRING	0x0000	0xFFFF
NSCP:installationTimeStamp	String Attribute	SYN_CI_STRING	0x0000	0xFFFF
NSCP:mailAccessDomain	String Attribute	SYN_CI_STRING	0x0000	0xFFFF
NSCP:mailAlternateAddress	String Attribute	SYN_CI_STRING	0x0000	0xFFFF
NSCP:mailAutoReplyMode	String Attribute	SYN_CI_STRING	0x0000	0xFFFF
NSCP:mailAutoReplyText	String Attribute	SYN_CI_STRING	0x0000	0xFFFF
NSCP:mailDeliveryOption	String Attribute	SYN_CI_STRING	0x0000	0xFFFF
NSCP:mailForwardingAddress	String Attribute	SYN_CI_STRING	0x0000	0xFFFF
NSCP:mailHost	String Attribute	SYN_CI_STRING	0x0000	0xFFFF
NSCP:mailMessageStore	String Attribute	SYN_CE_STRING	0x0000	0xFFFF

Continued

T A B L E   C . I

Base Attributes (continued)

ATTRIBUTE NAME	DEFINITION FLAGS	SYNTAX	LOWER LIMIT	UPPER LIMIT
NSCP:mailProgramDeliveryInfo	String Attribute	SYN_CE_STRING	0x0000	0xFFFF
NSCP:mailQuota	String Attribute	SYN_CI_STRING	0x0000	0xFFFF
NSCP:mgrpRFC822mailmember	String Attribute	SYN_CE_STRING	0x0000	0xFFFF
NSCP:ngComponent	n/a	SYN_DIST_NAME	0x0000	0xFFFF
NSCP:nsaclrole	String Attribute	SYN_CI_STRING	0x0000	0xFFFF
NSCP:nscreator	String Attribute	SYN_CI_STRING	0x0000	0xFFFF
NSCP:nsflags	String Attribute	SYN_CI_STRING	0x0000	0xFFFF
NSCP:nsLicenseEndTime	String Attribute	SYN_CI_STRING	0x0000	0xFFFF
NSCP:nsLicensedFor	String Attribute	SYN_CI_STRING	0x0000	0xFFFF
NSCP:nsLicenseStartTime	String Attribute	SYN_CI_STRING	0x0000	0xFFFF
NSCP:nsnewsACL	String Attribute	SYN_CI_STRING	0x0000	0xFFFF
NSCP:nsprettyname	String Attribute	SYN_CI_STRING	0x0000	0xFFFF
NSCP:serverHostName	String Attribute	SYN_CI_STRING	0x0000	0xFFFF
NSCP:serverProductName	String Attribute	SYN_CI_STRING	0x0000	0xFFFF
NSCP:serverRoot	String Attribute	SYN_CI_STRING	0x0000	0xFFFF
NSCP:serverVersionNumber	String Attribute	SYN_CI_STRING	0x0000	0xFFFF
NSCP:subtreeACl	String Attribute	SYN_CI_STRING	0x0000	0xFFFF
Obituary	Non-Removable Read-Only Attribute Sync Immediate	SYN_OCTET_STRING	0x0000	0xFFFF

ATTRIBUTE NAME	DEFINITION FLAGS	SYNTAX	LOWER LIMIT	UPPER LIMIT
Obituary Notify	Non-Removable Read-Only Attribute Sync Immediate	SYN_OCTET_STRING	0x0000	0xFFFF
Object Class	Non-Removable Read-Only Attribute Sync Immediate Public Read	SYN_CLASS_NAME	0x0000	0xFFFF
Operator	Non-Removable Sync Immediate Server Read	SYN_DIST_NAME	0x0000	0xFFFF
OU	Sized Attribute Non-Removable String Attribute Sync Immediate	SYN_CI_STRING	0x0001	0x0040
O	Sized Attribute Non-Removable String Attribute Sync Immediate	SYN_CI_STRING	0x0001	0x0040
Other GUID	Sized Attribute Non-Removable Sync Immediate Public Read	SYN_OCTET_STRING	0x0010	0x0010
Owner	Non-Removable Sync Immediate	SYN_DIST_NAME	0x0000	0xFFFF
Page Description Language	Sized Attribute Non-Removable String Attribute Sync Immediate	SYN_PR_STRING	0x0001	0x0040

Continued

T A B L E   C . I

Base Attributes (continued)

ATTRIBUTE NAME	DEFINITION FLAGS	SYNTAX	LOWER LIMIT	UPPER LIMIT
Page Description Languages	Public Read	SYN_INTEGER	0x0000	0xFFFF
Partition Creation Time	Single Valued Non-Removable Read-Only Attribute Sync Immediate Public Read	SYN_TIMESTAMP	0x0000	0xFFFF
Partition Control	Non-Removable Read-Only Attribute Sync Immediate Public Read	SYN_TYPED_NAME	0x0000	0xFFFF
Partition Status	Non-Removable Read-Only Attribute Public Read	SYN_OCTET_STRING	0x0000	0xFFFF
Password Allow Change	Single Valued Non-Removable Sync Immediate	SYN_BOOLEAN	0x0000	0xFFFF
Password Expiration Interval	Single Valued Non-Removable Sync Immediate	SYN_INTERVAL	0x0000	0xFFFF
Password Expiration Time	Single Valued Non-Removable Sync Immediate	SYN_TIME	0x0000	0xFFFF
Password Management	Single Valued Non-Removable Sync Immediate	SYN_UNKNOWN	0x0000	0xFFFF

ATTRIBUTE NAME	DEFINITION FLAGS	SYNTAX	LOWER LIMIT	UPPER LIMIT
Password Minimum Length	Single Valued Non-Removable Sync Immediate	SYN_INTEGER	0x0000	0xFFFF
Password Required	Single Valued Non-Removable Sync Immediate	SYN_BOOLEAN	0x0000	0xFFFF
Password Unique Required	Single Valued Non-Removable Sync Immediate	SYN_BOOLEAN	0x0000	0xFFFF
Passwords Used	Non-Removable Sync Immediate	SYN_OCTET_STRING	0x0000	0xFFFF
Path	Non-Removable Sync Immediate	SYN_PATH	0x0000	0xFFFF
Permanent Config Parms	Non-Removable Sync Immediate Public Read	SYN_OCTET_STRING	0x0000	0xFFFF
Physical Delivery Office Name	Sized Attribute Non-Removable String Attribute Sync Immediate	SYN_CI_STRING	0x0001	0x0080
Postmaster	Non-Removable Sync Immediate	SYN_DIST_NAME	0x0000	0xFFFF
Postal Address	Non-Removable Sync Immediate	SYN_PO_ADDRESS	0x0000	0xFFFF
Postal Code	Sized Attribute Non-Removable String Attribute Sync Immediate	SYN_CI_STRING	0x0000	0x0028

Continued

TABLE C.1

Base Attributes (continued)

ATTRIBUTE NAME	DEFINITION FLAGS	SYNTAX	LOWER LIMIT	UPPER LIMIT
Postal Office Box	Sized Attribute Non-Removable String Attribute Sync Immediate	SYN_CI_STRING	0x0000	0x0028
Primary Notification Service	Single Valued Public Read	SYN_TYPED_NAME	0x0000	0xFFFF
Primary Resource Service	Single Valued Public Read	SYN_TYPED_NAME	0x0000	0xFFFF
Print Job Configuration	Single Valued Non-Removable Sync Immediate	SYN_STREAM	0x0000	0xFFFF
Print Server	Single Valued Non-Removable Sync Immediate	SYN_TYPED_NAME	0x0000	0xFFFF
Printer	Non-Removable Sync Immediate	SYN_TYPED_NAME	0x0000	0xFFFF
Printer Agent Name	Single Valued Public Read	SYN_OCTET_STRING	0x0000	0xFFFF
Printer Configuration	Single Valued Non-Removable Sync Immediate	SYN_OCTET_STRING	0x0000	0xFFFF
Printer Control	Single Valued Non-Removable Sync Immediate	SYN_STREAM	0x0000	0xFFFF

ATTRIBUTE NAME	DEFINITION FLAGS	SYNTAX	LOWER LIMIT	UPPER LIMIT
Printer Manufacturer	Single Valued Sized Attribute String Attribute Public Read	SYN_CI_STRING	0x0001	0x0080
Printer Mechanism Types	Sized Attribute Public Read	SYN_INTEGER	0x0001	0xFFFF
Printer Model	Single Valued Sized Attribute String Attribute Public Read	SYN_CI_STRING	0x0001	0x0080
Printer Status	Single Valued Public Read	SYN_OCTET_STRING	0x0000	0xFFFF
Printer to PA ID Mappings	n/a	SYN_TYPED_NAME	0x0000	0xFFFF
Private Key	Single Valued Non-Removable Read-Only Attribute Sync Immediate	SYN_OCTET_STRING	0x0000	0xFFFF
Profile	Single Valued Non-Removable Sync Immediate	SYN_DIST_NAME	0x0000	0xFFFF
Profile Membership	Non-Removable Sync Immediate	SYN_DIST_NAME	0x0000	0xFFFF
PSM Name	Single Valued Public Read	SYN_DIST_NAME	0x0000	0xFFFF

Continued

TABLE C.1

Base Attributes (continued)

ATTRIBUTE NAME	DEFINITION FLAGS	SYNTAX	LOWER LIMIT	UPPER LIMIT
Public Key	Single Valued Non-Removable Read-Only Attribute Sync Immediate Public Read	SYN_OCTET_STRING	0x0000	0xFFFF
Purge Vector	Non-Removable Read-Only Attribute Public Read	SYN_TIMESTAMP	0x0000	0xFFFF
Queue	Non-Removable Sync Immediate	SYN_TYPED_NAME	0x0000	0xFFFF
Queue Directory	Single Valued Sized Attribute Non-Removable String Attribute Sync Immediate Server Read	SYN_CI_STRING	0x0001	0x00FF
Received Up To	Non-Removable Read-Only Attribute Sync Immediate Public Read	SYN_TIMESTAMP	0x0000	0xFFFF
Reference	Non-Removable Read-Only Attribute	SYN_DIST_NAME	0x0000	0xFFFF
Registry Advertising Name	Single Valued Sized Attribute String Attribute Public Read	SYN_CI_STRING	0x0001	0x0030
Registry Service Enabled	Single Valued	SYN_BOOLEAN	0x0000	0xFFFF

ATTRIBUTE NAME	DEFINITION FLAGS	SYNTAX	LOWER LIMIT	UPPER LIMIT
Registry Srvc Net Addr	Public Read	SYN_NET_ADDRESS	0x0000	0xFFFF
Registry Srvc Net Address	Single Valued	SYN_NET_ADDRESS	0x0000	0xFFFF
Replica	Non-Removable Read-Only Attribute Sync Immediate Public Read	SYN_REPLICA_POINTER	0x0000	0xFFFF
Replica Up To	Non-Removable Read-Only Attribute Sync Immediate Public Read	SYN_OCTET_STRING	0x0000	0xFFFF
Resolution	Single Valued Sized Attribute Public Read	SYN_INTEGER	0x0001	0x4240
Resource	Non-Removable Sync Immediate	SYN_DIST_NAME	0x0000	0xFFFF
Resource Mgmt Service Enabled	Single Valued	SYN_BOOLEAN	0x0000	0xFFFF
Resource Mgmt Srvc Net Addr	Public Read	SYN_NET_ADDRESS	0x0000	0xFFFF
Resource Mgmt Srvc Net Address	Single Valued Public Read	SYN_NET_ADDRESS	0x0000	0xFFFF
Resource Mgr Database Path	Single Valued Sized Attribute String Attribute	SYN_CI_STRING	0x0001	0x0080
Resource Mgr Database Volume	Single Valued	SYN_DIST_NAME	0x0000	0xFFFF

Continued

T A B L E C . I

Base Attributes (continued)

ATTRIBUTE NAME	DEFINITION FLAGS	SYNTAX	LOWER LIMIT	UPPER LIMIT
Revision	Single Valued Non-Removable Read-Only Attribute Public Read	SYN_COUNTER	0x0000	0xFFFF
Role Occupant	Non-Removable Sync Immediate	SYN_DIST_NAME	0x0000	0xFFFF
Run Setup Script	Single Valued	SYN_BOOLEAN	0x0000	0xFFFF
S	Sized Attribute Non-Removable String Attribute Sync Immediate	SYN_CI_STRING	0x0001	0x0080
SA	Sized Attribute Non-Removable String Attribute Sync Immediate	SYN_CI_STRING	0x0001	0x0080
SAP Name	Single Valued Sized Attribute Non-Removable String Attribute Sync Immediate	SYN_CI_STRING	0x0001	0x002F
SAS:Security DN	Single Valued Sync Immediate Server Read	SYN_DIST_NAME	0x0000	0xFFFF
SAS:Service DN	Single Valued Sync Immediate Server Read	SYN_DIST_NAME	0x0000	0xFFFF

ATTRIBUTE NAME	DEFINITION FLAGS	SYNTAX	LOWER LIMIT	UPPER LIMIT
Security Equals	Non-Removable Sync Immediate Server Read	SYN_DIST_NAME	0x0000	0xFFFF
Security Flags	Single Valued Non-Removable Sync Immediate	SYN_INTEGER	0x0000	0xFFFF
See Also	Non-Removable Sync Immediate	SYN_DIST_NAME	0x0000	0xFFFF
Serial Number	Sized Attribute Non-Removable String Attribute Sync Immediate	SYN_PR_STRING	0x0001	0x0040
Server	Non-Removable Sync Immediate Server Read	SYN_DIST_NAME	0x0000	0xFFFF
Server Holds	Non-Removable Sync Immediate	SYN_HOLD	0x0000	0xFFFF
Set Password After Create	Single Valued	SYN_BOOLEAN	0x0000	0xFFFF
Setup Script	Single Valued	SYN_STREAM	0x0000	0xFFFF
Sides Supported	Single Valued Sized Attribute Public Read	SYN_INTEGER	0x0001	0x0064
SLP Attribute	Single Valued String Attribute Sync Immediate Public Read	SYN_CI_STRING	0x0000	0xFFFF

Continued

TABLE C.1

Base Attributes (continued)

ATTRIBUTE NAME	DEFINITION FLAGS	SYNTAX	LOWER LIMIT	UPPER LIMIT
SLP Cache Limit	Single Valued Sync Immediate Public Read	SYN_INTEGER	0x0000	0xFFFF
SLP DA Back Link	Single Valued Sync Immediate Public Read	SYN_DIST_NAME	0x0000	0xFFFF
SLP Directory Agent DN	Single Valued Sync Immediate Public Read	SYN_DIST_NAME	0x0000	0xFFFF
SLP Language	Single Valued String Attribute Sync Immediate	SYN_CI_STRING	0x0000	0xFFFF
Public ReadSLP Lifetime	Single Valued Sync Immediate Public Read	SYN_INTEGER	0x0000	0xFFFF
SLP Scope Name	Single Valued String Attribute Sync Immediate Public Read	SYN_CI_STRING	0x0000	0xFFFF
SLP Scope Unit DN	Sync Immediate Public Read	SYN_DIST_NAME	0x0000	0xFFFF
SLP Start Purge Hour	Single Valued Sync Immediate Public Read	SYN_INTEGER	0x0000	0xFFFF
SLP Status	Single Valued Sync Immediate Public Read	SYN_INTEGER	0x0000	0xFFFF

ATTRIBUTE NAME	DEFINITION FLAGS	SYNTAX	LOWER LIMIT	UPPER LIMIT
SLP SU Back Link	Sync Immediate Public Read	SYN_DIST_NAME	0x0000	0xFFFF
SLP SU Type	String Attribute Sync Immediate Public Read	SYN_CI_STRING	0x0000	0xFFFF
SLP Type	Single Valued String Attribute Sync Immediate Public Read	SYN_CI_STRING	0x0000	0xFFFF
SLP URL	Single Valued String Attribute Sync Immediate Public Read	SYN_CI_STRING	0x0000	0xFFFF
SMS Protocol Address	Sync Immediate	SYN_OCTET_STRING	0x0000	0xFFFF
SMS Registered Service	Sync Immediate	SYN_OCTET_STRING	0x0000	0xFFFF
Status	Single Valued Non-Removable Sync Immediate Public Read	SYN_INTEGER	0x0000	0xFFFF
SU	Sized Attribute String Attribute Sync Immediate	SYN_CI_STRING	0x0001	0x007F
Supported Connections	Single Valued Non-Removable Sync Immediate	SYN_INTEGER	0x0000	0xFFFF

Continued

TABLE C.1

Base Attributes (continued)

ATTRIBUTE NAME	DEFINITION FLAGS	SYNTAX	LOWER LIMIT	UPPER LIMIT
Supported Gateway	Sized Attribute Non-Removable String Attribute Sync Immediate	SYN_CI_STRING	0x0001	0x1000
Supported Services	Sized Attribute Non-Removable String Attribute Sync Immediate	SYN_CI_STRING	0x0001	0x0040
Supported Typefaces	Sized Attribute Non-Removable String Attribute Sync Immediate	SYN_CI_STRING	0x0001	0x0040
Surname	Single Valued Sized Attribute Non-Removable String Attribute Sync Immediate Public Read	SYN_CI_STRING	0x0001	0x0040
SvcInfo	Single Valued Sync Immediate	SYN_OCTET_STRING	0x0000	0xFFFF
SvcType	Single Valued String Attribute Sync Immediate	SYN_CI_STRING	0x0000	0xFFFF
SvcTypeID	Single Valued Sync Immediate	SYN_OCTET_STRING	0x0000	0xFFFF

ATTRIBUTE NAME	DEFINITION FLAGS	SYNTAX	LOWER LIMIT	UPPER LIMIT
Synchronization Tolerance	Non-Removable, Sync Immediate, Public Read	SYN_TIMESTAMP	0x0000	0xFFFF
Synchronized Up To	Non-Removable, Read-Only Attribute, Public Read	SYN_TIMESTAMP	0x0000	0xFFFF
T	Sized Attribute, Non-Removable, String Attribute, Sync	SYN_CI_STRING	0x0001	0x0020
Telephone Number	Non-Removable, String Attribute, Sync Immediate	SYN_TEL_NUMBER	0x0000	0xFFFF
Timezone	Single Valued, Non-Removable, Sync Immediate, Public Read	SYN_OCTET_STRING	0x0000	0xFFFF
Title	Sized Attribute, Non-Removable, String Attribute, Sync Immediate	SYN_CI_STRING	0x0001	0x0040
Transitive Vector	Non-Removable, Read-Only Attribute, Public Read	SYN_OCTET_STRING	0x0000	0xFFFF
Trustees Of New Object	n/a	SYN_OBJECT_ACL	0x0000	0xFFFF
Type Creator Map	Single Valued, Non-Removable, Sync Immediate	SYN_STREAM	0x0000	0xFFFF

Continued

TABLE C.1
Base Attributes (continued)

ATTRIBUTE NAME	DEFINITION FLAGS	SYNTAX	LOWER LIMIT	UPPER LIMIT
Unknown	Non-Removable	SYN_UNKNOWN	0x0000	0xFFFF
Unknown Base Class	Single Valued Sized Attribute Non-Removable String Attribute	SYN_CI_STRING	0x0001	0x0020
Used By	Non-Removable Read-Only Attribute Sync Immediate Server Read	SYN_PATH	0x0000	0xFFFF
User	Non-Removable Sync Immediate Server Read	SYN_DIST_NAME	0x0000	0xFFFF
Uses	Non-Removable Read-Only Attribute Sync Immediate Server Read	SYN_PATH	0x0000	0xFFFF
UID	Single Valued Non-Removable Sync Immediate	SYN_INTEGER	0x0000	0xFFFF
Version	Single Valued Sized Attribute Non-Removable String Attribute Sync Immediate Public Read	SYN_CI_STRING	0x0001	0x0040

ATTRIBUTE NAME	DEFINITION FLAGS	SYNTAX	LOWER LIMIT	UPPER LIMIT
Volume	Single Valued Non-Removable Sync Immediate	SYN_DIST_NAME	0x0000	0xFFFF
Volume Space Restrictions	n/a	SYN_PATH	0x0000	0xFFFF
WANMAN:Cost	n/a	SYN_OCTET_STRING	0x0000	0xFFFF
WANMAN:Default Cost	Single Valued	SYN_INTEGER	0x0000	0xFFFF
WANMAN:LAN Area Membership	Single Valued	SYN_DIST_NAME	0x0000	0xFFFF
WANMAN:WAN Policy	n/a	SYN_OCTET_LIST	0x0000	0xFFFF
[Anything]	n/a	SYN_OCTET_STRING	0x0000	0xFFFF
[Nothing]	n/a	SYN_OCTET_STRING	0x0000	0xFFFF

NDS Resources

Throughout this book, we have referred to a number of different third-party products and NDS resources. We have added additional resource information in this appendix if you wish to expand your knowledge of NDS.

Novell Resources

* **Novell's NDS Product Page:** `http://www.novell.com/nds`

* **Novell's Security Information Page:**
  `http://www.novell.com/security`

* **Novell Consulting Services:** `http://consulting.novell.com`

* **Novell DeveloperNet Program:** `http://developer.novell.com`

* **LogicSource for NDS:**
  `http://support.novell.com/logicsource/nds`

* **Novell Support Connection:** `http://support.novell.com`

* **Novell Support Connection Forums:**
  `http://support.novell.com/forums/`
  `nntp://forums.novell.com`

Third-Party Tools

Bindview EMS
Bindview Development
5151 San Felipe, Suite 2200
Houston, TX 77056
(713) 561-4000
`http://www.bindview.com`

SecureConsole

Protocom Development, Ltd.

800-581-3502 (US)

+61 2 6208 4888 (Australia)

+44 1454 777 659 (United Kingdom)

http://www.serversystems.com

ScheMAX

Netoria, Inc.

1283 North State Street

Orem, UT 84057

(801) 227-0722

888-227-0711

http://www.netoria.com

DS Expert

NetPro Computing, Inc.

7150 E. Camelback Rd., Suite 100

Scottsdale, AZ 85251

(480) 941-3630

800-998-5090

http://www.netpro.com

GNU awk (gawk)

GNU Software

ftp://ftp.gnu.org/gnu/gawk

Site with pointers to DOS binary distributions are located at:
http://www.msc.cornell.edu/msccf/software/htmlchek/
awk-perl.html#miscawk

NDS Resources

- **NDS ToolKit**, DreamLan Consulting, Ltd.: http://www.dreamlan.com

- Jim Henderson's NDS Information Page:
  `http://www.bigfoot.com/~jhenderson/nds.html`

- Marcus Williamson's NDS Resources:
  `http://www.connectotel.com/netware`

- Darwin Collins' NDS Tools: `http://www.novellfans.com/`

Books

Novell's NDS Developer's Guide, by Chris Andrew, et al., Novell Press, ISBN: 0-7645-4557-4

Novell's Guide to NetWare 5 Networks, by Jeffrey F. Hughes and Blair W. Thomas, Novell Press, ISBN: 0-7645-4544-2

NDS Troubleshooting, by Jim Henderson and Peter Kuo, New Riders Publishing

The AWK Programming Language, by Alfred V. Aho, Brian W. Kernighan, Peter J. Weinberger, Addison-Wesley Publishing Company

Index

(continued)